ONE THOUSAND FAMOUS THINGS

BOOKS BY
ARTHUR MEE

SAINT GEORGE AND THE DRAGON

By Fortunino Matania

ONE THOUSAND FAMOUS THINGS

By ARTHUR MEE

HODDER AND STOUGHTON
LIMITED   LONDON

FIRST PUBLISHED 1937
FOURTH IMPRESSION 1950

PRINTED AND BOUND IN ENGLAND FOR
HODDER AND STOUGHTON, LTD., LONDON, BY
HAZELL, WATSON AND VINEY, LTD., AYLESBURY AND LONDON

Fame Immortal

FAME was never so busy. Morning, noon, and night her trumpet sounds across the world.

Time was when men must toil long years for a little fame, or must do some great thing like the winning of Trafalgar: " Gentlemen," said an Englishman on that fateful morning, " let us do something today that the world will talk of hereafter." Now a man has but to fight another man, or to be a little comical on the films, and half the world will run to see him. Shakespeare waited years for fame, and Cromwell centuries, but Hollywood and Fleet Street will make a painted lady famous in a day. We have come into a limelight world which makes the fool as famous as the wise.

It may seem that bad men have always been as famous as good men, but we have the authority of the poet for believing that

> Only the actions of the just
> Smell sweet and blossom in their dust.

The evil that men do lives after them, but it is the good that is famous. The reward of evil is not fame, but infamy. Fame will spring up in a day, but the fame that endures must set itself deep in the hearts or the minds of men. The fame that endures is more than the fact of being blazed abroad. It is not accidental, or a thing that comes by some strange chance: that way comes the bubble reputation of an hour; but the fame which lives and is worth while must have something good in it. A man may make mousetraps and die poor and unknown, but was it not Emerson who believed that if a man made a better mousetrap than any other man made the world would flock to his door? Always it is the quality that counts. When we say Let Us Now Praise Famous Men we mean men great and wise.

It is true that fame works strangely. We have seen it take a house-painter and make him suddenly the talk of Europe. It will neglect a man all his life and pick him up at the end. It will find a man starving in a garret as he writes and will make a note of what he writes, and long afterwards, when the man has starved to death, Fame will take this scrap of paper and set it ringing through the world. It will take a man poring *over a page of mathematics and will make a note of what he does, and years afterwards will take up the name of this forgotten man and tell the world that with his mathematics began the Wireless Age.*

That is fame immortal, not the fame of an hour, the trick of the kinema, the breath of Fleet Street. It is the sound that fills the world and echoes down the ages, thrilling with the memory of some great thing done, some fine word spoken, some noble spirit that has been abroad. It is Major Mordaunt's

> *Sound, sound the clarion, fill the fife,*
> *To all the sensual world proclaim :*
> *One crowded hour of glorious life*
> *Is worth an age without a name.*

It is Ben Jonson's fame that fills the heavens and the earth :

> *Her house is all of Echo made,*
> *Where never dies the sound :*
> *And as her brows the clouds invade,*
> *Her feet do strike the ground.*

It is the glory of our heritage that it is so rich in famous things. They haunt us everywhere. They are in poetry and art and in the world of practical achievement. They are written across our history. They are all over the face of our land.

Here we look at some of them. It is not claimed that everything in this book is as well known as Shakespeare or the Tower of London ; some of these things are counted famous only in the sense of quality, of being excellent or worthy of fame, the sense in which Southey used the word :

> *Why, that I cannot tell, said he,*
> *But twas a famous victory.*

But it is believed that most of these things have passed into fame in the sense that they are known to a great multitude. Sometimes it is a famous event that we have chosen to remember in some striking passage, sometimes a document, often a picture. If many famous things are missing, as they must be, they may perhaps be found in two volumes to which this comes as a third companion—a volume of One Thousand Beautiful Things and a volume of Everlasting Things such as we know men will be reading in a thousand years from now. It is claimed for this third volume only that it has in it a thousand things so famous that they are well known, or so excellent that they deserve to be known, or so important that they should be known.

These things are ours, part of the common stock of our possessions in a world that is so rich and wonderful, and so filled with fame.

Contents of This Book

The Pictures

*When the pictures are not facing the page given they
are inside the set of pictures beginning on that page*

Acknowledgments

The Editor desires to express his great indebtedness to the following authors, publishers, and holders of copyrights

To the proprietors of Punch for In Flanders Fields

To Lord St Davids for the poem by Colwyn Phillips

To Mrs Kettle for the poem by Tom Kettle

To Mr John Murray for Noel Hodgson's poem Before Action

To Mrs Owen and Chatto and Windus for Wilfred Owen's Miners

To Mrs Thomas for the poem by Edward Thomas

To Mr W. H. Davies and Jonathan Cape for The Kingfisher

To the Cambridge University Press for the lines by Charles Sorley

To Dean Alington for his lines to Charles Lister

To the executors of R. E. Vernede for his poem The Sea is His

To Lord Dunsany for the poem by Francis Ledwidge

To Messrs Heinemann for extracts from the Life of Walter Page

To Celia, Lady Congreve, and Country Life, for Wood Fires

To Mr Compton Mackenzie for Song of Parting

To Lady Conan Doyle for the poem by Sir Arthur Conan Doyle, and to John Murray the publisher

To Mrs Chesterton and J. M. Dent and Sons for Mr Chesterton's poem on The Donkey

To Sir John Arkwright for O Valiant Hearts, appearing in his poems published by Skeffington and Son

To Mr Frank Sidgwick and Mr C. C. Lynam for The Strenuous Life by Arthur Hugh Sidgwick

To the proprietors of The Times for the poem by Noel Oxland and The Triumph of the Cross

To Lord Desborough for Julian Grenfell's Into Battle, and to Lady Desborough for the picture by Zoffany

To the Hon Maurice Baring for the sonnet to Julian Grenfell appearing in his Selected Poems, published by Heinemann

To John Lane The Bodley Head for the two poems by Francis Burdett Money-Coutts, and for a poem by Edward Wyndham Tennant

To Mr Winston Churchill for passages from his History of the Great War, published by Thornton Butterworth

To the National Gallery, the National Portrait Gallery, and the Fine Arts Publishing Company for certain pictures

To Mr George Eumorfopolous for one of the treasures of his Tang collection

And to the following photographers: Herbert Felton, Frederick Hollyer, W. F. Taylor, Donald McLeish, John Swain, Messrs Anderson, Brogi, Bruckmann, and Wildenstein, and George Pulman & Sons

The picture of Queen Elizabeth on page 208 is in St Stephen's Hall in the Houses of Parliament

TO
MY WIFE

Let the Whole World Know

I WILL have the whole world to know that none but Englishmen shall chastise an Englishman.   *Cromwell's admiral, Robert Blake, to the Spanish Inquisition*

The Foundations

IF you have built castles in the air your work need not be lost ; that is where they should be.   Now put the foundations under them.

Thoreau

Speak About Palm Trees

IT is well to know the truth and speak it, but it is better to know the truth and speak about palm trees.   *An Arab Proverb*

Ah, Well

AH, well, there is just this world and the next, and then all our troubles will be over.

An old lady in Lady Oxford's Memoirs

Fight Something Ere We Die

COME ! Let us lay a crazy lance in rest,
And tilt at windmills under a wild sky !
For who would live so petty and unblest
That dare not tilt at something ere he die,
Rather than, screened by safe majority,
Preserve his little life to little ends,
And never raise a rebel battle-cry !

John Galsworthy

The Lonely Flower

I ONCE saw a botanist most tenderly replace a plant which he had inadvertently uprooted, though we were on a bleak hillside in Tibet, where no human being was likely to see the flower again.

Sir Francis Younghusband

So Many Foes

So many are your foes, their arrows shroud
The very sun with an eclipsing cloud.
We'll fight them in the dark then ! and the horde
Illumine with the lightning of the Sword.

Gerald Massey

The Miser

A MISER's mind thou hast,
Thou hast a prince's pelf:
Which makes thee wealthy to thine heir,
A beggar to thyself.

*Written in the Sixteenth Century
by George Turberville*

A Chant from Old Sarum

GOD be in my head
And in my understanding;

God be in my eyes
And in my looking;

God be in my mouth,
And in my speaking;

God be in my heart,
And in my thinking;

God be at mine end,
And at my departing.

*Sung by the monks of
Old Sarum 700 years ago*

The Last Pride of All

WITH thee were the dreams of my earliest love;
Every thought of my reason was thine:
In my last humble prayer to the Spirit above
Thy name shall be mingled with mine!

O! blest are the lovers and friends who shall live
The days of thy glory to see;
But the next dearest blessing that Heaven can give
Is the pride of thus dying for thee.   *Thomas Moore*

The Wit of David Garrick

FOR physic and farces his equal there scarce is:
His farces are physic, his physic a farce is.

HERE lies Nolly Goldsmith, for shortness called Noll,
Who wrote like an angel but talked like poor Poll.

Safety Last

THOUGH Love repine and Reason chafe,
There came a voice without reply:
*Tis man's perdition to be safe,
When for the truth he ought to die.*

Emerson

The Wise Man in the Shadow of Defeat

NOT unconsoled, I wait—in hope
  To see the moment when the righteous cause
Shall gain defenders zealous and devout
As they who have opposed her ; in which Virtue
Will to her efforts tolerate no bounds
That are not lofty as her rights ; aspiring
By impulse of her own ethereal zeal.
That spirit only can redeem mankind ;
And when that sacred spirit shall appear,
Then shall *our* triumph be complete as theirs,
Yet shall this confidence prove vain, the wise
Have still the keeping of their proper peace,
Are guardians of their own tranquillity.

Wordsworth's Excursion

Whose Dwelling is the Light of Setting Suns

FOR I have learned
  To look on nature, not as in the hour
Of thoughtless youth, but hearing oftentimes
The still, sad music of humanity,
Nor harsh nor grating, though of ample power
To chasten and subdue. And I have felt
A presence that disturbs me with the joy
Of elevated thoughts ; a sense sublime
Of something far more deeply interfused,
Whose dwelling is the light of setting suns,
And the round ocean, and the living air,
And the blue sky, and in the mind of man ;
A motion and a spirit, that impels
All thinking things, all objects of all thought,
And rolls through all things.

Wordsworth's Tintern Abbey

To One Dying in a Great Cause

LIVE and take comfort. Thou hast left behind
  Powers that will work for thee ; air, earth, and skies ;
There's not a breathing of the common wind
That will forget thee ; thou hast great allies :
Thy friends are exultations, agonies,
And love, and man's unconquerable mind.

Wordsworth on Toussaint L'Ouverture,
starved to death in a dungeon by Napoleon

You and the Past

EVERY ship that goes to America gets its chart from Columbus. Every novel is a debtor to Homer. Every carpenter who shaves with a foreplane borrows the genius of a forgotten inventor. Life is girt all round with the contributions of men who have perished to add their point of light to our sky. *Emerson*

A People Great and Strong

NOT gold, but only men can make
  A people great and strong;
Men who for truth and honour's sake
  Stand fast and suffer long.

Brave men who work while others sleep,
  Who dare while others fly—
They build a nation's pillars deep
  And lift them to the sky. *Emerson*

Two Men in the Dark

THEY tell you in London the story of the Frenchman and Englishman who quarrelled. Both were unwilling to fight, but their companions put them up to it. At last it was agreed that they should fight alone, in the dark, and with pistols.

The candles were put out, and the Englishman, to make sure not to hit anybody, fired up the chimney, *and brought down the Frenchman.*

Emerson

England's Place on the Earth

ENGLAND resembles a ship in its shape; and, if it were one, its best admiral could not have worked it, or anchored it in a more judicious or effective position. The shopkeeping nation, to use a shop word, has a good stand. England is anchored at the side of Europe, right in the heart of the modern world.   *Emerson*

The Company of the Wise

CONSIDER what you have in the smallest chosen library. A company of the wisest and wittiest men that could be picked out of all civil countries in a thousand years have set in best order the results of their learning and wisdom. The men themselves were hid and inaccessible, solitary, impatient of interruption, fenced by etiquette; but the thought which they did not uncover to their bosom friend is here written out in transparent words to us, the strangers of another age.   *Emerson*

The Secret Life

IT is a wonderful fact to reflect upon that every human creature is constituted to be a profound secret and mystery to every other.

Charles Dickens

Every Day from the Hands of God

ON week days he walked alone, but on Sundays he showed us the shrines of the wood gods and the home of Echo in the groves he loved.

When we were in bed my father would often come up, and, sitting by us in the twilight, chant, to our great delight, a Goodnight song, made up as he sang, to the trees, the birds, the flowers, the members of the family, even the cow and the cat.

He persistently kept meal-times pleasant: would allow no sour remnants of yesterday's wrong-doings to be served up again. Every day was to be fresh and new as a dewdrop from the hands of God.
Emerson's son on his father

Charles Dickens to Mr Lockhart

HE has risen like a rocket and he will come down like a stick.
John Gibson Lockhart on Charles Dickens

I WILL watch for that stick, Mr Lockhart, and when it comes down I will break it across your back. *Dickens on meeting
Lockhart afterwards*

Rich Indeed

WE are not rich in the bank, but we have always prospered, and we have quite enough. I never walk out with my husband but I hear the people praise him. I never go into a house of any degree but I hear his praises or see them in grateful eyes. I never lie down at night but I know that in the course of the day he has alleviated pain and soothed some fellow-creature in the time of need. I know that from the beds of those who were past recovery thanks have often gone up, in the last hour, for his patient ministration. Is not this to be rich? *A Doctor's Wife in Dickens*

Poor Scrooge

NOBODY ever stopped him in the street to say, with gladsome looks, "My dear Scrooge, how are you? When will you come to see me?" No beggars implored him to bestow a trifle, no children asked him what it was o'clock, no man or woman ever once in all his life inquired the way to such and such a place of Scrooge. Even the blind men's dogs appeared to know him; and when they saw him coming on would tug their owners into doorways. *Charles Dickens*

Why Runnest Thou so Fast?

AVON! Why runnest thou away so fast?
Rest thee before that Chancel where repose
The bones of him whose spirit moves the world.
*Walter Savage Landor to the river running
by the chancel where Shakespeare lies*

The Prayer of the BBC

*This is the inscription carved in Latin in the Entrance
Hall of Broadcasting House, the Headquarters of the BBC*

THIS Temple of the Arts and Muses is dedicated to Almighty God
by the first Governors of Broadcasting in the year 1931, Sir
John Reith being Director-General.

It is their prayer that good seed sown may bring forth a good
harvest, that all things hostile to peace or purity may be banished
from this house, and that the people, inclining their ears to whatsoever
things are beautiful and honest and of good report, may tread the
paths of wisdom and uprightness.

The Poet's Belief in Himself

WELL I remember how you smiled
To see me write your name upon
The soft sea-sand—*O ! what a child !
You think you're writing upon stone !*

I have since written what no tide
Shall ever wash away, what men
Unborn shall read o'er ocean wide
And find Ianthe's name again.

Walter Savage Landor

God Pardon Them

LIFE (priest and poet say) is but a dream ;
I wish no happier one than to be laid
Beneath a cool syringa's scented shade,
Or wavy willow, by the running stream,
Brimful of moral, where the dragon-fly
Wanders as careless and content as I.

Thanks for this fancy, insect king,
On purple crest and filmy wing,
Who with indifference givest up
The water-lily's golden cup ;
To come again and overlook
What I am writing in my book.

Believe me, most who read the line
Will read with hornier eyes than thine ;
And yet their souls shall live for ever,
And thine drop dead into the river !
God pardon them, O insect king,
Who fancy so unjust a thing !

Walter Savage Landor

Summer is Ending

THE feathers of the willow
Are half of them grown yellow
Above the swelling stream;
And ragged are the bushes,
And rusty now the rushes,
And wild the clouded gleam.

And thistle now is older,
His stalks begin to moulder,
His head is white as snow;
The branches all are barer,
The linnet's song is rarer,
The robin pipeth low.
Richard Watson Dixon

St Anthony to the Fishes

ST ANTHONY at church
Was left in the lurch,
So he went to the ditches
And preached to the fishes.

Sharp-snouted pikes,
Who keep fighting like tikes,
Now swam up harmonious
To hear St Antonius.

Good eels and sturgeon
Which aldermen gorge on,
Went out of their way
To hear preaching that day.

Fish great and fish small,
Lords, lackeys, and all,
Each looked at the preacher
Like a reasonable creature.

The sermon now ended,
Each turned and descended;
The pikes went on stealing,
The eels went on eeling;

Much delighted were they,
But preferred the old way.
Author unknown

The Garment of His Country

IF I thought there was a stain upon the remotest hem of the garment
of my country, I would devote my utmost labour to wipe it off.
Daniel Webster

The Last Will of Lady Joan Hungerford

MY body to be buried in the chapel of St Anne in the parish church of Farleigh-Hungerford, next to the grave of my husband. I will that with all possible speed after my decease my Executors cause some Masses to be said for my soul and for the souls of all the faithful deceased.

Also I desire on my burial day that 12 torches and 2 tapers burn about my body, and that 12 poor women holding the said torches be clothed in russet with linen hoods, and having stockings and shoes suitable.

I will that £10 be bestowed to buy black cloth for the clothing of my sons and daughters, as likewise the sons and daughters of all my domestic servants. I will that 200 marks now in the hands of my son Sir Walter Hungerford be given to found a perpetual chantry of one chaplain to celebrate divine service in the Chapel of St Anne in the north part of the said church of Farleigh for the health of my soul and the soul of my husband and the souls of all our ancestors for ever.

To Katharine the wife of my said son Walter my black mantle furred with miniver, and to Thomas his son a green bed embroidered with one greyhound. *Dated February 1, 1411, hanging by her tomb at Farleigh Castle*

Heir of All Things

YOU never enjoy the world aright till the sea itself floweth in your veins, till you are clothed with the heavens, and crowned with the stars; and perceive yourself to be the sole heir of the whole world; and more than so, because men are in it who are everyone sole heirs as well as you.

Till you can sing and rejoice and delight in God, as misers do in gold, and kings in sceptres, you never enjoy the world.

Till your spirit filleth the whole world, and the stars are your jewels; till you are as familiar with the ways of God in all Ages as with your walk and table; till you are intimately acquainted with that shady nothing out of which the world was made; till you love men so as to desire their happiness with a thirst equal to the zeal of your own; till you delight in God for being good to all—you never enjoy the world.

Till you more feel it than your private estate, and are more present in the hemisphere, considering the glories and the beauties there, than in your own house.

Till you remember how lately you were made, and how wonderful it was when you came into it; and more rejoice in the palace of your glory than if it had been made but today morning.

Thomas Traherne

THE ANNUNCIATION, BY DONATELLO

THE WONDERFUL FIGURES IN THE SINGING GALLERY BY LUCA DELLA RO

OUTS

R THE DUOMO IN FLORENCE AND NOW IN THE MUSEUM MARIA DEL FIORE
EDRAL

EROS, BY SIR ALFRED GILBERT

Thou, Little Sandpiper, and I

A CROSS the narrow beach we flit,
 One little sandpiper and I ;
And fast I gather, bit by bit,
 The scattered driftwood, bleached and dry.
The wild waves reach their hands for it,
 The wild wind raves, the tide runs high,
As up and down the beach we flit,
 One little sandpiper and I.

Above our heads the sullen clouds
 Scud black and swift across the sky ;
Like silent ghosts in misty shrouds
 Stand out the white lighthouses high.
Almost as far as eye can reach
 I see the close-reefed vessels fly,
As fast we flit along the beach,
 One little sandpiper and I.

I watch him as he skims along,
 Uttering his sweet and mournful cry.
He starts not at my fitful song
 Or flash of fluttering drapery.
He has no thought of any wrong ;
 He scans me with a fearless eye.
Staunch friends are we, well tried and strong,
 The little sandpiper and I.

Comrade, where wilt thou be tonight
 When the loosed storm breaks furiously ?
My driftwood fire will burn so bright !
 To what warm shelter canst thou fly ?
I do not fear for thee, though wroth
 The tempest rushes through the sky :
For are we not God's children both,
 Thou, little sandpiper, and I ?

Celia Thaxter

The Ringing Loom of Time

I N floods of being, in action's storm,
 Up and down I wave,
To and fro I flee,
Birth and the grave,
An infinite sea,
A changeful weaving,
An ardent living ;
The ringing loom of Time is my care,
And I weave God's living garment there.

Goethe's Faust

On a Contented Mind

WHEN all is done and said,
　In the end thus shall you find,
He most of all doth bathe in bliss
　That hath a quiet mind :
And, clear from worldly cares,
　Can deem to be content
The sweetest time in all his life
　In thinking to be spent.

The body subject is
　To fickle Fortune's power,
And to a million of mishaps
　Is casual every hour :
And Death in time doth change
　It to a clod of clay ;
Whenas the mind, which is divine,
　Runs never to decay.

Companion none is like
　Unto the mind alone ;
For many have been harmed by speech,
　Through thinking, few or none.
Fear oftentimes restraineth words,
　But makes not thought to cease ;
And he speaks best that hath the skill
　When for to hold his peace.

Our wealth leaves us at death ;
　Our kinsmen at the grave ;
Virtues of the mind unto
　The heavens with us we have.
Wherefore, for virtue's sake,
　I can be well content,
The sweetest time of all my life
　To deem in thinking spent.

Lord Vaux

I Know My Soul Hath Power to Know

I KNOW my soul hath power to know all things,
　Yet she is blind and ignorant in all :
I know I'm one of Nature's little kings,
　Yet to the least and vilest things am thrall.

I know my life's a pain and but a span ;
　I know my sense is mocked in everything ;
And, to conclude, I know myself a Man,
　Which is a proud and yet a wretched thing.

Sir John Davies

A Voice From the Last Generation

YOU will have temptation sent you—you, the labouring people of this country, and when you have become supreme to such a degree that there is no other power to balance and counteract the power you possess you will have approaching you a deep and searching moral control.

You will have to preserve the balance of your mind and character when you have fought the struggle with the capitalist and aristocrat and great mercantile classes. When you have become in a sense the political masters you have still before you one achievement to fulfil, one glory to attain and to appropriate to yourselves—to continue to be just. I venture to give you that warning of the future. It applies to the coming days more than to the days that are past.

W. E. Gladstone

The Thing He Could Not Find

ONE of the sorest things in life is to come to realise that one is just not good enough. Better perhaps than some, than many almost; but I do not care for matching myself against my kind. There is an ideal standard somewhere, and only that matters, and I cannot find it. *T. E. Lawrence*

Frail Man in a Changing World

I HAVE seen night turned into day in our cities and dwellings by the aid of gas. I have seen time and distance all but annihilated by the locomotive power of steam, by sea and land. I have seen the electric telegraph conveying from zone to zone the intercourse of man by sparks stolen as it were from heaven.

I have seen mighty monarchies fall. I have seen republics, founded on their ruins, crumble into dust. I have seen military despotism grow up and wither.

And shall man, frail man, amid all these changes of Nature and of policy, stand immovable, unaltered in his opinions and feelings? If a man is to refuse to yield to the pressure of the times and of the circumstances in which his lot is cast—if he is not open to conviction and, notwithstanding the altered state of affairs and the changed condition of things around him, refuses to alter his opinions, such a man may be fit for a lunatic asylum, but I say he does not possess the true recommendation for any deliberative assembly in the world.

Sir James Graham's last speech to the electors of Carlisle in 1859

What to Do Every Day

ONE ought every day at least to hear a little song, read a good poem, see a fine picture, and, if possible, speak a few reasonable words. *Goethe*

Time Cannot Efface It

IF we work upon marble, it will perish. If we work upon brass, time will efface it. If we rear temples, they will crumble to dust. But if we work upon men's immortal minds, if we imbue them with high principles, with the just fear of God and love of their fellowmen, we engrave on those tablets something which no time can efface, and which will brighten and brighten to all eternity.

Daniel Webster

Man's Inheritance

WHAT is the good of all that starry firmament and the revolving planets, of all Creation's labour and travail up to now, if it is not to enable a man to live in freedom, in happiness, and in activity among his surroundings ?

Goethe

Let Your Trouble Be

LET your trouble be,
    Light will follow dark:
Though the heaven falls,
    You may hear the lark.

Goethe

He Knows You Not, Ye Heavenly Powers

WHO ne'er his bread in sorrow ate,
    Who ne'er the mournful midnight hours
Weeping upon his bed hath sate,
    He knows you not, ye heavenly Powers.

Goethe

The Lowest Thing

NATIONAL hatred is a curious thing. You will always find it strongest and most passionate on the lowest level of civilisation. There is a stage where it disappears altogether, where, in a sense, we rise above the nations, and feel the joys and the sorrows of a neighbouring people as though they had come to our own.   *Goethe*

Salute to the Seasons

ALL our comfort is based on the regular recurrence of eternal things. The change from night to day, the succession of the seasons, of flowers and fruits, and of whatever else we look forward to enjoying at its allotted time—these are the mainspring of our life-machinery, and the more freely we open our hearts to their influence the happier we feel.   *Goethe*

Do It With Thy Might

WHAT is your duty ? Every day's demands of you.

Goethe

O, When Shall We Tell
Such a Tale Again?

FAIR stood the wind for France
When we our sails advance,
Nor now to prove our chance
   Longer will tarry ;
But putting to the main
At Caux, the mouth of Seine,
With all his martial train,
   Landed King Harry.

And taking many a fort,
Furnished in warlike sort,
Marched toward Agincourt
   In happy hour ;
Skirmishing day by day
With those that stopped his way
Where the French General lay
   With all his power.

Which in his height of pride,
King Henry to deride,
His ransom to provide
   To the king sending ;
Which he neglects the while,
As from a nation vile,
Yet, with an angry smile,
   Their fall portending.

And, turning to his men,
Quoth our brave Henry then :
Though they to one be ten,
   Be not amazèd ;
Yet have we well begun,
Battles so bravely won
Have ever to the sun
   By fame been raisèd.

And for myself, quoth he,
This my full rest shall be :
England ne'er mourn for me,
   Nor more esteem me :
Victor I will remain,
Or on this earth lie slain ;
Never shall she sustain
   Loss to redeem me.

They now to fight are gone ;
Armour on armour shone ;

Drum now to drum did groan :
    To hear was wonder ;
That with the cries they make
The very earth did shake ;
Trumpet to trumpet spake,
    Thunder to thunder.

Well it thine age became,
O noble Erpingham,
Which did the signal aim
    To our hid forces !
When, from a meadow by,
Like a storm suddenly,
The English archery
    Struck the French horses.

With Spanish yew so strong,
Arrows a cloth-yard long,
That like to serpents stung,
    Piercing the weather ;
None from his fellow starts,
But playing manly parts,
And, like true English hearts,
    Stuck close together.

Upon Saint Crispin's day
Fought was this noble fray,
Which fame did not delay
    To England to carry.
O, when shall Englishmen
With such acts fill a pen,
Or England breed again
    Such a King Harry ?
        Michael Drayton

Something in the English

IF you want to go into battle, have an Englishman at your right hand, and another at your left, and two immediately in front and two close behind.   There is something in the English which seems to guarantee security.   Never forget that, even when you are most irritated by the antics of these engaging madmen.   *Voltaire*

Play the Part Assigned to You

REMEMBER that thou art an actor in a play, the character of which is determined by the Playwright.   If he wishes the play to be short it is short ; if long it is long ; if he wishes you to play the part of a beggar, remember to act even this rôle adroitly, for this is your business—to play admirably the rôle assigned to you, though the selection of that rôle is Another's.   *Epictetus*

The Good Things of the World

WHEN we have been invited to a banquet we take what is set before us. If a guest should ask the host to set before him fish or sweet cakes he would be considered to be an unreasonable fellow, but in the world we ask the gods for what they do not give ; and we do this though the things are many which they have given.

Epictetus

Its Day Will Come

No lie ever grows old.
Euripides

Madonna's Prayer

HOLY angels and blest,
  Through those palms as ye sweep
Hold their branches at rest,
  For my Babe is asleep.

And ye Bethlehem palm-trees,
  As stormy winds rush
In tempest and fury,
  Your angry noise hush ;

More gently, more gently,
  Restrain your wild sweep ;
Hold your branches at rest ;
  My Babe is asleep.
Lope de Vega, 16th-century Spanish poet

Love's Farewell

SINCE there's no help, come let us kiss and part,
  Nay, I have done, you get no more of me ;
And I am glad, yea, glad with all my heart,
  That thus so cleanly I myself can free ;

Shake hands for ever, cancel all our vows,
  And when we meet at any time again,
Be it not seen in either of our brows
  That we one jot of former love retain.

Now at the last gasp of love's latest breath,
  When his pulse failing, passion speechless lies,
When faith is kneeling by his bed of death,
  And innocence is closing up his eyes,

Now if thou would'st, when all have given him over,
From death to life thou might'st him yet recover !
Michael Drayton

Rule, Britannia

WHEN Britain first, at Heaven's command,
   Arose from out the azure main ;
This was the charter of the land,
   And guardian angels sang this strain :
    Rule, Britannia, Britannia rule the waves ;
    Britons never, never, never shall be slaves !

The nations not so blest as thee,
   Must in their turns to tyrants fall :
While thou shalt flourish great and free,
   The dread and envy of them all.

Still more majestic shalt thou rise,
   More dreadful from each foreign stroke :
As the loud blast that tears the skies
   Serves but to root thy native oak.

Thee haughty tyrants ne'er shall tame ;
   All their attempts to bend thee down
Will but arouse thy generous flame ;
   But work their woe, and thy renown.

To thee belongs the rural reign ;
   Thy cities shall with commerce shine :
All thine shall be the subject main,
   And every shore it circles thine.

The Muses, still with freedom found,
   Shall to thy happy coast repair :
Blest isle ! with matchless beauty crowned,
   And manly hearts to guard the fair.
    Rule, Britannia, Britannia rule the waves ;
    Britons never, never, never shall be slaves !

              James Thomson

The Way the Calf Went Home

ONE day, through the primeval wood,
   A calf walked home, as good calves should ;
But made a trail all bent askew,
A crooked trail, as all calves do.
This forest trail became a lane,
That bent, and turned, and turned again,
And this, before men were aware,
A city's crowded thoroughfare ;
And men two centuries and a half
Trod in the footsteps of that calf.

              Samuel Walter Foss

MINERVA AT THE VATICAN

THE HOUSES OF PARLIAMENT

THE TOWER OF LONDON

Bad News for Croakers

In those days was Hezekiah sick unto death, and Isaiah came to him and said, Set thine house in order, for thou shalt die.

Then he turned his face to the wall, and prayed, saying, I beseech thee, O Lord, remember now how I have walked before thee in truth and with a perfect heart, and have done that which is good in thy sight. And Hezekiah wept sore.

And the word of the Lord came to him, saying, I have heard thy prayer ; I have seen thy tears : behold, I will heal thee. I will add unto thy days fifteen years.

WE have always liked the page in the Bible which tells us that the good king Hezekiah lived another fifteen years. Fifteen years of life is a wondrous thing, and it was given to that good king who made a conduit and brought water to Jerusalem before he slept with his fathers.

But today there is greater news, for fifteen years of life has been given to a nation. Our expectation of life has been raised in our generation from 40 to 55 years. *The promise made to Hezekiah has been fulfilled for the British people.*   *From a Newspaper*

God Bless Our Native Land

GOD bless our native land !
May heaven's protecting hand
    Still guard our shore ;
May Peace her power extend,
Foe be transformed to friend,
And Britain's rights depend
    On war no more.

May just and righteous laws
Uphold the public cause
    And bless our isle.
Home of the brave and free,
The land of liberty,
We pray that still on thee
    Kind heaven may smile.

And not this land alone,
But be Thy mercies known
    From shore to shore.
Lord, make the nations see
That men should brothers be,
And form one family
    The wide world o'er.
        William Hickson

The Conqueror

HE alone keeps his life and freedom who daily has to conquer them again. *Goethe*

The Song That is Heard No More

AMONG our ancient mountains,
  And from our lovely vales,
O let the prayer re-echo,
  God bless the Prince of Wales.
With hearts and voice awaken
  Those minstrel strains of yore,
Till Britain's name and glory
  Resound from shore to shore.

Should hostile bands or danger
  E'er threaten our fair isle,
May God's strong arm protect us,
  May Heaven still on us smile !
Above the throne of England
  May fortune's star long shine,
And round its sacred bulwarks
  The olive branches twine.

Welsh National Song

Precious Little One

MY heart is like a fountain true
  That flows and flows with love to you.
As chirps the lark unto the tree
So chirps my pretty Babe to me.

There's not a rose, where'er I seek,
As comely as my baby's cheek.
There's not a comb of honey bee
So full of sweets as Babe to me.

There's not a star that shines on high
Is brighter than my baby's eye.
There's not a boat upon the sea
Can dance as Baby does to me.

The queen has sceptre, crown, and ball,
You are my sceptre, crown, and all.
For all her robes of royal silk,
More fair your skin, as white as milk.

Ten thousand parks where deer do run.
Ten thousand roses in the sun,
Ten thousand pearls beneath the sea,
My Babe more precious is to me.

A Mother's Song by an Unknown Writer

They Will Come Again

THE burning of a little straw may hide the stars ; but the stars will reappear.

Voltaire

The Tired Woman's Epitaph

HERE lies a poor woman who always was tired ;
   She lived in a house where help was not hired.
Her last words on earth were, " Dear friends, I am going
Where washing ain't done, nor sweeping, nor sewing ;
But everything there is exact to my wishes ;
For where they don't eat there's no washing of dishes.
I'll be where loud anthems will always be ringing,
But, having no voice, I'll be clear of the singing.
Don't mourn for me now ; don't mourn for me never :
I'm going to do nothing for ever and ever."

Author unknown

There Is a Lady Sweet and Kind

THERE is a lady sweet and kind,
   Was never face so pleased my mind :
I did but see her passing by,
And yet I love her till I die.

Her gesture, motion, and her smiles,
Her wit, her voice, my heart beguiles :
Beguiles my heart, I know not why ;
And yet I love her till I die.

Cupid is wingèd and doth range
Her country, so my Love doth change :
But change she earth or change she sky,
Yet will I love her till I die.

*By an Unknown Writer
of the seventeenth century*

Marlowe and Raleigh in the Fields

As I entered into the field a handsome milkmaid cast away all care
and sang like a nightingale. Her voice was good, and the ditty
fitted for it. It was that smooth song *Come live with me and be my
love*, which was made by Kit Marlowe now at least fifty years ago ;
and the milkmaid's mother sang an answer to it, *If all the world and
love were young*, which was made by Sir Walter Raleigh in his
younger days. *Izaak Walton*

The Miracle of the Night

THE nightingale breathes such sweet loud music out of her little
instrumental throat that it might make mankind think miracles
are not ceased. He that at midnight, when the very labourer sleeps
securely, should hear the clear airs, the sweet descants, the natural
rising and falling, the doubling and redoubling of her voice, might
well be lifted above earth and say, " Lord, what music hast Thou
provided for the saints in heaven when Thou affordest bad men such
music on earth ? " *Izaak Walton*

The Possessor of the Earth

I COULD there sit quietly, and, looking on the waters, see fishes leaping at flies of several shapes and colours. Looking on the hills, I could behold them spotted with woods and groves. Looking down the meadows, I could see here a boy gathering lilies and ladysmocks and there a girl cropping columbines and cowslips, all to make garlands suitable to this present month of May.

As I thus sat, joying in mine own happy condition, I did thankfully remember what my Saviour said, that the meek possess the earth. *Izaak Walton*

The England Passing Away

THE paths trodden by the footsteps of ages were broken up; old things were passing away, and the faith and the life of ten centuries were dissolving like a dream.

Chivalry was dying; the abbey and the castle were soon together to crumble into ruins; and all the forms, desires, beliefs, convictions, of the old world were passing away, never to return. A new continent had risen up beyond the western sea. The floor of heaven, inlaid with stars, had sunk back into an infinite abyss of immeasurable space; and the firm earth itself, unfixed from its foundations, was seen to be but a small atom in the vastness of the Universe.

And now it is all gone—like an unsubstantial pageant faded; and between us and old England there lies a gulf of mystery which the prose of the historian will never adequately bridge. They cannot come to us, and our imagination can but feebly penetrate to them. Only among the aisles of the cathedrals, only as we gaze upon their silent figures sleeping on their tombs, some faint conceptions float before us of what these men were when they were alive; and perhaps in the sound of church bells, that peculiar creation of medieval age, which falls upon the ear like the echo of a vanished world.

J. A. Froude, writing of England 400 years ago

The Place Beloved

GOD gave all men all earth to love,
But since our hearts are small,
Ordained for each one spot should prove
Belovèd over all. *Rudyard Kipling*

The Cowards

THE worst of the worthy sort of people is that they are such cowards. A man groans over wrong; he shuts his lips, he takes his supper; he forgets. *Voltaire*

We Have Paid the Price

WE have fed our sea for a thousand years,
    And she calls us, still unfed ;
Though there's never a wave of all her waves
    But marks our English dead.

We've strawed our best to the wave's unrest,
    To the shark and the sheering gull ;
If blood be the price of Admiralty,
    Lord God, we ha' paid it full.   *Kipling*

The Smoke from a Wood Fire

A WHIFF of it can take us back to forgotten marches over unnamed
    mountains, to day-long halts beside flooded rivers in the rain,
wonderful mornings of youth, in brilliantly lighted lands where everything was possible, to uneasy wakings under the low desert moon, and
above all to God's own hour all the world over, when the stars have
gone out and it is too dark to see clear, and one lies and waits for a
new horizon to heave itself up against a new dawn.   Wood smoke
magic works on everyone according to his experience.
                                            Rudyard Kipling

Wood Fires

BEECH-WOOD fires are bright and clear
    If the logs are kept a year.
Oaken logs burn steadily
If the wood is old and dry.
Chestnut's only good, they say,
If for long it's laid away.
But ash new or ash old
Is fit for a queen with a crown of gold.

Birch and fir-logs burn too fast,
Blaze up bright but do not last.
Make a fire of elder-tree,
Death within your house you'll see.
It is by the Irish said
Hawthorn bakes the sweetest bread.
But ash green or ash brown
Is fit for a queen with a golden crown.

Elm-wood burns like churchyard mould,
E'en the very flames are cold.
Poplar gives a bitter smoke,
Fills your eye and makes you choke.
Apple-wood will scent your room
With an incense-like perfume.
But ash wet or ash dry
For a queen to warm her slippers by.
                        Celia Lady Congreve

The Simple Joys Are Dearer Far

THE midges dance aboon the burn ;
   The dews begin to fa' ;
The pairtricks down the rushy holm
   Set up their e'ening ca'.
Now loud and clear the blackbird's sang
   Rings through the briery shaw,
While, flitting gay, the swallows play
   Around the castle wa'.

Beneath the golden gloamin' sky
   The mavis mends her lay ;
The redbreast pours his sweetest strains
   To charm the lingering day ;
While weary yeldrins seem to wail
   Their little nestlings torn,
The merry wren, frae den to den,
   Gaes jinking through the thorn.

The roses fauld their silken leaves,
   The foxglove shuts its bell ;
The honeysuckle and the birk
   Spread fragrance through the dell.
Let others crowd the giddy court
   Of mirth and revelry,
The simple joys that Nature yields
   Are dearer far to me.

Robert Tannahill

George Greville's Proud Boast

I PURCHASED a magnificent collection of pictures by Vandyke and Rubens ; the works are not equalled, perhaps, in the kingdom. I made a noble approach to the Castle through the solid rock, built a porter's lodge, and founded a library of books, some valuable and scarce, all well chosen.

I made an armoury, and built walls round the court and pleasure-gardens. I built a noble greenhouse, and filled it with beautiful plants ; I placed in it a vase, considered the finest remains of Grecian Art for its size and beauty. I made a noble lake, from 300 to 400 feet broad and a mile long. I planted trees, now worth £100,000, besides 100 acres of ash. I built a stone bridge of 105 feet in span, every stone from 2000 to 3800 pounds weight ; the weight of the first tier on the centre was estimated at 100 tons. I gave the bridge to the town with no toll on it.

I will not enumerate a great many other things done by me. Let Warwick Castle speak for itself.

George Greville, Earl of Warwick

The Prisoner Bound

PRISONER, tell me, who was it bound you?

It was my master, said the prisoner. I thought I could outdo everybody in the world in wealth and power, and I amassed in my own treasure-house the money due to my king. When sleep overcame me I lay upon the bed that was for my lord, and on waking up I found I was a prisoner in my own treasure-house.

Prisoner, tell me, who was it wrought this unbreakable chain?

It was I, said the prisoner, who forged this chain very carefully. I thought my invincible power would hold the world captive, leaving me in a freedom undisturbed. Thus night and day I worked at the chain with huge fires and cruel, hard strokes. When at last the work was done and the links were complete and unbreakable I found that it held me in its grip. *Rabindranath Tagore*

Good-Night and Joy be With You All

THE weary sun's gaen down the west,
  The birds sit nodding on the tree ;
All Nature now prepares for rest,
  But rest prepared there's none for me.
The trumpet sounds to war's alarms,
  The drums they beat, the fifes they play,
Come, Mary, cheer me wi' thy charms,
  For the morn I will be far away.
Good-night, and joy—Good-night, and joy,
  Good-night, and joy be wi' you all ;
For since it's so that I must go,
  Good-night, and joy be wi' you all.
Robert Tannahill

The Willow Groweth Fast

THE willow groweth incredibly fast, it being a byword in Cambridgeshire that the profit of willows will buy the owner a horse before that of other trees will pay for his saddle. *Thomas Fuller*

The Little Lamb

ANNE, third daughter of King Charles the First, was born at Saint James, March 1637. She died in her infancy, when not quite four years old.

Being minded by those about her to call upon God, even when the grasp of Death was upon her, " I am not able (saith she) to say my long prayer, but I will say my short one. *Lighten mine eyes, O Lord, lest I sleep the sleep of death.*" This done, the little lamb gave up the ghost. *Thomas Fuller*

John Evelyn Goes Mourning to the Grave

DIED my dear son Richard, to our inexpressible grief and affliction, five years and three days old, but at that tender age a prodigy for wit and understanding, for beauty of body a very angel, for endowment of mind of incredible and rare hopes. He declaimed against the vanities of the world before he had seen any. He was all life, all prettiness, far from morose, sullen, or childish in anything he said or did.

The day before he died he called to me, and in a more serious manner than usual told me that for all I loved him so dearly I should give my house, land, and all my fine things to his brother Jack, he should have none of them. So early knowledge, so much piety and perfection. But thus God, having dressed up a saint fit for himself, would not longer permit him with us, unworthy of the future fruits of this incomparable hopeful blossom. Such a child I never saw; for such a child I bless God, in whose bosom he is. May I and mine become as this little child, who now follows the child Jesus, that Lamb of God, in a white robe whithersoever he goes.

Here ends the joy of my life, for which I go even mourning to the grave. *John Evelyn on the death of his little son*

The Little Boy Lost

DEAR SIR, I am in some little disorder by reason of the death of a little childe of mine, a boy that lately made me very glad, but now he rejoyces in his little orbe, while we think and sigh and long to be as safe as he is. *Jeremy Taylor to John Evelyn*

Rocked in the Cradle of the Deep

ROCKED in the cradle of the deep,
I lay me down in peace to sleep;
Secure I rest upon the wave,
For Thou, O Lord, hast power to save.

I know Thou wilt not slight my call,
For Thou dost mark the sparrow's fall;
And calm and peaceful is my sleep,
Rocked in the cradle of the deep.

And such the trust that still were mine,
Though stormy winds swept o'er the brine,
Or though the tempest's fiery breath
Roused me from sleep to wreck and death.

In ocean's caves still safe with Thee,
The germ of immortality;
And calm and peaceful is my sleep,
Rocked in the cradle of the deep.
Emma Willard

They Never Fail

THEY never fail who die
  In a great cause ; the block may soak their gore ;
Their heads may sodden in the sun ; their limbs
Be strung to city gates and castle walls ;
But still their spirit walks abroad.
  Though years
Elapse, and others share as dark a doom,
They but augment the deep and sweeping thoughts
That overpower all others, and conduct
The world at last to freedom. *Byron*

And Wilt Thou Leave Me Thus?

AND wilt thou leave me thus ?
  Say nay, say nay, for shame!
To save thee from the blame
Of all my grief and grame.
And wilt thou leave me thus ?
  Say nay ! Say nay !

And wilt thou leave me thus,
  That hath loved thee so long,
  In wealth and woe among ?
  And is thy heart so strong
As for to leave me thus ?
  Say nay ! Say nay !

And wilt thou leave me thus,
  That hath given thee my heart,
  Never for to depart,
  Neither for pain nor smart ?
And wilt thou leave me thus ?
  Say nay ! Say nay !

And wilt thou leave me thus,
  And have no more pity
  Of him that loveth thee ?
  Alas ! thy cruelty !
And wilt thou leave me thus ?
  Say nay ! Say nay !
  One of the first love songs in English,
  by Sir Thomas Wyatt the Elder

It Cannot Be Done

THE devil could drive woman out of Paradise, but the
  devil himself cannot drive the paradise out of woman.
  George Macdonald in Robert Falconer

The Dreamers of Jerusalem

*From a conversation between a Queen of Abyssinia
and James Bruce, discoverer of the source of the Nile.*

SEE, see, how every day of our life furnishes us with proofs of the perverseness and contradiction of human nature.

You are come from Jerusalem, through vile Turkish governments and hot unwholesome climates, to see a river and a bog, and you even take it ill when I discourage you from the pursuit of this fancy, in which you are likely to perish.

I, on the other hand, mother of kings, who have sat on the throne of this country more than thirty years, have for my only wish night and day that, after giving up everything in the world I could be conveyed to Jerusalem, and beg alms all my life after, if I could only be buried at last in the street within sight of the gate of that temple where our blessed Saviour lay.

A Passport for the Barbarians

MR GLADSTONE told us of a Chinese despatch which came under his notice when he was at the Board of Trade, and gave him food for reflection.

A ship laden with grain came to Canton. The administrator wrote to the Central Government at Peking to know whether the ship was to pay duty on its cargo.

The answer was to the effect that the Central Government of the Flowery Land was quite indifferent as a rule to the goings and comings of the Barbarians ; whether they brought a cargo or brought no cargo was a thing of supreme unconcern. "But this cargo, you say, is food for the people. There ought to be no obstacle to the entry of food for the people, so let it in. Your Younger Brother commends himself to you."   *Morley's Life of Gladstone*

These Two

WHEREVER you are, while I have life, my soul shall follow you, my ever dear Lord Marl; and wherever I am I should only kill the time wishing for night that I may sleep and hope the next day to hear from you.   *Sarah Jennings to her husband
the Duke of Marlborough in 1689*

IF I were young and handsome as I was, instead of old and faded as I am, and you could lay the empire of the world at my feet, you should never share the heart and hand that once belonged to John, Duke of Marlborough.   *Sarah Jennings when her hand
was sought by the Duke of Somerset*

Farewell to London Town

MY dear, the time has come to say
 Farewell to London town,
Farewell to each familiar street,
 The room where we looked down
Upon the people going by,
 The river flowing fast :
The innumerable shine of lamps,
 The bridges and—our past.

Our past of London days and nights,
 When every night we dreamed
Of Love and Art and Happiness,
 And every day it seemed
Ah ! little room, you held my life,
 In you I found my all ;
A white hand on the mantelpiece,
 A shadow on the wall.

My dear, what dinners we have had,
 What cigarettes and wine
In faded corners of Soho,
 Your fingers touching mine !
And now the time has come to say
 Farewell to London town ;
The prologue of our play is done,
 So ring the curtain down.

> From A Song of Parting, by
> H. C. Compton Mackenzie

The Laughing and the Weeping

LAUGH, and the world laughs with you,
 Weep, and you weep alone ;
For the sad old earth must borrow its mirth,
 But has trouble enough of its own.
Sing, and the hills will answer ;
 Sigh, it is lost on the air.
The echoes bound to a joyful sound,
 But shrink from voicing care.

Rejoice, and men will seek you,
 Grieve, and they turn and go
They want full measure of all your pleasure,
 But they do not need your woe.
Be glad, and your friends are many ;
 Be sad, and you lose them all :
There are none to decline your nectared wine,
 But alone you must drink life's gall.

> Ella Wheeler Wilcox

Put Not Your Trust in Princes

WHEN Soliman the Great was marching on Belgrade in 1521, an old woman came and complained to him that during her sleep his soldiers had stolen her oxen, which were all she had in the world.

" You must indeed have been wrapped in a deep sleep," said the Sultan, laughing, " if you did not hear the robbers."

" Yes," answered the old woman, " I was indeed sleeping peacefully, for I trusted Your Highness to watch over the public safety."

Soliman, admiring this speech, gave her compensation for the damage he ought to have prevented. *From an old book*

Five Signs of a Failing People

WHAT are the marks of low condition in a people ? I name five.

First, when people generally look upon the State as a charitable institution, which can be made to supply all their wants by putting enough votes in a ballot-box. That is a sure sign that they are declining in will-power and virility.

Second, when people generally take to scamping their work in the hours of labour, and to spending their leisure in playing the fool—a sure sign of social incompetence and intellectual poverty.

Third, when people generally lose discipline, so that, when a big thing has to be done or a difficult manoeuvre performed, instead of marching together, " one equal temper of heroic hearts," they get themselves tied up into mobs and bundles and fall to quarrelling with one another—a sure sign that they are badly bred and badly educated.

Fourth, when people generally buy their pleasures ready-made on the market, in the form of external excitement—a sure sign that personal skill is on the down grade and creativeness passing away.

Fifth, when religion becomes an interesting speculation, and the existence of right and wrong a vague rumour to be inquired into by experts—a sign that the compass is out of order and the light going out in the binnacle box.

These are the signs of low condition in a people. Whenever any of the five shows its head let us hit it, and hit it hard.

Dr L. P. Jacks

The Child in a Green Field

IT is better to be a child in a green field than a knight of many orders in a State ceremonial. *George Macdonald*

As the Sun Went Down

ONE told me Heraclitus, of thy death, and brought me to tears, and I remembered how often we two in talking put the sun to rest.

Callimachus

God Bless These Poor Folk

GOD bless these poor folk that are strivin'
By means that are honest and true,
For summat to keep 'em alive in
This world that we're scrambling through.

Owd Time he's a troublesome codger
Keeps nudgin' us on to decay,
And whispers, " Thou'rt nobbut a lodger ;
Get ready for going away."   *Edwin Waugh*

The Last Words of the Last Englishman's Wife

I AM afraid that nothing I can say will wean the Englishman from his teapot.

I have a vision of the day when England shall have at last really declined and fallen, and I see her last inhabitant and his wife sitting on the ruins of the Tower of London viewing the remains ; but they will view them over the edge of a teacup, from which the fumes, as of wet straw, will ascend to their nostrils, and one may be sure that even in that dim day they will conduct themselves with decorum.   The last Englishman's last wife's last words will be : " My dear, can I pour you another cup ? "   *From the Atlantic Monthly*

The Admiral Knocks at the Door

I HEARD a gentleman say, who was in the ship with him about six years ago, that as they were sailing over against the town of Hastings in Sussex, Sir Cloudesley Shovel called out, " Pilot, put near ; I have a little business on shore."

So he put near ; and Sir Cloudesley and this gentleman went to shore in a small boat ; and, having walked about half a mile, Sir Cloudesley came to a little house in All Saints Street.   " Come (says he), my business is here ; I came to see the good woman of this house."

Upon this they knocked at the door, and out came a poor old woman, upon which Sir Cloudesley kissed her, and then, falling down on his knees, begged her blessing, calling her mother.   He was mightily kind to her, and she to him, and after he had made his visit he left her ten guineas ; and took his leave with tears in his eyes, and departed to his ship.   *From an old diary*

The Divinity Within Us

THERE is surely a piece of Divinity in us—something that was before the elements, and owes no homage to the sun.

Sir Thomas Browne

She Could Not Bear

WE buried him at dawn of day;
    Ere set of sun his sister lay,
Self-slaughtered by his side.
Poor Basilo, she could not bear
Longer to breathe the vital air,
    When Melanippus died.
                Translated from Callimachus
                    by Herman Merivale

Alone With the Universe

BE able to be alone.   He who is thus prepared, the day is not uneasy
    nor the night black unto him.   Darkness may blind his eyes, not
his imagination.   In his bed he lies, like Pompey and his sons, in all
quarters of the earth; may speculate the Universe and enjoy the
whole world in the hermitage of himself.   Thus the old ascetic
Christians found a paradise in a desert, and with little converse on
earth held a conversation in heaven; thus they astronomised in
caves, and, though they beheld not the stars, had the glory of heaven
before them.   *Sir Thomas Browne*

On Judging Others

NO man can justly censure or condemn another, because, indeed,
    no man truly knows another.   This I perceive in myself; for
I am in the dark to all the world and my nearest friends behold me
but in a cloud.   Those that know me but superficially think less of
me than I do of myself; those of my near acquaintance think more;
God, Who truly knows me, knows that I am nothing.
                                                    Sir Thomas Browne

Absence

WITH leaden foot Time creeps along
    While Delia is away:
With her, nor plaintive was the song,
    Nor tedious was the day.

Ah, envious Power! reverse my doom;
    Now double thy career,
Strain every nerve, stretch every plume,
    And rest them when she's here!
                                            Richard Jago

John Bushby

HERE lies John Bushby, honest man!
    Cheat him, Devil, if you can.
                                        Robert Burns

The Prayer of Sir Thomas Browne

THE night is come like to the day,
Depart not thou, great God, away.

Let not my sins, black as the night,
Eclipse the lustre of thy light.
Keep still in my horizon, for to me
The sun makes not the day, but Thee.

Thou whose nature cannot sleep,
On my temples sentry keep ;
Guard me 'gainst those watchful foes,
Whose eyes are open while mine close.

Let no dreams my head infest,
But such as Jacob's temples blest.
While I do rest, my soul advance,
Make my sleep a holy trance,

That I may, my rest being wrought,
Awake into some holy thought,
And with as active vigour run
My course, as doth the nimble sun.

Sleep is a death, O make me try,
By sleeping, what it is to die.
And as gently lay my head
On my grave as now my bed.

Howe'er I rest, great God, let me
Awake again at last with thee.
And, thus assured, behold I lie
Securely or to wake or die.

These are my drowsy days, in vain
I do now wake to sleep again :
O come that hour when I shall never
Sleep again, but wake for ever.

Written in the seventeenth century

The Earl's Five Legacies

I GIVE all my deer to Earl Salisbury, who I know will preserve them,
because he denied the King a buck out of one of his own parks.

I give nothing to Lord Say ; which legacy I give to him because
I know he will bestow it on the poor.

To Tom May I give five shillings ; I intended him more, but whoever
has seen his History of the Parliament thinks five shillings too much.

I give Lieutenant-General Cromwell one word of mine, because
hitherto he never kept his own !

I give up the ghost. *From a will made by the Earl of Pembroke*

Five Things from Long Ago

W*HAT is that which is most beautiful?*
The Universe, for it is the work of God.
What is most powerful?
Necessity, because it triumphs over all things.
What is most difficult?
To know oneself.
What is most easy?
To give advice.
What is necessary to happiness?
A sound body and a contented mind.

Thales of Miletus, Seventh Century B.C.

The Friend Who Puts Us to Shame

M AN is the god of the dog. He knows no other ; he can understand no other.

And see how he worships him—with what reverence he crouches
at his feet, with what love he fawns upon him, with what dependence
he looks up to him, with what cheerful alacrity he obeys him. His
whole soul is wrapt up in his god. All the powers of his nature are
devoted to his service, and are ennobled by the intercourse. Divines
tell us that it just ought to be so with the Christian, but the dog
puts the Christian to shame. *Robert Burns*

A Prayer in the Prospect of Death

O THOU unknown Almighty Cause
Of all my hope and fear !
In whose dread presence, ere an hour,
Perhaps I must appear !

If I have wandered in those paths
Of life I ought to shun ;
As something, loudly in my breast,
Remonstrates I have done ;

Thou know'st that Thou hast formed me
With passions wild and strong ;
And listening to their witching voice
Has often led me wrong.

Where human weakness has come short,
Or frailty stept aside,
Do thou, All-Good ! for such Thou art,
In shades of darkness hide.

Where with intention I have erred,
No other plea I have,
But Thou art good ; and Goodness still
Delighteth to forgive. *Robert Burns*

WOMEN AT PRAYER, BY ALPHONSE LEGROS

THE NATIVITY, BY FRA ANGELICO

SALISBURY CATHEDRAL

SHAKESPEARE'S CHURCH

Two Rich Men

THERE is a story of a man whom others called poor and who had just enough fortune to support himself in going about the country in the simplest way and studying and enjoying the life and beauty of it. He was once in the company of a great millionaire who was engaged in business, working at it daily and getting richer every year, and the poor man said to the millionaire: I am a richer man than you are.

How do you make that out? said the millionaire.

Why (he replied), I have got as much money as I want and you have not. *Lord Grey of Fallodon*

The Soul's Best Friend

FAREWELL, thou busy world! and may
We never meet again;
Here can I eat, and sleep, and pray,
And do more good in one short day
Than he who his whole age outwears
Upon the most conspicuous theatres,
Where naught but vanity and vice do reign.

Great God! how sweet are all things here!
How beautiful the fields appear!
How cleanly do we feed and lie!
Lord! what good hours do we keep!
How quietly we sleep! *Charles Cotton on arriving
in the country from the town*

She is a Winsome Wee Thing

SHE is a winsome wee thing,
She is a handsome wee thing,
She is a bonnie wee thing,
This sweet wee wife o' mine.

I never saw a fairer,
I never loved a dearer,
And neist my heart I'll wear her,
For fear my jewel tine.

She is a winsome wee thing,
She is a handsome wee thing,
She is a bonnie wee thing,
This sweet wee wife o' mine.

The warld's wrack, we share o't,
The warstle and the care o't;
Wi' her I'll blithely bear it,
And think my lot divine.
Robert Burns

F.T.—3

Heart Could Not Wish for More

MY blessings on ye, honest wife,
I ne'er was here before :
Ye've wealth o' gear for spoon and knife,
Heart could not wish for more.

Heaven keep you clear of sturt and strife,
Till far ayont four score,
And while I toddle on through life
I'll ne'er gae by your door !

Robert Burns

Mary Queen of Scots Waiting for Death

O SOON to me may summer suns
Nae mair light up the morn,
Nae mair to me the autumn winds
Wave o'er the yellow corn.
And in the narrow house of death
Let winter round me rave,
And the next flowers that deck the spring
Bloom on my peaceful grave.

Robert Burns

Afton Water

FLOW gently, sweet Afton, among thy green braes,
Flow gently, I'll sing thee a song in thy praise ;
My Mary's asleep by thy murmuring stream,
Flow gently, sweet Afton, disturb not her dream.

Thou stock-dove whose echo resounds thro' the glen,
Ye wild whistling blackbirds in yon thorny den,
Thou green-crested lapwing, thy screaming forbear,
I charge you disturb not my slumbering fair.

How lofty, sweet Afton, thy neighbouring hills,
Far mark'd, with the courses of clear winding rills ;
There daily I wander as noon rises high,
My flocks and my Mary's sweet cot in my eye.

How pleasant thy banks and green valleys below,
Where wild in the woodlands the primroses blow ;
There oft as mild ev'ning weeps over the lea,
The sweet-scented birk shades my Mary and me.

Robert Burns

The Heavens Above and the Law Within

TWO things fill the mind with ever new and increasing wonder and
awe—the starry heavens above me and the moral law within me.

Immanuel Kant

A Grace Before Dinner

O THOU, who kindly dost provide
  For every creature's want !
We bless thee, God of Nature wide,
  For all thy goodness lent :
And, if it please thee, Heavenly Guide,
  May never worse be sent ;
But whether granted, or denied,
  Lord, bless us with content !

Robert Burns

On Commissary Goldie's Brains

L ORD, to account who dares thee call,
  Or e'er dispute thy pleasure ?
Else why within so thick a wall
  Enclose so poor a treasure ?

Robert Burns

Should Auld Acquaintance be Forgot?

S HOULD auld acquaintance be forgot
  And never brought to mind ?
Should auld acquaintance be forgot
  And auld lang syne ?

  For auld lang syne, my jo,
    For auld lang syne,
  We'll tak' a cup o' kindness yet,
    For auld lang syne.

And surely ye'll be your pint-stoup,
  And surely I'll be mine ;
And we'll tak' a cup o' kindness yet
  For auld lang syne.

We twa hae run about the braes,
  And pu'd the gowans fine ;
But we've wandered mony a weary fit
  Sin' auld lang syne.

We twa hae paidled i' the burn
  Frae morning sun till dine ;
But seas between us braid hae roared
  Sin' auld lang syne.

And there's a hand, my trusty fiere,
  And gie's a hand o' thine ;
And we'll tak' a right gude-willie waught
  For auld lang syne.   *Robert Burns*

For All That and All That

Is there, for honest poverty,
  That hangs his head, and a' that ?
The coward-slave, we pass him by,
  We dare be poor for a' that !
    For a' that and a' that ;
      Our toils obscure and a' that ;
    The rank is but the guinea stamp,
      The man's the gowd for a' that.

What though on hamely fare we dine,
  Wear hodden-gray and a' that ;
Gie fools their silks and knaves their wine,
  A man's a man for a' that.
    For a' that and a' that,
      Their tinsel show and a' that ;
    The honest man, though e'er sae poor,
      Is king o' men for a' that.

A king can mak a belted knight,
  A marquis, duke, and a' that ;
But an honest man's aboon his might,
  Guid faith, he mauna fa' that !
    For a' that and a' that,
      Their dignities and a' that,
    The pith o' sense and pride o' worth
      Are higher rank than a' that.

Then let us pray that come it may,
  As come it will for a' that,
That sense and worth, o'er a' the earth,
  May bear the gree, and a' that ;
    For a' that and a' that,
      It's coming yet for a' that,
    When man to man, the warld o'er,
      Shall brothers be for a' that. Robert Burns

Magna Est Veritas

Here, in this little Bay,
  Full of tumultuous life and great repose,
Where, twice a day,
The purposeless, glad ocean comes and goes,
Under high cliffs, and far from the huge town,
I sit me down.
For want of me the world's course will not fail :
When all its work is done the lie shall rot :
The truth is great, and shall prevail
When none cares whether it prevail or not.
                                    Coventry Patmore

Peeling a Potato

IF you see a young girl you would like to marry manage somehow to see her peel potatoes.

If she cuts the peelings very thick you will know she is extravagant ; if she leaves in the eyes she is lazy ; if she washes them in only one water she is dirty ; if she uses much fat to boil them she is greasy ; if she lets them burn she is careless. Leave such a girl ; she would not make a man happy.

But if you find a girl who knows how to take a potato, peel it, wash it, and boil it, marry her whether she be pretty or ugly, poor or rich ; she will make you happy. *An Arab's philosophy*

The Heaps Saved from the Great Fire

THE smoke and fiery vapour continued so intense that my hair was almost singed. The by-lanes and narrower streets were filled up with rubbish, nor could one possibly have known where he was but by the ruins of some church or hall that had some remarkable tower or pinnacle remaining.

I went toward Islington and Highgate, where one might have seen two hundred thousand people of all ranks and degrees dispersed and lying along by their heaps of what they could save from the fire, ready to perish from hunger and destitution, yet not asking one penny for relief, which to me appeared a stranger sight than any I had yet beheld. *John Evelyn*

The World on an Even Keel

IF anybody will take down the map of the world and study it he will see at once that the world is ballasted by the English-speaking countries, how, as long as they remain friends, holding the trade routes and the main material resources of the world under their control, the world must needs sail on an even keel. *John Galsworthy*

Fouling Civilisation

PEOPLE who are sending this nauseating film stuff across the world are fouling civilisation. Our criminal courts and hospitals are left to clear up the litter, while money-bugs clear off with the money-bags.

One can respect misguided enthusiasm and honest error, but here are men deliberately exploiting every human nobility for cash. An England peopled with their sexual spectres could not live.

I am no kill-joy, and for that reason I do not want to see happiness and beauty and idealism shattered. I prefer to see dirt outlawed by an informed public opinion. *J. A. R. Cairns*

Shakespeare's Countryman

NOT without honour my days ran,
　　Nor yet without a boast shall end,
For I was Shakespeare's countryman,
And were you not my friend ?

William Watson

Queen Elizabeth Speaks

MY hands were stained with blood, my heart was proud and cold,
　　My soul is black with shame . . . but I gave Shakespeare gold.
So after aeons of flame I may, by grace of God,
Rise up to kiss the dust that Shakespeare's feet have trod.

Joyce Kilmer

Alone With Shakespeare

WHEN I went out of office after eleven years, very tired and for the time not fit for anything, I spent some weeks alone in the country. During that time I read several of Shakespeare's plays. The impression produced upon me by his incredible power and range was really that of awe ; I felt almost afraid to be alone in the room with him, as if I were in the presence of something supernatural.

Lord Grey of Fallodon

Finis

A THOUSAND years of European history thus came to a close. . . . The empire that had once extended from the Carpathians to Spain had vanished from the eyes of men. The great edifice had collapsed with less noise than accompanies the fall of some aged tapestry from the wall that has been its home for countless years.

The Empire was in truth not unlike a faded piece of tapestry. . . . The colours faded. The gaily-clad knights and ladies lost their animation and became somewhat ridiculous in their stiff and formal attitudes. The wall that supported the tapestry began to crumble ever so gradually with the passage of time. Outside the dim room a new life and new civilisation had sprung up. It had even begun to invade the room itself with strange new pieces of furniture that made the tapestry look still more faded and worn. One day the supports that had upheld the tapestry through so many years quietly gave way, and it lay like a dusty old piece of cloth upon the floor.

As with the tapestry, so with the Hapsburg Monarchy. Age had sapped its virility. For long it stood tottering upon its crumbling foundations. As the wind lays some aged forest giant upon the ground, so the World War swept away the Hapsburgs and their Empire into the limbo that awaits outworn institutions. *Felix nube* —if he read that famous phrase in exile, Karl's lips must have been twisted into a smile at once ironic and pitiful.

*On the Hapsburg Monarchy—the last words of the
last article in the last number of the Edinburgh
Review, on closing its career after more than a century*

All Things Pass

I PASSED one day by a very ancient and wonderfully populous city, and asked one of its inhabitants how long it had been founded. It is indeed a mighty city (replied he); we know not how long it has existed, and our ancestors were on this subject as ignorant as ourselves.

Five centuries afterwards, as I passed by the same place, I could not perceive the slightest vestige of the city. I demanded of a peasant who was gathering herbs upon its former site how long it had been destroyed.

In sooth, a strange question (replied he); the ground here has never been different from what you now behold it. Was there not of old (said I) a splendid city here? Never (answered he), so far as we have seen; and never did our fathers speak to us of any such.

On my return there five hundred years afterwards I found the sea in the place; and on its shores were a party of fishermen, of whom I inquired how long the land had been covered by the waters.

Is this a question (say they) for a man like you? This spot has always been what it is now.

I again returned five hundred years afterwards; the sea had disappeared. I inquired of a man how long this change had taken place, and he gave me the same answer as I had received before.

Lastly, on coming back again after an equal lapse of time, I found there a flourishing city, more populous and more rich in beautiful buildings than the city I had seen the first time; and when I would fain have informed myself concerning its origin the inhabitants answered me: " Its rise is lost in remote antiquity; we are ignorant how long it has existed, and our fathers were on this subject as ignorant as ourselves." *An Arabian writer of the Thirteenth Century*

The Worm Must Not Complain

HE who makes himself a worm cannot complain if he is crushed.
Immanuel Kant

The Dreamers

AH, there be souls none understand,
  Like clouds, they cannot touch the land,
Drive as they may by field or town.

Call these not fools; the test of worth
Is not the hold you have on earth.
Lo, there be gentlest souls, sea blown,
That know not any harbour known,
And it may be the reason is
They touch on fairer shores than this.
Joaquin Miller

All You Have at the End

GIVE honour and love for evermore
　To this great man gone to rest ;
Peace on the dim Plutonian shore,
Rest in the land of the blest.

I reckon him greater than any man
That ever drew sword in war ;
I reckon him nobler than king or khan,
Braver and better by far.

And wisest he in this whole wide land
Of hoarding till bent and grey,
For all you can hold in your cold dead hand
Is what you have given away.

So whether to wander the stars or to rest
For ever hushed and dumb,
He gave with a zest and he gave his best :
Give him the best to come.

*Joaquin Miller on Peter Cooper, inventor
and philanthropist, who died in 1883*

The Mystic and the Beggar

*A book of the fourteenth century tells this
conversation between a Mystic and a Beggar*

GOD give you a good day, my friend, said the Mystic.
　I thank God I never had a bad day, said the Beggar.
God give you a happy life, said the Mystic.
I thank God I am never unhappy, said the Beggar.
But who are you ? asked the Mystic, surprised by his reply.
I am a king, said the Beggar.
But where is your kingdom ? said the Mystic.
To whom the Beggar once again answered, *In my own heart.*

The Something that Comes to the Aid of a Man

A RAPTURE may visit a man suddenly faced with peril and opportunity in a battle or an accident. He is released—that is all
you can say. Fear and desire, his two keepers through life, to
preserve and enchain him, are suddenly gone, and he goes to self-
sacrifice as lightly as a child draws its breath, with so perfect a
freedom from all sense of effort, danger, or pain that presently he is
surprised and abashed, and feels like a secret impostor when people
credit him with heroism.
C. E. Montague

The Things We Love and Bless

DAUGHTER, daughter! don't call names; you are always abusing my pleasures, which is what no mortal will bear. Trash, lumber, sad stuff, are the titles you give my favourite amusements. If I called a white staff a stick of wood, a gold key gilded brass, and the ensigns of illustrious orders coloured strings, this may be philosophically true, but would be very ill received. We have all our playthings; happy are they that can be contented with those they can obtain.

Lady Mary Montagu

The Lost Leader

JUST for a handful of silver he left us,
   Just for a riband to stick in his coat,
Found the one gift of which Fortune bereft us,
   Lost all the others she lets us devote;
They, with the gold to give, doled him out silver,
   So much was theirs who so little allowed:
How all our copper had gone for his service!
   Rags—were they purple, his heart had been proud.

We that had loved him so, followed him, honoured him,
   Lived in his mild and magnificent eye,
Learned his great language, caught his clear accents,
   Made him our pattern to live and to die:
Shakespeare was of us, Milton was for us,
   Burns, Shelley, were with us—they watch from their graves!
He alone breaks from the van and the freemen,
   He alone sinks to the rear and the slaves.

We shall march prospering—not through his presence;
   Songs may inspirit us—not from his lyre;
Deeds will be done while he boasts his quiescence,
   Still bidding crouch whom the rest bade aspire:
Blot out his name then, record one lost soul more,
   One task more declined, one more footpath untrod,
One more devil's triumph and sorrow for angels,
   One wrong more to man, one more insult to God!

Life's night begins: let him never come back to us!
   There would be doubt, hesitation, and pain,
Forced praise on our part, the glimmer of twilight,
   Never glad confident morning again.
Best fight on well, for we taught him—strike gallantly,
   Menace our heart ere we master his own;
Then let him receive the new knowledge and wait us,
   Pardoned in heaven, the first by the throne.

Robert Browning

God Took Them

It is a little odd, in going through Browning's poems and letters, to come upon these two beautiful things. In the letter he is describing the death of his wife, who passed away in Florence, where she lies on a little hill above that beautiful city.

God Took Me

OVERHEAD the tree-tops meet,
Flowers and grass spring 'neath one's feet;
There was nought above me, and nought below,
My childhood had not learned to know:
For what are the voices of birds
(Ay, and of beasts) but words, our words,
Only so much more sweet?

The knowledge of that with my life begun.
But I had so near made out the Sun,
And counted your stars, the Seven and One,
Like the fingers of my hand:
Nay, I could all but understand
Wherefore through heaven the white Moon ranges;
And just when out of her soft fifty changes
No unfamiliar face might overlook me,
Suddenly God took me.

God Took Her

GOD took her. She suffered very little pain, and was spared the misery of knowing she was about to leave us; she was smilingly assuring me she was better to within a few minutes of the last.

Then came what my heart will keep till I see her again, and longer, the most perfect expression of her love to me within my whole knowledge of her—always smilingly, happily, and with a face like a girl's; and in a few minutes she died in my arms, her head on my cheek.

God took her to Himself as you would lift a sleeping child from a dark, weary bed into the light.

The Rubbish Heap of Oxyrhynchus

In a rubbish heap at Oxyrhynchus in Egypt there were found last century about 1800 fragments of papyri, some with new sayings of Jesus, and one with this letter from a boy to his father.

Theonas writes to his father Theon: Greeting

IT was a fine thing of you not to take me with you to town. If you won't take me with you to Alexandria I won't write you a letter or speak to you. Mother said to Archelaus: "He upsets me. Take him away!" So send for me, I implore you. If you won't send I won't eat, I won't drink. There now. Farewell. Deliver to Theon from his son Theonas.

The Little Thing and the Great Thing

THAT low man seeks a little thing to do,
  Sees it and does it :
This high man, with a great thing to pursue,
  Dies ere he knows it.
That low man goes on adding one to one,
  His hundred's soon hit :
This high man, aiming at a million,
  Misses a unit.
That has the world here—should he need the next,
Let the world mind him !
This throws himself on God, and, unperplexed,
  Seeking shall find Him.   *Robert Browning*

Farewell from Paradise

I AM the nearest nightingale
  That singeth in Eden after you ;
And I am singing loud and true
And sweet ; I do not fail.
I sit upon a cypress bough,
Close to the gate, and I fling my song
Over the gate and through the mail
Of the warden angels marshalled strong :
Over the gate and after you !
And the warden angels let it pass,
Because the poor brown bird, alas,
  Sings in the garden, sweet and true.
And I build my song of high pure notes,
  Note over note, height over height,
  Till I strike the arch of the Infinite,
And I bridge abysmal agonies
With strong, clear calms of harmonies,
And something abides, and something floats,
And in the song which I sing after you.
  Fare ye well, farewell !   *Mrs Browning*

Waiting by the Temple

*This love-letter to a gladiator was found in the ruins of the Street
of Abundance in Pompeii ; it was written 2000 years ago.*

ART thou Phoebus Apollo in the body of Hercules ? Indeed thou
art a god to me. Thy beauty and strength have blotted from
my eyes all other men. I am young and the suitors I despise say
that I am beautiful. I will await thee, beloved one, near the Temple
of Isis.

When I Have Fears That I May Cease to Be

WHEN I have fears that I may cease to be
    Before my pen has cleaned my teeming brain,
Before high-pilèd books, in charactery,
Hold like rich garners the full ripened grain ;
When I behold, upon the night's starred face,
Huge cloudy symbols of a high romance,
And think that I may never live to trace
Their shadows, with the magic hand of chance ;
And when I feel, fair creature of an hour,
That I shall never look upon thee more,
Never have relish in the faery power
Of unreflecting love—then on the shore
Of the wide world I stand alone, and think
Till love and fame to nothingness do sink.

                      Keats

Red and White Roses

READ in these roses the sad story
    Of my hard fate and your own glory.
In the white you may discover
The paleness of a fainting lover ;
In the red the flames still feeding
On my heart with fresh wounds bleeding.
The white will tell you how I languish,
And the red express my anguish :
The white my innocence displaying,
The red my martyrdom betraying :
The frowns that on your brow resided,
Have those roses thus divided.
Oh ! let your smiles but clear the weather,
And then they both shall grow together.

          A poem with a bunch of roses
          to a lady, by Thomas Carew

Do Not Leave Me Thus

A letter written on papyrus in the third century by a soldier's son to his mother

WHEN my father came to me, he did not give me an obolus or a cloak or anything. All will laugh at me. "His father is a soldier," they will say, "and yet he gives him nothing."

My father said, "When I get home I will send you everything," but he has sent me nothing. Why ?

The mother of Valerius sent him a pair of girdles and a jar of oil, and a basket of dainties, and 200 drachmae. Wherefore, I beg you, mother, send to me. Do not leave me thus.

The Proof

IF the man who turnip cries,
Cry not when his father dies,
Tis a proof that he had rather
Have a turnip than his father.

Dr Johnson

Little Brother

AMONG the beautiful pictures
That hang on Memory's wall
Is one of a dim old forest,
That seemeth best of all.
I once had a little brother,
With eyes that were dark and deep ;
In the lap of that old dim forest
He lieth in peace asleep ;
Light as the down of the thistle,
Free as the winds that blow,
We roved there the beautiful summers,
The summers of long ago ;
But his feet on the hills grew weary,
And, one of the autumn eves,
I made for my little brother
A bed of the yellow leaves.
Sweetly his pale arms folded
My neck in a meek embrace,
As the light of immortal beauty
Silently covered his face ;
And when the arrows of sunset
Lodged in the tree-tops bright,
He fell, in his saint-like beauty,
Asleep by the gates of light.
Therefore of all the pictures
That hang on Memory's wall,
The one of the dim old forest
Seemeth the best of all.

Alice Cary

Two Lines in Two Centuries

NATURE and Nature's laws lay hid in night :
God said, *Let Newton be,* and all was light.
Alexander Pope in the Eighteenth Century

IT did not last. The Devil, howling *Ho !*
Let Einstein be, restored the status quo.
J. C. Squire in the Twentieth Century

The Idle Singer of an Empty Day

OF Heaven or Hell I have no power to sing:
  I cannot ease the burden of your fears,
Or make quick-coming death a little thing,
  Or bring again the pleasure of past years;
  Nor for my words shall ye forget your tears,
Nor hope again for aught that I can say,
The idle singer of an empty day.

But rather, when a-weary of your mirth,
  From full hearts still unsatisfied ye sigh,
And, feeling kindly unto all the earth,
  Grudge every minute as it passes by,
  Made the more mindful that the sweet days lie—
Remember me a little then I pray,
The idle singer of an empty day.

*The verse with which William Morris
leads us on to his Earthly Paradise*

The Undiscovered Ocean

I SEEM to have been only like a boy playing on the seashore and
diverting myself in now and then finding a smoother pebble or a
prettier shell than ordinary, while the great ocean of truth lay all
undiscovered before me.   *Sir Isaac Newton*

Joyce Kilmer to a Very Beautiful Ladye

FROM what old ballad or from what rich frame
  Did you descend to glorify the Earth?
Was it from Chaucer's singing book you came?
  Or did Watteau's small brushes give you birth?

Nothing so exquisite as that slight hand
  Could Raphael or Leonardo trace;
Nor could the poets know in Fairyland
  The changing wonder of your lyric face.

I would possess a host of lovely things,
  But I am poor and such joys may not be;
So God Who lifts the poor and humble kings
  Sent loveliness itself to dwell with me.

Written by Joyce Kilmer for Aline his wife

I Eat My Peas With Honey

I EAT my peas with honey;
  I've done it all my life:
It makes the peas taste funny,
  But keeps them on the knife.

Rhyme by a Writer Unknown

Little One Coming

IF it is a boy, well and good ; if it is a girl, throw it away.

About the time of Christ an Egyptian labourer was writing
this message to his wife, who was expecting a child to be born

Man Should Not Hunt Mankind to Death

MAN should not hunt mankind to death,
But strike the enemies of man.
Kill vices if you can :
They are your wildest beasts,
And when they thickest fall
You make the gods true feasts.

Ben Jonson

Ben Jonson Invites a Friend to His Poor House

TONIGHT, grave sir, both my poor house and I
Do equally desire your company :
Not that we think us worthy such a guest,
But that your worth will dignify our feast.
With those that come, whose grace may make that seem
Something which else would hope for no esteem.
It is the fair acceptance, sir, creates
The entertainment perfect, not the cates.
Yet shall you have, to rectify your palate,
An olive, capers, or some better sallet
Ushering the mutton : with a short-legged hen,
If we can get her full of eggs, and then,
Limons, and wine for sauce : to these a coney
Is not to be despaired of for our money ;
Nor shall our cups make any guilty men,
But at our parting will be as when
We innocently met.   No simple word
That shall be uttered at our mirthful board
Shall make us sad next morning, or affright
The liberty that we'll enjoy tonight.

Ben Jonson to Queen Elizabeth

LET Flattery be dumb and Envy blind
In her dread presence : Death himself admire her.
And may her virtues make him forget
The use of his inevitable hand.
Fly from her, Age ; sleep, Time, before her throne :
Our strongest walls fall down when she is gone.

Epilogue spoken before Queen Elizabeth at Ben
Jonson's play Everyman Out of His Humour

He Who Taught Himself

HE who was taught only by himself had a fool for a master.
Ben Jonson

At the End of the War

AMONG the calamities of war may be justly numbered the diminution of the love of truth by the falsehoods which interest dictates and credulity encourages.

A peace will equally leave the warrior and the relater of wars destitute of employment; and I know not whether more is to be dreaded from streets filled with soldiers accustomed to plunder, or from garrets filled with scribblers accustomed to lie. *Dr Johnson*

The Thing That is Worth All We Have

BOSWELL: People go through the world very well and carry on the business of life to good advantage without learning.

Johnson: Why, sir, that may be true in cases where learning cannot possibly be of any use; for instance, this boy rows us as well without learning as if he could sing the song of Orpheus to the Argonauts who were the first sailors.

Johnson then called to the boy: What would you give, my lad, to know about the Argonauts who were the first sailors?

Sir, said the boy, I would give what I have.

Johnson was much pleased with his answer, and we gave him a double fare. My friend then turning to me: " Sir," he said, " a desire of knowledge is the natural feeling of mankind, and every human being whose mind is not debauched will be willing to give all that he has to get knowledge." *From Boswell's Life of Johnson*

The Englishman and the Frenchman

A FRENCHMAN must always be talking, whether he knows anything of the matter or not; an Englishman is content to say nothing when he has nothing to say. *Dr Johnson*

A Recipe for Good Talk

THERE must, in the first place, be knowledge, there must be materials. In the second place there must be a command of words. In the third place there must be imagination, to place things in such views as they are not commonly seen in. In the fourth place there must be presence of mind, and a resolution that is not to be overcome by failure. This last is an essential requisite; for want of it many people do not excel in conversation. Now I want it; I throw up the game upon losing a trick.
Dr Johnson, the great talker

Prospect from Scotland

THE noblest prospect a Scotsman ever sees is the highroad that leads him to England.   *Dr Johnson*

Introducing the Vicar of Wakefield

I RECEIVED one morning a message from poor Goldsmith that he was in great distress, and, as it was not in his power to come to me, begging that I would come to him as soon as possible. I sent him a guinea and promised to come to him directly.

I accordingly went as soon as I was dressed, and found that his landlady had arrested him for his rent, at which he was in a violent passion. I perceived that he had already changed my guinea and had got a bottle of Madeira and a glass before him. I put the cork into the bottle, desired he would be calm, and began to talk to him of the means by which he might be extricated.

He then told me that he had a novel ready for the press, which he produced to me. I looked into it and saw its merit; told the landlady I should soon return; and, having gone to a bookseller, sold it for sixty pounds. I brought Goldsmith the money and he discharged his rent, not without rating his landlady in a high tone for having used him so ill. *Dr Johnson's discovery of the Vicar of Wakefield*

March Comes On

THE stormy March is come at last,
  With wind, and cloud, and changing skies;
I hear the rushing of the blast
  That through the snowy valley flies.

Ah, passing few are they who speak,
  Wild, stormy month, in praise of thee;
Yet though thy winds are loud and bleak,
  Thou art a welcome month to me.

For thou, to northern lands, again
  The glad and glorious sun dost bring;
And thou hast joined the gentle train
  And wear'st the gentle name of Spring.

Then sing aloud the gushing rills
  In joy that they again are free.
And, brightly leaping down the hills,
  Renew their journey to the sea.

Thou bring'st the hope of those calm skies,
  And that soft time of sunny flowers,
When the wide bloom on earth that lies
  Seems of a brighter world than ours.
                              William Cullen Bryant

Some Call it Evolution

A FIRE-MIST and a planet,
　　A crystal and a cell,
A jelly-fish and a saurian,
　　And a cave where the cave-men dwell;
Then a sense of law and beauty,
　　A face turned from the clod:
Some call it Evolution,
　　And others call it God.

Like tides on the crescent sea-beach
　　When the moon is new and thin,
Into our hearts high yearnings
　　Come welling and surging in,
Come from the mystic ocean,
　　Whose rim no foot has trod:
Some of us call it Longing,
　　And others call it God.

A haze on the far horizon,
　　The infinite, tender sky,
The ripe, rich tint of the cornfields,
　　And the wild geese flying high,
And over upland and lowland
　　The charm of the golden-rod:
Some of us call it Autumn,
　　And others call it God.

A picket frozen on duty,
　　A mother starved for her brook,
Socrates drinking the hemlock,
　　And Jesus on the rood,
And millions who, humble and nameless,
　　The straight hard pathway trod:
Some call it Consecration,
　　And others call it God.

William Herbert Carruth

Our Earthly Rulers Falter

O GOD of earth and altar
　　Bow down and hear our cry,
Our earthly rulers falter
　　Our people drift and die;
The walls of gold entomb us
　　The swords of scorn divide,
Take not thy thunder from us,
　　But take away our pride.

G. K. Chesterton

William Byrd's Prayer

PROSTRATE, O Lord, I lie,
　Behold me, Lord, with pity,
Stop not thine ears against my cry,
　My sad and mourning ditty,
Breathed from an inward soul
　From a heart heartily contrite,
An offering sweet, a sacrifice,
　In Thy high heavenly sight.

Observe not sins, O Lord,
　For who may then abide it?
But let Thy mercy cancel them,
　Thou hast not man denied it,
Man melting with remorse and thoughts,
　Thought past repenting.
O lighten, Lord, and hear our songs,
　Our sins full sore lamenting.

The wonders of Thy works
　Above all reason reacheth,
And yet Thy mercy above all
　This, us Thy spirit teacheth.
Then let no sinner fall
　In depth of soul's despair,
Since never soul so foul there was
　But mercy made it fair.

To His Lost Wife

SLEEP on, my love, in thy cold bed
　Never to be disquieted!
My last good-night! Thou wilt not wake
Till I thy fate shall overtake:
Till age, or grief, or sickness must
Marry my body to that dust
It so much loves; and fill the room
My heart keeps empty in that tomb.

Stay for me there: I will not fail
To meet thee in that hollow vale.
And think not much of my delay:
I am already on the way,
And follow thee with all the speed
Desire can make, or sorrows breed.
Each minute is a short degree
And every hour a step towards thee.
　　　Henry King, Bishop of Chichester

God's Long Wait

WHETHER my discoveries will be read by posterity, or by my contemporaries, is a matter that concerns them more than me. I may be well contented to wait one century for a reader, when God Himself during so many thousand years has waited for an observer.

John Kepler

Men Should be Careful

MEN should be careful lest they cause women to weep, for God counts their tears. *The Talmud*

Two Frogs

OWING to the drying-up of a lake two frogs were forced to quit and to seek for water elsewhere. As they were upon the search they discovered a very deep well. Come, says one to the other, let us go down here. You say well, says her companion; but what if the water should fail us here, too? How shall we get out?

Tis good advice to look before we leap. *Aesop*

The Wolf in a Sheep's Coat

THERE goes a story of a wolf that wrapped himself up in a sheep's skin and worried lambs for a good while under that disguise; but the shepherd met with him at last, and trussed him up, sheepskin and all, upon an eminent gibbet for a spectacle and an example. The neighbours made a wonderment of it, and asked him what he meant by hanging up his sheep. Oh, says he, that's only the skin of a sheep that was made use of to cover the heart, malice and body of a wolf that shrouded himself under it.

People are not to be judged by their looks, but by the character of their lives and by their works. *Aesop*

Mr Valiant Passes Over

IT was noised about that Mr Valiant-for-Truth was sent for. When he understood it he called for his friends and told them of it. Then he said, I am going to my Father's; and, though with great difficulty I got hither, yet now I do not repent me of all the trouble I have been at to arrive where I am.

My sword I give to him that shall succeed me in my pilgrimage, and my courage and skill to him that can get it. My marks and scars I carry with me, to be a witness for me that I have fought his battles who now will be my rewarder.

When the day that he must go hence was come many accompanied him to the riverside, into which as he went he said, *Death, where is thy sting?* and as he went down deeper he said, *Grave, where is thy victory?* So he passed over, and all the trumpets sounded for him on the other side. *Pilgrim's Progress*

The Ten Commandments

THOU shalt not have another God than me :
    Thou shalt not to an image bow thy knee.
Thou shalt not take the name of God in vain :
See that the Sabbath thou do not profane.
Honour thy father and thy mother too :
In act or thought see thou no murder do.
From evil habits keep thy body clean :
Thou shalt not steal, though thou be very mean.
Bear no false witness, keep thee without spot :
What is thy neighbour's see thou covet not.

John Bunyan

John Bunyan's Riddle

THEN were they very merry, and sat at the table a long time, talking of many things. Then said the old gentleman, My good landlord, while we are cracking your nuts, if you please, do you open this riddle :

A man there was (though some did count him mad),
The more he cast away the more he had.

Then they all gave good heed, wondering what Gaius would say. So he sat still awhile, and then replied :

He who bestows his goods upon the poor,
Shall have as much again, and ten times more.

Then said Joseph, I did not think you could have found it out. Oh, said Gaius, I have been trained up in this way a great while ; nothing teaches like experience.   *Pilgrim's Progress*

On His Pilgrim's Progress

THIS book will make a traveller of thee
    If by its counsel thou wilt ruled be.
It will direct thee to the Holy Land
If thou wilt its directions understand.
Yea, it will make the slothful active be ;
The blind also delightful things to see.
Art thou for something rare and profitable ?
Or wouldst thou see a truth within a fable ?
Art thou forgetful ? Or would'st thou remember
From New Year's Day to the last of December ?
Then read my fancies ; they will stick like burrs,
And may be to the helpless Comforters.

John Bunyan

John Prints It

I SET my pen to paper with delight,
And quickly had my thoughts in black and white,
For having now my method by the end,
Still as I pulled it came ; and so I penned
It down, until at last it came to be,
For length and breadth the bigness which you see.

Well, when I had thus put my ends together,
I showed them others, that I might see whether
They would condemn them or them justify ;
And some said *Let them live* ; some *Let them die* :
Some said *John, print it* ; others said *Not so* :
Some said *It might do good* ; others said *No*.

Now I was in a strait, and did not see
Which was the best thing to be done by me :
At last I thought, *Since you are thus divided,*
I print it will ; and so the case decided.

John Bunyan

Who Would True Valour See

WHO would true valour see,
　Let him come hither ;
One here will constant be,
　Come wind, come weather :
There no discouragement
Shall make him once relent,
His first avowed intent,
　To be a pilgrim.

Whoso beset him round
　With dismal stories,
Do but themselves confound,
　His strength the more is.
No lion can him fright,
He'll with a giant fight,
But he will have a right
　To be a pilgrim.

Hobgoblin nor foul fiend
　Can daunt his spirit ;
He knows he at the end
　Shall life inherit.
Then fancies fly away,
He'll not fear what men say,
He'll labour night and day
　To be a pilgrim.

John Bunyan

Rhymes of John Bunyan

The Weathercock

BRAVE weathercock, I see thou set'st thy nose
Against the wind which way soe'er it blows.

The Penny Loaf

THY price one penny is in time of plenty ;
In famine doubled tis, from one to twenty.
Yea, no man knows what price on thee to set
When there is but one penny loaf to get.

The Apple Tree

A COMELY sight indeed it is to see
A world of blossoms on an apple tree.

On the Way to Paradise

SOME boys have wit enough to sport and play
Who at their books are blockheads day by day.
Some men are arch enough at any vice
But dunces in the way to Paradise.

The Cackler

THE hen so soon as she an egg doth lay
Spreads the fame of her doing as she may.
About the yard she cackling now doth go
To tell what twas she at her nest did do.

Just thus it is with some professing men ;
If they do aught that good is, like our hen,
They can't but cackle on't where'er they go ;
What their right hand doth their left hand must know.

A Blessing on His Book

Now may this little book a blessing be
To those that love this little book and me ;
And may its buyer have no cause to say
His money is but lost or thrown away.

King Charles's Men Dreaming of Wings

THE philosophers of King Charles's reign were busy on finding out
the art of flying. The famous Bishop Wilkins was so confident
of success in it that he says he does not question but in the next age
it will be as usual to hear a man call for his wings when he is going a
journey as it is now to call for his boots.

Written by Joseph Addison 250 years ago

John Bunyan to Certain Ladies

BEAUTY at best is but as fading flowers,
Bright now, anon with darksome clouds it lowers.
Tis but skin-deep, and therefore must decay ;
Time's blowing on it sends it quite away.

The Great Bar to Happiness

SIN is the great block and bar to our happiness, the procurer of all miseries to man both here and hereafter. Take away sin and nothing can hurt us. *John Bunyan*

An Invitation to a Little Bird

MY little bird, how canst thou sit
And sing amidst so many thorns ?
Let me but hold upon thee get ;
My love with honour thee adorns.

Thou art at present little worth ;
Five farthings none will give for thee.
But, prithee, little bird, come forth,
Thou of more value art to me.

My father's palace shall be thine,
Yea, in it thou shalt sit and sing ;
My little bird, if thou'lt be mine,
The whole year round shall be thy spring.

I'll teach thee all the notes at Court,
Unthought-of music thou shalt play ;
And all that thither do resort
Shall praise thee for it every day.

I'll keep thee safe from cat and cur,
No touch of harm shall come to thee ;
Yea, I will be thy succourer,
My bosom shall thy cabin be.

But lo ! behold, the bird is gone ;
These charmings would not make her yield.
The child's left at the bush alone,
The bird flies yonder o'er the field.

John Bunyan

Go, Little Book

GO, little Book ! from this my solitude ;
I cast thee on the waters,—go thy ways :
And if, as I believe, thy vein be good,
The world will find thee after many days.
Be it with thee according to thy worth :
Go, little Book ! in faith I send thee forth.

Southey

The Bit of Dust and Ashes

THE angels rejoice to see a bit of dust and ashes overcome principalities and powers. *John Bunyan*

The Pennyworth of the Poor

IF thou sellest do not commend ; if thou buyest do not dispraise ; but give the thing thou hast to do with its just value and worth. Be moderate in all thy sellings, and be sure let the poor have a pennyworth. *John Bunyan*

Remember the Wise

REMEMBER the wise ; for they have laboured, and you are entering into their labours.

Every fact you are taught is a voice from beyond the tomb, an heirloom from men whose bodies are now in the dust. Most of them were poor ; many died and saw no fruit of their labours ; some were persecuted, some were slain. Of some the very names are forgotten. But their works live, and grow and spread over fresh generations of youth, showing them fresh steps toward that temple of wisdom which is the knowledge of things as they are ; the knowledge of those eternal laws by which God governs the heavens and the Earth, things seen and unseen, from the rise and fall of mighty nations to the growth and death of moss on yonder moors. *Charles Kingsley*

Some Future Day

SOME future day when what is now is not,
When all old faults and follies are forgot,
And thoughts of difference passed like dreams away,
We'll meet again upon some future day.

When all that hindered, all that vexed our love,
As tall rank weeds will climb the blade above,
When all but it has yielded to decay,
We'll meet again upon some future day.

When we have proved, each on his course alone,
The wider world, and learnt what's now unknown,
Have made life clear, and worked out each a way,
We'll meet again,—we shall have much to say.

With happier mood, and feelings born anew,
Our boyhood's bygone fancies we'll review,
Talk o'er old talks, play as we used to play,
And meet again on many a future day.

Some day, which oft our hearts shall yearn to see,
In some far year, though distant yet to be,
Shall we indeed (ye winds and waters, say)
Meet yet again upon some future day ?
Arthur Hugh Clough

The Earthquake Pill

I REMEMBER when our whole island was shaken with an earthquake some years ago there was an impudent mountebank who sold pills which, as he told country people, were very good against an earthquake.   *Addison*

In Windswept Space

SOMEWHERE, in desolate windswept space,
    In Twilight Land, in No Man's Land,
Two hurrying Shapes met face to face,
    And bade each other stand.

And who are you ? cried one, agape,
    Shuddering in the gloaming light.
I know not, said the second Shape,
    I only died last night !
       Thomas Bailey Aldrich

The Worldly Hope Men Set Their Hearts Upon

THE worldly hope men set their hearts upon
    Turns ashes or it prospers ; and anon,
Like snow upon the desert's dusty face,
Lighting a little hour or two, is gone.

Think, in this battered caravanserai
Whose doorways are alternate night and day,
    How Sultan after Sultan with his pomp
Abode his hour or two, and went his way.

They say the lion and the lizard keep
The courts where Jamshýd gloried and drank deep ;
    And Bahrám, that great hunter—the wild ass
Stamps o'er his head, and he lies fast asleep.

I sometimes think that never blows so red
The rose as where some buried Caesar bled ;
    That every hyacinth the garden wears
Dropt in its lap from some once lovely head.
       From Omar Khayyám

Great Empires and Little Minds

MAGNANIMITY in politics is but seldom the truest wisdom. A great empire and little minds go ill together.   *Edmund Burke*

Edmund Burke to an Honourable Gentleman

THE honourable gentleman is indebted to his memory for his wit and to his imagination for his facts.   *Burke in Parliament*

The Moving Finger Writes

THE moving finger writes ; and, having writ,
 Moves on : nor all thy piety nor wit
Shall lure it back to cancel half a line,
Nor all thy tears wash out a word of it.

From Omar Khayyám

The Wish of Edmund Burke

Standing in a little garden in Bristol, Edmund Burke says,

I WISH to be a member of Parliament to have my share of doing good and resisting evil.

Edmund Burke on John Howard

HIS plan is original, and it is as full of genius as it is of humanity. He has visited all Europe, not to survey the sumptuousness of palaces or the stateliness of temples ; not to make accurate measurements of ancient grandeur, nor to form a scale of the curiosities of modern art ; not to collect medals or to collate manuscripts ; but to dive into the depth of dungeons, to plunge into the infection of hospitals, to survey the mansions of sorrow and pain ; to take the gauge and dimensions of misery, depression, and contempt ; to remember the forgotten, to attend to the neglected, to visit the forsaken, and to compare and collate the distresses of men in all countries.

The Tyranny of Democracy

OF this I am certain, that in a democracy the majority of the citizens is capable of exercising the most cruel oppressions upon the minority, and that the oppression of the minority will extend to far greater numbers, and will be carried on with much greater fury, than ever from the dominion of a single sceptre. *Edmund Burke*

The Only Way

I AM aware that the age is not what we all wish, but I am sure that the only means to check its degeneracy is heartily to concur in whatever is best in our time. *Edmund Burke*

Do Not Be Deceived by the Great Noise

BECAUSE half a dozen grasshoppers under a fern make the field ring with their importunate chink, while thousands of great cattle, reposed beneath the shadow of the British oak, chew the cud and are silent, pray do not imagine that those who make the noise are the only inhabitants of the field, that of course they are many in number, or that, after all, they are other than the little, shrivelled, meagre, hopping, though loud and troublesome, insects of the hour.

Edmund Burke

Flying Down the Depths of Time

LITTLE snatch of ancient song,
  What has made thee live so long ?
Flying on thy wings of rhyme
Lightly down the depths of time.

W. E. H. Lecky

He Planted a Thought in the Minds of Men

HE planted an oak in his father's park
  And a thought in the minds of men,
And he bade farewell to his native shore,
  Which he never will see again.

Oh, merrily stream the tourist throng
  To the glow of the Southern sky ;
A vision of pleasure beckons them on,
  But he went there to die.

The oak will grow and its boughs will spread
  And many rejoice in its shade,
But none will visit the distant grave,
  Where a stranger youth is laid ;

And the thought will live when the oak has died,
  And quicken the minds of men,
But the name of the thinker has vanished away,
  And will never be heard again.

W. E. H. Lecky

Above the Wrecks of Time

ALL *things perish, and the strongest*
  Often do not last the longest.
The stately ship is seen no more,
The fragile skiff attains the shore ;
And while the great and wise decay,
And all their trophies pass away,
Some sudden thought, some careless rhyme,
Still floats above the wrecks of time.

W. E. H. Lecky

The Swan Song

SWANS sing before they die : twere no bad thing
  Did certain persons die before they sing.

Samuel Taylor Coleridge

A Child's Prayer

ERE on my bed my limbs I lay
God grant me grace my prayers to say !
O God, preserve my mother dear
In health and strength for many a year.
And O preserve my father too,
And may I pay him reverence due ;
And may I my best thoughts employ
To be my parents' hope and joy !
And O preserve my brothers both
From evil doings and from sloth,
And may we always love each other,
Our friends, our father, and our mother !
And still, O Lord, to me impart
An innocent and grateful heart,
That after my last sleep I may
Awake to Thy eternal day.

Samuel Taylor Coleridge

Through the World We Two Will Go

THY hand in mine, thy hand in mine,
And through the world we two will go,
Our faces set to every foe,
With love before us as a sign,
Thy hand in mine, thy hand in mine.

My heart in thine, my heart in thine,
Through life, through happy death the same.
We two will kneel before the shrine
And keep alight the sacred flame.
My heart in thine, my heart in thine.

Mary Coleridge

She is Not Fair to Outward View

SHE is not fair to outward view
As many maidens be ;
Her loveliness I never knew
Until she smiled on me ;
O, then I saw her eye was bright,
A well of love, a spring of light.

But now her looks are coy and cold,
To mine they ne'er reply,
And yet I cease not to behold
The love-light in her eye :
Her very frowns are fairer far
Than smiles of other maidens are.

Hartley Coleridge

He Prayeth Best Who Loveth Best

O WEDDING-GUEST ! this soul hath been
  Alone on a wide wide sea :
So lonely twas, that God Himself
Scarce seemed there to be.

O sweeter than the marriage-feast,
Tis sweeter far to me,
To walk together to the kirk
With a goodly company !

To walk together to the kirk,
And all together pray,
While each to his great Father bends,
Old men, and babes, and loving friends,
And youths and maidens gay !

Farewell, farewell ! but this I tell
To thee, thou Wedding-Guest !
He prayeth well, who loveth well
Both man and bird and beast.

He prayeth best, who loveth best
All things both great and small :
For the dear God who loveth us,
He made and loveth all.

The Mariner, whose eye is bright,
Whose beard with age is hoar,
Is gone ; and now the Wedding-Guest
Turned from the bridegroom's door.

He went like one that hath been stunned,
And is of sense forlorn :
A sadder and a wiser man,
He was the morrow morn.

Last Words of The Ancient Mariner,
by Samuel Taylor Coleridge

All is Still as Death

This scene in the aisle of a temple, described in Congreve's Mourning
Bride, was declared by Dr Johnson to be the best description he had ever read.

ALL is hushed, and still as death—tis dreadful !
  How reverend is the face of this tall pile,
Whose ancient pillars rear their marble heads
To bear aloft its arched and ponderous roof,
By its own weight made steadfast and immovable,
Looking tranquillity ! It strikes an awe
And terror on my aching sight ; the tombs
And monumental caves of death look cold,
And shoot a chillness to my trembling heart.

William Congreve

O, May the Dream be True

THERE is an awful quiet in the air,
  And the sad earth, with moist imploring eye,
Looks wide and wakeful at the pondering sky,
Like Patience slow subsiding to Despair.
But see, the blue smoke, as a voiceless prayer,
Sole witness of a secret sacrifice,
Unfolds its tardy wreaths, and multiplies
Its soft chameleon breathings in the rare
Capacious ether—so it fades away,
And nought is seen beneath the pendent blue,
The undistinguishable waste of day.
So have I dreamed ! (oh, may the dream be true !)
That praying souls are purged from mortal hue,
And grow as pure as He to whom they pray.
Hartley Coleridge

Come Gently On

No funeral gloom, my dears, when I am gone,
  Corpse-gazings, tears, black raiment, graveyard grimness ;
Think of me as withdrawn into the dimness,
Yours still, you mine ; remember all the best
Of our past moments, and forget the rest ;
And so, to where I wait, come gently on.
William Allingham

Time Heals All Woes but His

IN time the ox becomes accustomed to the plough that tills the field,
  and yields his neck to be pressed by the curving yoke   In time the
spirited horse obeys the flowing reins, and, with quiet mouth, receives
the hard bit.   In time the anger of the Punic lions is assuaged.

Length of time, too, causes that the grape swells out on the spreading clusters, and that the berries can hardly contain the juice they hold
within.   Time, too, pushes forth the seed into the whitening ears of
corn ; and makes the apple not to be of sour flavour.   Tis time that
blunts the edge of the plough that renews the land ; tis time that
wears the hard flint and the adamant. This, too, by degrees mitigates
raging anger ; this lessens sadness and elevates the sorrowing heart.
Length of time, as it glides on with silent foot, is able to lessen everything but my cares.   *Ovid in exile*

Let There Be No Lament

LET no one honour me with tears, nor bury me with lamentation.
  Why ?   Because I fly from lip to lip, living in the mouths of men.
Ovid

Late Singer of a Sunless Day

LATE singer of a sunless day,
  I know not if with pain
Or pleasure more, I hear thy lay
  Renew its vernal strain.

As gleams of youth, when youth is o'er
  And bare the summer bowers,
Thy song brings back the years of yore,
  And unreturning hours.

So was it once ! So yet again
  It never more will be !
Yet sing ; and lend us in thy strain
  A moment's youth with thee.
Francis Turner Palgrave

Like Light Through the Window

SILENCE the voice of Christianity and the world is well-nigh dumb, for gone is that sweet music which kept in order the rulers of the people, which cheers the poor widow in her lonely toil, and comes like light through the windows of morning to men who sit stooping and feeble, with failing eyes and a hungering heart. *Theodore Parker*

Charles Lamb Sleeps

HERE the children fell a-crying, and asked if their little mourning which they had on was not for Uncle John, and they looked up and prayed me not to go on about their uncle, but to tell them some stories about their pretty dead mother.

Then I told how for seven long years, in hope sometimes, sometimes in despair, yet persisting ever, I courted the fair Alice ; and as much as children could understand, I explained to them what coyness, and difficulty, and denial meant in maidens—when suddenly, turning to Alice, the soul of the first Alice looked out at her eyes with such a reality of re-presentment that I became in doubt which of them stood there before me, or whose that bright hair was ; and while I stood gazing both the children gradually grew fainter to my view, receding, and still receding till nothing at last but two mournful features were seen in the uttermost distance, which, without speech, strangely impressed upon me the effects of speech : " We are nothing ; less than nothing, and dreams. We are only what might have been, and must wait upon the tedious shores of Lethe millions of ages before we have existence, and a name "—and, immediately awaking, I found myself quietly seated in my bachelor arm-chair, where I had fallen asleep.
Charles Lamb

THE CROUCHING MAN IN A VERONA CHURCH

KING CHARLES, BY VAN DYCK

To A Young Girl Dying

With a gift of fresh palm leaves

THIS is Palm Sunday : mindful of the day,
    I bring palm branches, found upon my way :
But these will wither ; thine shall never die,
The sacred palms thou bearest to the sky !
Dear little saint, though but a child in years,
Older in wisdom than my gray compeers !
We doubt and tremble,—*we*, with bated breath,
Talk of this mystery of life and death :
Thou, strong in faith, art gifted to conceive
Beyond thy years, and teach us to believe !

Then, take my palms, triumphal, to thy home,
Gentle, white palmer, never more to roam !
Only, sweet sister, give me, ere thou goest,
Thy benediction,—for my love thou knowest !
We, too, are pilgrims, travelling towards the shrine :
Pray that our pilgrimage may end like thine !

Thomas William Parsons

The Little Clerk

THE whimsical clerk has been promoted far above the solemn pro-
fessional authors ; his world is still alive, still smiles before us.
The pipes and glasses and rubbers of whist and talks round the fire—
he has preserved them all and has become the familiar companion of
whole generations.   A hundred years have passed, and his fireside is
not darkened, but warms a host of friends.

J. B. Priestley on Charles Lamb

Then Life and All Shall Cease

A CHILD's a plaything for an hour ;
    Its pretty tricks we try
For that or for a longer space ;
    Then tire, and lay it by.

But I knew one, that to itself
    All seasons could control ;
That would have mocked the sense of pain
    Out of a grieved soul.

Thou straggler into loving arms,
    Young climber up of knees,
When I forget thy thousand ways,
    Then life and all shall cease.

Charles Lamb

Somewhere There Waiteth in This World

SOMEWHERE there waiteth in this world of ours
  For one lone soul another lonely soul,
Each choosing each through all the weary hours,
  And meeting strangely at one sudden goal,
Then blend they, like green leaves with golden flowers,
Into one beautiful perfect whole ;
And life's long night is ended, and the way
Lies open onward to eternal day.

Sir Edwin Arnold

Homage to a Little House

OH, my father, my mother, who lived so humbly in this little house,
  it is to you I owe everything.

Thy enthusiasm, my brave-hearted mother, thou hast instilled in
me. If I have always associated the greatness of Science with the
greatness of France it is because I was impregnated with the feelings
thou hast inspired.

And thou, dearest father, whose life was as hard as thy hard trade,
thou hast shown to me what patience and protracted effort can
accomplish. It is to thee that I owe perseverance in daily work. To
look upward, learn to the utmost, to seek to rise ever higher, such
was thy teaching.

Be ye blessed, my dear parents, for what ye have been, and may
the homage done today to your little house be yours.

*Louis Pasteur, when placing
a tablet on his birthplace*

It Might Have Been

I ONCE met a kind man
  Who laughed with me,
I'd have liked him for a brother,
  For his jollity.

He mentioned Beersheba
  And Galilee,
And other places lying deep
  In the cool country.

A little boy told me,
  Stopping in his play,
That it might have been Christ
  Who talked to me that day.

Harold Lewis Cook

The Cobbler and the Saint

*This story was told by Hugh Latimer,
who was burned at the stake for his faith.*

ST ANTHONY, being in the wilderness, led there a very hard and strict life, insomuch as none at that time did the like. To whom came a voice from heaven, saying, " Anthony, thou art not so perfect as is a cobbler that dwelleth at Alexandria."

Anthony, hearing this, rose up forthwith, took his staff, and travelled till he came to Alexandria, where he found the cobbler.

The cobbler was astonished to see so reverend a father come to his house. Then Anthony said unto him, " Come and tell me thy whole conversation and how thou spendest thy time."

" Sir (said the cobbler), as for me, good works have I none, for my life is but simple and slender. I am but a poor cobbler. In the morning when I rise I pray for the whole city wherein I dwell, especially for all such neighbours and poor friends as I have. After, I set at my labour, where I spend the whole day in getting my living. And I keep me from all falsehood, for I hate nothing so much as I do deceitfulness ; wherefore when I make any man a promise I keep it and perform it truly. And thus I spend my time poorly, with my wife and children, whom I teach, as far as my wit will serve me, to fear God. And this is the sum of my simple life."

St Anthony, who lived in a ruin at the top of a hill in a wilderness, was over a hundred years old when he died. But who did more work for the world, we may wonder, the busy cobbler making shoes or the idle saint reflecting on his ruined hill?

The Yeoman On His Farm

MY father was a yeoman and had no lands of his own, only he had a farm of three or four pound by year at the uttermost, and hereupon he tilled so much as kept half a dozen men.

He had walk for a hundred sheep, and my mother milked thirty kine. He was able, and did find the king a harness, with himself and his horse, while he came to the place that he should receive the king's wages. I can remember that I buckled his harness when he went into Blackheath field. He kept me at school or else I had not been able to have preached before the king's majesty now. He married my sisters with five pound apiece, so that he brought them up in godliness and fear of God. He kept hospitality for his poor neighbours, and some alms he gave to the poor.

All this he did of the said farm, where he that now hath it payeth sixteen pound by year or more and is not able to do anything for his prince, nor himself, nor for his children, or give a cup of drink to the poor.   *Hugh Latimer*

The Most Diligent Prelate in England

WHO is the most diligent bishop and prelate in all England that passeth all the rest in doing his office ?

I can tell, for I know him who it is ; I know him well. There is one that passeth all the others, and is the most diligent prelate and preacher in all England. Will ye know who it is ? I will tell you : it is the devil. He is the most diligent preacher of all. He is never out of his diocese. Ye shall never find him unoccupied. He keepeth residence at all times. Ye shall never find him out of the way. Call for him when you will, he is ever at home. The diligentest preacher in all the realm, he is ever at his plough. No lording nor loitering can hinder him ; he is ever applying his business. Ye shall never find him idle, I warrant you. *Hugh Latimer*

Six Years, Six Little Years

Grieved by his father's evil ways, Mycerinus, King of Egypt, ruled his people justly and well, but to him came an Oracle saying that he was to live but six years longer.

MY father loved injustice, and lived long ;
  Crowned with gray hairs he died, and full of sway.
I loved the good he scorned, and hated wrong,
  The Gods declare my recompense today.
I looked for life more lasting, rule more high,
And when six years are measured, lo, I die !

The rest I give to joy. Even while I speak,
  My sand runs short ; and (as yon star-shot ray,
Hemmed by two banks of cloud, peers pale and weak,
  Now, as the barrier closes, dies away)
Even so do past and future intertwine,
Blotting this six-years space, which yet is mine.

Six years, six little years, six drops of time,
  Yet suns shall rise, and many moons shall wane,
And old men die, and young men pass their prime.
Matthew Arnold

My Country

ENGLAND, with all thy faults, I love thee still,
  My country ! and while yet a nook is left
Where English names and manners may be found,
Shall be constrained to love thee. Though thy clime
Be fickle, and thy year, most part, deformed
With dripping rains, or withered by a frost,
I would not yet exchange thy sullen skies
And fields without a flower, for warmer France
With all her vines ; nor for Ausonia's groves
Of golden fruitage and her myrtle bowers.
Cowper

Years Hence

YEARS hence, perhaps, may dawn an age
  More fortunate, alas ! than we,
Which without hardness will be sage,
  And gay without frivolity.
Matthew Arnold

Rest In Peace

STREW on her roses, roses,
  And never a spray of yew.
In quiet she reposes :
  Ah ! would that I did too.

Her mirth the world required :
  She bathed it in smiles of glee.
But her heart was tired, tired,
  And now they let her be.

Her life was turning, turning,
  In mazes of heat and sound ;
But for peace her soul was yearning,
  And now peace laps her round.

Her cabined, ample Spirit,
  It fluttered and failed for breath.
Tonight it doth inherit
  The vasty Hall of Death.
Matthew Arnold

So Small a Thing ?

IS it so small a thing
  To have enjoyed the sun,
To have lived light in the spring,
  To have loved, to have thought,
    to have done ?   *Matthew Arnold*

The Lustre of Your Name

BORN, as you are, citizens of a great State, and brought up, as you
have been, with habits equal to your birth, you should be ready to
face the greatest disasters, and still to keep unimpaired the lustre of
your name.

The hand of Heaven must be borne with resignation, that of the
enemy with fortitude. Remember that if your country has the
greatest name in all the world it is because she never bent before
disaster. Do not betray any sign of being oppressed by your present
sufferings, since they whose minds are least sensitive to calamity, and
whose hands are most quick to meet it, are the greatest men of the
greatest communities. *Pericles to the Ancient Greeks*

The Man Who Cared

*These lines are simple and natural to us now, but in the eighteenth century,
when Cowper wrote them, they were a noble act of courage by one of the few men
who cared about a widespread wrong.*

OH for a lodge in some vast wilderness,
   Some boundless contiguity of shade,
Where rumour of oppression and deceit,
Of unsuccessful or successful war,
Might never reach me more.   My ear is pained,
My soul is sick, with every day's report
Of wrong and outrage with which earth is filled.
There is no flesh in man's obdurate heart ;
It does not feel for man ; the natural bond
Of brotherhood is severed as the flax
That falls asunder at the touch of fire.
He finds his fellow guilty of a skin
Not coloured like his own ; and, having power
To enforce the wrong, for such a worthy cause
Dooms and devotes him as his lawful prey.
Thus man devotes his brother, and destroys ;
And, worse than all, and most to be deplored,
As human nature's broadest, foulest blot.
Chains him, and tasks him, and exacts his sweat
With stripes that mercy, with a bleeding heart,
Weeps when she sees inflicted on a beast.
Then what is man ?   And what man, seeing this,
And having human feelings, does not blush,
And hang his head, to think himself a man ?
I would not have a slave to till my ground,
To carry me, to fan me while I sleep,
And tremble when I wake, for all the wealth
That sinews bought and sold have ever earned.

No : dear as freedom is, and in my heart's
   Just estimation prized above all price,
I had much rather be myself the slave,
And wear the bonds, than fasten them on him.
We have no slaves at home.   Then why abroad ?
Slaves cannot breathe in England ; if their lungs
Receive our air, that moment they are free ;
They touch our country, and their shackles fall.
That's noble, and bespeaks a nation proud
And jealous of the blessing.   Spread it then,
And let it circulate through every vein
Of all your empire ; that where Britain's power
Is felt mankind may feel her mercy too.

                                        William Cowper

O Nanny, Wilt Thou Gang Wi' Me?

O NANNY, wilt thou gang wi' me,
   Nor sigh to leave the flaunting town ?
Can silent glens have charms for thee,
   The lowly cot and russet gown ?
Nae langer drest in silken sheen,
   Nae langer decked wi' jewels rare,
Say, canst thou quit each courtly scene
   Where thou wert fairest of the fair ?

O Nanny, when thou'rt far awa,
   Wilt thou not cast a look behind ?
Say, canst thou face the flaky snow,
   Nor shrink before the winter wind ?
O can that soft and gentle mien
   Severest hardships learn to bear,
Nor, sad, regret each courtly scene
   Where thou wert fairest of the fair ?

O Nanny, canst thou love so true
   Through perils keen wi' me to gae ?
Or, when thy swain mishap shall rue,
   To share with him the pang of wae ?
Say, should disease or pain befall,
   Wilt thou assume the nurse's care,
Nor, wishful, those gay scenes recall
   Where thou wert fairest of the fair ?

And when at last thy love shall die,
   Wilt thou receive his parting breath ?
Wilt thou repress each struggling sigh
   And cheer with smiles the bed of death ?
And wilt thou o'er his much-loved clay
   Strew flowers, and drop the tender tear ?
Nor then regret those scenes so gay
   Where thou wert fairest of the fair ?
                              Thomas Percy

The Conqueror or the Crier ?

THEMISTOCLES, being asked whether he had rather be Homer or
   Achilles, replied, " Would you rather be a conqueror at the
Olympian games or the crier who proclaims the victors ? "
                              Plutarch

The Difference

A DESCENDANT of Harmodius was taunting Iphicrates with his low
   birth. " The difference between us is this," he replied ; " my
family begins with me, and yours ends with you."   *Plutarch*

The Just Man

AN illiterate man came to Aristides, and asked him to write on the billet for his banishment the name Aristides.

" Do you know him ? " asked the minister.   " No, I don't ; but I hate to hear him always called the Just."

Aristides made no reply, but wrote his own name as he was requested.   *Plutarch*

The City No One Knows

IF we traverse the world it is possible to find cities without walls, without letters, without kings, without wealth, without coin, without schools and theatres ; but a city without a temple no one ever saw.   *Plutarch*

The Ten

CAECILIUS METELLUS, being advised to attack a strong position which he was assured could be taken with the loss of only ten men, replied, " I will, if you will be one of the ten."   *Plutarch*

Spring is No More

THE young men have been taken from the city ; the spring has gone out of the year.   *Pericles*

In the Name of Pericles

HE perished, but his wreath was won,
    He perished in his height of fame ;
Then sank the cloud on Athens' sun,
    Yet still she conquered in his name.
Filled with his soul she could not die ;
    Her conquest was posterity.
                                George Croly on Pericles

The Peaks We Cannot Scale

FORGIVE !
    And tell me that sweet tale,
How you and I one day may live
    In some diviner vale.

In some diviner vale, dear child,
    Than this in which we lie
And watch the monstrous mountains piled
    And clouded into sky.

Yet even there, far out of reach
    Are peaks we cannot scale,
For God has something still to reach
    In that diviner vale.
                                Francis Burdett Money-Coutts

Epitaph On a Fair Woman

IN this green chest is laid away
The fairest frock she ever wore ;
It clothed her both by night and day
And none shall wear it evermore.

Francis Burdett Money-Coutts

The Ploughman in the Fields of Ayr

I SEE amid the fields of Ayr,
A ploughman, who, in foul and fair,
Sings at his task
So clear, we know not if it is
The laverock's song we hear, or his,
Nor care to ask.

For him the ploughing of those fields
A more ethereal harvest yields
Than sheaves of grain ;
Songs flush with purple bloom the rye,
The plover's call, the curlew's cry,
Sing in his brain.

Touched by his hand, the wayside weed
Becomes a flower ; the lowliest reed
Beside the stream
Is clothed with beauty ; gorse and grass
And heather, where his footsteps pass,
The brighter seem.

And then to die so young and leave
Unfinished what he might achieve !
Yet better sure
Is this, than wandering up and down
An old man in a country town,
Infirm and poor.

For now he haunts his native land
As an immortal youth ; his hand
Guides every plough ;
He sits beside each ingle-nook,
His voice is in each rushing brook
Each rustling bough.

His presence haunts this room tonight
A form of mingled mist and light
From that far coast.
Welcome beneath this roof of mine !
Welcome ! this vacant chair is thine,
Dear guest and ghost !

Longfellow

Dead He Lay Among His Books

DEAD he lay among his books !
The peace of God was in his looks.

As the statues in the gloom
Watch o'er Maximilian's tomb,

So those volumes from their shelves
Watched him, silent as themselves.

Ah ! his hand will nevermore
Turn their storied pages o'er ;

Never more his lips repeat
Songs of theirs, however sweet.

Let the lifeless body rest !
He is gone who was its guest.

Traveller ! in what realms afar,
In what planet, in what star,

In what vast aerial space,
Shines the light upon thy face ?

In what gardens of delight
Rest thy weary feet tonight ?

Friend ! but yesterday the bells
Rang for thee their loud farewells ;

And today they toll for thee,
Lying dead beyond the sea ;

Lying dead among thy books,
The peace of God in all thy looks !   *Longfellow*

I Hear the Voice of Christ Say Peace

WERE half the power that fills the world with terror,
Were half the wealth bestowed on camps and courts,
Given to redeem the human mind from error,
There were no need of arsenals nor forts :

The warrior's name would be a name abhorred,
And every nation that should lift again
Its hand against a brother on its forehead
Would wear for evermore the curse of Cain !

Down the dark future, through long generations,
The echoing sounds grow fainter and then cease ;
And, like a bell, with solemn, sweet vibrations,
I hear once more the voice of Christ say Peace !

Peace ! and no longer from its brazen portals
The blast of war's great organ shakes the skies ;
But, beautiful as songs of the immortals,
The holy melodies of love arise.   *Longfellow*

Peace, the Lovers are Asleep

To those whom death again did wed
This grave's the second marriage bed.
For though the hand of fate could force
Twixt soul and body a divorce,
It could not sever man and wife,
Because they both lived but one life.
Peace, good reader, do not weep ;
Peace, the lovers are asleep.
They, sweet turtles, folded lie
In the last knot that love could tie.
Let them sleep, let them sleep on,
Till the stormy night be gone
And the eternal morrow dawn
Then the curtains will be drawn,
And they wake into a light
Whose day shall never die in night.

*An epitaph by Richard Crashaw on husband
and wife who died and were buried together*

I Am Five Centuries Old

Taddeo Gaddi built me. I am old,
Five centuries old. I plant my foot of stone
Upon the Arno, as St Michael's own
Was planted on the dragon. Fold by fold,
Beneath me as it struggles, I behold
Its glistening scales. Twice hath it overthrown
My kindred and companions. Me alone
It moveth not ; but is by me controlled.
I can remember when the Medici
Were driven from Florence ; longer still ago
The final wars of Ghibelline and Guelf.
Florence adorns me with her jewelry ;
And when I think that Michael Angelo
Hath leaned on me, I glory in myself.

Longfellow on an old bridge

I Heard the Trailing Garments of the Night

I heard the trailing garments of the Night
Sweep through her marble halls !
I saw her sable skirts all fringed with light
From the celestial walls !

I felt her presence, by its spell of night,
Stoop o'er me from above ;
The calm majestic presence of the Night,
As of the one I love.

Longfellow

A Lady With a Lamp Shall Stand

WHENE'ER a noble deed is wrought,
  Whene'er is spoken a noble thought,
Our hearts, in glad surprise,
To higher levels rise.

The tidal wave of deeper souls
Into our inmost being rolls,
  And lifts us unawares
  Out of all meaner cares.

Honour to those whose words or deeds
Thus help us in our daily needs,
  And by their overflow
  Raise us from what is low !

Thus thought I, as by night I read
Of the great army of the dead,
  The trenches cold and damp,
  The starved and frozen camp,

The wounded from the battle-plain
In dreary hospitals of pain,
  The cheerless corridors,
  The cold and stony floors.

Lo ! in that house of misery
A lady with a lamp I see
  Pass through the glimmering gloom,
  And flit from room to room.

And slow, as in a dream of bliss,
The speechless sufferer turns to kiss
  Her shadow, as it falls
  Upon the darkening walls.

As if a door in heaven should be
Opened and then closed suddenly,
  The vision came and went,
  The light shone and was spent.

On England's annals, through the long
Hereafter of her speech and song,
  That light its rays shall cast
  From portals of the past.

A Lady with a Lamp shall stand
In the great history of the land,
  A noble type of good,
  Heroic womanhood.

Longfellow on Florence Nightingale

The Heights by Great Men
Reached and Kept

SAINT AUGUSTINE ! well hast thou said,
  That of our vices we can frame
A ladder, if we will but tread
  Beneath our feet each deed of shame !

All common things, each day's events,
  That with the hour begin and end,
Our pleasures and our discontents,
  Are rounds by which we may ascend.

All thoughts of ill ; all evil deeds
  That have their root in thoughts of ill ;
Whatever hinders or impedes
  The action of the nobler will,

All these must first be trampled down
  Beneath our feet, if we would gain
In the bright fields of fair renown
  The right of eminent domain.

We have not wings, we cannot soar ;
  But we have feet to scale and climb
By slow degrees, by more and more,
  The cloudy summits of our time.

The heights by great men reached and kept
  Were not attained by sudden flight,
But they, while their companions slept,
  Were toiling upward in the night.
From Longfellow's Ladder of St Augustine

Retribution

THOUGH the mills of God grind slowly
  Yet they grind exceeding small ;
Though with patience he stands waiting,
  With exactness grinds he all.
Translated by Longfellow

Build Thee More Stately Mansions,
O My Soul

BUILD thee more stately mansions, O my soul,
  As the swift seasons roll !
  Leave thy low-vaulted past !
Let each new temple, nobler than the last,
Shut thee from heaven with a dome more vast,
  Till thou at length art free,
Leaving thine outgrown shell by life's unresting sea !
Oliver Wendell Holmes

All Are Architects of Fate

ALL are architects of Fate,
  Working in these walls of Time :
Some with massive deeds and great,
  Some with ornaments of rhyme.

Nothing useless is or low ;
  Each thing in its place is best ;
And what seems but idle show
  Strengthens and supports the rest.

For the structure that we raise
  Time is with materials filled ;
Our todays and yesterdays
  Are the blocks with which we build.

Truly shape and fashion these,
  Leave no yawning gaps between ;
Think not, because no man sees,
  Such things will remain unseen.

In the elder days of art
  Builders wrought with greatest care
Each minute and unseen part,
  For the gods see everywhere.

Let us do our work as well,
  Both the unseen and the seen ;
Make the house where gods may dwell
  Beautiful, entire, and clean.
                        Longfellow

In the Heart of a Friend

I SHOT an arrow into the air,
  It fell to earth, I knew not where ;
For, so swiftly it flew, the sight
Could not follow it in its flight.

I breathed a song into the air,
It fell to earth, I knew not where ;
For who has sight so keen and strong
That it can follow the flight of song ?

Long, long afterward, in an oak
I found the arrow, still unbroke ;
And the song, from beginning to end,
I found again in the heart of a friend.
                        Longfellow

The Day Breaks

A WIND came up out of the sea,
  And said, O mists, make room for me.

It hailed the ships, and cried, Sail on,
Ye mariners, the night is gone.

And hurried landward far away,
Crying, Awake ! It is the day.

It said unto the forest, Shout !
Hang all your leafy banners out !

It touched the wood bird's folded wing,
And said, O bird, awake and sing !

And o'er the farms, O chanticleer,
Your clarion blow ; the day is near.

It whispered to the fields of corn :
Bow down, and hail the coming morn.

It shouted through the belfry tower,
Awake, O bell, proclaim the hour !

It crossed the churchyard with a sigh,
And said, Not yet ; in quiet lie.

Longfellow

Lives of Great Men All Remind Us

L IVES of great men all remind us
  We can make our lives sublime,
And, departing, leave behind us
  Footprints on the sands of Time,

Footprints, that perhaps another,
  Sailing o'er life's solemn main,
A forlorn and shipwrecked brother,
  Seeing, shall take heart again.

Let us, then, be up and doing,
  With a heart for any fate ;
Still achieving, still pursuing,
  Learn to labour and to wait.

Longfellow

Heroes and Kings

H EROES and kings, your distance keep,
  In peace let one poor poet sleep,
Who never flattered folks like you :
Let Horace blush, and Virgil too.

Alexander Pope

Thus Let Me Live

HAPPY the man whose wish and care
    A few paternal acres bound,
Content to breathe his native air
        In his own ground.

Whose herds with milk, whose fields with bread,
Whose flocks supply him with attire;
Whose trees in summer yield him shade,
        In winter, fire.

Blest who can unconcernedly find
Hours, days, and years slide soft away
In health of body, peace of mind,
        Quiet by day,

Sound sleep by night; study and ease
Together mixed; sweet recreation,
And innocence, which most does please,
        With meditation.

Thus let me live, unseen, unknown;
Thus, unlamented, let me die;
Steal from the world, and not a stone
        Tell where I lie.

Alexander Pope

To Little Peggy

MY noble lovely little Peggy,
    Let this, my first epistle, beg ye,
At dawn of morn and close of even,
To lift your heart and hands to heaven.

And, dearest child, along the day,
In everything you do and say,
Obey and please my lord and lady,
So God shall love and angels aid ye.

If to these precepts you attend
No second letter need I send,
And so I rest your constant friend.

Matthew Prior

Quit

To John I owed great obligation;
    But John unhappily thought fit
To publish it to all the nation:
    Sure John and I are more than quit.

Matthew Prior

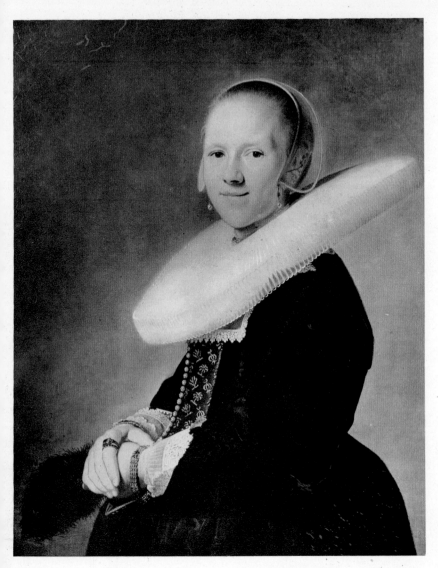

PORTRAIT OF A LADY, BY JOHANNES VERSPRONCK

THE MERRY FIDDLER, BY FRANK HALS

Laugh On

LAUGH on, fair Cousins, for to you
  All life is joyous yet ;
Your hearts have all things to pursue,
  And nothing to regret ;
And every flower to you is fair,
  And every month is May :
You've not been introduced to Care :
  Laugh on, laugh on, today !

Perhaps your eyes may grow more bright
  As childhood's hues depart ;
You may be lovelier to the sight
  And dearer to the heart ;
You may be sinless still, and see
  This earth still green and gay ;
But what you are you will not be.
  Laugh on, laugh on, today !

O'er me have many winters crept
  With less of grief than joy ;
But I have learned and toiled and wept ;
  I am no more a boy.
I've never had the gout, tis true ;
  My hair is hardly grey ;
But now I cannot laugh like you :
  Laugh on, laugh on, today.

I used to have as glad a face,
  As shadowless a brow ;
I once could run as blithe a race
  As you are running now ;
But never mind how I behave :
  Don't interrupt your play ;
And though I feel so very grave
  Laugh on, laugh on, today !
                    Winthrop Mackworth Praed

There He Left a Friend

HIS magic was not far to seek,
  He was so human.   Whether strong or weak,
Far from his kind he neither sank nor soared,
But sate an equal guest at every board :
No beggar ever felt him condescend,
No prince presume ; for still himself he bare
At manhood's simple level, and where'er
He met a stranger, there he left a friend.
                    Russell Lowell on Agassiz

Since I Am Not What I Was

VENUS, take my votive glass :
    Since I am not what I was,
What from this day I shall be,
Venus, let me never see.

Matthew Prior on a lady
offering her glass to Venus

Reinforcements

WHEN little boys with merry noise
    In the meadows shout and run ;
And little girls, sweet woman buds,
    Brightly open in the sun ;
I may not of the world despair,
    Our God despaireth not, I see ;
For blithesomer in Eden's air
    These lads and maidens could not be.

Why were they born, if Hope must die ?
    Wherefore this health, if Truth should fail ?
And why such Joy, if Misery
    Be conquering us and must prevail ?
Arouse ! our spirit may not droop !
    These young ones fresh from Heaven are ;
Our God hath sent another troop,
    And means to carry on the war.

Thomas Toke Lynch

Go, Ask the Poor

HIS epitaph shall mock the shortlived stone,
    No lichen shall its lines efface,
He needs these few and simple lines alone
    To mark his resting place :

Here lies a Poet.   Stranger, if to thee
    His claim to memory be obscure,
If thou wouldst learn how truly great was he,
    Go, ask it of the poor.

James Russell Lowell

Be Noble

BE noble ; and the nobleness that lies
    In other men sleeping, but never dead,
Will rise in majesty to meet thine own.

James Russell Lowell

Kossuth

A RACE of nobles may die out,
  A royal line may leave no heir ;
Wise Nature sets no guards about
  Her pewter plate and wood ware.

But they fail not, the kinglier breed,
  Who starry diadems attain ;
To dungeon, axe, and stake succeed
  Heirs of the old heroic strain.

And he, let come what will of woe,
  Hath saved the land he strove to save ;
No Cossack hordes, no traitor's blow,
  Can quench the voice shall haunt his grave.

I Kossuth am : O Future, thou
  That clear'st the just and blott'st the vile,
O'er this small dust in reverence bow,
  Remembering what I was erewhile.

I was the chosen trump wherethrough
  Our God sent forth awakening breath ;
Came chains ?   Came death ?   The strain He blew
  Sounds on, outliving chains and death.
                              James Russell Lowell

Plain and Flat

E z fer war I call it murder,
    There you hev it plain an' flat ;
I don't want to go no furder
    Than my testyment fer that ;
God hez sed so plump an' fairly,
    It's ez long ez it is broad,
An' you've got to git up airly
    Ef you want to take in God.
                              James Russell Lowell

To Brother Robert Burns

D EAR Bard and Brother, let who may
    Against thy faults be railing,
(Though far, I pray, from us be they
    That never had a failing).

One toast I'll give, and that not long,
    Which thou wouldst pledge if present,
To him whose song, in nature strong,
    Makes man of prince and peasant.
                    James Russell Lowell at a Burns Centenary

As Life Runs on the Road Grows Strange

As life runs on the road grows strange
　　With faces new, and near the end
The milestones into headstones change,
　　Neath every one a friend.

James Russell Lowell on his 68th birthday

I Will Not Go Back

I WILL be harsh as truth and as uncompromising as justice.
I am in earnest. I will not equivocate. I will not excuse.
I will not retreat a single inch, and I will be heard.

William Lloyd Garrison

The Time Would Come

I HAVE begun many things many times and have often succeeded
at last. I will sit down now, but the time will come when you will
hear me.　　　　　*Disraeli's first speech in Parliament*

O Small Beginnings, Ye Are Great and Strong

IN a small chamber, friendless and unseen,
　　Toiled o'er his types one poor unlearned young man ;
The place was dark, unfurnitured, and mean,
　　Yet there the freedom of a race began.

We stride the river daily at its spring,
　　Nor, in our childish thoughtlessness, foresee,
What myriad vassal streams shall tribute bring,
　　How like an equal it shall greet the sea.

O small beginnings, ye are great and strong,
　　Based on a faithful heart and weariless brain !
Ye build the future fair, ye conquer wrong,
　　Ye earn the crown, and wear it not in vain.

James Russell Lowell to William Lloyd Garrison

His Happiest Times

I CHOSE you and I loved you in my happiest times.

The broken-hearted Raleigh to his wife

The Prince Without Mercy

IF all the pictures and patterns of a merciless prince were lost in the
world, they might all again be painted out of the story of this king,
Henry the Eighth.　　　　　*Sir Walter Raleigh*

A Beggar Through This World Am I

A BEGGAR through this world am I,
  From place to place I wander by;
Fill up my pilgrim's scrip for me,
For Christ's sweet sake and charity!
A little of thy steadfastness,
Rounded with leafy gracefulness,
Old oak, give me:
That the world's blasts may round me blow,
And I yield gently to and fro,
While my stout-hearted trunk below
And firm-set roots unmoved be.
Some of thy stern, unyielding might,
Enduring still through day and night
Rude tempest-shock and withering blight:
That I may keep at bay
The changeful April sky of chance,
And the strong tide of circumstance:
Give me, old granite gray.
Some of thy mournfulness serene,
Some of the never-dying green,
Put in this scrip of mine,
That grief may fall like snowflakes light,
And deck me in a robe of white,
Ready to be an angel bright:
O sweetly mournful pine!
A little of thy merriment,
Of thy sparkling, light content,
Give me, my cheerful brook;
That I may still be full of glee
And gladsomeness, where'er I be,
Though fickle fate hath prisoned me
In some neglected nook.
Ye have been very kind and good
To me, since I've been in the wood;
Ye have gone nigh to fill my heart;
But goodbye, kind friends, every one,
I've far to go ere set of sun:
Of all good things I would have part,
The day was high ere I could start,
And so my journey's scarce begun.
Heaven help me! how could I forget
To beg of thee, dear violet!
Some of thy modesty,
That flowers here as well, unseen,
As if before the world thou'dst been,
O give, to strengthen me.   *James Russell Lowell*

When a Deed is Done For Freedom

WHEN a deed is done for Freedom, through the broad earth's
    aching breast
Runs a thrill of joy prophetic, trembling on from east to west,
And the slave, where'er he cowers, feels the soul within him climb
To the awful verge of manhood, as the energy sublime
Of a century bursts full-blossomed on the thorny stem of Time.

For mankind are one in spirit, and an instinct bears along,
Round the Earth's electric circle, the swift flash of right or wrong ;
Whether conscious or unconscious, yet Humanity's vast frame
Through its ocean-sundered fibres feels the gush of joy or shame ;
In the gain or loss of one race all the rest have equal claim.

Once to every man and nation comes the moment to decide,
In the strife of Truth with Falsehood, for the good or evil side ;
Some great cause, God's new Messiah, offering each the bloom or blight,
Parts the goats upon the left hand and the sheep upon the right,
And the choice goes by for ever twixt that darkness and that light.

Hast thou chosen, O my people, on whose party thou shalt stand
Ere the Doom from its worn sandals shakes the dust against our land ?
Though the cause of Evil prosper, yet tis Truth alone is strong,
And, albeit she wander outcast now, I see around her throng
Troops of beautiful tall angels, to enshield her from all wrong.

Careless seems the great Avenger ; history's pages but record
One death-grapple in the darkness twixt old systems and the Word ;
Truth for ever on the scaffold, Wrong for ever on the throne—
Yet that scaffold sways the future, and behind the dim unknown
Standeth God within the shadow, keeping watch above His own.

James Russell Lowell

La Belle Dame Sans Merci

MY heart was never broken till this day, that I hear the Queen goes
    so far off, whom I have followed so many years with so great
love and desire in so many journeys, and am now left behind her in a
dark prison all alone.   While she was yet near at hand that I might
hear of her in two or three days my sorrows were less, but even now
my heart is cast into the depths of all misery.

I that was wont to behold her riding like Alexander, hunting like
Diana, walking like Venus, the gentle wind blowing her fair hair
about her pure cheeks like a nymph, sometimes sitting in the shade
like a goddess, sometimes singing like an angel, sometimes playing
like Orpheus !   Behold the sorrow of this world !

She is gone in whom I trusted, and of me hath not one thought of
mercy, nor any respect of that that was.

*Sir Walter Raleigh writing from
the Tower to Robert Cecil*

His Love Admits No Rival

SHALL I like a hermit dwell
On a rock or in a cell,
Calling home the smallest part
That is missing of my heart,
To bestow it where I may
Meet a rival every day ?
If she undervalue me
What care I how fair she be ?

Were her tresses angel gold,
If a stranger may be bold,
Unrebukèd, unafraid,
To convert them to a braid,
And with little more ado
Work them into bracelets too ;
If the mine be grown so free
What care I how rich it be ?
Sir Walter Raleigh

Put Off Your Mail, O Kings

PUT off, put off your mail, O kings,
And beat your brands to dust !
Your hands must learn a surer grasp,
Your hearts a better trust.

O, bend aback the lance's point,
And break the helmet bar ;
A noise is in the morning wind,
But not the note of war.

Upon the grassy mountain paths,
The glittering hosts increase :
They come ! They come ! How fair their feet !
They come who publish peace.

And victory, fair victory,
Our enemies are ours !
For all the clouds are clasped in light,
And all the earth with flowers.

Aye, still depressed and dim with dew ;
But wait a little while,
And with the radiant, deathless rose,
The wilderness shall smile.

And every tender, living thing
Shall feed by streams of rest ;
Nor lambs shall from the flock be lost,
Nor nestling from the nest.
John Ruskin

The Disgrace

IT does not disgrace a gentleman to become an errand-boy or a day labourer; but it does disgrace him much to become a knave or a thief.   *John Ruskin*

The Richest Country and the Richest Man

THERE is no wealth but Life—Life including all its powers of love, of joy, and of admiration.

That country is the richest which nourishes the greatest number of noble and happy human beings; that man is the richest who, having perfected the functions of his own life to the utmost, has also the widest helpful influence, both personal and by means of his possessions over the lives of others.   *John Ruskin*

A Mistake of Good People

EVERY day I am more sure of the mistake made by good people universally in trying to pull fallen people up instead of keeping the yet safe ones from tumbling after them; and in always spending their pains on the worst instead of on the best materials. *John Ruskin*

Our England from a Garden

IN London I am but a bird of passage. I own no house; I am not a tenant. I just live in a house from which I can be ejected any moment without compensation.

From it I can see the Horse Guards Parade, which reminds me of the General Strike; the Foreign Office, which reminds me of trouble in China and Mr Chen; the India Office, which reminds me of the Swarajists; the War Office and the Admiralty, which remind me of Estimates.

And then I think of what I can see from my own garden in the most beautiful view in all England. I see the hills known to all of you, beginning in the north-east, the Clent; and beyond, in Warwickshire, Edgehill, where the English squire passed with horse and hounds between the two armies; Bredon, the beginning of the Cotswolds, like a cameo against the sky, and the wonderful straight blue line of the Malverns, little shapes of Ankerdine and Berrow Hill, and, perhaps most beautiful and graceful, his two neighbours Woodbury and Abberley; and Clee Hills, opening up another beautiful and romantic world and presenting a circle of beauty which I defy any part of England to match.

There are our possessions. There is no need among ourselves to tell of them: they lie in our hearts, and I think possibly one of the reasons that we love them so much is that so little is known of them outside our own country. *Stanley Baldwin when Prime Minister*

She Sat Beside Me Yesternight

SHE sat beside me yesternight,
  With lip and eye so sweetly smiling,
So full of soul, of life, of light,
  So beautifully care-beguiling,
That she had almost made me gay,
Had almost charmed the thought away
(Which, like the poisoned desert wind,
Came sick and heavy o'er my mind),
That memory soon mine all would be,
And she would smile no more for me.

Written of a child of sixteen by
John Ruskin in his old age

Sir John Oldcastle Passes Out of the World

UPON the day appointed he was brought out of the tower with his arms bound behind him having a very cheerful countenance. Then was he lain upon a hurdle as though he had been a most heinous traitor to the crown, and so drawn forth into St Giles Field, where they had set up a new pair of gallows.

As he was comen to the place of execution and was taken from the hurdle, he fell down devoutly upon his knees, desiring Almighty God to forgive his enemies. Then stood he up and beheld the multitude, exhorting them in most godly manner to follow the laws of God.

Then was he hanged up there in chains of iron, and so consumed alive in the fire, praising the name of God so long as his life lasted. This terrible kind of death, with gallows, chains, and fire, appeareth not very precious in the eyes of men. The righteous seemeth to die, saith the wise man, in the sight of them which are unwise, and their end is taken for very destruction. But though they suffer pain before men, saith he, yet is their expectation full of immortality. As gold in the furnace does God try his elect. Right dear in the sight of God, saith David, is the death of his true servants.

From Foxe's Book of Martyrs, on the death of Sir John Oldcastle, the hero to whose memory Shakespeare apologised for misrepresenting him

The Perfect Peace There Was in Britain

THERE was such perfect peace in Britain wheresoever the dominion of King Edwin extended that a woman with her new-born babe might walk throughout the island from sea to sea without receiving any harm. That king took such care for the good of his nation that in several places where he had seen clear springs near the highways he caused stakes to be fixed, with brass dishes hanging on them for travellers. *Bede, writing in the Seventh Century*

The Old Gentlemen on the Wheelbarrow

I OFTEN wonder if all the people in this country realise the changes that are coming over the industrial system in England.

It happens that I have seen a great deal of this evolution taking place before my own eyes. I worked for many years in an industrial business and had under me what was then considered a large number of men.

It was a place where I had known from childhood every man on the ground, where I was able to talk to men, not only about troubles in the works, but troubles at home, where strikes and lock-outs were unknown, and where the fathers and grandfathers of the men had worked and their sons went automatically into the business. It was also a place where nobody ever got the sack, and where we had a natural sympathy for those who were less concerned in efficiency than this generation is. There were a large number of old gentlemen who used to spend the day sitting on the handle of a wheelbarrow and smoking their pipes.

Oddly enough, it was not an inefficient community. It was the last survivor of that type of works, and ultimately was swallowed up in one of those great combinations to which the industries of the country are tending. *Stanley Baldwin*

England Given Away

AT first the island had no other inhabitants but the Britons, from whom it derived its name. When they had made themselves masters of the greatest part of the island it happened that the nation of the Picts, putting to sea in a few long ships, were driven by the winds on the northern coasts of Ireland, where, finding the nation of the Scots, they begged to be allowed to settle among them.

The Scots answered that the island could not contain them both ; but " we can give you good advice (said they) what to do. There is another island not far from ours, which we often see at a distance when the days are clear. If you will go thither you will obtain settlements ; or, if they should oppose you, you shall have our assistance."

The Picts accordingly, sailing over into Britain, began to inhabit the northern parts.

Now the Picts had no wives, and asked them of the Scots, who would not grant them upon any other terms than that, when any difficulty should arise, they should choose a king from the female royal race rather than from the male, which custom has been observed to this day.

In process of time Britain received a third nation, the Scots, who, migrating from Ireland, secured to themselves those settlements among the Picts which they still possess. *Bede's History of England*

They Who Were About to Die

WE who remember Drake and Oxenham, Cavendish and Raleigh, have forgotten names as illustrious, deeds as valiant, and voyages as momentous, which were sent out by the merchant adventurers of London.

We remember how Sir Hugh Willoughby, sent out to find the North-east Passage round Siberia, dropped down the river on his way. It was only three days before the death of the young King Edward the Sixth. The ships were hung with streamers as they passed Greenwich Palace ; the dying king was brought out to see the little fleet sail out ; salutes were fired, the flag was dropped to bid farewell.

The Admiral about to die saluted his King about to die.

Yet three days and Edward lay still and quiet in death. Yet six months and the gallant Willoughby sat still and quiet in death. He sat in his cabin in his arm-chair, with his papers before him, frozen to death ; and so he was found.　　　　　　　　　　*Sir Walter Besant*

The Fallen Friend

THOUGH raised to the summit of power from a low origin, he betrayed no insolence or contempt towards his inferiors and was grateful to remember all the obligations which, during his more humble fortune, he had owed to anyone. He had served as a private in the Italian wars when he received some good offices from a merchant who had entirely forgotten his person as well as the service which he had rendered him.

Cromwell in his grandeur happened at London to cast his eye on his benefactor now reduced to poverty by misfortune. He immediately sent for him, reminded him of their ancient friendship, and by his grateful assistance reinstated him in his former prosperity and opulence.　　　　　　　*David Hume on Thomas Cromwell*

When She Smiled

WHEN she smiled it was a pure sunshine that anyone chose to bask in if they could ; but anon came a storm and the thunder fell in wondrous manner on all alike.　*Queen Elizabeth by her godson,*
Sir John Harington

The Great Man's Little House

CONVERSATION *between Sir Nicholas Bacon and Queen Elizabeth at Gorhambury :* My Lord, what a little house you have gotten.

Madam, my house is well, but it is you that have made me too great for my house.

The Pilot that Weathered the Storm

It was in a dark hour for our country that one statesman wrote this tribute to another. A treaty of Peace with France had been signed and Pitt was at a birthday dinner at Walmer Castle when Canning read this poem to the guests, written by himself.

IF hushed the loud whirlwind that ruffled the deep,
　　The sky, if no longer loud tempests deform ;
When our perils are past, shall our gratitude sleep ?
　　No ! Here's to the Pilot that Weathered the Storm.

At the footstool of power let flattery fawn,
　　Let faction her idols extol to the skies ;
To virtue, in humble retirement withdrawn,
　　Unblamed may the tribute of gratitude rise.

And shall not his memory to Britain be dear,
　　Whose example with envy all nations behold,
A statesman unbiassed by interest or fear
　　By power uncorrupted, untainted by gold ?

Who, when terror and doubt through the Universe reigned,
　　While rapine and treason their standards unfurled,
The heart and the hopes of his country maintained,
　　And one kingdom preserved midst the wreck of the world.

Unheeding, unthankful, we bask in the blaze
　　While the beams of the sun in full majesty shine ;
When he sinks into twilight with fondness we gaze,
　　And mark the mild lustre that gilds his decline.

Lo ! Pitt, when the course of thy greatness is o'er,
　　Thy talents, thy virtues, we fondly recall !
Now justly we prize thee, when lost we deplore ;
　　Admired in thy zenith but loved in thy fall.

O ! take, then, for dangers by wisdom repelled,
　　For evils by courage and constancy braved,
O take, for a throne by thy counsels upheld,
　　The thanks of a people thy firmness has saved.

And O, if again the rude whirlwind should rise,
　　The dawning of Peace should fresh darkness deform,
The regrets of the good, and the fears of the wise
　　Shall turn to the Pilot that Weathered the Storm !

George Canning

Thomas Cromwell to Henry the Eighth

I, A most woeful prisoner, am ready to submit to death when it please God and Your Majesty ; and yet the frail flesh incites me to call to Your Grace for mercy and pardon of mine offences.

Written at the Tower with the heavy heart and trembling hand of Your Highness's most miserable prisoner and poor slave, Thomas Cromwell. Most gracious prince, I cry for mercy, mercy, mercy.

Seven Weeks

QUEEN ELIZABETH to Mr Speaker Popham : Now, Mr Speaker, what has passed in the Lower House ?

Mr Speaker : If it please your majesty, seven weeks.

Galileo Blind

ALAS, your dear friend and servant Galileo has been for the last month hopelessly blind ; so that this heaven, this earth, this universe, which I by my marvellous discoveries and clear demonstrations had enlarged a hundred thousand times beyond the belief of the wise men of bygone ages, henceforward for me is shrunk into such a small space as is filled by my own bodily sensations.

Galileo to a friend

What Garfield Thought of Garfield

I DO not care much what others say and think about me. But there is one man's opinion which I very much value, and that is the opinion of James Garfield. Others I need not think about. I can get away from them, but I have to be with him all the time. He is with me when I rise up and when I lie down ; when I eat and talk ; when I go out and come in. It makes a great difference whether he thinks well of me or not.

President Garfield

The King's Last Sleep

AFTER the bishop was gone to his lodging the King continued reading and praying more than two hours after. The King commanded Mr Herbert to lie beside him on a pallat, where he took small rest, that being the last night his sovereign master enjoyed. But nevertheless the King for four hours slept soundly and awaking about two hours before the dawn of day he opened his curtain to call Mr Herbert, there being a great cake of wax set in a silver basin that burned all night so that he perceived him somewhat disturbed in sleep but bade him rise—For (said his Majesty) I will get up having a great work to do this day. However, he would know why he was so troubled in his sleep.

He replied, May it please your majesty I was dreaming. I would know your dream, said the King, which being told his Majesty said it was remarkable. Herbert, this is my second marriage day. I would be as trim today as may be for before night I hope to be espoused to my blessed Jesus.

He then appointed what clothes he would wear. Let me have a shirt on more than ordinary by reason the season is so sharp as probably may make me shake, which some observers will imagine proceeds from fear. I would have no such imputation. I fear not death. Death is not terrible to me. I bless God I am prepared.

Sir Thomas Herbert, King Charles's last attendant

Deceit

O WHAT a tangled web we weave
When first we practice to deceive !
Sir Walter Scott

Sir Walter Going Out of the World

I AM drawing near to the close of my career; I am fast shuffling off the stage.

I have been perhaps the most voluminous writer of the day, and it is a comfort to me to think that I have tried to unsettle no man's faith, to corrupt no man's principle, and that I have written nothing on my deathbed I should wish blotted out. *Sir Walter Scott, dying*

Surely We May Endure

IF God bears with the very worst of us, we may surely endure each other. *Sir Walter Scott*

A Word About King Charles

WHAT, after all, are the virtues ascribed to Charles ? A religious zeal, not more sincere than that of his son, and fully as weak and narrow-minded, and a few of the ordinary household decencies which half the tombstones in England claim for those who lie beneath them. A good father ! A good husband ! Ample apologies indeed for fifteen years of persecution, tyranny, and falsehood !

We charge him with having broken his coronation oath ; and we are told that he kept his marriage vow ! We accuse him of having given up his people to the merciless inflictions of the most hot-headed and hard-hearted of prelates ; and the defence is that he took his little son on his knee and kissed him ! We censure him for having violated the articles of the Petition of Right, after having, for good and valuable consideration, promised to observe them ; and we are informed that he was accustomed to hear prayers at six o'clock in the morning ! It is to such considerations as these, together with his Vandyke dress, his handsome face, and his peaked beard, that he owes, we verily believe, most of his popularity with the present generation.

For ourselves, we own that we do not understand the common phrase, A good man but a bad king. We can as easily conceive a good man and an unnatural father, or a good man and a treacherous friend. We cannot, in estimating the character of an individual, leave out of our consideration his conduct in the most important of all human relations ; and if in that relation we find him to have been selfish, cruel, and deceitful, we shall take the liberty to call him a bad man, in spite of all his temperance at table, and all his regularity at chapel. *Macaulay*

County Guy

A H ! County Guy, the hour is nigh,
  The sun has left the lea,
The orange flower perfumes the bower,
  The breeze is on the sea.
The lark, his lay who thrilled the day,
  Sits hushed his partner nigh ;
Breeze, bird, and flower confess the hour,
  But where is County Guy ?

The village maid steals through the shade,
  Her shepherd's suit to hear ;
To beauty shy, by lattice high,
  Sings high-born Cavalier.
The star of Love, all stars above,
  Now reigns o'er earth and sky ;
And high and low the influence know,
  But where is County Guy ?

Sir Walter Scott

Looking on From Age to Age

THERE is not, and there never was on this earth, a work of human policy so well deserving of examination as the Roman Catholic Church.

No other institution is left standing which carries the mind back to the times when the smoke of sacrifice rose from the Pantheon, and when camelopards and tigers bounded in the Flavian amphitheatre. The proudest royal houses are but of yesterday when compared with the line of the Supreme Pontiffs. That line we trace back in an unbroken series, from the Pope who crowned Napoleon in the nineteenth century to the Pope who crowned Pepin in the eighth ; and far beyond the time of Pepin the august dynasty extends till it is lost in the twilight of fable. The republic of Venice came next in antiquity. But the republic of Venice was modern when compared with the Papacy ; and the republic of Venice is gone, and the Papacy remains.

The Papacy remains, not in decay, not a mere antique, but full of life and youthful vigour.

She saw the commencement of all the governments and of all the ecclesiastical establishments that now exist in the world ; and we feel no assurance that she is not destined to see the end of them all. She was great and respected before the Saxon had set foot on Britain, before the Frank had passed the Rhine, when Grecian eloquence still flourished in Antioch, when idols were still worshipped in the temple of Mecca. And she may still exist in undiminished vigour when some traveller from New Zealand shall, in the midst of a vast solitude, take his stand on a broken arch of London Bridge to sketch the ruins of St Paul's.

Macaulay

He Did Not Wear a Silken Cope

HE did not take his seat on a bishop's throne, or wear a silken cope, but he mounted the scaffold and was clothed in a garment of flame.   *On William Tyndale, by Dr Merle D'Aubigné*

The Prince of Buffoons

VOLTAIRE is the prince of buffoons. His merriment is without disguise or restraint. He gambols, he grins, he shakes his sides, he points the finger, he turns up the nose, he shoots out the tongue.

The nature of Voltaire was indeed not inhuman, but he venerated nothing. Neither in the masterpieces of art nor in the purest examples of virtue, neither in the First Great Cause nor in the awful enigma of the grave, could he see anything but subjects for drollery. The more solemn and august the theme, the more monkey-like was his grimacing and chattering.   *Macaulay*

Oliver and His Men

CROMWELL had passed his youth and the prime of his manhood in a civil situation. He never looked on war till he was more than forty. He had first to form himself and then to form his troops. Out of raw levies he created an army, the bravest and the best disciplined, the most orderly in peace, and the most terrible in war, that Europe had ever seen.

He called this body into existence. He led it to conquest. He never fought a battle without gaining it. He never gained a battle without annihilating the force opposed to him. Yet his victories were not the highest glories of his military system. The respect which his troops paid to property, their attachment to the laws and religion of their country, their submission to the civil power, their temperance, their industry, are without parallel.

At the command of the established Government, which had no means of enforcing obedience, fifty thousand soldiers, whose backs no enemy had ever seen, laid down their arms and retired into the mass of the people, thenceforth to be distinguished only by superior diligence, sobriety, and regularity in the pursuits of peace from the other members of the community which they had saved.

If the spirit of any man ever remained behind him on the Earth the spirit of the great Oliver is with our England still. *Macaulay*

Shakespeare's Portraits

WE most admire him for this, that while he has left us a greater number of striking portraits than all other dramatists put together, he has scarcely left us a single caricature.   *Macaulay*

Come On, All You Young Men

COME on now, all you young men, all over the world.   You are needed more than ever now to fill the gap of a generation shorn by the war.   You have not an hour to lose.   You must take your places in life's fighting line.   Twenty to twenty-five.   These are the years!   Don't be content with things as they are.   The earth is yours, and the fullness thereof.   *Winston Churchill*

As Sure as Macaulay

I WISH I were as sure about any one thing as Macaulay is about everything.   *Lord Melbourne*

I Am the Grass

PILE the bodies high at Austerlitz and Waterloo.
    Shovel them under and let me work.
I am the grass ; I cover all.

And pile them high at Gettysburg
And pile them high at Ypres and Verdun.
Shovel them under and let me work.
Two years, ten years, and passengers ask the Conductor :
    What place is this ?
    Where are we now ?

I am the grass.   Let me work.   *Carl Sandburg*

Beauty Bright

HERE lies Merrily Joules,
    A beauty bright,
Who left Isaac Joules
Her heart's delight.
          Epitaph in a Somerset churchyard

On Robin's Grave

TREAD lightly here, for here, tis said,
    When piping winds are hushed around,
A small note wakes from underground,
Where now his tiny bones are laid.
No more in lone and leafless groves,
With ruffled wing and faded breast,
His friendless, homeless spirit roves ;
Gone to the world where birds are blessed
Where never cat glides o'er the green,
Or schoolboy's giant form is seen ;
But Love, and Joy, and smiling Spring
Inspire their little souls to sing.
          Epitaph by Samuel Rogers on an urn in a garden

See'st Thou that Cloud?

SEE'ST thou that cloud as silver clear,
Plump, soft, and swelling everywhere?
Tis Julia's bed, and she sleeps there.

Robert Herrick

Content in the Country

HERE, here I live with what my board
Can with the smallest cost afford;
Though ne'er so mean the viands be,
They will content my Prue and me.
Or pea, or bean, or wort, or beet,
Whatever comes, content makes sweet.
Here we rejoice because no rent
We pay for our poor tenement,
Wherein we rest, and never fear
The landlord or the usurer.
The quarter-day does ne'er affright
Our peaceful slumbers in the night.
We eat our own, and batten more,
Because we feed on no man's score;
But pity those whose flanks grow great
Swelled with the lard of others' meat.
We bless our fortunes when we see
Our own beloved privacy:
And like our living, where we're known
To very few, or else to none.

Robert Herrick

Five Threes

A LITTLE saint best fits a little shrine,
A little prop best fits a little vine;
As my small cruse best fits my little wine.

A little seed best fits a little soil,
A little trade best fits a little toil;
As my small jar best fits my little oil.

A little bin best fits a little bread,
A little garland fits a little head;
As my small stuff best fits my little shed.

A little hearth best fits a little fire,
A little chapel fits a little choir;
As my small bell best fits my little spire.

A little stream best fits a little boat,
A little lead best fits a little float;
As my small pipe best fits my little note.

Robert Herrick

Pray be Silent

HERE a pretty baby lies,
  Snug asleep with lullabies ;
Pray be silent and not stir
The easy earth that covers her.

Robert Herrick

More Rich Than Cleopatra's Tomb

I SAW a fly within a bead
  Of amber cleanly buried :
The urn was little, but the room
More rich than Cleopatra's tomb.

Robert Herrick

Robert Herrick Sings

I SING of brooks, of blossoms, birds, and bowers,
  Of April, May, of June, and July flowers ;
I sing of maypoles, hock-carts, wassails, wakes,
Of bridegrooms, brides, and of their bridal-cakes.
I write of youth, of Love, and have access
By these, to sing of cleanly wantonness.
I sing of dews, of rains, and, piece by piece,
Of balm, of oil, of spice, and ambergris.
I sing of times trans-shifting ; and I write
How roses first came red and lilies white.

Gather Ye Rosebuds While Ye May

GATHER ye rosebuds while ye may :
  Old Time is still a-flying ;
And this same flower that smiles today
  Tomorrow will be dying.

The glorious lamp of heaven, the sun,
  The higher he's a-getting,
The sooner will his race be done,
  The nearer he's to setting.

That age is best which is the first,
  When youth and blood are warmer ;
But, being spent, the worse and worst
  Times still succeed the former.

Then be not coy, but use your time,
  And whilst ye may go marry ;
For having lost but once your prime,
  You may for ever tarry.

Robert Herrick

A Brother Remembers His Sister

To the Pure Soul of My
SISTER HENRIETTE
Who Died at Byblos, 24th of September, 1861

Do you remember, in the bosom of God where you are now at rest, those long days at Ghazir, where, alone with you, I wrote these pages which drew their inspiration from the places we had visited together ?

Sitting silently by my side you read over every page, and copied it as soon as written ; at our feet stretched the sea, the villages, the ravines, and the mountains. When the overpowering light of day had given place to the unnumbered army of the stars your thoughtful doubts led me back to the sublime object of our common thoughts.

One day you told me that you would love this book, because it had been written with you, and also because it was after your own heart. If at times you feared for it the narrow judgments of the man of frivolous mind, you were always full of assurance that truly religious souls would end by finding pleasure in it. In the midst of these sweet meditations the Angel of Death smote both of us with his pinion ; the slumber of fever seized us at the self-same hour ; I awakened alone.

Now you sleep in the land of Adonis, near holy Byblos and the sacred waters whither the women of the ancient mysteries were wont to come and mingle their tears. O, my good genius, reveal to me, whom you loved, these verities that have kingship over death, that shield us from the dread of it, that almost make us love it !

Ernest Renan's dedication of his Life of Jesus

The Morning Star

Thou wert the morning star among the living,
  Ere thy fair light had fled :
Now, having died, thou art as Hesperus giving
  New splendour to the dead.

Shelley's version of Plato's lines to Stella

Let Me Grow Lovely, Growing Old

Let me grow lovely, growing old,
  So many old things do :
Laces and ivory and gold,
  And silks, need not be new.

And there is healing in old trees,
  Old streets a glamour hold,
Why may not I, as well as these,
  Grow lovely, growing old ?

Karle Wilson Baker

The Excellent Mrs Partington

I DO not mean to be disrespectful, but the attempt of the Lords to stop the progress of reform reminds me very forcibly of the great storm of Sidmouth, and of the conduct of the excellent Mrs Partington on the occasion.

In the winter of 1824 there set in a great flood upon that town. The tide rose to an incredible height, the waves rushed in upon the houses, and everything was threatened with destruction ! In the midst of this sublime and terrible storm Dame Partington, who lived upon the beach, was seen at the door of her house with mop and pattens, trundling her mop, squeezing out the seawater, and vigorously pushing away the Atlantic Ocean. The Atlantic was roused. Mrs Partington's spirit was up ; but I need not tell you that the contest was unequal. The Atlantic Ocean beat Mrs Partington. She was excellent with a slop or a puddle, but she should not have meddled with a tempest.

Gentlemen, be at your ease. Be quiet and steady. You will beat Mrs Partington. *Sidney Smith at Taunton in 1832*

Ye Little Birds that Sit and Sing

YE little birds that sit and sing
   Amidst the shady valleys,
And see how Phillis sweetly walks
Within her garden alleys :
Go, pretty birds, about her bower ;
Sing, pretty birds, she may not lower ;
Ah me ! methinks I see her frown !
Ye pretty wantons, warble.

Go, tell her through your chirping bills,
As you by me are bidden,
To her is only known my love,
Which from the world is hidden.
Go, pretty birds, and tell her so ;
See that your notes strain not too low,
For still methinks I see her frown ;
Ye pretty wantons, warble.

O fly ! make haste ! see, see, she falls
Into a pretty slumber !
Sing round about her rosy bed
That, waking, she may wonder :
Say to her, tis her lover true
That sendeth love to you, to you !
And when you hear her kind reply,
Return with pleasant warblings.
Thomas Heywood

There Was a Little Girl

THERE was a little girl
  And she had a little curl
Right in the middle of her forehead.
  When she was good
  She was very very good,
But when she was bad she was horrid.

  One day she went upstairs
  When her parents, unawares,
In the kitchen were occupied with meals.
  And she stood upon her head
  In her little truckle-bed,
And then began hooraying with her heels.

  Her mother heard the noise,
  And she thought it was the boys
A-playing at a combat in the attic ;
  But when she climbed the stair,
  And found Jemima there,
She took and she did spank her most emphatic.

Old Rhyme by writer unknown

He Would Not Live Again

*Wordsworth having asked Southey if he would like to live
his youth over again, Southey answered in these lines.*

DO I regret the past ?
  Would I again live o'er
The morning hours of life ?
Nay, William, nay, not so !
In the warm joyaunce of the summer sun
  I do not wish again
  The changeful April day.
Nay, William, nay, not so !
Safe havened from the sea
  I would not tempt again
  The uncertain ocean's wrath.
Praise be to him who made me what I am,
  Other I would not be.
No, William, no, I would not live again
  The morning hours of life ;
  I would not be again
  The slave of hope and fear ;
  I would not learn again
The wisdom by experience hardly taught.

All That is Best in the World

POETRY makes immortal all that is best and most
beautiful in the world. *Shelley*

Poor Jim Dick

WHEN I was a small boy there was a black boy in the neighbourhood by the name of Jim Dick. I and my playfellows tormented the poor black by calling him Negro, Blackamoor, and other names.

The poor fellow appeared excessively grieved at our conduct and soon left us. Later on, skating in the neighbourhood, I had the misfortune to break my skates, and I could not go without borrowing Jim's skates. I went to him and asked him for them. " Oh, yes, Robert, you may have them and welcome," was his answer. When I went to return them I told Jim I had returned his skates and was under great obligations to him for his kindness. With tears in his eyes he said, " Robert, don't ever call me a Blackamoor again ! " and immediately left the room.

The words pierced my heart and I burst into tears, and from that time I resolved never again to abuse a poor black. *Robert Southey*

Bird of the Wilderness

BIRD of the wilderness,
Blithesome and cumberless,
Sweet be thy matin o'er mountain and lea !
Emblem of happiness,
Blest is thy dwelling-place,
O to abide in the desert with thee !
Wild is thy lay and loud,
Far in the downy cloud,
Love gives it energy, love gave it birth ;
Where, on thy dewy wing,
Where art thou journeying ?
Thy lay is in Heaven, thy love is on Earth.

O'er fell and fountain sheen,
O'er moor and mountain green,
O'er the red streamer that heralds the day,
Over the cloudlet dim,
Over the rainbow's rim,
Musical cherub, soar, singing, away !
Then, when the gloaming comes,
Low in the heather blooms,
Sweet will thy welcome and bed of love be.
Emblem of happiness,
Blest is thy dwelling-place,
O to abide in the desert with thee !
James Hogg

Pessimism

MAN, *so far as natural science by itself is able to teach us,* is no longer the final cause of the Universe, the Heaven-descended heir of all the ages. His very existence is an accident, his story a brief and transitory episode in the life of one of the meanest of the planets.

Of the combination of causes which first converted a dead organic compound into the living progenitors of humanity Science indeed as yet knows nothing. It is enough that from such beginnings famine, disease, and mutual slaughter, fit nurses of the future lords of creation, have gradually evolved a race with conscience enough to feel that it is vile and intelligence enough to know that it is insignificant.

We survey the past, and see that its history is of blood and tears, of helpless blundering, of wild revolt, of stupid acquiescence, of empty aspirations. We sound the future, and learn that after a period, long compared with the individual life, but short indeed compared with the divisions of time open to our investigation, the energies of our system will decay, the glory of the sun will be dimmed, and the earth, tideless and inert, will no longer tolerate the race which has for a moment disturbed its solitude.

Man will go down into the pit, and all his thoughts will perish. The uneasy consciousness which in this obscure corner has for a brief space broken the contented silence of the Universe will be at rest. Matter will know itself no longer. Imperishable monuments and immortal deeds, death itself and love stronger than death, will be as though they had never been. Nor will anything that *is* be better or be worse for all that the labour, genius, devotion, and suffering of the man have striven through countless generations to effect.

*Lord Balfour on what Science
without Faith has to teach us*

The Infinite and Eternal Energy

BUT one truth must grow ever clearer—the truth that there is an Inscrutable Existence everywhere manifested, to which we can neither find nor conceive beginning or end. Amid the mysteries which become the more mysterious the more they are thought about, there will remain the one absolute certainty that we are ever in the presence of an Infinite and Eternal Energy from which all things proceed.

Herbert Spencer

The Awful Mystery

I THINK it is one of the most awful of mysteries that we have lives apart from those we love most, that we can go on living after the connection, which seems to be life itself, is snapped. Certainly something, some vital part in us, does die then.

Sir J. M. Barrie

Who Counsels Peace at this Momentous Hour?

WHO counsels peace at this momentous hour,
    When God hath given deliverance to the oppressed,
        And to the injured power ?
Who counsels peace, when Vengeance like a flood
    Rolls on, no longer now to be repressed ;
        When innocent blood
From the four corners of the world cries out
        For justice upon one accursèd head ;
    When Freedom hath her holy banners spread
        Over all nations, now in one just cause
        United ; when with one sublime accord
        Europe throws off the yoke abhorred,
        The Loyalty and Faith of Ancient Laws
        Follow the avenging sword ?

Woe, woe to England ! woe and endless shame,
        If this heroic land,
False to her feelings and unspotted fame,
Hold out the olive to the Tyrant's hand !
Woe to the world, if Buonaparte's throne
        Be suffered still to stand !
For by what names shall Right and Wrong be known ;
    What new and courtly phrases must we feign
For falsehood, murder, and all monstrous crimes,
        If that perfidious Corsican maintain
        Still his detested reign,
And France, who yearns, even now to break her chain
    Beneath his iron rule be left to groan ?

*Written by Robert Southey during the
negotiations with Napoleon in 1814*

Rider Haggard Commits Himself to the Everlasting Arms

So ends the chronicle of Henry Rider Haggard, a lover of the kindly race of men, a lover of children, a lover of his friends (and no hater of his enemies), a lover of flowers, a lover of the land and of all creatures that dwell thereon, but most of all, perhaps, a lover of his country, which, with heart and soul and strength, he has tried to serve to the best of his small powers and opportunities.

" Thus, then, poor sinner though I am, trustfully as a wearied child that at the coming of the night creeps to its mother's knee, do I commit my spirit to the comfort of those Everlasting Arms that were and are its support through all the fears of Earth, and, as I believe, have nursed it from of old."

The last words of the last book of Rider Haggard

The Realities and the Shadow

When Wilkes was in the Escurial, looking at Titian's famous picture of The Last Supper, an old Jeronimite said to him :

I HAVE sat daily in sight of that picture for now nearly threescore years ; during that time my companions have dropped off one after another—all who were my seniors, all who were my contemporaries, and many or most of those who were younger than myself ; more than one generation has passed away, and there the figures in the picture have remained unchanged ! I look at them till I sometimes think that they are the realities and we but shadows.

Robert Southey

The Passing-On of George Meredith

HE strode up the hill whirling his staff, for which he had no longer any other use. His hearing was again so acute that from far away on the Dorking road he could hear the rumbling of a coach.

It had been disputed whether he should be buried in Westminster Abbey or in a quiet churchyard, and there came to him somehow a knowledge (it was the last he ever knew of little things) that people had been at variance as to whether a casket of dust should be laid away in one hole or in another, and he flung back his head with the old glorious action, and laughed a laugh " broad as a thousand beeves at pasture."

Box Hill was no longer deserted. When a great man dies—and this was one of the greatest since Shakespeare—the immortals await him at the top of the nearest hill. He looked up and saw his peers. They were all young, like himself. He waved the staff in greeting. One, a mere stripling, " slight unspeakably," R. L. S. detached himself from the others, crying gloriously, " Here's the fellow I have been telling you about ! " and ran down the hill to be the first to take his Master's hand. In the meanwhile an empty coach was rolling on to Dorking.

J. M. Barrie

Good-Night

GOOD-NIGHT ! Good-night ! parting is such sweet sorrow That I shall say Good-night till it be morrow.

Shakespeare's Juliet

Who Would Escape ?

POLONIUS : The actors are come. I will use them according to their desert.

Hamlet : God's bodykins, man, much better : use every man after his desert and who should 'scape whipping ? *Shakespeare*

We Build the Ladder by which We Rise

I COUNT this thing to be grandly true,
That a noble deed is a step toward God,
Lifting the soul from the common sod
To a purer air and a broader view.

We hope, we aspire, we resolve, we trust,
When the morning calls us to life and light,
But our hearts grow weary, and, ere the night,
Our lives are trailing the sordid dust.

Only in dreams is a ladder thrown
From the weary earth to the sapphire walls ;
But the dream departs, and the vision falls,
And the sleeper wakes on his pillow of stone.

Heaven is not reached at a single bound :
But we build the ladder by which we rise
From the lowly earth to the vaulted skies,
And we mount to its summit round by round.
Josiah Gilbert Holland

Isle of Beauty, Fare Thee Well

SHADES of evening close not o'er us,
Leave our lonely bark awhile ;
Morn, alas ! will not restore us
Yonder dim and distant isle.
Still my fancy can discover
Sunny spots where friends may dwell ;
Darker shadows round us hover,
Isle of Beauty, fare thee well !

Tis the hour when happy faces
Smile around the taper's light ;
Who will fill our vacant places ?
Who will sing our songs tonight ?
Through the mist that floats above us
Faintly sounds the vesper bell,
Like a voice from those who love us,
Breathing fondly, Fare thee well !

When the waves are round me breaking,
As I pace the deck alone,
And my eye is vainly seeking
Some green leaf to rest upon ;
When on that dear land I ponder,
Where my old companions dwell,
Absence makes the heart grow fonder,
Isle of Beauty, fare thee well !
Thomas Haynes Bayly

She Wore a Wreath of Roses

SHE wore a wreath of roses
　　The night that first we met ;
Her lovely face was smiling
　　Beneath her curls of jet.
Her footstep had the lightness
　　Her voice the joyous tone,—
The tokens of a youthful heart,
　　Where sorrow is unknown.
I saw her but a moment,
　　Yet methinks I see her now,
With the wreath of summer flowers
　　Upon her snowy brow.

A wreath of orange-blossoms,
　　When next we met, she wore ;
The expression of her features
　　Was more thoughtful than before ;
And standing by her side was one
　　Who strove, and not in vain,
To soothe her, leaving that dear home
　　She ne'er might view again.
I saw her but a moment,
　　Yet methinks I see her now,
With the wreath of orange-blossoms
　　Upon her snowy brow.

And once again I see that brow ;
　　No bridal-wreath is there,
The widow's sombre cap conceals
　　Her once luxuriant hair.
She weeps in silent solitude,
　　And there is no one near
To press her hand within his own,
　　And wipe away the tear.
I see her broken-hearted ;
　　Yet methinks I see her now,
In the pride of youth and beauty,
　　With a garland on her brow.
　　　　　　　　Thomas Haynes Bayly

A Poor Woman in a Foreign Land

MY lords, I am a poor woman, lacking wit to answer to any such noble persons of wisdom as you be in so weighty a matter ; therefore, I pray you, be good to me, poor woman, destitute of friends here in a foreign land.　　*Katharine of Aragon to the Cardinals*

A Hundred Years to Come

WHERE, where will be the birds that sing,
A hundred years to come ?
The flowers that now in beauty spring,
A hundred years to come ?
The rosy cheek,
The lofty brow,
The heart that beats
So quickly now ?
Where, where will be our hopes and fears,
Joy's pleasant smiles and sorrow's tears,
A hundred years to come ?

Who'll press for gold the crowded street,
A hundred years to come ?
Who'll tread yon aisle with willing feet,
A hundred years to come ?
Pale, trembling age
And fiery youth,
And childhood with
Its brow of truth ;
The rich, the poor, on land and sea :
Where will the mighty millions be,
A hundred years to come ?

We all within our graves will sleep,
A hundred years to come ;
No living soul for us will weep,
A hundred years to come ;
And others then
Our lands will till,
And other men
Our homes will fill,
And other birds will sing as gay,
And bright the sun shine as today,
A hundred years to come.

Hiram Dodd Spencer

O, Call Back Yesterday

ONE day too late, I fear me, noble lord,
Hath clouded all thy happy days on earth :
O, call back yesterday, bid time return,
And thou shalt have twelve thousand fighting men !
Today, today, unhappy day, too late,
O'erthrows thy joys, friends, fortune, and thy state ;
For all the Welshmen, hearing thou wert dead,
Are gone to Bolingbroke, dispersed and fled.

Salisbury in Shakespeare's Richard the Second

The Shepherd in His Serenity

CORIN : And how do you like this shepherd's life, Master Touchstone ?

Touchstone : Truly, shepherd, in respect of itself, it is a good life, but in respect that it is a shepherd's life it is naught. Now, in respect it is in the fields it pleases me well ; but in respect it is not in the court it pleases me naught. Wast ever in court, shepherd ?

Corin : No truly. I am a true labourer : I earn that I eat, get that I wear, owe no man hate, envy no man's happiness, glad of other men's good, content with my harm, and the greatest of my pride is to see my ewes graze and my lambs suck.

Shakespeare in As You Like It

Shall Caesar Send a Lie ?

CAESAR : Shall Caesar send a lie ?
Have I in conquest stretched mine arm so far
To be afeared to tell graybeards the truth ?

Shakespeare

After Life's Fitful Fever He Sleeps Well

DUNCAN is in his grave ;
After life's fitful fever he sleeps well ;
Treason has done his worst : nor, steel, nor poison,
Malice domestic, foreign levy, nothing,
Can touch him further.   *Macbeth*

The Bright Day is Done

FINISH, good lady ; the bright day is done,
And we are for the dark.

Cleopatra's lady-in-waiting

The Fault is in Ourselves

BRUTUS : Another general shout !
I do believe that these applauses are
For some new honours that are heaped on Caesar.

Cassius : Why, man, he doth bestride the narrow world
Like a Colossus, and we petty men
Walk under his huge legs and peep about
To find ourselves dishonourable graves.
Men at some time are masters of their fates :
The fault, dear Brutus, is not in our stars,
But in ourselves, that we are underlings.

Julius Caesar

The Day is Near

THE time of universal peace is near :
Prove this a prosperous day.
Shakespeare

The Philosophy of Sir Toby Belch

DOST thou think because thou art virtuous there shall be no
more cakes and ale ? *Sir Toby Belch in Twelfth Night*

Tomorrow

TOMORROW, and tomorrow, and tomorrow,
Creeps in this petty pace from day to day,
To the last syllable of recorded time ;
And all our yesterdays have lighted fools
The way to dusty death. Out, out, brief candle !
Life's but a walking shadow, a poor player
That struts and frets his hour upon the stage,
And then is heard no more ; it is a tale
Told by an idiot, full of sound and fury,
Signifying nothing. *Shakespeare*

She Never Told Her Love

SHE never told her love
But let concealment, like a worm i' the bud,
Feed on her damask cheek ; she pined in thought,
And with a green and yellow melancholy
She sat like Patience on a monument,
Smiling at grief. *Twelfth Night*

Bottom the Weaver Comes Upon a Wonder

TITANIA : Thou art as wise as thou art beautiful.
Bottom : Not so, neither : but if I had wit enough to
get out of this wood I have enough to serve mine own turn.

Titania : Out of this wood do not desire to go :
Thou shalt remain here, whether thou wilt or no.
I am a spirit of no common rate :
The summer still doth tend upon my state ;
And I do love thee : therefore, go with me ;
I'll give thee fairies to attend on thee,
And they shall fetch thee jewels from the deep,
And sing while thou on pressèd flowers dost sleep :
And I will purge thy mortal grossness so
That thou shalt like an airy spirit go.
Midsummer Night's Dream

Bottom's Dream

BOTTOM: When my cue comes, call me, and I will answer. I have had a most rare vision. I have had a dream, past the wit of man to say what dream it was : man is but an ass if he go about to expound this dream. Methought I was—there is no man can tell what. Methought I was, and methought I had—but man is but a patched fool if he will offer to say what methought I had. The eye of man hath not heard, the ear of man hath not seen, man's hand is not able to taste, his tongue to conceive, nor his heart to report, what my dream was. I will get Peter Quince to write a ballad of this dream : it shall be called Bottom's Dream.

Midsummer Night's Dream

Dost Thou So Hunger for Mine Empty Chair?

One of the poignant moments of drama in Shakespeare is that when the dying Henry the Fourth imagines his son to be longing for the crown and rebukes him in these moving words.

PRINCE: I never thought to hear you speak again.
    King: Thy wish was father, Harry, to that thought :
I stay too long by thee ; I weary thee.
Dost thou so hunger for mine empty chair
That thou wilt needs invest thee with my honours
Before thy hour be ripe ? O foolish youth !
Thou seek'st the greatness that will overwhelm thee.
Stay, but a little ; for my cloud of dignity
Is held from falling with so weak a wind
That it will quickly drop ; my day is dim.
What ! canst thou not forbear me half an hour ?
Then get thee gone and dig my grave thyself,
And bid the merry bells to ring thine ear
That thou art crownèd, not that I am dead.
Let all the tears that should bedew my hearse
Be drops of balm to sanctify thy head.
Only compound me with forgotten dust ;
Give that which gave thee life unto the worms.
Pluck down my officers, break my decrees ;
For now a time is come to mock at form :
Harry the Fifth is crowned : up, vanity !
Down, royal state ! all you sage counsellors, hence,
And to the English court assemble now
From every region, apes of idleness !
O my poor kingdom, sick with civil blows !
When that my care could not withhold thy riots,
What wilt thou do when riot is thy care ?
O, thou wilt be a wilderness again,
Peopled with wolves, thy old inhabitants !

From Henry the Fourth

SIR JOSHUA REYNOLDS, BY HIMSELF

SHAKESPEARE, BY RICHARD BURBAGE

SIR WALTER RALEIGH, BY AN UNKNOWN ARTIST

SIR WALTER SCOTT, BY SIR EDWIN LANDSEER

This England Never Did Nor Never Shall

THIS England never did, nor never shall,
     Lie at the proud foot of a conqueror,
But when it first did help to wound itself.
Now these her princes are come home again,
Come the three corners of the world in arms,
And we shall shock them.   Nought shall make us rue,
If England to itself do rest but true.

Shakespeare's King John

Did Shakespeare Say This?

SHAKESPEARE was godfather to one of Ben Jonson's children, and after the christening, being in a deep study, Jonson came to cheer him up, and asked him why he was so malancholy.

No faith, Ben (says he), not I, I have been considering a great while what should be the fittest gift for me to bestow upon my godchild, and I am resolved at last.

I prythee what? says he.

I' faith, Ben (says he), I'll e'en give him a dozen good latten spoons, and thou shalt translate them.

*An old story of the time, the only
conversation recorded of Shakespeare*

On the Word of a King

WAS there ever such stuff as the great part of Shakespeare?   Is it not sad stuff?   But one must not say so.

George the Third to Miss Burney

Handel Blind

WHEN Handel was blind he composed his Samson, in which there is that most touching of all songs, Total Eclipse :

*Total Eclipse! no sun, no moon,
All dark amidst the blaze of noon!
O glorious light! no cheering ray
To glad my eyes with welcome day!
Why thus deprived Thy prime decree?
Sun, moon, and stars are dark to me.*

Mr Beard was the great tenor singer of the day, who was to sing this song.   Handel sent for him.   Mr Beard, he said, I cannot sing it as it should be sung, but I can tell you how it ought to be sung.

And then he sang it, with what strange pathos need not be told. Beard stood listening, and when it was finished said, with tears in his eyes, But, Mr Handel, I can never sing it like that.

Story told by Edward Fitzgerald

Grief Can Wait

WEEP not, my wanton, smile upon my knee,
When you art old there's grief enough for thee.
Robert Greene in Shakespeare's day

The Upstart Crow

THERE is an upstart crow beautiful with our feathers, that, with his tiger's heart wrapped in a player's hide, supposes he is as well able to bombast out a blank verse as the best of you. . . . It is a pity men of such rare wits should be subject to the pleasures of such rude grooms.   *Robert Greene's churlish reference*
to his rival William Shakespeare

England's Moat

IT may be said now to England, Martha, Martha, thou art busy about many things, but one thing is necessary. To the question What shall we do to be saved in this world ? there is no other answer but this, *Look to your moat.*

The first article of an Englishman's political creed must be that he believeth in the sea. Without that there needeth no General Council to pronounce him incapable of salvation here.

We are in an island, confined to it by God Almighty, not as a penalty but a grace, and one of the greatest that can be given to mankind.   *Lord Halifax in the Seventeenth Century*

Here's an Acre Rich Indeed

MORTALITY, behold and fear !
What a change of flesh is here !
Think how many royal bones
Sleep within this heap of stones :
Here they lie had realms and lands
Who now want strength to stir their hands :
Where from their pulpits sealed with dust
They preach " In greatness is no trust."
Here's an acre sown indeed
With the richest, royallest seed
That the earth did e'er suck in
Since the first man died for sin.
Here the bones of birth have cried :
Though gods they were, as men they died !
Here are sands, ignoble things,
Dropt from the ruined sides of kings ;
Here's a world of pomp and state
Buried in dust, once dead by fate.
Written in Shakespeare's day by Francis Beaumont

Lie Lightly, Earth

LAY a garland on my hearse,
Of the dismal yew ;
Maidens, willow branches bear ;
Say I died true ;
My love was false, but I was firm
From my hour of birth.
Upon my buried body lie
Lightly, gentle earth !

Beaumont and Fletcher

And Shall Trelawny Die ?

A GOOD sword and a trusty hand !
A merry heart and true !
King James's men shall understand
What Cornish lads can do.

And have they fixed the where and when ?
And shall Trelawny die ?
Here's twenty thousand Cornish men
Will know the reason why !

Out spake their captain brave and bold,
A merry wight was he :
If London Tower were Michael's hold
We'll set Trelawny free !

We'll cross the Tamar, land to land,
The Severn is no stay,
With one and all, and hand in hand,
And who shall bid us Nay ?

Trelawny he's in keep and hold,
Trelawny he may die ;
But here's twenty thousand Cornish bold
Will know the reason why !

Robert Stephen Hawker

Life Has No More to Give

SAY not, because he did no wondrous deed,
Amassed no worldly gain,
Wrote no great book, revealed no hidden truth,
Perchance he lived in vain ;
For there was grief within a thousand hearts
The hour he ceased to live :
He held the love of women and of men
Life has no more to give !

Charlotte Becker

England Invincible

ENGLAND has been destroyed every ten or fifteen years, from the time of the Armada to the present day, in the prophecies of men.

Every few years she has been about to be overthrown by sea; she has been about to be ploughed up by the land; she has been about to be stripped of her resources in India and in other parts of the globe. Nations have formed alliances against her; the armies and fleets of the civilised world have gone about her; her interests have been repeatedly and violently assailed, and yet she stood, as she now stands, mistress of the seas, and the strongest power on Earth.   *Henry Ward Beecher*

The Crows at Washington

SLOW flapping to the western sun
  By twos and threes in setting rows,
As twilight shadows dimly close,
   The crows fly over Washington.

I stand and watch with clouded eyes
   These dim battalions move along;
Out of the distance memory cries
   Of days when life and hope were strong,
When love was prompt and wit was gay;
Even then, at evening, as today,
   I watched, while twilight hovered dim
   Over Potomac's curving rim,
This selfsame flight of homing crows
Blotting the sunset's fading rose
   Above the roofs of Washington.
         John Hay

Never More

NEVER, oh, never more shall I behold
  A sunrise on the glacier: stars of morn
Paling in primrose round the crystal horn;
Soft curves of crimson mellowing into gold
O'er sapphire chasm, and silvery snowfield cold;
Fire that o'erfloods the horizon; beacons borne
From wind-worn peak to storm-swept peak forlorn;
Clear hallelujahs through heaven's arches rolled.
Never, oh, never more these feet shall feel
The firm elastic tissue of upland turf,
Or the crisp edge of the high rocks; or cling
Where the embattled cliffs beneath them reel
Through cloud-wreaths eddying like the Atlantic surf,
Far, far above the wheeling eagle's wing.
        John Addington Symonds

Good-Night, Friend

WHEN you meet a countryman after dusk he greets you and wishes you *Good-night*; and you return his greeting and call him *Friend*. It seems as though a feeling something like brotherhood rose up in every heart at the approach of the hour when we are all to be gathered together beneath the wings of sleep. *Augustus Hare*

Nouveau Riche

MY babe and I in muddy ditch
  Lie newly side by side;
Praised be the God who made me rich,
  But keep my soul from pride.

Lean arms I clasp and bitter rags
  For shelter round my boy;
Forgive the queen in me that brags,
  Oh You who sent the joy.
        Janet Begbie

Old Ironsides

AY, tear her tattered ensign down!
  Long has it waved on high,
And many an eye has danced to see
  That banner in the sky;
Beneath it rung the battle shout,
  And burst the cannon's roar;
The meteor of the ocean air
  Shall sweep the clouds no more.

Her deck, once red with hero's blood,
  Where knelt the vanquished foe,
Where winds were hurrying o'er the flood,
  And waves were white below,
No more shall feel the victor's tread,
  Or know the conquered knee;
The harpies of the shore shall pluck
  The eagle of the sea.

O better that her shattered hulk
  Should sink beneath the wave;
Her thunders shook the mighty deep,
  And there should be her grave;
Nail to the mast her holy flag,
  Set every threadbare sail,
And give her to the god of storms,
  The lightning and the gale.
        Oliver Wendell Holmes

Hail and Farewell

At a breakfast party in St John's College, Cambridge, this Hail and Farewell was read to the guest, Oliver Wendell Holmes.

BY all sweet memory of the saints and sages
　Who wrought among us in the days of yore;
By youth who, turning now life's early pages,
　Ripen to match the worthies gone before;
On us, O son of England's greatest daughter,
　A kindly word from heart and tongue bestow;
Then chase the sunsets o'er the western water
　And bear our blessing with you as you go.

A Poet and His Trees

IF it is something to make two blades of grass grow where only one was growing, it is much more to have been the occasion of the planting of an oak which shall defy twenty scores of winters, or of an elm which shall canopy with its green cloud of foliage half as many generations of mortal immortalities.

I have written many verses, but the best poems I have produced are the trees I planted on the hillside that overlooks the broad meadows. Nature finds rhymes for them in the recurring measures of the seasons. Winter strips them of their ornaments and gives them, as it were, in prose translation; and Summer clothes them in all the splendour of their leafy language. *Oliver Wendell Holmes*

A Child Asleep

THOU sleepest—but when wilt thou wake, fair child?
　When the fawn awakes in the forest wild?
When the lark's wing mounts with the breeze of morn?
When the first rich breath of the rose is born?
Lonely thou sleepest! yet something lies
Too deep and still on thy soft-sealed eyes;
Mournful, though sweet, is thy rest to see:
When will the hour of thy rising be?

Not when the fawn wakes; not when the lark
On the crimson cloud of the morn floats dark.
Grief with vain passionate tears hath wet
The hair, shedding gleams from thy pale brow yet;
Love, with sad kisses unfelt, hath pressed
Thy meek-dropt eyelids and quiet breast;
And the glad spring, calling out bird and bee,
Shall colour all blossoms, fair child, but thee.
Thou'rt gone from us, bright one! That *thou* should'st die,
And life be left to the butterfly!

*Felicia Hemans, on looking at a
Chantrey monument of a child sleeping*

There Was Heard the Sound of a Coming Foe

THERE was heard the sound of a coming foe,
  There was sent through Britain a bended bow ;
And a voice was poured on the free winds far,
As the land rose up at the sign of war.

Heard you not the battle horn ?
Reaper, leave thy golden corn,
Leave it for the birds of heaven.
Swords must flash, and spears be riven.
Leave it for the winds to shed :
Arm, ere Britain's turf grow red !

And the reaper armed, like a freeman's son ;
And the bended bow and the voice passed on.

Hunter, leave the mountain-chase,
Take the falchion from its place ;
Let the wolf go free today,
Leave him for a nobler prey.
Let the deer ungalled sweep by :
Arm thee ! Britain's foes are nigh !

And the hunter armed ere the chase was done ;
And the bended bow and the voice passed on.

Chieftain, quit the joyous feast,
Stay not till the song hath ceased.
Though the mead be foaming bright,
Though the fires give ruddy light,
Leave the hearth, and leave the hall :
Arm thee ! Britain's foes must fall.

And the chieftain armed, and the horn was blown ;
And the bended bow and the voice passed on.

Prince, thy father's deeds are told,
In the ower and in the hold :
Where the goatherd's lay is sung,
Where the minstrel's harp is strung,
Foes are on thy native sea :
Give our bards a tale of thee.

And the prince came armed, like a leader's son ;
And the bended bow and the voice passed on.

Mother, stay not thou thy boy,
He must learn the battle's joy.
Sister, bring the sword and spear,
Give thy brother words of cheer.
Maiden, bid thy lover part,
Britain calls the strong in heart.

And the bended bow and the voice passed on ;
And the bards made song for a battle won.   *Felicia Hemans*

The Happy Homes of England

THE stately homes of England !
How beautiful they stand,
Amidst their tall ancestral trees,
O'er all the pleasant land
The deer across their greensward bound,
Through shade and sunny gleam,
And the swan glides past them with the sound
Of some rejoicing stream.

The merry homes of England !
Around their hearths by night
What gladsome looks of household love
Meet in their ruddy light !
There woman's voice flows forth in song,
Or childish tale is told,
Or lips move tunefully along
Some glorious page of old.

The blessed homes of England !
How softly on their bowers
Is laid the holy quietness
That breathes from Sabbath hours !
Solemn, yet sweet, the church bell's chime
Floats through their woods at morn ;
All other sounds in that still time
Of breeze and leaf are born.

The cottage homes of England !
By thousands on her plains
They are smiling o'er the silvery brooks
And round the hamlet's fanes.
Through glowing orchards forth they peep,
Each from its nook of leaves ;
And fearless there the lowly sleep,
As the birds beneath their eaves.

The free, fair homes of England !
Long, long in hut and hall
May hearts of native proof be reared
To guard each hallowed wall !
And green for ever be the groves,
And bright the flowery sod,
Where first the child's glad spirit loves
Its country and its God !

Felicia Hemans

Seeing Trees

A FOOL sees not the same trees as a wise
man sees.   *William Blake*

James Russell Lowell to Oliver Wendell Holmes

OUTLIVE us all ! Who else like you
Could sift the seedcorn from our chaff,
And make us, with the pen we knew,
Deathless at least in epitaph ?

A 75th birthday greeting

The Gods be Praised, I'm Poor no More

THE Gods be praised, I'm poor no more !
Henceforth, my friends, consider me
A gentleman of property ;
My days of bread and scrape are o'er.

Farewell to Fortune's flouts and frowns,
I've fifty crowns, I've fifty crowns !
Yes, every year
I pocket clear
A revenue of fifty crowns.

Comrades, the universe is mine !
I could, if so I chose, maintain
The splendour of a sovereign,
And with a hundred orders shine.

My roof shall never want a guest ;
Relations, friends, of every hue,
Par excellence, my comrades, you,
All shall be feted on the best.

Farewell to Fortune's flouts and frowns,
I've fifty crowns, I've fifty crowns !
Yes, every year
I pocket clear
A revenue of fifty crowns.

Pierre Jean de Béranger

On, On, My Little Boat

BY tranquil breezes, night and morn,
Along a tranquil tide,
My little barque is lightly borne,
Wherever Fate may guide.
With swelling sail she wings away
Afar, afar we float.
(Sweet zephyr, softly round her play !)
On, on, my little boat !
With Fortune's wind a port we'll find,
On, on, my little boat !

Pierre Jean de Béranger

The Feet of Angels Bright

THE sun descending in the west,
   The evening star does shine ;
The birds are silent in their nest,
   And I must seek for mine.

Farewell green fields and happy grove,
   Where flocks have ta'en delight.
Where lambs have nibbled, silent move
   The feet of angels bright.

They look in every thoughtless nest
   Where birds are covered warm ;
They visit caves of every beast,
   To keep them all from harm.

William Blake

Little Rhymes by William Blake

To see a world in a grain of sand,
   And a heaven in a wild flower ;
Hold infinity in the palm of your hand,
   And eternity in an hour.

A Robin Redbreast in a cage
Puts all Heaven in a rage.

A dog starved at his master's gate
Predicts the ruin of the State.

Each outcry of the hunted hare
A fibre from the brain doth tear.

A skylark wounded on the wing
Doth make a cherub cease to sing.

He who shall hurt a little wren
Shall never be beloved by men.

He who the ox to wrath has moved
Shall never be by woman loved.

Kill not the moth nor butterfly,
For the last judgment draweth nigh.

When gold and gems adorn the plough,
To peaceful arts shall Envy bow.

The poor man's farthing is worth more
Than all the gold on Afric's shore.

A truth that's told with bad intent
Beats all the lies you can invent.

He who doubts from what he sees
Will ne'er believe, do what you please.

From Auguries of Innocence

To Sweet Delight

EVERY night and every morn
  Some to misery are born ;
Every morn and every night
Some are born to sweet delight.

William Blake

Joy and Woe are Woven Fine

JOY and woe are woven fine,
  A clothing for the soul divine ;
  Under every grief and pine
Runs a joy with silken twine.
It is right it should be so ;
Man was made for joy and woe ;
And when this we rightly know
Safely through the world we go.

William Blake

Here Lies John Trot

HERE lies John Trot, the friend of all mankind :
  He has not left one enemy behind.
Friends were quite hard to find, old authors say,
But now they stand in everybody's way.

William Blake

The Poet Looks Forward to His Fame

MORE durable than brass the frame
  Which here I consecrate to Fame ;
Higher than pyramids that rise
With royal pride to brave the skies ;
Nor years, though numberless the train,
Nor flight of seasons, wasting rain,
Nor winds, that loud in tempests break,
Shall e'er its firm foundation shake.

AND now I have completed a work which neither the anger of Jove,
  nor fire, nor steel, nor consuming Time will be able to destroy !
Let that day which has no power but over this body put an end to the
term of my uncertain life when it will.   Yet, in my better part, I shall
be raised immortal above the lofty stars, and indelible shall be my
name.   And whenever the Roman power is extended throughout the
vanquished Earth I shall be read by the lips of nations, and if the
presage of poets have aught of truth, throughout all years shall I
survive in fame.   *Two translations of Horace's farewell to
his book, written before the first century*

Sweet Day so Calm and Bright

SWEET day so cool, so calm, so bright,
The bridal of the earth and sky,
The dew shall weep thy fall tonight ;
    For thou must die.

Sweet rose, whose hue, angry and brave,
Bids the rash gazer wipe his eye,
Thy root is ever in its grave,
    And thou must die.

Sweet spring, full of sweet days and roses,
A box where sweets compacted lie,
My music shows ye have your closes,
    And all must die.

Only a sweet and virtuous soul,
Like seasoned timber, never gives ;
But though the whole world turn to coal,
    Then chiefly lives.   *George Herbert*

The Man Unshaken

THE man tenacious of his purpose in a righteous cause is not shaken
from his firm resolve by the frenzy of his fellow citizens bidding
what is wrong, not by the face of threatening tyrant, not by Auster,
stormy master of the restless Adriatic, not by the mighty hand of
thundering Jove. Were the vault of heaven to break and fall upon
him its ruins would smite him undismayed.   *Horace*

Tom Brown Goes to School

TOM, my boy, remember that you are going, at your own request,
to be chucked into this great school like a young bear, with
all your troubles before you—earlier, perhaps, than we should have
sent you.

If schools are what they were in my time you'll see a great many
cruel things done, and hear a deal of bad talk. But never fear. Tell
the truth ; keep a brave and kind heart ; never say or listen to anything you wouldn't have your mother hear, and you'll never feel
ashamed to come home.   *Thomas Hughes*

The Chessboard

THE chessboard is the world ; the pieces are the phenomena of the
Universe ; the rules of the game are what we call the Laws of
Nature. The player on the other side is hidden from us. We know
that his play is always fair, just, and patient, but also we know to our
cost that he never overlooks a mistake or makes the smallest allowance
for ignorance.   *Professor Huxley*

The Good Fight of Charles Darwin

ONE could not converse with Darwin without being reminded of Socrates. There was the same desire to find someone wiser than himself, the same belief in the sovereignty of reason, the same ready humour, the same sympathetic interest in all the ways and works of men.

None have fought better and none have been more fortunate than Charles Darwin. He found a great truth trodden underfoot, reviled by bigots, and ridiculed by all the world ; he lived long enough to see it irrefragably established in science, inseparably incorporated with the common thoughts of men, and only hated and feared by those who would revile, but dare not. What shall a man desire more than this ?

Once more the image of Socrates rises unbidden, and the noble peroration of the Apology rings in our ears as if it were Charles Darwin's farewell :

The hour of departure has arrived, and we go our ways—I to die and you to live. Which is the Better, God only knows. Professor Huxley

Of All the Senseless Babble

I AM utterly incapable of conceiving the existence of matter if there is no mind in which to picture that existence.

Of all the senseless babble I have ever had occasion to read, the demonstrations of those philosophers who undertake to tell us all about the nature of God would be the worst if they were not surpassed by the still greater absurdities of the philosophers who try to prove that there is no God. *Professor Huxley*

The Absolute Justice of Things

THE ledger of the Almighty is strictly kept and every one of us has the balance of his operations paid over to him at the end of every minute of his existence.

The absolute justice of the system of things is as clear to me as any scientific fact. The gravitation of sin to sorrow is as certain as that of the earth to the sun, or more so. *Professor Huxley*

Professor Huxley's Word to Youth

PROFESSOR HUXLEY having explained to a confident youth that no man can explain the universe, the youth asked the professor :

What, then, is the use of all your learning if you know nothing at the end of it ?

Huxley : I know nothing and you know nothing, but I know why I know nothing and you don't, and that is the difference between us.

The Panama Gang

HERE we are, gentlemen ; here's the whole gang of us,
    Pretty near through with the job we are on ;
Size up our work (it will give you the hang of us)
    South to Balboa and north to Colon.
Yes, the canal is our letter of reference ;
    Look at Culebra and glance at Gatun ;
What can we do for you—got any preference,
    Wireless to Saturn or bridge to the moon ?

Don't send us back to a life that is flat again,
    We who have shattered a continent's spine ;
Office work—oh, but we couldn't do that again !
    Haven't you something that's more in our line ?
Got any river they say isn't crossable ?
    Got any mountains that can't be cut through ?
We specialise in the wholly impossible,
    Doing things nobody ever could do !

Take a good look at the whole husky crew of us,
    Engineers, doctors, and steam-shovel men ;
Taken together you'll find quite a few of us
    Soon to be ready for trouble again.
Bronzed by the tropical sun that is blistery,
    Chockful of energy, vigour, and tang,
Trained by a task that's the biggest in history,
    Who has a job for this Panama Gang ?

Berton Braley

If the Earth Should Fall Tonight

IF this little world tonight
    Suddenly should fall through space
In a hissing, headlong flight,
    Shrivelling from off its face,
As it falls into the sun
    In an instant every trace
Of the little crawling things—
    Ants, philosophers, and lice,
Cattle, cockroaches, and kings,
    Beggars, millionaires and mice,
Men and maggots all as one
    As it falls into the sun . . .
Who can say but at the same
    Instant from some planet far,
A child may watch us and exclaim :
    See the pretty shooting star.

Oliver Herford

The Names Come Ringing Down the Way

A ROUND the good world's wide expanse
   Are places great and small
Whose names fair tingle with romance,
   And I would see them all ;
There's Cairo, Fez, and Ispahan,
   Bangkok and Singapore,
And Trebizonde and Cagayan
   And Rio and Lahore.

There's Sarawak and Callao,
   Algiers and Kandahar,
Khartoum, Rangoon, and Tokio,
   Bombay and Zanzibar ;
About the name of each there clings
   Enchantment's golden veil,
The wonder of strange folk and things,
   The glamour of the trail !

For some are north and some are south,
   And some are east and west,
And some are cursed with heat and drouth,
   And some with balm are blessed ;
But Capetown, Rhodes, or Frisco Bay,
   Shanghai, Seville, or Rome,
Their names come singing down the way
   To tempt me forth from home ;
Their magic's ringing down the way
   To lure me forth from home !
                                        Berton Braley

The People Chosen of God

I NEVER shall forget the emotion which filled me at the sight of
  London.   There she sat, the great empress of the seas, giving laws
to isles and continents, stretching afar over kings and peoples, not like
those of old, the rod of oppression, but the beneficent sceptre of her
riches and her liberty.

And I heard the hum of her vast industry, and through the streets
there poured the living sea of men and vehicles.

Then by-and-by there dawned a day, a day which was not like
other days ; no noisy wagons now in the streets, no throngs hurrying
to business ; the giant machine that had been roaring and thundering
the day before had suddenly stood still as if before the vision of God.
I look across the ocean, and there again I find this Anglo-Saxon race
clad in like grandeur under forms the most unlike.   It is, I love to
think, the people chosen of God to renew the face of the earth, and to
prepare for those old truths and institutions which cannot pass away
newer and more enduring garments.   *Père Hyacinthe*

Emily Brontë's Prayer

RICHES I hold in light esteem,
And Love I laugh to scorn ;
And lust of fame was but a dream
That vanished with the morn :

And, if I pray, the only prayer
That moves my lip for me
Is, " Leave the heart that now I bear,
And give me liberty ! "

Yea, as my swift days near their goal,
Tis all that I implore :
In life and death a chainless soul,
With courage to endure.

The Courage to Endure

THE windows of an old stone house on a hilltop looked out upon the grey and purple Yorkshire moors.

The day was hot, and the door was left open towards the lane that ran by the church to the fields. Three sisters lived in the stone house with their father, the clergyman of the parish, and one of the girls thought she heard the panting of a dog in the lane. Going to the door, she saw a pointer with tongue hanging distressfully out and back bruised and scarred.

She called the poor creature in, with the intention of giving it food and water. As she stooped to pat its head the pointer snapped and bit her arm, drawing blood, and then rushed away. The girl, who was Emily Brontë, felt the bite, but thought little of it.

Presently, however, villagers passed that way and gave the alarm that a mad dog was at large in the streets of Haworth, and Emily Brontë at once became conscious of the danger of hydrophobia. She walked into the laundry, where a maid was busy starching and ironing. There, with its point resting in the fire, was an Italian iron, and this Miss Brontë took, thrusting the red-hot point into the wounds caused by the dog's teeth. Having thus cauterised the wounds, she went upstairs, without a word, to regain her calm.

She lived to become famous with her sisters, and one of her poems has been said to be the best poem ever written by woman.

From a Brontë biography

That Proud Island

ACROSS the sea in calm majesty lies that proud island whose existence consoles me for a thousand Continental crimes, and vindicates for me the goodness of Providence. *Victor Hugo*

THE BELFRY OF BRUGES

TOM TOWER, OXFORD   MAGDALEN TOWER, OXFORD

THE BACKS AT CAMBRIDGE

The Day Will Come

A DAY will come when you France, you Russia, you Italy, you England, you Germany, all you nations of the Continent, shall, without losing your distinctive qualities and your glorious individuality, blend in a higher unity, and form a European fraternity, even as Normandy, Brittany, Burgundy, all the French provinces, blended into France.

A day will come when bullets and bombs shall be replaced by ballots, by the universal suffrage of the people, by the sacred arbitraments of a great sovereign Senate, which shall be to Europe what the Parliament is to England, what the Diet is to Germany, what the Legislative Assembly is to France.

A day will come when a cannon shall be exhibited in our museums as an instrument of torture is now, and men shall marvel that such things could be.

A day will come when we shall see those two immense groups the United States of America and the United States of Europe extending hand to hand over the ocean, exchanging their products, their commerce, their industry, their art, their genius, clearing the earth, colonising deserts, ameliorating Creation under the eye of the Creator.

Victor Hugo

The Thing That is Greater Than All

M ARIUS, almost without drawing breath, went on in a burst of enthusiasm :

Let us be just, my friends ! To be the Empire of such an Emperor, what a destiny for a nation, when that nation was France, and her genius was added to his ! To rise and rule, to march in triumph, with the capitals of the world for halting-places and kings for grenadiers, to dethrone dynasties, to change the map of Europe by a charge, to feel that your hand was on the sword-hilt of God, to follow a leader who was Hannibal, Caesar, Charlemagne, in one, a man who could dazzle you every morning with fresh victories, wake you by the guns of the Invalides, fling great names into gulfs of light, names that will shine for ever, Marengo, Arcola, Austerlitz, Jena, Wagram ! To set constellations of glory blazing in the skies of history, to make the French Empire the peer of the Roman, to be the greatest nation and give birth to the greatest army, to send out the legions over the earth as a mountain sends forth its eagles, to triumph, to dominate, to threaten, to be the one nation in Europe crowned and haloed with glory, to sound a flourish across the centuries, to conquer the world twice over, by conquest and by charm—it was stupendous, sublime ! What could be greater ?

To be free, said Combfrere.   *Victor Hugo in Les Miserables*

In Our Century

IN the twentieth century war will be dead, the scaffold will be dead, hatred will be dead, frontier boundaries will be dead, dogmas will be dead ; man will live. He will possess something higher than all these—a great country, the whole earth, and a great hope, the whole heaven.   *Victor Hugo*

The Party Which Does Not Exist

I REPRESENT a party which does not yet exist, the party of the Twentieth Century, out of which will come first of all the United States of Europe and after that the United States of the World.
                                                            Victor Hugo

The Light from Unknown Worlds

I FEEL in myself the future life. I am like a forest once cut down ; the new shoots are stronger and livelier than ever. I am rising, I know, toward the sky. The sunshine is on my head. The Earth gives me its generous sap, but Heaven lights me with the reflection of unknown worlds.

You say the soul is nothing but the resultant of the bodily powers. Why, then, is my soul more luminous when my bodily powers begin to fail ? Winter is on my head, but eternal spring is in my heart. I breathe at this hour the fragrance of the lilacs, the violets, and the roses, as at twenty. The nearer I approach the end the plainer I hear around me the immortal symphonies of the worlds. It is marvellous yet simple. It is a fairy tale, and it is history.

For half a century I have been writing my thoughts in prose and in verse ; history, philosophy, drama, romance, tradition, satire, ode, and song ; I have tried all. But I feel I have not said the thousandth part of what is in me.

When I go down to the grave I can say, like many others, *I have finished my day's work.* But I cannot say *I have finished my life.* My day's work will begin again the next morning. The tomb is not a blind alley ; it is a thoroughfare. It closes on the twilight, it opens on the dawn.   *Victor Hugo*

The Ancient Warrior

FOR Witherington my heart is woe
  That ever he slain should be,
For when his legs were hewn in two
  He fought upon his knee.

*From the Ballad of Chevy Chase, which moved
Sir Philip Sidney more than a trumpet*

A Little Sun, A Little Rain

A LITTLE sun, a little rain,
   A soft wind blowing from the west,
And woods and fields are sweet again,
   And warmth within the mountain's breast.

A little love, a little trust,
   A soft impulse, a sudden dream,
And life as dry as desert dust,
   Is fresher than a mountain stream.
                              Stopford Brooke

Cranmer's Last Day

CRANMER'S strangely mingled nature found a power in its very weakness when he was brought into the Church of St Mary at Oxford to repeat his recantation on the way to the stake.

" Now," ended his address to the hushed congregation before him, " now I come to the great thing that troubleth my conscience more than any other thing that ever I said or did in my life, and that is the setting abroad of writings contrary to the truth, which here I now renounce and refuse as things written for fear of death to save my life, if it might be. And, forasmuch as my hand offended in writing contrary to my heart, my hand shall therefore be the first punished, for if I come to the fire it shall be the first burned."

" This was the hand that wrote it," he again exclaimed at the stake, " therefore it shall suffer first punishment "; and holding it steadily in the flame, he never stirred nor cried till life was gone.
                              John Richard Green

Chaucer to His Empty Purse

To you, my Purse, and to no other wight
   Complain I, for ye be my lady dear !
I am so sorry now that ye be light,
For certain but ye make me heavy cheer
I were as lief be laid upon my bier,
For which unto your mercy thus I cry :
Be heavy again, or else must I die.

Now voucheth safe this day ere it be night
That I of you the blissful sound may hear,
Or see your colour as the sun is bright
That with its yellowness had ne'er a peer.
Queen of my comfort and of good company,
Be heavy again, or else must I die.
                              A free rendering of Chaucer

The Conqueror Conquered

HE recked little of men's love or hate. His grim look, his pride, his silence, his wild outbursts of passion, spread terror through his court.

His very wrath was solitary. " To no man spake he, and no man dared speak to him," when the news reached him of Harold's accession to the throne. He found society only when he passed from the palace to the loneliness of the woods. He loved the wild deer as though he had been their father.

Death itself took its colour from the savage solitude of his life. Priests and nobles fled as the last breath left him, and the Conqueror's body lay naked and lonely on the floor. *John Richard Green*

Geoffrey Chaucer to His Immortal Soul

FAR from mankind, my weary soul, retire,
Still follow truth, contentment still desire.
Who climbs on high at best his weakness shows,
Who rolls in riches all to fortune owes.
Read well thyself, and mark thy early ways,
Vain is the muse, and envy waits on praise.

Wavering as winds the breath of fortune blows,
No power can turn it and no prayers compose.
Deep in some hermit's solitary cell
Repose and ease and contemplation dwell.
Let conscience guide thee in the days of need,
Judge well thy own, and then thy neighbour's deed.

What heaven bestows with thankful eyes receive ;
First ask thy heart, and then through faith believe.
Slowly we wander o'er a toilsome way,
Shadows of life and pilgrims of a day.
Who restless in this world receives a fall,
Look upon high, and thank thy God for all !
Geoffrey Chaucer

Philip Sidney—By a Friend

THOUGH I lived with him, and knew him from a child, I never knew him other than a man, with such staidness of mind and lovely and familiar gravity as carried grace and reverence above greater years, his talk ever of knowledge, and his very play tending to enrich the mind. *Fulke Greville on Sir Philip Sidney*

Lament over Sidney

COME to me grief for ever,
Come to me tears day and night,
Sidney, O Sidney, is dead.
By a writer unknown

Lift Up Your Heart

LEAVE me, O Love, which reachest but to dust ;
  And thou, my mind, aspire to higher things ;
Grow rich in that which never taketh rust ;
  Whatever fades, but fading pleasure brings.

Draw in thy beams, and humble all thy might
  To that sweet yoke where lasting freedoms be ;
Which breaks the clouds, and opens forth the light
  That doth both shine and give us sight to see.

O take fast hold ; let that light be thy guide
  In this small course which birth draws out of death,
And think how ill becometh him to slide
  Who seeketh heaven and comes of heavenly breath.

Then farewell, World ; thy uttermost I see :
Eternal Love, maintain thy life in me.

Sir Philip Sidney

The Tale Which Holdeth Children from their Play

Now therein of all Sciences (I speak still of humane, and according to the humane conceits) is our poet the monarch. For he doth not only show the way, but giveth so sweet a prospect into the way as will entice any man to enter into it.

Nay, he doth, as if your journey should lie through a fair Vineyard, at the first give you a cluster of Grapes, that, full of that taste, you may long to pass further.

He beginneth not with obscure definitions, which must blur the margent with interpretations, and load the memory with doubtfulness ; but he cometh to you with words set in delightful proportion, either accompanied with, or prepared for, the well-enchanting skill of Musick ; and with a tale forsooth he cometh unto you ; with a tale which holdeth children from play, and old men from the chimney-corner.

And, pretending no more, doth intend the winning of the mind from wickedness to virtue : even as the child is often brought to take most wholesome things by hiding them in such other as have a pleasant taste ; which, if one should begin to tell them the nature of aloes or rhubarb they should receive, would sooner take their physick at their ears than at their mouth.

So it is in men (most of which are childish in the best things, till they be cradled in their graves) ; glad they will be to hear the tales of Hercules, Achilles, Cyrus, and Aeneas ; and, hearing them, must needs hear the right description of wisdom, valour, and justice ; which, if they had been barely, that is to say philosophically, set out they would swear they be brought to school again.

Sir Philip Sidney

My True Love Hath My Heart

MY true love hath my heart, and I have his,
By just exchange one for another given :
I hold his dear, and mine he cannot miss ;
There never was a better bargain driven :
My true love hath my heart and I have his.

His heart in me keeps him and me in one ;
My heart in him his thoughts and senses guides.
He loves my heart, for once it was his own,
I cherish his because in me it bides :
My true love hath my heart and I have his.

Sir Philip Sidney

On the Doorsteps of the Rich

SIMONIDES, asked by a lady whether it is better to be wise or wealthy, said :

To be wealthy, for I see the wise sitting on the doorsteps of the rich.

The Little Gleam Between Two Eternities

MEN speak too much about the world. Each one of us here, let the world go how it will, and be victorious or not victorious, has he not a life of his own to lead—one life, a little gleam of time between two eternities ?

For the saving of the world I will trust confidently to the Maker of the work ; and look a little to my own saving, which I am more competent to ! *Carlyle*

Courage, Brother

OUR grand business undoubtedly is not to see what lies dimly at a distance, but to do what lies clearly at hand. Courage, brother. Get honest, and times will mend. *Carlyle*

The Man Who Did a Little Thing

HE who first shortened the labour of copyists by device of movable types was disbanding hired armies, and cashiering most kings and senates, and creating a whole new democratic world : he had invented the art of printing. *Carlyle*

The Impossible

EVERY noble work is at first impossible. *Carlyle*

The Miracle

THIS world, after all our sciences, is still a miracle—wonderful, inscrutable, magical to whosoever will think of it. *Carlyle*

The Poorest Day

THE poorest day that passes over us is the conflux of two Eternities ; it is made up of currents that issue from the remotest Past and flow onwards into the remotest Future. *Carlyle*

Two Men Talking

ALFRED TENNYSON: In my old age I should like to get away from all this tumult and turmoil of civilisation and live on the top of a tropical mountain. I should, at least, like to see the splendours of the Brazilian forests before I die.

Thomas Carlyle : I would also like to quit it all.

Alfred Tennyson : If I were a young man I would head a colony out somewhere or other.

Thomas Carlyle : Oh, ay, so would I, to India or somewhere ; but the scraggiest bit of heath in Scotland is more to me than all the forests of Brazil. I am just twinkling away.

A conversation in 1879, given in Tennyson's Life

The Men of the Village of Dumdrudge

WHAT is the net purport and upshot of war ? There dwell and toil in the British village of Dumdrudge, usually some five hundred souls. From these there are successively selected, during the French war, say thirty able-bodied men.

Dumdrudge at her own expense has suckled and nursed them ; she has, not without difficulty and sorrow, fed them up to manhood, and even trained them to crafts, so that one can weave, another build, another hammer, and the weakest can stand under thirty stone avoirdupois.

Nevertheless, amid much weeping and swearing, they are selected ; all dressed in red ; and shipped away, at the public charges, say to the south of Spain ; and fed there till wanted.

And now to that same spot in the south of Spain, are thirty similar French artisans, from a French Dumdrudge, in like manner wending : till at length, after infinite effort, Thirty stands fronting Thirty, each with a gun in his hand. Straightway the word Fire ! is given, and they blow the souls out of one another ; and in place of sixty brisk, useful craftsmen, the world has sixty dead carcasses, which it must bury, and anew shed tears for.

Had these men any quarrel ? Busy as the devil is, not the smallest ! They lived far enough apart ; were the entirest strangers ; nay, in so wide a Universe there was even some mutual helpfulness between them. How then ? Simpleton ! their Governors had fallen out, and instead of shooting one another had the cunning to make these poor blockheads shoot. *Thomas Carlyle*

Ten Mistakes a Day

I BELIEVE it is pretty well acknowledged that I am the best general in Europe, yet I make ten mistakes a day. Ten, he repeated, holding up his fingers. *Conversations of Napoleon*

The Value of Five Minutes

THE reason I beat the Austrians is that they did not know the value of five minutes. *Napoleon*

Our Affair

NAPOLEON TO A BRITISH AMBASSADOR: I will make war on you.
Ambassador : That, Sire, is your affair.
Napoleon : I will annihilate you.
Ambassador : That, Sire, is our affair.

The Fallen Conqueror

A VICTIM to the factions which distract my country, and to the enmity of the greatest Powers of Europe, I have terminated my political career, and I come, like Themistocles, to throw myself upon the hospitality of the British people.

I put myself under the protection of their laws, which I claim from your Royal Highness, as the most powerful, the most constant, and the most generous of my enemies. *Napoleon to the Prince Regent after Waterloo*

Is This the Man of Thousand Thrones ?

TIS done—but yesterday a king !
And armed with kings to strive—
And now thou art a nameless thing :
So abject—yet alive !
Is this the man of thousand thrones,
Who strewed our earth with hostile bones,
And can he thus survive ?
Since he, miscalled the Morning Star,
Nor man nor fiend hath fallen so far.
Lord Byron

The Conqueror

DO you know what amazes me more than anything else ? The impotence of force to organise anything. There are only two powers in the world, the sword and the spirit. In the long run the sword will always be conquered by the spirit. *Napoleon*

In Some Unlucky Minute

CLORIS ! If I were Persia's king,
    I'd make my graceful queen of thee ;
While Fanny, wild and artless thing,
    Should but thy humble handmaid be.

There is but one objection in it,
    That verily, I'm much afraid,
I should in some unlucky minute
    Forsake the mistress for the maid !
                        Thomas Moore

The Rapids Are Near and Daylight Past

FAINTLY as tolls the evening chime
    Our voices keep tune and our oars keep time.
Soon as the woods on the shore look dim
We'll sing at St Anne's our parting hymn.
Row, brothers, row, the stream runs fast,
The rapids are near and the daylight's past.

Why should we yet our sail unfurl ?
There is not a breath the blue wave to curl ;
But when the wind blows off the shore
Oh, sweetly we'll rest our weary oar.
Blow, breezes, blow, the stream runs fast,
The rapids are near and the daylight's past.

Utawa's tide ! this trembling moon
Shall see us float over thy surges soon.
Saint of this green isle, hear our prayers,
Oh, grant us cool heavens and favouring airs !
Blow, breezes, blow, the stream runs fast,
The rapids are near and the daylight's past.
                Canadian Boat Song, by Thomas Moore

An Epitaph

THE body of Benjamin Franklin, printer,
    Like the cover of an old book,
Its contents torn out,
And stript of its lettering and gilding,
    Lies here, food for worms ;
Yet the work itself shall not be lost,
For it will (he believes) appear once more
        In a new
    And more beautiful edition,
        Corrected and amended
            by
        The Author.

Nothing Half So Sweet

THERE's nothing half so sweet in life
As Love's young dream.

Thomas Moore

She is Far From the Land

SHE is far from the land where her young hero sleeps,
And lovers around her are sighing ;
But coldly she turns from their gaze and weeps,
For her heart in his grave is lying.

She sings the wild song of her dear native plains,
Every note which he loved awaking ;
Ah, little they think who delight in her strains
How the heart of the minstrel is breaking.

He had lived for his love, for his country he died,
They were all that to life had entwined him ;
Nor soon shall the tears of his country be dried,
Nor long will his love stay behind him.

Oh, make her a grave where the sunbeams rest
When they promise a glorious morrow ;
They'll shine o'er her sleep like a smile from the West,
From her own loved island of sorrow.

*Written by Thomas Moore of Sarah Curran, who
left Ireland after her lover's execution for rebellion*

Lord, Who Shall Bear That Day ?

LORD, who shall bear that day, so dread, so splendid,
When we shall see Thy angel hovering o'er
This sinful world, with hand to heaven extended,
And hear him swear by Thee that time's no more ?
When earth shall feel thy fast consuming ray—
Who, mighty God, oh who shall bear that day ?

When through the world Thy awful call hath sounded—
" Wake, oh ye dead, to judgment wake, ye dead ! "
And from the clouds, by seraph eyes surrounded,
The Saviour shall put forth His radiant head ;
While earth and heaven before Him pass away—
Who, mighty God, oh who shall bear that day ?

When, with a glance, the eternal Judge shall sever
Earth's evil spirits from the pure and bright,
And say to *those*, " Depart from Me for ever ! "
To *these*, " Come, dwell with Me in endless light !
When each and all in silence take their way—
Who, mighty God, oh who shall bear that day ?

Thomas Moore

Joan of Arc's Farewell to Home

FAREWELL, ye mountains, ye belovèd glades,
  Ye lone and peaceful valleys, fare ye well !
Through you Joanna never more may stray,
For aye Joanna bids you now farewell.
Ye meads which I have watered, and ye trees
Which I have planted, still in beauty bloom !
Farewell, ye grottoes, and ye crystal springs !
Sweet echo, vocal spirit of the vale,
Who sang responsive to my simple strain,
Joanna goes, and ne'er returns again.

He who in glory did on Horeb's height
Descend to Moses in the bush of flame,
And bade him stand in Royal Pharaoh's sight ;
Who once to Israel's pious shepherd came,
And sent him forth, his champion in the fight ;
Who aye hath loved the lowly shepherd train ;
He, from these leafy boughs, thus spake to me :
Go forth ! Thou shalt on Earth my witness be.
Thou in rude armour must thy limbs invest,
A plate of steel upon thy bosom bear.
Vain earthly love may never stir thy breast,
Nor passion's sinful glow be kindled there.
But war's triumphant glory shall be thine,
Thy martial fame all women shall outshine !
For when in fight the stoutest hearts despair,
When direful ruin threatens France, forlorn,
Then thou aloft my oriflamme shalt bear,
And swiftly as the reaper mows the corn,
Thou shalt lay low the haughty conqueror ;
His fortune's wheel thou rapidly shalt turn,
To Gaul's heroic sons deliverance bring,
Relieve beleaguered Rheims, and crown thy king !

The Heavenly Spirit promised me a sign :
He sends the helmet—it hath come from Him.
Its iron filleth me with strength divine ;
I feel the courage of the cherubim.
As with the rushing of a mighty wind
It drives me forth to join the battle's din ;
The clanging trumpets sound, the chargers rear,
And the loud war-cry thunders in mine ear.

By the German poet Schiller

The Poet of Paradise

MILTON almost requires a solemn service of music to
be played before you enter upon him. *Charles Lamb*

Joan to Her Judges

WILL you say that you have no judge upon earth ?

I will say nothing to you about it. I have a good master, who is Our Lord, and to Him I will submit all.

If you do not submit to the Church you will be pronounced a heretic, and burned at the stake.

I will not say otherwise than I have said, and if I saw the fire before me I would say it again.

" Superba responsio " wrote the clerk in the margin of the record.

An Unknown Soldier Wins His Immortality

JOAN asked for a cross. None was able to furnish one. But an English soldier broke a stick in two and crossed the pieces and tied them together, and this cross he gave her, moved to it by the good heart that was in him ; and she kissed it and put it in her bosom.   *From a Life of Joan*

The Creed of Benjamin Franklin

HERE is my Creed. I believe in one God, Creator of the Universe. That He governs it by His Providence. That He ought to be worshipped. That the most acceptable service we render Him is doing good to His children. That the soul of Man is immortal, and will be treated with justice in another life respecting its conduct in this.

The Angel to Methuselah

ARISE, *Methuselah, and build thee a house, for thou shalt live yet five hundred years longer.*

Methuselah : If I am to live but five hundred years longer it is not worth while to build me a house ; I will sleep in the air as I have been used to do.   *A story made up by Benjamin Franklin*

Man is More than Breath

NO man can stand in the tropic forests without feeling that they are temples filled with the various productions of the God of Nature, and that there is more in man than the breath of his body.
                              Charles Darwin

Intolerable Thought

BELIEVING as I do that man in the distant future will be a far more perfect creature than he now is, it is an intolerable thought that he and all other sentient beings are doomed to complete annihilation after such long-continued slow progress. To those who fully admit the immortality of the human soul, the destruction of our world will not appear so dreadful.   *Charles Darwin*

Let There be Light

LET there be light ! proclaimed the Almighty Lord.
   Astonished Chaos heard the potent word.
Through all his realms the kindling ether runs,
And the mass starts into a million suns ;
Earths round each sun with quick explosions burst,
And second planets issue from the first ;
Bend, as they journey with projectile force,
In bright ellipses their reluctant course ;
Orbs wheel in orbs, round centres centres roll,
And form, self-balanced, one reluctant whole ;
Onward they move amid their bright abode,
Space without bound, the bosom of their God.
Written by Erasmus Darwin in the Eighteenth Century

These Two

ALEXANDER : I am come hither, Diogenes, to succour and relieve thee,
   because I see thee in great penury and need of many things.

Diogenes in his tub : Whether of us two is in the more penury—
I, that besides my scrip and my cage do miss nothing at all, or thou
who, not being contented with the inheritance of thy father's kingdom,
doest put thyself in a venture and hazard so many perils and dangers
to enlarge the limits of thine empire so much that not all the world
seemeth able to satisfy thy desire ?   *From Erasmus*

The Spirit of Saint Peter

I SAW with my own eyes Pope Julius marching at the head of a
  triumphal procession as if he were Pompey or Caesar.

St Peter subdued the world with faith, not with arms or soldiers
or military engines.   St Peter's successors would win as many victories
if they had Peter's spirit.   *Erasmus*

The Strong Man Afraid

CHRIST I know.   Luther I know not.
   They pretend that Luther has borrowed from me.   I beseech
you protect me from such calumnies.   I have said nothing except
that Luther ought to be answered and not crushed.   I would have
the church purified of evil lest the good in it suffer . . . We must
bear almost anything rather than throw the world in confusion.   I
was the first to oppose the publication of Luther's books.   I recom-
mended Luther himself to publish nothing revolutionary.   I feared
always that revolution would be the end, and I would have done
more had I not been afraid that I might be found fighting against
the spirit of God.   *Erasmus*

No Land on Earth Like Ours

OH, splendid England, home and citadel of virtue and learning! No land in all the world is like England. In no country would I love better to spend my days.

Erasmus

To One Who is Coming to England

YOU are going to England. You will not fail to be pleased. You will find the people there most agreeable and gracious; only be careful not to presume upon their intimacy. They will condescend to your level, but do not you therefore suppose that you stand upon theirs. The noble lords are gods in their own eyes; for the other classes, be courteous, give your right hand, do not take the wall, but trust no one that you do not know. Above all, speak no evil of England to them. They are proud of their country above all nations in the world, as they have good reason to be.

Erasmus writing to a friend

John Milton on John Milton

A critic having written offensively of Milton as a " monster huge and hideous, void of sight," the poet wrote this reply.

I DO not believe that I was ever once noted for deformity by anyone who ever saw me; but the praise of beauty I am not anxious to obtain. My stature certainly is not tall, but it rather approaches the middle than the diminutive. Yet what if it were diminutive when so many men, illustrious both in peace and war, have been the same? And how can that be called diminutive which is great enough for every virtuous achievement?

Nor, though very thin, was I ever deficient in courage or in strength; and I was wont constantly to exercise myself in the use of the broadsword as long as it comported with my habit and my years. Armed with this weapon, as I usually was, I should have thought myself quite a match for anyone, though much stronger than myself; and I felt perfectly secure against the assault of any open enemy. At this moment I have the same courage, the same strength, though not the same eyes; yet so little do they betray any external appearance of injury that they are as unclouded and bright as the eyes of those who most distinctly see. In this instance alone I am a dissembler against my will.

My face, which is said to indicate a total privation of blood, is of a complexion entirely opposite to the pale and the cadaverous; so that, though I am more than forty years old, there is scarcely anyone to whom I do not appear ten years younger than I am; and the smoothness of my skin is not in the least affected by the wrinkles of age.

Adam and Eve Leave Paradise

IN either hand the hastening angel caught
  Our lingering parents, and to the Eastern gate
Led them direct, and down the cliff as fast
To the subjected plain—then disappeared.
They, looking back, all the eastern side beheld
Of Paradise, so late their happy seat,
Waved over by that flaming brand, the gate
With dreadful faces thronged and fiery arms.
Some natural tears they dropped, but wiped them soon ;
The world was all before them, where to choose
Their place of rest, and Providence their guide.
They, hand in hand, with wandering steps and slow,
Through Eden took their solitary way.

Last words of Paradise Lost

Milton's First Poem

LET us with a gladsome mind
  Praise the Lord, for He is kind :
For His mercies ay endure,
Ever faithful, ever sure.

Let us blaze His name abroad
For of gods He is the God :

He with all-commanding might
Filled the new-made world with light :

He the golden-tresséd sun
Caused all day his course to run :

The hornéd moon to shine by night,
Mid her spangled sisters bright :

All things living He doth feed,
His full hand supplies their need :

Let us, with a gladsome mind,
Praise the Lord, for He is kind :
For His mercies shall endure
Ever faithful, ever sure.

Milton in His Pride

THEY accuse me of blindness, because I have lost my eyes in the
  service of liberty. They tax me with cowardice, and while I
had the use of my eyes and my sword I never feared the boldest
among them. Finally, I am upbraided with deformity, while no one
was more handsome in the age of beauty. I do not even complain
of my want of sight ; in the night with which I am surrounded the
light of the Divine Presence shines with a more brilliant lustre.

Nothing is Here for Tears

COME, come, no time for lamentation now,
Nor much more cause ; Samson hath quit himself
Like Samson, and heroically hath finished
A life heroic ; on his enemies
Fully revenged, hath left them years of mourning,
And lamentation to the sons of Caphtor,
Through all Philistian bounds ; to Israel
Honour hath left, and freedom, let but them
Find courage to lay hold on this occasion ;
To himself and father's house eternal fame ;
And, which is best and happiest yet, all this
With God not parted from him, as was feared,
But favouring and assisting to the end.
Nothing is here for tears, nothing to wail
Or knock the breast, no weakness, no contempt,
Dispraise, or blame, nothing but well and fair,
And what may quiet us in a death so noble.
Milton in Samson Agonistes

The Great Fall

FROM morn
To noon he fell, from noon to dewy eve,
A summer's day ; and with the setting sun
Dropt from the zenith, like a falling star.
Milton in Paradise Lost

Ye Winds That From Four Quarters Blow

HIS praise, ye winds, that from four quarters blow,
Breathe soft or loud ; and wave your tops, ye pines,
With every plant, in sign of worship wave !
Fountains and ye that warble as ye flow,
Melodious murmurs, warbling tune his praise.
Join voices all ye living souls ! Ye birds
That, singing up to Heaven's gate ascend,
Bear on your wings and in your notes his praise ;
Ye that in waters glide, and ye that walk
The earth, and stately tread, or lowly creep,
Witness if I be silent, morn or even,
To hill, or valley, fountain, or fresh shade
Made vocal by my song, and taught his praise.
Hail ! universal Lord ; be bounteous still
To give us only good ; and, if the night
Have gathered aught of evil or concealed.
Disperse it, as now light dispels the dark.
Milton

AFTER THE STORM, BY JOSEF ISRAELS

MISS MURRAY, BY SIR THOMAS LAWRENCE

Lucy Gray

OFT I had heard of Lucy Gray :
    And when I crossed the wild
I chanced to see, at break of day,
    The solitary child.

No mate, no comrade Lucy knew ;
    She dwelt on a wide moor,
The sweetest thing that ever grew
    Beside a human door.

You yet may spy the fawn at play,
    The hare upon the green ;
But the sweet face of Lucy Gray
    Will never more be seen.

Tonight will be a stormy night,
    You to the town must go ;
And take a lantern, child, to light
    Your mother through the snow.

That, Father, will I gladly do :
    'Tis scarcely afternoon,
The minster-clock has just struck two,
    And yonder is the moon !

At this the father raised his hook,
    And snapped a faggot-band ;
He plied his work ; and Lucy took
    The lantern in her hand.

Not blither is the mountain roe ;
    With many a wanton stroke
Her feet disperse the powdery snow,
    That rises up like smoke.

The storm came on before its time :
    She wandered up and down ;
And many a hill did Lucy climb :
    But never reached the town.

    .   .   .   .   .   .

Yet some maintain that to this day
    She is a living child ;
That you may see sweet Lucy Gray
    Upon the lonesome wild.

O'er rough and smooth she trips along,
    And never looks behind ;
And sings a solitary song
    That whistles in the wind.

                              Wordsworth

Faithful Only He

So spake the Seraph Abdiel, faithful found
Among the faithless, faithful only he;
Among innumerable false unmoved,
Unshaken, unseduced, unterrified,
His loyalty he kept, his love, his zeal;
Nor number nor example with him wrought
To swerve from truth, or change his constant mind.

Paradise Lost

Wordsworth's Perfect Lady

She was a Phantom of delight
When first she gleamed upon my sight;
A lovely Apparition, sent
To be a moment's ornament.

. . . . . .

I saw her upon nearer view,
A Spirit, yet a Woman too!
A Creature not too bright or good
For human nature's daily food.

. . . . . .

And now I see with eye serene
The very pulse of the machine;
A Being breathing thoughtful breath,
A Traveller between life and death;
The reason firm, the temperate will,
Endurance, foresight, strength, and skill;
A perfect Woman, nobly planned,
To warn, to comfort, and command;
And yet a Spirit still, and bright
With something of angelic light.

Thou, while thy babes around thee cling,
Shalt show us how divine a thing
A Woman may be made.
Thy thoughts and feelings shall not die,
Nor leave thee, when grey hairs are nigh,
A melancholy slave;
But an old age serene and bright,
And lovely as a Lapland night,
Shall lead thee to thy grave.

Passages from two poems

Woe to that Nation

Woe to the nation whose military power is irresistible.

Wordsworth

It is Not to be Thought Of

IT is not to be thought of that the flood
Of British freedom, which, to the open sea
Of the world's praise, from dark antiquity
Hath flowed, " with pomp of waters, unwithstood,"
Roused though it be full often to a mood
Which spurns the check of salutary bands,
That this most famous stream in bogs and sands
Should perish, and to evil and to good
Be lost for ever. In our halls is hung
Armoury of the invincible knights of old :
We must be free or die who speak the tongue
That Shakespeare spake ; the faith and morals hold
Which Milton held. In everything we are sprung
Of Earth's first blood, have titles manifold.

Wordsworth

William Wordsworth to John Milton

THY soul was like a star, and dwelt apart :
Thou hadst a voice whose sound was like the sea :
Pure as the naked heavens, majestic, free,
So didst thou travel on life's common way,
In cheerful godliness ; and yet thy heart
The lowliest duties on herself did lay.

The Splendour of the Morning

EARTH has not anything to show more fair :
Dull would he be of soul who could pass by
A sight so touching in its majesty . . .
Never did sun more beautifully steep
In his first splendour valley, rock, or hill ;
Ne'er saw I, never felt, a calm so deep !
The river glideth at his own sweet will :
Dear God ! the very houses seem asleep,
And all that mighty heart is lying still.

Wordsworth

The Beauty of the Evening

IT is a beauteous evening, calm and free ;
The holy time is quiet as a nun
Breathless with adoration ; the broad sun
Is sinking down in its tranquillity ;
The gentleness of heaven is on the sea :
Listen ! the mighty being is awake . . .

Wordsworth

The Laurels Pass from Age to Youth

ALREADY am I worn with care and age,
And just abandoning the ungrateful Stage ;
But you, whom every muse and grace adorn,
Whom I foresee to better fortune born,
Be kind to my remains ; and, oh, defend
Against your judgment your departed friend.
Let not the insulting foe my fame pursue,
But guard those laurels which descend to you.

John Dryden to William Congreve

How to Live

LET us endeavour so to live that when we come to die even the
undertaker will be sorry.   *Mark Twain*

Caesar Among the Pirates

IN earlier days Julius Caesar was taken by pirates. What then ?
He threw himself into their ship, established the most extraordinary
intimacies, told them stories, declaimed to them ; if they did not
applaud his speeches, he threatened them with hanging—which he
performed afterwards—and, in a short time, was master of all on
board.   *Emerson*

The Good Man Does Lives After Him

HE who digs a well, constructs a stone fountain, plants a grove of
trees by the roadside, plants an orchard, builds a durable house,
reclaims a swamp, or so much as puts a stone seat by the wayside,
makes the land so far lovely and desirable, makes a fortune which
he cannot carry with him, but which is useful to his country long
afterwards.   *Emerson*

The Cloak from Arthur's Court

IN the old fables we read of a cloak brought from fairyland as a gift
for the fairest and purest in Prince Arthur's Court. It was to be
her prize whom it would fit. Everyone was eager to try it on, but
it would fit nobody : for one it was a world too wide, for the next it
dragged on the ground, and for the third it shrunk to a scarf. They,
of course, said that the devil was in the mantle, but really the truth
was in the mantle, and was exposing the ugliness which each would
fain conceal. All drew back with terror from the garment. The
innocent Genelas alone could wear it.

In like manner, every man is provided, *in his thought,* with a
measure of man which he applies to every passenger. Unhappily,
not one in many thousands comes up to the stature and proportions
of the model.   *Emerson*

Give Us Our Daily Bread

O LORDS ! O rulers of the nation !
O softly clothed ! O richly fed !
O men of wealth and noble station !
Give us our daily bread.

For you we are content to toil,
For you our blood like rain is shed.
Then lords and rulers of the soil,
Give us our daily bread.

Your silken robes, with endless care,
Still weave we ; still unclothed, unfed,
We make the raiment that ye wear.
Give us our daily bread.

In the red forge-light do we stand,
We early leave—late seek our bed,
Tempering the steel for your right hand.
Give us our daily bread.

We sow your fields, ye reap the fruit,
We live in misery and in dread.
Hear but our prayer, and we are mute,
Give us our daily bread.

Throughout old England's pleasant fields,
There is no spot where we may tread,
No house to us sweet shelter yields.
Give us our daily bread.

Fathers are we ; we see our sons,
We see our fair young daughters, dead :
Then hear us, O ye mighty ones !
Give us our daily bread.

Tis vain—with cold, unfeeling eye
Ye gaze on us, unclothed, unfed,
Tis vain—ye will not hear our cry,
Nor give us daily bread.

We turn from you, our lords by birth,
To him who is our Lord above ;
We are all made of the same earth,
Are children of one love.

Then Father of this world of wonders !
Judge of the living and the dead !
Lord of the lightnings and the thunders,
Give us our daily bread.

Wathen Mark Wilks Call,
writing in the Corn Law days

The Glory and the Dream

I WAS often unable to think of external things as having external existence, and I communed with all I saw as something not apart from, but inherent in, my own nature.

Many times while going to school have I grasped at a wall or a tree to recall myself from this abyss of idealism.

Wordsworth on his childhood

A Cry of Woe From the Long Ago

This poem was written with a pen made from rook's feathers picked up in a prison yard in the days of the Chartist agitation

WE plough and sow, we're so very, very low,
  That we delve in the dirty clay,
Till we bless the plain with the golden grain,
  And the vale with the fragrant hay.
Our place we know, we're so very low,
  Tis down at the landlord's feet :
We're not too low the bread to grow,
  But too low the bread to eat.

Down, down we go, we're so very, very low,
  To the hell of the deep-sunk mines,
But we gather the proudest gems that glow
  When the crown of a despot shines.
And whenever he lacks—upon our backs
  Fresh loads he deigns to lay :
We're far too low to vote the tax,
  But not too low to pay.

We're low, we're low, we're very, very low,
  Yet from our fingers glide
The silken flow and the robes that glow
  Round the limbs of the sons of pride.
And what we get and what we give,
  We know, and we know our share :
We're not too low the cloth to weave,
  But too low the cloth to wear !

Ernest Jones

Flower in the Crannied Wall

FLOWER in the crannied wall,
  I pluck you out of the crannies,
I hold you here, root and all, in my hand,
Little flower—but if I could understand
What you are, root and all, and all in all,
I should know what God and man is.

Tennyson

To the Great Name

To all our statesmen, so they be
  True leaders of the land's desire !
To both our Houses, may they see
  Beyond the borough and the shire !
We sailed wherever ship could sail,
  We founded many a mighty State ;
Pray God our greatness may not fail
  Through craven fears of being great.
      Hands all round !
  God the traitor's hope confound !
To this great cause of Freedom drink, my friends,
  And the great name of England, round and round.

A Toast by Tennyson

One Still Strong Man

Ah God, for a man with heart, head, hand,
  Like some of the simple great ones gone
For ever and ever by,
One still strong man in a blatant land,
Whatever they call him, what care I,
Aristocrat, democrat, autocrat—one
Who can rule and dare not lie.

Tennyson

For Ever and For Ever

Flow down, cold rivulet, to the sea,
  Thy tribute wave deliver ;
No more by thee my steps shall be,
  For ever and for ever.

Flow, swiftly flow, by lawn and lea,
  A rivulet, then a river :
Nowhere by thee my steps shall be,
  For ever and for ever.

But here will sigh thine alder tree,
  And here thine aspen shiver ;
And here by thee will hum the bee,
  For ever and for ever.

A thousand suns will stream on thee,
  A thousand moons will quiver ;
But not by thee my steps shall be,
  For ever and for ever.

Tennyson

The Land That Freedom Chose

You ask me, why, though ill at ease,
  Within this region I subsist,
  Whose spirits falter in the mist,
And languish for the purple seas.

It is the land that freemen till,
  That sober-suited Freedom chose,
  The land where, girt with friends or foes,
A man may speak the thing he will.

A land of settled government,
  A land of just and old renown,
  Where Freedom slowly broadens down
From precedent to precedent.

Tennyson on his Native Land

Bound by Gold Chains

More things are wrought by prayer
  Than this world dreams of. Wherefore let thy voice
Rise like a fountain for me night and day.
For what are men better than sheep or goats
That nourish a blind life within the brain
If, knowing God, they lift not hands of prayer
Both for themselves and those who call them friend ?
For so the whole round Earth is every way
Bound by gold chains about the feet of God. *Tennyson*

Till Crowds be Sane and Crowns be Just

A people's voice ! we are a people yet,
  Though all men else their nobler dreams forget,
Confused by brainless mobs and lawless Powers
Thank Him who isled us here, and roughly set
His Briton in blown seas and storming showers,
We have a voice with which to pay the debt
Of boundless love and reverence and regret
To those great men who fought, and kept it ours.
And keep it ours, O God, from brute control ;
O Statesmen, guard us, guard the eye, the soul
Of Europe, keep our noble England whole,
And save the one true seed of freedom sown
Betwixt a people and their ancient throne,
That sober freedom out of which there springs
Our loyal passion for our temperate kings ;
For, saving that, ye help to save mankind
Till public wrong be crumbled into dust,
And drill the raw world for the march of mind
Till crowds at length be sane and crowns be just.

Tennyson's Ode on the Death of Wellington

The Proud Voice of King Arthur

WHEN the Roman left us, and their law
Relaxed its hold upon us, and the ways
Were filled with rapine, here and there a deed
Of prowess done redressed a random wrong.
But I was first of all the kings who drew
The knighthood-errant of this realm and all
The realms together under me, their Head,
In that fair Order of my Table Round,
A glorious company, the flower of men,
To serve as model for the mighty world,
And be the fair beginning of a time.
I made them lay their hands in mine and swear
To reverence the King, as if he were
Their conscience, and their conscience as their King,
To break the heathen and uphold the Christ,
To ride abroad redressing human wrongs,
To speak no slander, no, nor listen to it,
To honour his own word as if his God's.
To lead sweet lives in purest chastity,
To love one maiden only, cleave to her,
And worship her by years of noble deeds,
Until they won her ; for indeed I knew
Of no more subtle master under heaven
Than is the maiden passion for a maid,
Not only to keep down the base in man,
But teach high thought, and amiable words
And courtliness, and the desire of fame,
And love of truth, and all that makes a man. *Tennyson*

A Credo

IT is hard to believe in God, but it is harder not to believe. I believe in God not from what I see in Nature but from what I find in man. *Tennyson*

The Increasing Purpose

YET I doubt not through the ages one increasing purpose runs,
And the thoughts of men are widened with the process of the sums
Tennyson in Locksley Hall

Ah, That it Were Possible

AH, Christ, that it were possible,
For one short hour to see
The souls we loved, that they might tell us
What and where they be ! *Tennyson*

Spare Me the Whispering, Crowded Room

I ASK not that my bed of death
From bands of greedy heirs be free ;
For these besiege the latest breath
Of fortune's favoured sons, not me.

I ask not each kind soul to keep
Tearless, when of my death he hears.
Let those who will, if any, weep !
There are worse plagues on earth than tears.

I ask but that my death may find
The freedom to my life denied ;
Ask but the folly of mankind
Then, then at last, to quit my side.

Spare me the whispering, crowded room,
The friends who come, and gape, and go ;
The ceremonious air of gloom :
All which makes death a hideous show.

Bring none of these ; but let me be,
While all around in silence lies,
Moved to the window near, and see
Once more before my dying eyes,

Bathed in the sacred dews of morn
The wide aerial landscape spread,
The world which was ere I was born,
The world which lasts when I am dead ;

There let me gaze, till I become
In soul, with what I gaze on, wed !
To feel the universe my home ;
To have before my mind (instead

Of the sick room, the mortal strife,
The turmoil for a little breath)
The pure eternal course of life,
Not human combatings with death.

Thus feeling, gazing, might I grow
Composed, refreshed, ennobled, clear ;
Then willing let my spirit go
To work or wait elsewhere or here !
From A Wish, by Matthew Arnold

Better to Fight

IT is better to fight for the good than to rail at
the ill.   *Tennyson*

The Soul of Judas Iscariot

Twas the soul of Judas Iscariot,
    Strange, and sad, and tall,
Stood all alone at dead of night
    Before a lighted hall.

And the wold was white with snow,
    And his footmarks black and damp,
And the ghost of the silvern moon arose,
    Holding her yellow lamp.

And the icicles were on the eaves,
    And the walls were deep with white,
And the shadows of the guests within
    Passed on the window light.

The shadows of the wedding guests
    Did strangely come and go,
And the body of Judas Iscariot
    Lay stretched along the snow ;

The body of Judas Iscariot
    Lay stretched along the snow ;
Twas the soul of Judas Iscariot
    Ran swiftly to and fro.

To and fro, and up and down,
    He ran so swiftly there,
As round and round the frozen Pole
    Glideth the lean white bear.

.   .   .

Twas the Bridegroom sat at the table-head,
    And the lights burnt bright and clear :
Oh, who is that, the Bridegroom said,
    Whose weary feet I hear ?

Twas one looked from the lighted hall,
    And answered soft and slow :
It is a wolf runs up and down
    With a black track in the snow.

The Bridegroom in his robe of white
    Sat at the table-head :
Oh, who is that who moans without ?
    The blessed Bridegroom said.

Twas one looked from the lighted hall,
    And answered fierce and low :
Tis the soul of Judas Iscariot
    Gliding to and fro.

Twas the soul of Judas Iscariot
  Did hush itself and stand,
And saw the Bridegroom at the door,
  With a light in his hand.

The Bridegroom stood in the open door,
  And he was clad in white,
And far within the Lord's Supper
  Was spread so broad and bright.

The Bridegroom shaded his eyes and looked,
  And his face was bright to see :
What dost thou here at the Lord's Supper
  With thy body's sins ? said he.

Twas the soul of Judas Iscariot
  Stood black, and sad, and bare :
I have wandered many nights and days ;
  There is no light elsewhere.

Twas the wedding guests cried out within,
  And their eyes were fierce and bright :
Scourge the soul of Judas Iscariot
  Away into the night !

The Bridegroom stood in the open door,
  And he waved hands still and slow,
And the third time that he waved his hands
  The air was thick with snow.

And of every flake of falling snow,
  Before it touched the ground,
There came a dove, and a thousand doves
  Made sweet sound.

Twas the body of Judas Iscariot
  Floated away full fleet,
And the wings of the doves that bare it off
  Were like its winding-sheet.

Twas the Bridegroom stood at the open door,
  And beckoned, smiling sweet ;
Twas the soul of Judas Iscariot
  Stole in and fell at his feet.

The Holy Supper is spread within,
  And the many candles shine,
And I have waited long for thee
  Before I poured the wine !

The supper wine is poured at last,
  The lights burn bright and fair,
Iscariot washes the Bridegroom's feet,
  And dries them with his hair.
                    Robert Buchanan

No Pleasure is Comparable to This

WHAT is truth ? said jesting Pilate, and would not wait for an answer.

Truth is a naked and open daylight that doth not show the masks and mummeries and triumphs of the world half so stately and daintily as candlelight.

The poet saith excellently well—It is a pleasure to stand upon the shore and to see ships tossed upon the sea ; a pleasure to stand in the window of a castle and to see a battle, and the adventures below ; but no pleasure is comparable to the standing upon the vantage ground of truth and to see the errors and wanderings and mists and tempests in the vale below, so always that this prospect be with pity and not with pride.

Certainly it is heaven upon earth to have a man's mind move in charity, rest in providence, and turn upon the poles of truth.

Francis Bacon

O, It Was Very Fair

It has been said that there is not in English literature a more tender picture of an English scene than this by Mrs Browning, who found the face of the country " as if God's finger touched but did not press " in making England.

SUCH an up and down
Of verdure—nothing too much up or down,
A ripple of land ; such little hills, the sky
Can stoop to tenderly and the wheatfields climb ;
Such nooks of valleys lined with orchises,
Fed full of noises by invisible streams.
I flattered all the beauteous country round,
As poets use, the skies, the clouds, the fields,
The happy violets hiding from the roads
The primroses run down to, carrying gold ;
The tangled hedgerows, where the cows push out
Impatient horns and tolerant churning mouths
Twixt dripping ash-boughs—hedgerows all alive
With birds and gnats and large white butterflies
Which look as if the may-flower had caught life
And palpitated forth upon the wind ;
Hills, vales, woods, netted in a silver mist,
Farms, granges, doubled up among the hills ;
And cattle grazing in the watered vales,
And cottage chimneys smoking from the woods,
And cottage gardens smelling everywhere,
Confused with smell of orchards . . .
And, ankle-deep in English grass, I leaped,
And clapped my hands, and called all very fair.

Elizabeth Browning

The Strange Desire

IT is a strange desire to seek power and to lose liberty, or to seek power over others and to lose power over a man's self.

— Francis Bacon

Cobwebs

LAWS are like cobwebs, which catch the small flies but are broken through by the great ones.

Old Saying preserved by Francis Bacon

The Gentlemen of the Jury

THE *Judge called to the jury :*
Gentlemen of the jury, you see this man about whom so great an uproar hath been made in this town ; you have also heard what these worthy gentlemen have witnessed against him ; also you have heard his reply and confession.

It lieth now in your breasts to hang him or save his life ; but yet I think meet to instruct you in our law. There was an Act made in the days of Pharaoh that, lest those of a contrary religion should multiply and grow too strong for him, their males should be thrown into the river. There was also an Act made in the days of Nebuchadnezzar that whoever would not fall down and worship his golden image should be thrown into a fiery furnace. There was also an Act made in the days of Darius that whoso for some time called upon any god but him should be cast into the lions' den. Now the substance of these laws this rebel has broken.

Then went the jury out, whose names were Mr Blindman, Mr No-Good, Mr Malice, Mr Love-Lust, Mr Live-Loose, Mr Heady, Mr High-Mind, Mr Enmity, Mr Liar, Mr Cruelty, Mr Hate-Light, and Mr Implacable, who every one gave in his private verdict against him among themselves, and afterwards unanimously concluded to bring him in guilty before the judge. And first Mr Blindman, the foreman, said, I see clearly that this man is a heretic. Then said Mr No-Good, Away with such a fellow from the earth. Ay, said Mr Malice, for I hate the very looks of him. Then said Mr Love-Lust, I could never endure him. Nor I, said Mr Live-Loose, for he would always be condemning my way. Hang him, hang him, said Mr Heady. A sorry scrub, said Mr High-Mind. My heart riseth against him, said Mr. Enmity. He is a rogue, said Mr Liar. Hanging is too good for him, said Mr Cruelty. Let us despatch him out of the way, said Mr Hate-Light. Then said Mr Implacable, Might I have all the world given me I could not be reconciled to him: therefore let us forthwith bring him in guilty of death.

And so they did : thus came Faithful to his end.

Pilgrim's Progress

The Spectators

IN the theatre of human life it is only for God and angels to be spectators. *Francis Bacon*

The Four Prisoners

SIR JOHN RAINSFORD besought Queen Eizabeth that four prisoners might have their liberty. The Queen asked who they were and he said, Matthew, Mark, Luke, and John, who had long been imprisoned in the Latin tongue, and now he desired that they might go abroad among the people in English. *Recorded by Francis Bacon*

Madam Bubble

STANDFAST : As I was musing there was one in very pleasant attire, but old, who presented herself to me, and offered me her purse and her bed.

Now the truth is I was both weary and sleepy ; I am also as poor as an owlet, and that perhaps the witch knew. Well, I repulsed her once and again, but she put by my repulses and smiled. Then I began to be angry, but she mattered that nothing at all. Then she made offers again, and said if I would be ruled by her she would make me great and happy, for, said she, " I am the mistress of the world, and men are made happy by me." Then I asked her name and she told me it was Madam Bubble.

Honest : Madam Bubble ! Is she not a tall, comely dame, something of a swarthy complexion ?

Standfast : Right, you hit it ; she is just such a one.

Honest : Doth she not wear a great purse by her side, and is not her hand often in it, fingering her money, as if that was her heart's delight ?

Standfast : It is just so.

Greatheart : This woman is a witch, and it is by virtue of her sorceries that this ground is enchanted. This is she that maintaineth in their splendour all the enemies of pilgrims ; she hath brought off many a man from a pilgrim's life. She is a great gossiper. She is always, both she and her daughters, at one pilgrim's heels or another, now commending and then preferring the excellences of this life. She is a bold and impudent slut : she will talk with any man. She laugheth poor pilgrims to scorn, but highly commends the rich. If there be one cunning to get money in a place she will speak well of him from house to house. She loveth banqueting and feasting mainly well ; she is always at one full table or another.

She has given it out in some places that she is a goddess, and therefore some do worship her. She has her time and open places for cheating ; and she will say, and avow it, that none can show a good comparable to hers. She promiseth to dwell with children's children if they will but love her and make much of her. She will cast out of her purse gold like dust in some places, and to some persons. She loves to be sought after and spoken well of. She is never weary of commending her commodities; and she loves them most that think best of her. She will promise to some crowns and kingdoms if they will but take her advice; yet many hath she brought to the halter, and ten thousand times more to destruction.

Standfast : Oh! what a mercy it is that I did resist her; for whither might she have drawn me?

Greatheart : Whither! nay, none but God knows. But, in general, to be sure she would have drawn thee into destruction. Wherefore, good Mr Standfast, be as your name is, and when you have done all, Stand.

At this discourse, there was among the pilgrims a mixture of joy and trembling, but at length they brake out, and sang:

> What danger is the pilgrim in!
> How many are his foes!
> How many ways there are to sin,
> No living mortal knows.
>
> Some of the ditch shy are, yet can
> Lie tumbling in the mire:
> Some, though they shun the frying-pan,
> Do leap into the fire.

Pilgrim's Progress

The Thought of His Little Blind Child

I FOUND myself a man encompassed with infirmities. The parting with my wife and poor children hath often been to me in this place as the pulling the flesh from my bones, and that not only because I am somewhat too fond of these great mercies, but also because I should have often brought to my mind the many hardships, miseries, and wants that my poor family was like to meet with should I be taken from them, especially my poor blind child, who lay nearer my heart than all beside. Oh! the thought of the hardship my poor blind one might go under would break my heart to pieces.

Poor child, thought I, what sorrow art thou like to have for thy portion in this world! Thou must be beaten; must beg; suffer hunger, cold, nakedness, and a thousand calamities; though I cannot now endure the wind should blow upon thee. But yet (recalling myself) thought I, I must venture you all with God, though it goeth to the quick to leave you. Oh! I saw in this condition I was as a man who was pulling down his house upon the head of his wife and children, yet, thought I, *I must do it, I must do it.* John Bunyan

THE THIRD EARL COWPER WITH COUNTESS COWPER AND
THE GORE FAMILY, BY ZOFFANY

THE ITALIAN COMEDIANS, BY WATTEAU

DUTCH INTERIOR, BY DE HOOCH

THE PEARL NECKLACE, BY VERMEER

Vanity Fair

I SAW in my dream that when they were got out of the wilderness they saw a town before them ; the town is Vanity, and there is a fair kept, called Vanity Fair. It is kept all the year long.

The fair is no new-erected business, but a thing of ancient standing ; I will show you the original of it. Almost five thousand years agone there were pilgrims walking to the Celestial City, as these two honest persons are : and Beelzebub, Apollyon, and Legion, with their companions, perceiving by the path that their way to the city lay through this town of Vanity, contrived here to set up a fair, wherein should be sold all sorts of vanity, and that it should last all the year long. At this fair are all such merchandise sold as houses, lands, trades, places, honours, preferments, titles, countries, kingdoms, pleasures ; and delights of all sorts. And moreover at this fair there are at all times to be seen jugglings, cheats, games, plays, fools, apes, knaves, and rogues, and that of every kind.

Now the way to the Celestial City lies just through the town where this fair is kept, and he that will go to the city, and yet not go through this town, must needs go out of the world.

These pilgrims must needs go through this fair, but behold, even as they entered, all the people in the fair were moved, and the town itself in a hubbub about them, and that for several reasons.

First, the pilgrims were clothed with such raiment as was diverse from the raiment of any that traded in that fair. Secondly, as they wondered at their apparel, so they did likewise at their speech, for few could understand what they said. Thirdly, that which did not a little amuse the merchandisers was that these pilgrims set very light by all their wares ; they cared not so much as to look upon them ; and if they called upon them to buy they would put their fingers in their ears, and cry, Turn away mine eyes from beholding vanity ! and look upwards, signifying that their trade and traffic was in heaven.

One chanced mockingly, beholding the carriages of the men, to say unto them, What will ye buy ? but they, looking gravely upon him, said, We buy the truth. At that there was an occasion taken to despise the men the more, some mocking, some taunting, some calling upon others to smite them.   *Pilgrim's Progress*

Stars of the Night

THEIR noonday never knows
  What names immortal are,
Tis night alone that shows
  How star surpasseth star.
          John Bannister Tabb

Bunyan's Last Ride

WHERE content dwells even a poor cottage is a kingly palace. This happiness Mr Bunyan had all his life long, not so much minding this world as knowing he was here as a pilgrim and stranger and had no tarrying city, but looked for one not made with hands, eternal in the highest heavens. At length, worn out with sufferings, age, and much teaching, the day of his dissolution drew near, and death, that unlocks the prison of the soul to enlarge it for a more glorious mansion, put a stop to his acting his part on the stage of mortality.

Even the last act of his was a labour of love and charity. A young gentleman, a neighbour of Mr Bunyan's, happening into the displeasure of his father, and being much troubled in mind upon that account (for he heard his father purposed to disinherit him, or otherwise deprive him of what he had to leave) pitched upon Mr Bunyan as a fit man to make way for his submission, and prepare his father's mind to receive him. He, willing to do any good office as it could be requested, readily undertook it. Riding to Reading in Berkshire, he there used such pressing arguments and reasons against anger and passion, as also for love, and reconciliation, that the father was mollified, and his heart yearned for his son.

But Mr Bunyan, returning to London and being overtaken with excessive rains, coming to his lodgings extremely wet, fell sick of a violent fever, which he bore with much constancy and patience, and expressed himself as if he desired nothing more than to be with Christ, in that case esteeming death as gain. Finding his vital strength decay, having settled his mind and affairs as well as the shortness of time and the violence of his disease would permit, with a constant and Christian patience, he resigned his soul into the hands of his most merciful Redeemer, following his pilgrim from the City of Destruction to the New Jerusalem.

He died at the house of one Mr Struddock, a grocer, at the Star on Snow Hill, in the parish of St Sepulchre, London, on the 12th of August, 1688, in the sixtieth year of his age, after ten days' sickness; and was buried in the new burying-place near the Artillery Ground, where he sleeps till the morning of the resurrection.

By George Cokayne, a Baptist of Bunyan's day

The Shining Figure of the Temple

I WILL tell you a story that I have read of Martha and Mary. The name of the author I have forgot, but the thing was this.

Martha, said my author, was a very holy woman, much like Lazarus her brother, but Mary was a wanton. After Martha had waited long, tried many ways to bring her sister to good, all ineffectually, at last she comes upon her thus:

Sister (quoth she), I pray thee go with me to the temple today, to hear one preach a sermon.

What kind of preacher is he ? said she.

Martha replied, It is one Jesus of Nazareth ; he is the handsomest man that ever you saw with your eyes.   Oh ! he shines in beauty, and is a most excellent preacher.

Now what does Mary, after a little pause, but goes up into her chamber, and with her pins and her clothes decks up herself as fine as her fingers could make her.   This done, away she goes, not with her sister Martha but as much unobserved as she could, to the sermon, or rather to see the preacher.   So he comes in, and she looks, and the first glimpse pleased her.   Well, Jesus addresseth himself to his sermon, and she looks earnestly on him.

Now at that time, saith my author, Jesus preached about the Lost Sheep, the Lost Groat, and the Prodigal Son.   When he came to show what care the shepherd took for one lost sheep, and how the woman swept to find her piece which was lost, and what joy there was at their finding, Mary began to be taken by the ears, and forgot what she came about, musing what the preacher would make of it. But when he came to the application, and showed that by the lost sheep was meant a great sinner, that by the shepherd's care was meant God's love for great sinners, and that by the joy of the neigh- bours was showed what joy there was among the angels in heaven over one great sinner that repenteth, she began to be taken by the heart.   As he spake these last words she thought he pitched his innocent eyes just upon her, and looked as if he spake what was now said to her, wherefore her heart began to tremble, being shaken with affection and fear.   Then her eyes ran down with tears apace, wherefore she was forced to hide her face with her handkerchief, and so sat sobbing and crying all the rest of the sermon.

Sermon being done, up she gets and away she goes, and withal enquired where this Jesus the preacher dined that day ?   One told her at the house of Simon the Pharisee, so away goes she, first to her chamber, and there strips herself of her wanton attire ; then falls upon her knees to ask God forgiveness for all her wicked life.

This done, in a modest dress she goes to Simon's house, where she finds Jesus sat at dinner.   So she gets behind him, and weeps, and drops her tears upon his feet like rain, and washes them, and wipes them with the hair of her head.   She also kissed his feet with her lips and anointed them with ointment . . . And he said unto her, Thy sins are forgiven.   *John Bunyan*

To the Death

I DO not agree with a word that you say, but I will defend to the death your right to say it.   *Voltaire*

The First Poem of the First Day

THERE had not here as yet,
  Save cavern-shade,
Aught been ;
But this wide abyss
Stood deep and dim,
Strange to its Lord,
Idle and useless ;
On which looked with his eyes
The King firm of mind,
And beheld those places
Void of joys ;
Saw the dark cloud
Lower in eternal night,
Swart under heaven,
Dark and waste,
Until this worldly creation
Through the word existed
Of the Glory-King.

Here first shaped
The Lord Eternal
Chief of all creatures,
Heaven and Earth,
The firmament upreared,
And this spacious land
Established,
By his strong powers,
The Lord Almighty.
The Earth as yet was
Not green with grass ;
Ocean covered
Swart in eternal night,
Far and wide,
The dusky ways.

Then was the glory-bright
Spirit of heaven's Guardian
Borne over the deep
With utmost speed :
The Creator of angels bade,
The Lord of Life,
Light to come forth
Over the spacious deep.
Quickly was fulfilled
The high King's behest ;
For him was holy light

Over the waste,
As the Maker bade.
Then sundered
The Lord triumphs
Over the ocean-flood
Light from darkness,
Shade from brightness,
Then gave names to both
The Lord of Life.
Light was first
Through the Lord's word
Named day ;
Beauteous, bright creation !
Well pleased
The Lord at the beginning
The pro-creative time.
The first day saw
The dark shade
Swart prevailing
Over the wide abyss.

Caedmon's Song of Creation

The First English Song

THE name which throws glory over Whitby is the name of a cowherd from whose lips flowed the first great English song.

Caedmon had learnt nothing of the art of verse, the alliterative jingle so common among his fellows ; wherefore, being sometimes at feasts, when all agreed for glee's sake to sing in turn, he no sooner saw the harp come towards him than he rose from the board and went homewards.

Once when he had done thus, and gone from the feast to the stable where he had that night charge of the cattle, there appeared to him in his sleep One who said, greeting him by name, Sing, Caedmon, some song to Me. I cannot sing, he answered ; for this cause I left the feast and came hither. He who talked with him answered, However that be, you shall sing to Me. What shall I sing ? rejoined Caedmon. The beginning of created things, replied He.

In the morning the cowherd stood before the abbess and told his dream. Abbess and brethren alike concluded that heavenly grace had been conferred on him by the Lord. They translated for Caedmon a passage in Holy Writ, bidding him, if he could, put the same into verse. The next morning he gave it them composed in excellent verse, whereon the abbess, understanding the divine grace in the man, bade him quit the secular life and take on him the monastic life. Piece by piece the sacred story was thus thrown into Caedmon's poem. *John Richard Green*

Songs of 1000 Years

It may be said of Caedmon that his gentle figure sleeps in the cradle of our English literature. He sang the Song of Creation in the seventh century. Here is a free rendering of the imagery in his beautiful way of telling the story.

As yet was nought save shadows of darkness; the spacious Earth lay hidden, deep and dim, alien to God, unpeopled and unused.

Thereon the Steadfast King looked down and beheld it, a place empty of joy. He saw dim chaos hanging in eternal night, obscure beneath the heavens. Here first with mighty power the Everlasting Lord, the Helm of all created things, Almighty King, made Earth and Heaven, raised up the sky, and founded the spacious land. The Earth was not yet green with grass; the dark waves of the sea flowed over it; midnight darkness was upon it, far and wide.

In radiant glory God's holy spirit moved upon the waters with wondrous might. The Lord of angels, Giver of Life, bade light shine forth.

One thousand years after came another English poet, who read the story of Caedmon and wrote Creation's Song again. He was John Milton, and his majestic words have crowned that Temple of Literature of which Caedmon laid the first stone.

HEAVEN opened wide
Her ever-during Gates, Harmonious sound
On golden hinges moving, to let forth
The King of Glorie in his powerful Word
And Spirit coming to create new worlds.
Silence, ye troubled waves, and thou Deep, peace,
Said then the Omnific Word : Your discord end,
Nor staid, but on the Wings of Cherubim
Uplifted, in paternal glorie rode
Far into Chaos and the world unborn ;
For Chaos heard his voice : him all his train
Followed in bright procession to behold
Creation, and the wonders of his might.
Then staid the fervid wheels, and in his hand
He took the golden compasses, prepared
In God's eternal store, to circumscribe
This Universe, and all created things.
One foot he centred, and the other turned
Round through the vast profundity obscure,
And said : *Thus far extend, thus far thy bounds.*
This be thy just circumference, O World.
Thus God the Heaven created, thus the Earth,
Matter unformed and void.   Darkness profound
Covered the Abyss ; but on the watery calm
His brooding wings the Spirit of God outspread,
And Earth self-balanced on her centre hung.
Let there be Light, said God, and forthwith Light
Sprang from the Deep, and from her Native East
To journey through the airy gloom began
Sphered in a radiant Cloud.

The Faery Voyager to the Dim Unknown

The bitter tragedy of Hartley Coleridge lay hidden in the future when Wordsworth wrote these lines of his little friend aged six.

O THOU whose fancies from afar are brought,
   Who of thy words dost make a mock apparel,
And fittest to unutterable thought
The breeze-like motion and the self-born carol ;
Thou faery voyager that dost float
In such clear water that thy boat
May rather seem
To brood on air than on an earthly stream,
Suspended in a stream as clear as sky,
Where earth and heaven do make one imagery ;
O blessed vision, happy child,
Thou art so exquisitely wild,
I think of thee with many fears
For what may be thy lot in future years.

I thought of times when Pain might be thy guest,
Lord of thy house and hospitality ;
And Grief, uneasy lover, never rest
But when she sate within the touch of thee.
O, too industrious folly !
O, vain and causeless melancholy !
Nature will either end thee quite,
Or, lengthening out thy season of delight,
Preserve for thee, by individual right,
A young lamb's heart among the full-grown flocks.
What hast thou to do with sorrow,
Or the injuries of tomorrow ?
Thou art a dewdrop which the morn brings forth,
Ill fitted to sustain unkindly shocks,
Or to be trailed along the soiling earth ;
A gem that glitters while it lives,
And no forewarning gives,
But at the touch of wrong, without a strife,
Slips in a moment out of life.

It is Better

IT is better to suffer wrong than to do it.
                              Dr Johnson

The Fisherman's Prayer

LORD, grant this day I catch a fish
   So large that even I
In telling of it afterwards
Shall have no need to lie.
                              Author unknown

Oliver Goldsmith's Pictures of the Village
The Schoolmaster

BESIDE yon straggling fence that skirts the way,
With blossomed furze unprofitably gay,
There, in his noisy mansion, skilled to rule,
The village master taught his little school.
A man severe he was, and stern to view ;
I knew him well, and every truant knew.
Well had the boding tremblers learned to trace
The day's disasters in his morning face ;
Full well they laughed, with counterfeited glee
At all his jokes, for many a joke had he ;
Full well the busy whisper, circling round,
Conveyed the dismal tidings when he frowned,
Yet he was kind, or if severe in aught,
The love he bore to learning was in fault.
The village all declared how much he knew ;
Twas certain he could write, and cypher too.
In arguing, too, the parson owned his skill,
For e'en though vanquished he could argue still ;
While words of learned length and thundering sound
Amazed the gazing rustics ranged around,
And still they gazed, and still the wonder grew,
That one small head could carry all he knew.

The Inn

NEAR yonder thorn, that lifts its head on high,
Where once the signpost caught the passing eye,
Low lies that house where nut-brown draughts inspired,
Where greybeard mirth and smiling toil retired ;
Where village statesmen talked with looks profound,
And news much older than their ale went round.
Imagination fondly stoops to trace
The parlour splendours of that festive place ;
The whitewashed wall, the nicely-sanded floor,
The varnished clock that clicked behind the door ;
The chest, contrived a double debt to pay,
A bed by night, a chest of drawers by day ;
The hearth, except when winter chilled the day,
With aspen boughs, and flowers, and fennel gay ;
While broken teacups, wisely kept for show,
Ranged o'er the chimney, glistened in a row.
Vain transitory splendours ! Could not all
Reprieve the tottering mansion from its fall ?
Obscure it sinks, nor shall it more impart
An hour's importance to the poor man's heart.

From The Deserted Village

Oliver Goldsmith's Portrait Gallery
Here Lies Edmund Burke

HERE lies our good Edmund, whose genius was such,
We scarcely can praise it or blame it too much ;
Who, born for the Universe, narrowed his mind,
And to party gave up what was meant for mankind.
Though fraught with all learning, yet straining his throat
To persuade Tommy Townshend to lend him a vote ;
Who, too deep for his hearers, still went on refining,
And thought of convincing, while they thought of dining ;
Though equal to all things, for all things unfit,
Too nice for a statesman, too proud for a wit ;
For a patriot too cool ; for a drudge disobedient ;
And too fond of the right to pursue the expedient.

Here Lies David Garrick

Here lies David Garrick, describe me who can,
An abridgement of all that was pleasant in man ;
As an actor, confessed without rival to shine ;
As a wit, if not first, in the very first line :
Yet with talents like these, and an excellent heart,
The man had his failings, a dupe to his art.
Like an ill-judging beauty, his colours he spread,
And beplastered with rouge his own natural red.
On the stage he was natural, simple, affecting ;
Twas only that when he was off he was acting.

Here Lies Sir Joshua Reynolds

Here Reynolds is laid, and, to tell you my mind,
He has not left a better or wiser behind :
His pencil was striking, resistless, and grand ;
His manners were gentle, complying, and bland,
Still born to improve us in every part,
His pencil our faces, his manners our heart.
To coxcombs averse, yet most civilly steering,
When they judged without skill he was still hard of hearing :
When they talked of their Raphaels, Correggios, and stuff,
He shifted his trumpet and only took snuff.

Charles Lamb is Free

*Perhaps the happiest day in the sad life of Charles Lamb was the day on which
he was released from the drudgery of a clerk, March 29, 1825.   After thirty-three
years he was free, and he wrote this on his freedom.*

I HAD grown to my desk as it were ; and the wood had entered into
my soul.   Now I no longer hunt for pleasure ; I let it come to me.
I have time for everything ; I can interrupt a man of much occupation
when he is busiest.   I can insult over him with an invitation to take

a day's pleasure with me at Windsor this fine May morning.   I walk about, not to or from.

In the delight of his new-found freedom, Lamb wrote these letters.

This to Wordsworth :

I came home for ever on Tuesday in last week.   It was like passing from life into eternity.   Every year to be as long as three ; that is, to have three times as much real time in it—time that is my own. Mary wakes every morning with an obscure feeling that some good has happened to us.

This to Wordsworth's wife's sister :

For some days I was staggered ;   could not comprehend the magnitude of my deliverance ;   was confused, giddy ;   knew not whether I was on my head or my heels ;   but those giddy feelings have now gone away, and my weather-glass stands at a degree or two above content.   I go about quiet, and have none of that restless hunting after recreation which made holidays formerly uneasy joys. All being holydays I feel as if I had none, as they do in heaven, where tis all red-letter days.

This to Bernard Barton the poet :

I am free, B.B.—free as air.

> The little bird that wings the sky
> Knows no such Liberty !

I went and sat among 'em all at my old thirty-three years' desk yester morning, and deuce take me if I had not yearnings at leaving all my old pen-and-ink fellows, merry, sociable lads, at leaving them in the lurch, fag, fag, fag.   The comparison of my own superior felicity gave me anything but pleasure.

A Cloud Passes Over Bridget

In this essay Lamb is looking at a piece of old blue china, with its young Mandarin handing tea to a little lady, when a cloud passes over his cousin Bridget's face and she begins regretting these luxuries and remembering the old days of their poverty.

I wish the good old times would come again (she said) when we were not quite so rich.

I do not mean that I want to be poor ; but there was a middle state in which, I am sure, we were a great deal happier.   A purchase is but a purchase now that you have money enough and to spare. Formerly it used to be a triumph.   When we coveted a cheap luxury (and, O ! how much ado I had to get you to consent in those times) we were used to have a debate two or three days before, and to weigh the *for* and *against,* and think what we might spare it out of, and what saving we could hit upon, that should be an equivalent. A thing was worth buying then, when we felt the money that we paid for it.

Do you remember the brown suit, which you made to hang upon you till all your friends cried shame upon you, it grew so threadbare —and all because of that folio Beaumont and Fletcher, which you dragged home late at night from Barker's in Covent Garden ? Do you remember how we eyed it for weeks before we could make up our minds to the purchase, and had not come to a determination till it was near ten o'clock of the Saturday night, when you set off from Islington, fearing you should be too late—and when the old book-seller with some grumbling opened his shop, and by the twinkling taper (for he was setting bedwards) lighted out the relic from his dusty treasures—and when you lugged it home, wishing it were twice as cumbersome—and when you presented it to me—and when we were exploring the perfectness of it (*collating*, you called it)—and while I was repairing some of the loose leaves with paste, which your impatience would not suffer to be left till daybreak—was there no pleasure in being a poor man ?

Or can those neat black clothes which you wear now, and are so careful to keep brushed, since we have become rich and finical, give you half the honest vanity with which you flaunted it about in that overworn suit for four or five weeks longer than you should have done, to pacify your conscience for the mighty sum of fifteen (or sixteen shillings, was it ?) which you had lavished on the old folio ? Now you can afford to buy any book that pleases you, but I do not see that you ever bring me home any nice old purchases now.

Then do you remember our pleasant walks at Enfield, and Potter's Bar, and Waltham, when we had a holyday—holydays and all other fun are gone now we are rich—and the little handbasket in which I used to deposit our day's fare of savoury cold lamb and salad—and how you would pry about at noontide for some decent house where we might go in and produce our store . . .

Now, when we go out a day's pleasuring, which is seldom, more-over, we *ride* part of the way, and go into a fine inn, and order the best of dinners, never debating the expense—which, after all, never has half the relish of those chance country snaps, when we were at the mercy of uncertain usage and a precarious welcome.

You are too proud to see a play anywhere now but in the pit. Do you remember where it was we used to sit, when we squeezed out our shillings apiece to sit three or four times in a season in the one-shilling gallery—where you felt all the time that you ought not to have brought me—and more strongly I felt obligation to you for having brought me—and the pleasure was the better for a little shame, and when the curtain drew up, what cared we for our place in the house, or what mattered it where we were sitting, when our thoughts were with Rosalind in Arden, or Viola at the Court of Illyria ?

Now we can only pay our money and walk in. You cannot see, you say, in the galleries now. I am sure we saw, and heard, too, well enough then—but sight and all, I think, is gone with our poverty.

Trailing Clouds of Glory Do We Come

Our birth is but a sleep and a forgetting :
    The Soul that rises with us, our life's Star,
Hath had elsewhere its setting,
    And cometh from afar :
Not in entire forgetfulness,
And not in utter nakedness,
But trailing clouds of glory do we come
    From God, who is our home ;
Heaven lies about us in our infancy !
Shades of the prison-house begin to close
    Upon the growing Boy,
But he beholds the light, and whence it flows,
    He sees it in his joy ;
The Youth, who daily farther from the east
    Must travel, still is Nature's priest,
    And by the vision splendid
    Is on his way attended ;
At length the Man perceives it die away,
And fade into the light of common day.

    O joy ! that in our embers
    Is something that doth live,
    That nature yet remembers
    What was so fugitive !
The thought of our past years in me doth breed
Perpetual benediction ; not indeed
For that which is most worthy to be blest :
Delight and liberty, the simple creed
Of childhood, whether busy or at rest,
With new-fledged hope still fluttering in his breast
    Not for these I raise
    The song of thanks and praise ;
    But for those obstinate questionings
    Of sense and outward things,
    Fallings from us, vanishings ;
    Blank misgivings of a Creature
Moving about in worlds not realised,
High instincts before which our mortal Nature
Did tremble like a guilty thing surprised :
    But for those first affections,
    Those shadowy recollections,
  Which, be they what they may,
Are yet the fountain-light of all our day,
Are yet a master-light of all our seeing ;
  Uphold us, cherish, and have power to make
Our noisy years seem moments in the being
Of the eternal Silence ; truths that wake,
    To perish never ;

Which neither listlessness, nor mad endeavour,
  Nor Man nor Boy,
Nor all that is at enmity with joy,
Can utterly abolish or destroy !
    Hence in a season of calm weather,
      Though inland far we be,
Our souls have sight of that immortal sea
    Which brought us hither,
      Can in a moment travel thither,
And see the children sport upon the shore,
And hear the mighty waters rolling evermore.

Then sing, ye Birds, sing, sing a joyous song !
  And let the young Lambs bound
  As to the tabor's sound !

And O, ye Fountains, Meadows, Hills, and Groves,
Forebode not any severing of our loves !
Yet in my heart of hearts I feel your might ;
I only have relinquished one delight
To live beneath your more habitual sway.
I love the Brooks which down their channels fret,
Even more than when I tripped lightly as they ;
The innocent brightness of a new-born Day
      Is lovely yet ;
The Clouds that gather round the setting sun
Do take a sober colouring from an eye
That hath kept watch o'er man's mortality,
Another race hath been, and other palms are won.
Thanks to the human heart by which we live,
Thanks to its tenderness, its joys, and fears,
To me the meanest flower that blows can give
Thoughts that do often lie too deep for tears.
            From Wordsworth's Ode to Immortality

The Most Magnificent Faces Since The Golden Age

LET those who are disposed to follow the present evil fashion of
disparaging the great Victorians make a collection of their
heads in photographs or engravings and compare them with those
of their own little favourites.   Let them set up in a row good portraits
of Tennyson, Charles Darwin, Gladstone, Manning, Newman,
Martineau, Lord Lawrence, Burne-Jones, and, if they like, a dozen
lesser luminaries, and ask themselves candidly whether men of this
stature are any longer among us.

I will not speculate on the causes which, from time to time,
throw up a large number of great men in a single generation.   I will
only ask you to agree with me that since the Golden Age of Greece
no age can boast so many magnificent types of the human countenance as the reign of Queen Victoria.   *W. R. Inge*

Life is Sweet, Brother

LIFE is sweet, brother. *Do you think so ?*
Think so ! There's night and day, brother, both sweet things ;
sun, moon, and stars, brother, all sweet things ; there's likewise the
wind on the heath. Life is very sweet, brother ; who would wish
to die ? *The gipsies in George Borrow's Lavengro*

The Good Of It

EXPELLED on account of his tyranny, Dionysius the Second of
Syracuse, who had been the host and pupil of Plato, was asked
by a cynic during his exile, " Of what service is the philosophy of
Plato to you now ? " to which he answered :

*It assists me to behold the vicissitudes of fortune without astonish-
ment, and to suffer her severities without complaint.*

The Bad Old Days

I KNOW it is an old folly to make peevish complaints of the times,
and charge the common failures of human nature on a particular
age. One may nevertheless venture to affirm that the present hath
brought forth new and portentous villainies, not to be paralleled
in our own or any other history.

We have been long preparing for some great catastrophe. Vice
and villainy have by degrees grown reputable among us ; our
infidels have passed for fine gentlemen, and our venal traitors for
men of sense who knew the world. We have made a jest of public
spirit, and cancelled all respect for whatever our laws and religion
repute sacred. The old English modesty is quite worn off, and
instead of blushing for our crimes we are ashamed only of piety
and virtue. Our symptoms are so bad that, notwithstanding all the
care and vigilance of the legislature, it is to be feared the final period
of our State approaches.

God grant the time be not near when men shall say :

*This island was once inhabited by a religious, brave, sincere people,
of plain, uncorrupt manners, respecting inbred worth rather than titles
and appearances, assertors of liberty, lovers of their country, jealous of
their own rights, and unwilling to infringe the rights of others ; im-
provers of learning and useful arts, enemies to luxury, tender of other
men's lives and prodigal of their own ; inferior in nothing to the old
Greeks or Romans.*

*Such were our ancestors during their rise and greatness ; but they
degenerated, grew servile flatterers of men in power, became venal,
corrupt, injurious, which drew upon them the hatred of God and man,
and occasioned their final ruin.* *Bishop Berkeley writing in 1721*

One April Day

Wordsworth and his sister Dorothy, walking one April day in the lovely country round their Lakeland home, came upon a host of daffodils. This is what brother and sister felt about it, and put into words when they got home.

WHEN we were in the woods above Gowbarrow Park we saw a few daffodils close by the water-side. We fancied that the sea had floated the seeds ashore, and that the little colony had so sprung up. But as we went along there were more and yet more; and at last, under the boughs of the trees, we saw there was a long belt of them along the shore.

I never saw daffodils so beautiful. They grew among the mossy stones about them. Some rested their heads on the stones, as on a pillow, for weariness; the rest tossed and danced, and seemed as if they verily laughed with the wind that blew over the lake; they looked so gay and glancing, ever changing.   *Dorothy Wordsworth*

I WANDERED lonely as a cloud
   That floats on high o'er vales and hills,
When all at once I saw a crowd,
   A host of golden daffodils,
Beside the lake, beneath the trees,
Fluttering and dancing in the breeze.

Continuous as the stars that shine
   And twinkle on the Milky Way,
They stretched in never-ending line
   Along the margin of a bay:
Ten thousand saw I at a glance,
Tossing their heads in sprightly dance.

The waves beside them danced; but they
   Out-did the sparkling waves in glee:
A poet could not but be gay
   In such a jocund company;
I gazed and gazed, but little thought
What wealth the show to me had brought:

For oft when on my couch I lie,
   In vacant or in pensive mood,
They flash upon that inward eye
   Which is the bliss of solitude;
And then my heart with pleasure fills,
And dances with the daffodils.
                William Wordsworth

To All You Ladies

To all you ladies now at land
    We men at sea indite ;
But first would have you understand
    How hard it is to write :
The Muses now, and Neptune too,
We must implore to write to you.

For though the Muses should prove kind,
    And fill our empty brain,
Yet if rough Neptune rouse the wind
    To wave the azure main,
Our paper, pen, and ink, and we,
Roll up and down our ships at sea.

Then if we write not by each post,
    Think not we are unkind ;
Nor yet conclude our ships are lost
    By Dutchmen or by wind :
Our tears we'll send a speedier way,
The tide shall bring them twice a day.

The King with wonder and surprise
    Will swear the seas grow bold,
Because the tides will higher rise
    Then e'er they did of old :
But let him know it is our tears
Bring floods of grief to Whitehall stairs.

Let wind and weather do its worst,
    Be you to us but kind ;
Let Dutchmen vapour, Spaniards curse,
    No sorrow we shall find :
Tis then no matter how things go,
Or who's our friend, or who's our foe.

In justice you cannot refuse
    To think of our distress,
When we for hopes of honour lose
    Our certain happiness :
All those designs are but to prove
Ourselves more worthy of your love.

And now we've told you all our loves,
    And likewise all our fears,
In hopes this declaration moves
    Some pity for our tears :
Let's hear of no inconstancy :
We have too much of that at sea.

                    Charles Sackville, Earl of Dorset,
                    in the Seventeenth Century

LADY HAMILTON AS DIANA, BY ROMNEY

JOAN OF ARC, BY ROSSETTI

Robert Burns Gives Thanks

*T*HIS *is how Robert Burns thanked a gentleman who had sent him a newspaper and promised to continue it :*

Kind Sir, I've read your paper through,
And, faith, to me, twas really new !
How guess'd ye, Sir, what maist I wanted ?
This mony a day I've grained and gaunted,
To ken what French mischief was brewin' ;
Or what the drumlie Dutch were doin' ;

Or how our merry lads at hame,
In Britain's court, kept up the game :
How royal George, the Lord leuk o'er him !
Was managing St Stephen's quorum ;

A' this and mair I never heard of ;
And, but for you, I might despair'd of.
So gratefu' back your news I send you,
And pray a' guid things may attend you !

As the paper did not come regularly he sent this protest :

Dear Peter, dear Peter,
We poor sons of metre
Are often negleckit, ye ken ;
For instance, your sheet, man,
(Though glad I'm to see't, man,)
I get it no ae day in ten.

Written in a Country Churchyard

*C*AN storied urn or animated bust
Back to its mansion call the fleeting breath ?
Can Honour's voice provoke the silent dust,
Or Flattery soothe the dull, cold ear of Death ?

Perhaps in this neglected spot is laid
Some heart once pregnant with celestial fire ;
Hands that the rod of empire might have swayed,
Or waked to ecstasy the living lyre.

But Knowledge to their eyes her ample page,
Rich with the spoils of time, did ne'er unroll ;
Chill Penury repressed their noble rage,
And froze the genial current of the soul.

Full many a gem of purest ray serene
The dark, unfathomed caves of ocean bear :
Full many a flower is born to blush unseen,
And waste its sweetness on the desert air.

Some village Hampden, that with dauntless breast
The little tyrant of his fields withstood,
Some mute, inglorious Milton here may rest,
Some Cromwell, guiltless of his country's blood.

F.T.—12

Th' applause of listening senates to command,
 The threats of pain and ruin to despise,
To scatter plenty o'er a smiling land,
 And read their history in a nation's eyes,

Their lot forbade : nor circumscribed alone
 Their growing virtues, but their crimes confined ;
Forbade to wade through slaughter to a throne,
 And shut the gates of mercy on mankind :

The struggling pangs of conscious truth to hide,
 To quench the blushes of ingenuous shame,
Or heap the shrine of Luxury and Pride
 With incense kindled at the Muse's flame.

Far from the madding crowd's ignoble strife
 Their sober wishes never learned to stray ;
Along the cool, sequestered vale of life
 They kept the noiseless tenour of their way.

> *From Gray's Elegy, written*
> *in Stoke Poges Churchyard*

Pride of Nottingham

You didn't know of Bendigo !   Well, that knocks me out !
 Who's your board school teacher ?   What's he been about ?
Chock-a-block with fairy tales, full of useless cram,
And never heard o' Bendigo, the pride of Nottingham !

Bendy he turned Methodist—he said he felt a call,
He stumped the country preachin' and you bet he filled the hall,
If you seed him in the pulpit, a bleatin' like a lamb,
You'd never know bold Bendigo, the pride of Nottingham !

His hat was like a funeral, he'd got a waiter's coat,
With a hallelujah collar and a choker round his throat ;
His pals would laugh and say in chaff that Bendigo was right
In takin' on the devil, since he'd no one else to fight.

But he was very earnest, improvin' day by day,
A-workin' and a-preachin' just as his duty lay ;
But the devil he was waitin', and in the final bout
He hit him hard below his guard and knocked poor Bendy out.

Now I'll tell you how it happened.   He was preachin' down at Brum,
He was billed just like a circus—you should see the people come,
The chapel it was crowded, and in the foremost row
There was half a dozen bruisers who'd a grudge at Bendigo.

There was Tommy Platt of Bradford, Solly Jones of Perry Bar,
Long Connor from the Bull Ring, the same wot drew with Carr,
Jack Ball the fightin' gunsmith, Joe Murphy from the News,
And Iky Moss the bettin' boss, the Champion of the Jews.

A very pretty handful a-sittin' in a string,
Full of beer and impudence, ripe for anything,
Sittin' in a string there, right under Bendy's nose,
If his message was for sinners, he would make a start on those.

Soon he heard them chaffin' : " Hi, Bendy !   Here's a go ! "
" How much are you coppin' by this Jump-to-Glory show ? "
" Stow it, Bendy !   Left the Ring !   Mighty spry of you !
Didn't everybody know the Ring was leavin' you ? "

Bendy fairly sweated as he stood above and prayed,
" Look down, O Lord, and grip me with a strangle-hold ! " he said.
" Fix me with a strangle-hold !   Put a stop on me !
I'm slippin', Lord, I'm slippin' and I'm clingin' hard to Thee ! "

But the roughs they kept on chaffin' and the uproar it was such
That the preacher in the pulpit might be talkin' double Dutch,
Till a working man he shouted out, a-jumpin' to his feet,
" Give us a lead, your reverence, and heave 'em in the street."

Then Bendy said, " Good Lord, since first I left my sinful ways,
Thou knowest that to Thee alone I've given up my days,
But now, dear Lord " (and here he laid his Bible on the shelf)
" I'll take with your permission just five minutes for myself."

He vaulted from the pulpit like a tiger from a den,
They say it was a lovely sight to see him floor his men ;
Right and left and left and right, straight and true and hard,
Till the Ebenezer Chapel looked more like a knacker's yard.

Platt was standin' on his back, and lookin' at his toes,
Solly Jones of Perry Bar was feelin' for his nose,
Connor of the Bull Ring had all that he could do
Rakin' for his ivories that lay about the pew.

Jack Ball the fightin' gunsmith was in a peaceful sleep,
Joe Murphy lay across him, all tied up in a heap,
Five of them was twisted in a tangle on the floor,
And Iky Moss, the bettin' boss, had sprinted for the door.

Five repentant fightin' men, sitting in a row,
Listenin' to words of grace from Mister Bendigo,
Listenin' to his reverence, all as good as gold,
Pretty little baa-lambs, gathered to the fold.

So that's the way that Bendy ran his mission in the slum,
And preached the Holy Gospel to the fightin' men of Brum,
" The Lord (said he) has given me His message from on high,
And if you interrupt Him I will know the reason why."

But to think of all your schoolin', clean wasted, thrown away,
Darned if I can make out what you're learnin' all the day,
Grubbin' up old fairy tales, fillin' up with cram,
And didn't know of Bendigo, the pride of Nottingham !

From Bendy's Sermon, by Arthur Conan Doyle

Picture of a Happy Man

We all know the first of these Pictures of a Happy Life, written by Sir Henry Wotton in 1614, but how many know the second, written two years before by John Davies?

How happy is he born and taught
    That serveth not another's will ;
Whose armour is his honest thought,
    And simple truth his utmost skill !

Whose passions not his masters are ;
    Whose soul is still prepared for death,
Untied unto the world by care
    Of public fame or private breath ;

Who envies none that chance doth raise,
    Nor vice ; who never understood
How deepest wounds are given by praise ;
    Nor rules of state but rules of good.

Who hath his life from rumours freed ;
    Whose conscience is his strong retreat ;
Whose state can neither flatterers feed,
    Nor ruin make oppressors great.

Who God doth late and early pray
    More of His grace than gifts to lend ;
And entertains the harmless day
    With a religious book or friend.

This man is freed from servile bands
    Of hope to rise or fear to fall :
Lord of himself, though not of lands,
    And, having nothing, yet hath all.

*It would appear certain that in writing the
above Sir Henry Wotton had just read this :*

How blest is he (though ever crossed)
    That can all crosses blessings make ;
That finds himself ere he be lost ;
    And lose that found for virtue's sake.

Yea, blest is he in life and death,
    That fears not death, nor loves this life ;
That sets his will his wit beneath ;
    And hath continual peace in strife.

That lives too low for envy's looks ;
    And yet too high for loathed contempt ;
Who makes his friends good men and books,
    And nought without them doth attempt.

That fears no frowns, nor cares for fawns
    Of Fortune's favourites or foes,
That neither checks with kings nor pawns ;
    And yet still wins what checkers lose.

That never looks but grace to find ;
    Nor seeks for knowledge to be known :
That makes a kingdom of his mind,
    Wherein, with God, he reigns alone.

This man is great with little state,
    Lord of the World epitomised :
Who with staid front out-faceth Fate ;
    And, being empty, is sufficed.

Green Meadows and Shining Streams

This is a picture of this famous island eight centuries ago,
written by Geoffrey of Monmouth about the year 1150.

BRITAIN, best of islands, lieth in the Western Ocean betwixt Gaul and Ireland, and containeth 800 miles in length and 200 in breadth.

Whatsoever is fitting for the use of mortal men the island doth afford in unfailing plenty, for she aboundeth in metals of every kind ; fields hath she, stretching far and wide, and hillsides meet for tillage of the best, whereon, by reason of the fruitfulness of the soil, the divers crops in their season do yield their harvests.

Forests also hath she, filled with every manner of wild deer, in the glades whereof groweth grass that the cattle may find therein meet change of pasture, and flowers of many colours that do proffer their honey unto the bees that flit ever busily about them. Meadows hath she, set in pleasant places, green at the foot of misty mountains, wherein be sparkling wellsprings clear and bright, flowing forth with a gentle whispering ripple in shining streams that sing sweet lullaby unto them that lie upon their banks.

Watered is she, moreover, by lakes and rivers wherein is much fish, and, besides the narrow sea of the southern coast whereby men make voyage unto Gaul, by three noble rivers, Thames, Severn, and Humber, the which she stretcheth forth as it were three arms, whereby she taketh in the traffic from oversea brought hither from every land in her fleets.

By twice ten cities, moreover, and twice four was she graced in days of old, whereof some with shattered walls in desolate places be now fallen into decay, while some, still whole, do contain churches of the saints, with towers builded wondrous fair on high, wherein companies of religious, both men and women, do their service unto God after the traditions of the Christain faith.

Let Me Go to Paradise With the Asses

These quaintly moving lines are by a quaintly original man—Francis Jammes, a poet of France, living at the foot of the Pyrenees, loving animals and insects, and trees and flowers, and all things of the open air. And especially he loves himself and his own life, for "he is always telling you he is Francis Jammes," a critic says.

O GOD, when You send for me, let it be
  Upon some festal day of dusty roads.
I wish, as I did ever here below,
By any road that pleases me, to go
To Paradise, where stars shine all day long.
Taking my stick out on the great highway,
To my dear friends the asses I shall say :

I am Francis Jammes going to Paradise,
For there is no hell where the Lord God dwells.
Come with me, my sweet friends of azure skies,
You poor, dear beasts who whisk off with your ears
Mosquitoes, peevish blows, and buzzing bees.

Let me appear before You with these beasts,
Whom I so love because they bow their head
Sweetly, and halting join their little feet
So gently that it makes you pity them.
Let me come followed by their million ears,
By those that carried panniers on their flanks,
And those that dragged the car of acrobats,
Those that had battered cans upon their backs,
She-asses, limping, full as leather bottles,
And those, too, that they breech because of blue
And oozing wounds round which the stubborn flies
Gather in swarms.   God, let me come to You
With all these asses into Paradise.

Let angels lead us where Your rivers soothe
Their tufted banks, and cherries tremble, smooth
As in the laughing flesh of tender maids.
And let me, where Your perfect peace pervades,
Be like Your asses, bending down above
The heavenly waters through eternity,
To mirror their sweet, humble poverty
In the clear waters of eternal love.

Alexander Writes to Aristotle

Aristotle having published some books on abstruse scientific subjects, Alexander sent him this note.

YOU did wrong in publishing the acroamatic parts of science. In what shall we differ from others if the sublimer knowledge which we gained from you be made common to all the world ? For my part I had rather excel the bulk of mankind in the superior parts of learning than in the extent of power and dominion.   Farewell.

The Traveller and the River

Traveller

WHY dost thou wildly rush and roar,
  Mad River, O Mad River ?
Wilt thou not pause and cease to pour
Thy hurrying, headlong waters o'er
  This rocky shelf forever ?

What secret trouble stirs thy breast ?
  Why all this fret and flurry ?
Dost thou not know that what is best
In this too restless world is rest
  From overwork and worry ?

The River

What would'st thou in these mountains seek,
  O stranger from the city ?
Is it perhaps some foolish freak
Of thine, to put the words I speak
  Into a plaintive ditty ?

Traveller

Yes ; I would learn of thee thy song,
  With all its flowing numbers,
And, in a voice as fresh and strong
As thine is, sing it all day long,
  And hear it in my slumbers.

The River

A brooklet nameless and unknown
  Was I at first, resembling
A little child, that all alone
Comes venturing down the stairs of stone
  Irresolute and trembling.

Later, by wayward fancies led,
  For the wide world I panted ;
Out of the forest dark and dread
Across the open fields I fled
  Like one pursued and haunted.

I tossed my arms, I sang aloud,
  My voice exultant blending
With thunder from the passing cloud,
The wind, the forest bent and bowed,
  The rush of rain descending.

I heard the distant ocean call,
   Imploring and entreating ;
Drawn onward, o'er this rocky wall
I plunged, and the loud waterfall
   Made answer to the greeting.

And now, beset with many ills,
   A toilsome life I follow ;
Compelled to carry from the hills
These logs to the impatient mills
   Below there in the hollow.

Yet something ever cheers and charms
   The rudeness of my labours ;
Daily I water with these arms
The cattle of a hundred farms,
   And have the birds for neighbours.

Men call me mad, and well they may,
   When, full of rage and trouble,
I burst my banks of sand and clay,
And sweep their wooden bridge away,
   Like withered reeds or stubble.

Now go and write thy little rhyme,
   As of thine own creating.
Thou seest the day is past its prime ;
I can no longer waste my time ;
   The mills are tired of waiting.

                        Longfellow

The Kingfisher

IT was the Rainbow gave thee birth,
   And left thee all her lovely hues ;
And, as her mother's name was Tears,
   So runs it in thy blood to choose
For haunts the lonely pools, and keep
In company with trees that weep.

Go you and, with such glorious hues,
   Live with proud Peacocks in green parks ;
On lawns as smooth as shining glass,
   Let every feather show its marks ;
Get thee on boughs and clap thy wings
Before the windows of proud kings.

Nay, Lovely Bird, thou art not vain ;
   Thou hast no proud ambitious mind ;
I also love a quiet place
   That's green, away from all mankind ;
A lonely pool, and let a tree
Sigh with her bosom over me.   *W. H. Davies*

The Unseen Warrior Calls

A MIST was driving down the British Channel,
  The day was just begun,
And through the window-panes, on floor and panel,
  Streamed the red autumn sun.

It glanced on flowing flags and rippling pennon,
  And the white sails of ships ;
And, from the frowning rampart, the black cannon
  Hailed it with feverish lips.

Sandwich and Romney, Hastings, Hythe, and Dover,
  Were all alert that day
To see the French war-steamers speeding over
  When the fog cleared away.

Sullen and silent, and like couchant lions,
  Their cannon, through the night,
Holding their breath, had watched, in grim defiance,
  The sea-coast opposite.

And now they roared at drum-beat from their stations
  On every citadel ;
Each answering each, with morning salutations,
  That all was well.

And down the coast, all taking up the burden,
  Replied the distant forts,
As if to summon from his sleep the Warden
  And Lord of the Cinque Ports.

Him shall no sunshine from the fields of azure,
  No drum-beat from the wall,
No morning gun from the black fort's embrasure,
  Awaken with its call !

No more, surveying with an eye impartial
  The long line of the coast,
Shall the gaunt figure of the old Field-Marshal
  Be seen upon his post.

For in the night, unseen, a single warrior,
  In sombre harness mailed,
Dreaded of man, and surnamed the Destroyer,
  The rampart wall had scaled.

He passed into the chamber of the sleeper,
  The dark and silent room,
And as he entered darker grew, and deeper,
  The silence and the gloom.

He did not pause to parley or dissemble,
  But smote the Warden hoar ;
Ah, what a blow ! that made all England tremble,
  And groan from shore to shore.

Meanwhile, without, the surly cannon waited,
The sun rose bright o'erhead ;
Nothing in Nature's aspect intimated
That a great man was dead.

Longfellow

So When a Great Man Dies

GARLANDS upon his grave,
And flowers upon his hearse,
And to the tender heart and brave
The tribute of this verse.

His was the troubled life
The conflict and the pain,
The grief, the bitterness of strife,
The honour without stain.

Like Winkelried, he took
Into his manly breast
The sheaf of hostile spears, and broke
A path for the oppressed.

Then from the fatal field,
Upon a nation's heart
Borne like a warrior on his shield !
So should the brave depart.

Death takes us by surprise,
And stays our hurrying feet ;
The great design unfinished lies,
Our lives are incomplete.

But in the dark unknown
Perfect their circles seem,
Even as a bridge's arch of stone
Is rounded in the stream.

Alike are life and death,
When life in death survives,
And the uninterrupted breath
Inspires a thousand lives.

Were a star quenched on high,
For ages would its light,
Still travelling downward from the sky,
Shine on our mortal sight.

So when a great man dies,
For years beyond our ken
The light he leaves behind him lies
Upon the paths of men.

Longfellow

His Dog is Dead

O MATE of man ! Blest being ! You that shared
  Your master's hunger and his meals as well !
You that in days of old in pilgrimage fared
  With young Tobias and the angel Rafael.

Servant that loved me with a love intense,
  As saints love God, my great exemplar be !
The mystery of your deep intelligence
  Dwells in a guiltless, glad eternity.

Dear Lord ! If You should grant me by Your grace
  To see You face to face in heaven, O then
Grant that a poor dog look into the face
  Of him who was his god here among men !

                                    Francis Jammes

Now Came Still Evening On

Now came still Evening on, and Twilight grey
  Had in her sober livery all things clad . . .
When Adam thus to Eve : Fair consort, the hour
Of night, and all things now retired to rest,
Mind us of like repose ; since God hath set
Labour and rest, as day and night, to men
Successive, and the timely dew of sleep,
Now falling with soft slumberous weight, inclines
Our eyelids . . . Night bids us rest.
To whom thus Eve, with perfect beauty adorned :
My author and disposer, what thou bidd'st
Unargued I obey. So God ordains :
God is thy law, thou mine : to know no more
Is woman's happiest knowledge, and her praise.
With thee conversing I forget all time,
All seasons, and their change ; all please alike.
Sweet is the breath of Morn, her rising sweet,
With charm of earliest birds ; pleasant the Sun,
When first on this delightful land he spreads
His orient beams, on herb, tree, fruit, and flower,
Glistering with dew ; fragrant the fertile Earth
After soft showers ; and sweet the coming-on
Of grateful Evening mild ; then silent Night,
With this her solemn bird, and this fair Moon,
And these the gems of Heaven, her starry train :
But neither breath of Morn, when she ascends
With charm of earliest birds ; nor rising Sun
On this delightful land ; nor herb, fruit, flower,
Glistering with dew ; nor fragrance after showers ;
Nor grateful Evening mild ; nor silent night,

With this her solemn bird ; nor walk by moon.
Or glittering starlight, without thee is sweet.
But wherefore all night long shine these ?   For whom
This glorious sight, when sleep hath shut all eyes ?
To whom our general ancestor replied :
Daughter of God and Man, accomplished Eve,
Those have their course to finish round the Earth
By morrow evening, and from land to land
In order (though to nations yet unborn
Ministering light prepared) they set and rise,
Lest total Darkness should by night regain
Her old possession and extinguish life
In nature and all things.
These, then, though unbeheld in deep of night,
Shine not in vain. Nor think, though men were none,
That Heaven would want spectators, God want praise.
Millions of spiritual creatures walk the Earth
Unseen, both when we wake and when we sleep :
All these with ceaseless praise his works behold
  Both day and night.
Thus talking, hand in hand alone they passed
On to their blissful bower.

Milton's Paradise Lost

Lords and Commons, Consider What a Nation This is

LORDS and Commons of England, consider what nation it is whereof ye are, and whereof ye are the governors—a nation not slow and dull, but of a quick, ingenious, and piercing spirit, acute to invent, subtle and sinewy to discourse, not beneath the reach of any point the highest that human capacity can soar to.   Is it for nothing that the grave and frugal Transylvanian sends out yearly from as far as the mountainous borders of Russia, and beyond the Hercynian wilderness not their youth, but their staid men, to learn our language and our theologic arts ?

Yet that which is above all this, the favour and the love of Heaven, we have great argument to think in a peculiar manner propitious towards us. Why else was this nation chosen before any other, that out of her as out of Zion should be sounded forth the first tidings and trumpet of Reformation to all Europe ?   Now once again, by all concurrence of signs and the general instinct of holy and devout men, God is decreeing to begin some new and great reformation in His church, even to the reforming of Reformation itself.   What does He, then, but reveal Himself to His servants and (as His manner is) first to His Englishmen?

Behold now this vast city—a city of refuge, the mansion house of liberty, encompassed and surrounded with His protection.   The shop of war hath not there more anvils and hammers waking to fashion out the plates and instruments of armed justice in defence of beleagured truth than there be pens and heads there, sitting by their studious lamps, musing, searching, revolving new notions and ideas wherewith to present, as with their homage and their fealty, their approaching Reformation ; others as fast reading, trying all things, assenting to the force of reason and convincement.

What could a man require more from a nation so pliant and so prone to seek knowledge ? What wants there to such a pregnant soil but wise and faithful labourers to make a knowing people, a nation of prophets, of sages, and of worthies ? I doubt not if some great and worthy stranger should come among us, wise to discern the mould and temper of a people and how to govern it, observing the high hopes and aims, the diligent alacrity of our thoughts and reasonings in the pursuance of truth and freedom, but that he would cry out as Pyrrhus did, admiring Roman docility and courage, " If such were my people, I would not despair the greatest design that could be attempted, to make a kingdom happy."

Methinks I see in my mind a noble and puissant nation rousing herself like a strong man after sleep, and shaking her invincible locks. Methinks I see her as an eagle mewing her mighty youth, and kindling her undazzled eyes at the full midday beam ; purging and unscaling her long-abused sight at the fountain itself of heavenly radiance ; while the whole noise of timorous and flocking birds, with those also that love the twilight, flutter about, amazed at what she means.

Milton's Areopagitica

New Suits for Sir Walter Raleigh

SIR WALTER RALEIGH was bred in Oriel College in Oxford, and then coming to Court found some hopes of the Queen's favours falling upon him. This made him write in a glass window, obvious to the Queen's eye :

Fain would I climb, yet fear I to fall.

Her Majesty, either espying or being shown it, did underwrite :

If thy heart faileth thee, climb not at all.

However, he at length climbed up by the stairs of his own desert. But his introduction to Court bare an elder date : from this occasion : This Captain Raleigh coming out of Ireland to the English Court in good habit (his clothes being then a considerable part of his estate) found the Queen walking, till, meeting with a plashy place, she seemed to scruple going thereon. Presently Raleigh cast and spread his new plush coat on the ground, whereon the Queen trod gently rewarding him afterwards with many suits for his so free and seasonable tender of so fair a footcloth. *From an old book*

These Were Fanatics

THERE may be a fanaticism for evil as well as for good. I will not deny that there are persons among us loving liberty too well for their personal good in a selfish generation. Such there may be, and, for the sake of their example, would there were more!

In calling them fanatics you would cast contumely upon the noble army of martyrs from the earliest day down to this hour; upon the great tribunes of human rights by whom life, liberty, and happiness on earth have been secured; upon the long line of devoted patriots who through history have truly loved their country; and upon all who, in noble aspirations for the general good and in forgetfulness of self, have stood out before their age and gathered into their generous bosoms the shafts of tyranny and wrong in order to make a pathway for truth.

You discredit Luther, when alone he nailed his articles to the door of the church at Wittenberg, and then, to the imperial demand that he should retract firmly replied, Here I stand; I cannot do otherwise, so help me God! You discredit Hampden, when alone he refused to pay the few shillings of ship-money, and shook the throne of Charles. You discredit Milton, when amid the corruptions of a heartless Court he lived on, the lofty friend of liberty, above question or suspicion. You discredit Russell and Sidney, when for the sake of their country they calmly turned from family and friends to tread the narrow steps of the scaffold. You discredit the early founders of American institutions, who preferred the hardships of a wilderness surrounded by a savage foe to injustice on beds of ease. You discredit our fathers, who, few in numbers and weak in resources yet strong in their cause, did not hesitate to brave the mighty power of England, already encircling the globe with her morning drum-beats.

Yes, sir, of such are the fanatics of history.

Charles Sumner, who stood alone in the U.S. Senate as the bold enemy of slavery and made this speech there in 1856.

Truth Loses No Battles

GIVE me the liberty to know, to utter, and to argue freely according to conscience, above all liberties.

Though all the winds of doctrine were let loose to play upon the Earth, so Truth be in the field, we do injuriously to misdoubt her strength. Let her and Falsehood grapple. Who ever knew Truth put to the worse in a free and open encounter? Who knows not that Truth is strong next to the Almighty? She needs no policies, no stratagems, nor licensings, to make her victorious; those are the shifts and defences that error uses against her power. Give her but room, and do not bind her when she sleeps. *Milton*

A Word from Sir Walter Raleigh

*Macaulay's "Slobbering James the First" sent Sir Walter Raleigh to the scaffold,
but before he died Raleigh wrote this poem to prove that the king could not slay him.*

Goe, soule, the body's guest,
  Upon a thanklesse arrant ;
Feare not to touche the best,
  The truth shall be thy warrant :
    Goe, since I needs must dye,
    And give the world the lye.

Goe tell the court it glowes
  And shines like rotten wood ;
Goe tell the church it showes
  What's good, and doth no good :
    If church and court reply,
    Then give them both the lye.

Tell potentates they live
  Acting by others actions ;
Not loved unlesse they give,
  Not strong but by their factions ;
    If potentates reply
    Give potentates the lye.

Tell fortune of her blindnesse ;
  Tell nature of decay ;
Tell friendship of unkindnesse ;
  Tell justice of delay ;
    And if they dare reply
    Then give them all the lye.

So, when thou hast, as I
  Commanded thee, done blabbing,
Although to give the lye
  Deserves no less than stabbing,
    Yet stab at thee who will
    No stab the soule can kill.

April

April, April,
  Laugh thy girlish laughter ;
Then, the moment after,
  Weep thy girlish tears !
April, that mine ears
  Like a lover greetest,
If I tell thee, sweetest,
  All my hopes and fears,
April, April,
  Laugh thy golden laughter,
But, the moment after,
  Weep thy golden tears !   *William Watson*

Sir Walter Raleigh and Sir Francis Bacon Think of Death

IF we seek a reason in the boundless ambition in mortal man we may add to that which hath been already said, that the kings and princes of the world have always laid before them the actions, but not the ends, of those great ones which preceded them.

They are always transported with the glory of the one, but they never mind the misery of the other till they find the experience in themselves. They neglect the advice of God while they enjoy life but follow the counsel of Death upon his first approach. Death, which hateth and destroyeth man, is believed ; God, which hath made him and loves him, is always deferred.

I have considered, saith Solomon, all the works that are under the sun, and behold all is vanity and vexation of spirit ; but who believe it till Death tells it us ? It is Death alone that can suddenly make man to know himself. He tells the proud and insolent that they are but Abjects, and humbles them at the instant ; makes them cry, complain, and repent, yea, even to hate their forepassed happiness. He takes the account of the rich and proves him a beggar. He holds a glass before the eyes of the most beautiful, and makes them see therein their deformity.

O eloquent, just, and mighty Death, whom none could advise, thou hast persuaded ; what none hath dared, thou hast done ; and whom all the world hath flattered, thou only hast cast out of the world and despised. Thou hast drawn together all the far-stretched great-ness, all the pride, cruelty, and ambition of man, and covered it all over with these two narrow words, *Hic jacet.*

From Raleigh's History of the World

MEN fear death as children fear to go in the dark ; and, as that natural fear in children is increased with tales, so is the other. Certainly the contemplation of Death as the wages of sin and passage to another world is holy and religious, but the fear of it as a tribute due unto Nature is weak. It is as natural to die as to be born.

Above all, believe it, the sweetest canticle is *Nunc dimittis* when a man hath obtained worthy ends and expectations. Death hath this also, that it openeth the gate to good fame and extinguisheth envy.

Sir Francis Bacon

The Song of a Wife

I SERVE for a day, for a week, for a year,
  For lifetime, for ever, while man dwelleth here.

Thomas Tusser's Sixteenth
Century Book of Housewifery

THE SEA OF GALILEE

THE GARDEN OF GETHSEMANE

SYDNEY HARBOUR

VICTORIA FALLS

Thomas Tusser's Ladder to Prosperity

To take thy calling thankfully,
  And shun the path to beggary.
To grudge in youth no drudgery,
To come by knowledge perfectly.
To count no travel slavery,
That brings in penny saverly.
To follow profit earnestly,
But meddle not with pilfery.
To get by honest practisy,
And keep thy gettings covertly.
To lash not out too lashingly,
For fear of pinching penury.
To get good plot to occupy,
And store and use it husbandly.
To shew to landlord courtesy,
And keep thy covenants orderly.
To hold that thine is lawfully,
For stoutness or for flattery.
To wed good wife for company,
And live in wedlock honestly.
To furnish house with housholdry,
And make provision skilfully.
To join to wife good family,
And none to keep for bravery.
To suffer none live idly,
For fear of idle knavery.
To courage wife in huswifery,
And use well-doers gently.
To keep no more but needfully,
And count excess unsavoury.
To raise betimes the lubberly,
Both snorting Hob and Margery.
To walk thy pastures usually,
To spy ill neighbours' subtilty.
To hate revengement hastily,
For losing love and amity.
To love thy neighbour neighbourly,
And show him no discourtesy.
To answer stranger civilly,
But shew him not thy secrecy.
To use no man deceitfully,
To offer no man villainy.
To learn how foe to pacify,
But trust him not too hastily.
To keep thy touch substantially,
And in thy word use constancy.

To make thy bonds advisedly,
And come not bound through suerty.
To meddle not with usury,
Nor lend thy money foolishly.
To hate to live in infamy,
Through craft and living shiftingly.
To shun all kind of treachery,
For treason endeth horribly.
To learn to shun ill company,
And such as live dishonestly.
To banish house of blasphemy,
Lest crosses cross, unluckily.
To stop mischance through policy,
For chancing too unhappily.
To bear thy crosses patiently,
For worldly things are slippery.
To lay to keep from misery.
Age coming on, so creepingly.
To pray to God continually,
For aid against thine enemy.
To spend thy Sabbath holily,
And help the needy poverty.
To live in conscience quietly,
And keep thyself from malady.
To ease thy sickness speedily,
Ere help be past recovery.
To seek to God for remedy,
For witches prove unluckily.
These be the steps, unfeignedly,
To climb to thrift by husbandry.

*From Thomas Tusser's book of good counsel to
countrymen and housewives of the Sixteenth Century*

Bad News

My lord, what can I say to you? I am sore vexed, but your pretty cottage is burnt to the ground. What will you say, my lord?　　*The Housekeeper to Lord Grey of Fallodon*

If I Should Die Tonight

If I should die tonight,
My friends would look upon my quiet face
Before they laid it in its resting place,
And deem that death had left it almost fair;
And, laying snow-white flowers against my hair,
Would smooth it down with tearful tenderness,
And fold my hands with lingering caress,
Poor hands, so empty and so cold tonight!

If I should die tonight,
My friends would call to mind with loving thought
Some kindly deed the icy hands had wrought ;
Some gentle word the frozen lips had said ;
Errands on which the willing feet had sped ;
The memory of my selfishness and pride,
My hasty words, would all be put aside,
And so I should be loved and mourned tonight.

If I should die tonight,
Even hearts estranged would turn once more to me,
Recalling other days remorsefully.
The eyes that chill me with averted glance,
Would look upon me as of yore perchance,
And soften in the old familiar way ;
For who could war with dumb unconscious clay ?
So I might rest, forgiven of all, tonight.

Oh, friends, I pray tonight,
Keep not your kisses from my dead cold brow,
The way is lonely—let me feel them now,
Think gently of me ; I am travel-worn ;
My faltering feet are pierced with many a thorn.
Forgive, oh hearts estranged, forgive, I plead !
When dreamless rest is mine I shall not need
The tenderness for which I long tonight.

Arabella Eugenia Smith

Everything Did With Him Talk

How like an angel came I down !
    How bright are all things here !
When first among his works I did appear
O how their glory did me crown !
The world resembled his eternity
In which my soul did walk,
And everything that I did see
Did with me talk.

The skies in their magnificence,
The lively, lovely air,
Oh, how divine, how soft, how sweet, how fair !
The stars did entertain my sense,
And all the works of God so bright and pure,
So rich and great did seem,
As if they ever must endure
In my esteem.

A native health and innocence
Within my bones did grow,

And while my God did all His glories show
I felt a vigour in my sense
That all was spirit.   I within did flow
With seas of life, like wine ;
I nothing in the world did know
But twas divine.

Harsh ragged objects were concealed,
Oppressions, tears, and cries,
Sins, griefs, complaints, dissensions, weeping eyes,
Were hid ; and only things revealed
Which heavenly spirits and the angels prize.
The state of innocence
And bliss, not trades and poverties,
Did fill my sense.

The streets were paved with golden stones,
The boys and girls were mine,
Oh, how did all their lovely faces shine !
The sons of men were Holy Ones
In joy and beauty, then appeared to me,
And everything which here I found,
While like an angel I did see,
Adorned the ground.

Rich diamond and pearl and gold
In every place was seen ;
Rare splendours, yellow, blue, red, white, and green,
Mine eyes did everywhere behold.
Great wonders clothed with glory did appear,
Amazement was my bliss.
That and my wealth was everywhere :
No joy to this !

Cursed and devised proprieties,
With envy, avarice,
And fraud, those fiends that spoil even Paradise,
Fled from the splendour of mine eyes.
And so did hedges, ditches, limits, bounds,
I dreamed not ought of those,
But wandered over all men's grounds,
And found repose.

Proprieties themselves were mine,
And hedges ornaments ;
Walls, boxes, coffers, and their rich contents
Did not divide my joys, but all combine.
Clothes, ribbons, jewels, laces, I esteemed
My joys by others worn ;
For me they all to wear them seemed
When I was born.   *Thomas Traherne*

Suddenly One Day

SUDDENLY one day
  The last ill shall fall away.
The last little beastliness that is in our blood
Shall drop from us as the sheath drops from the bud,
And the great spirit of man shall struggle through
And spread huge branches underneath the blue.
In any mirror, be it bright or dim,
Man will see God staring back at him.

T. P. C. Wilson

The Undying
In memory of T. P. C. W.

THE quiet passing ships ;
  A shadowed hillside,
And his spirit,
And the slow wash of the tide.

The fire of the heather ;
The stars waning dim,
And his spirit,
Always the spirit of him.

Stronger than grief or death,
Hurt, or the power to kill,
Comes insistent, triumphant,
His spirit still.   *Marjorie Wilson, to a
brother killed in the War*

A Memory

MY wandering heart is over the fields
  With my sisters the Sun and the Rain ;
But fetters are holding my body close,
  And my hands, in the hands of Pain.

Sweet are the slim-stalked hare-bell flowers
  Where the low gold grasses blow ;
But an alien gaoler keeps my door
  And he will not let me go.

Birds and the trees keep holiday,
  And my broken body stays ;
But not iron key or prison wall
  Can bar my love-filled days.

No pacing warder with steely grip
  Can my spirit keep apart
From the days when my head was crowned with stars
  And a glory was in my heart.

Marjorie Wilson, on being told that she must die

The Honest Friend

On the whole it is easy to understand the dog and to learn to read his thoughts. The dog cannot dissimulate, cannot deceive, cannot lie, because he cannot speak. The dog is a saint. He is straightforward and honest by nature.

He looks upon his master as his king, almost as his god. He expects his god to be severe if need be, but he expects him to be just. He knows that his god can read his thoughts, and he knows it is no good to conceal them.

He knows by instinct when he is not wanted ; lies quite still for hours when his king is hard at work. But when his king is sad and worried he knows that his time has come, and he creeps up and lays his head on his lap. " Don't worry. Never mind if they all abandon you. Let us go for a walk and forget all about it ! "

Axel Munthe

He Wrote the Bridge of Sighs

No courtier this, and nought to courts he owed,
  Fawned not on thrones, hymned not the great and callous,
Yet, in one strain that few remember, showed
  He had the password to King Oberon's palace,

And seeing a London seamstress's grey fate,
  He of a human heartstring made a thread,
And stitched him such a royal robe of state
  That eastern kings are poorlier habited.

He saw wan Woman toil with famished eyes ;
  He saw her bound, and strove to sing her free.
He saw her fallen, and wrote The Bridge of Sighs,
  And on it crossed to immortality.

William Watson

The Poet to His Master

O let me leave the plains behind,
  And let me leave the vales below ;
Into the highlands of the mind,
  Into the mountains let me go.

My Keats, my Spenser, loved I well ;
  Gardens and statued lawns were these ;
But not for ever would I dwell
  In arbours and in pleasances.

Here are the heights, crest beyond crest,
  Loftiest of all things cloud-encurled :
And I will watch from Everest
  The onsweep of the surgeful world.

William Watson on Shakespeare

December 31, 1933

OUTSIDE the door the New Year knocks ;
    His fingers are so small and cold.
I will not open yet to him,
    For last year is not quite all told,
    Nor made—my farewells to the Old.

Old Year, when you were young as he
    Who waits outside my door tonight,
I stood with happy hands that clasped
    My friends' hands.   Gay with dance and light
    We were when last Old Year took flight.

And one, since then, has flown the seas,
    Though most still walk the roads of home ;
To one delight and joy have been ;
    The clouds of grief have shadowed some,
    And unto one a Call has come.

Old Year, who for a moment froze
    My heart with that stern news, before
You pass into Remembering and
    Become the Past for evermore,
    And Young Year enters at the door,

Know this : Before the next swift year
    Has travelled quite its circuit through,
I too may journey in your wake
    To seek Eternity, I too
    May be in Time's great heart, as you.

Then little will they know who speak
    Such words as say that I am dead.
Only shall I have cast my cloak,
    My ragged garment shall have shed,
    To wear the robes of God instead.
                    By Marjorie Wilson, dying

Hail

HAIL to the coming singers !
    Hail to the brave light-bringers !
Forward I reach and share
All that they sing and dare.

The airs of heaven blow o'er me ;
A glory shines before me
Of what mankind shall be :
Pure, generous, brave, and free.

Ring, bells in unreared steeples,
The joy of unborn peoples !
                    Whittier

I Loved a Lass, A Fair One

I LOVED a lass, a fair one,
   As fair as e'er was seen ;
She was indeed a rare one,
   Another Sheba Queen :
But, fool as then I was,
   I thought she loved me too :
But now, alas ! she's left me,
   Falero, lero, loo !

Her hair like gold did glister,
   Each eye was like a star,
She did surpass her sister,
   Which passed all others far ;
She would me honey call,
   She'd—O she'd kiss me too !
But now, alas ! she's left me,
   Falero, lero, loo !

Her cheeks were like the cherry,
   Her skin was white as snow ;
When she was blithe and merry
   She angel-like did show ;
Her waist exceeding small,
   The fives did fit her shoe :
But now, alas ! she's left me,
   Falero, lero, loo !

In summer time or winter
   She had her heart's desire ;
I still did scorn to stint her
   From sugar, sack, or fire ;
The world went round about,
   No cares we ever knew :
But now, alas ! she's left me,
   Falero, lero, loo !

To maiden's vows and swearing
   Henceforth no credit give ;
You may give them the hearing,
   But never them believe ;
They are as false as fair,
   Unconstant, frail, untrue :
For mine, alas ! hath left me,
   Falero, lero, loo !
        George Wither in the 17th Century

Sir Philip Sidney's Advice From His Father

SINCE this is my first letter that ever I did write to you, I will not that it be all empty of some advices which my natural care of you provoketh me to wish you to follow, as documents to you in this your tender age.

Let your first action be the lifting up of your mind to Almighty God by hearty prayer; and feelingly digest the words you speak in prayer, with continual meditation and thinking of Him to Whom you pray, and of the matter for which you pray. And use this as an ordinary act, and at an ordinary hour; whereby the time itself shall put you in remembrance to do that which you are accustomed to do.

Apply your study to such hours as your discreet master doth assign you, earnestly; and the time I know he will so limit, as shall be both sufficient for your learning and safe for your health. And mark the sense and the matter of that you read, as well as the words. So shall you both enrich your tongue with words and your wit with matter: and judgment will grow as years grow in you.

Be humble and obedient to your master, for unless you frame yourself to obey others (yea, and feel in yourself what obedience is) you shall never be able to teach others how to obey you.

Be courteous of gesture, and affable to all men, with diversity of reverence according to the dignity of the person; there is nothing that winneth so much with so little cost.

Use moderate diet, so as, after your meal, you may find your wit fresher and not duller, and your body more lively and not more heavy. Seldom drink wine. Use exercise of body, yet such as is without peril of your joints or bones; it will increase your force and enlarge your breath. Delight to be cleanly, as well in all parts of your body as in your garments; it shall make you grateful in each company.

Give yourself to be merry; for you degenerate from your father if you find not yourself most able in wit and body and to do anything when you be most merry; but let your mirth be ever void of all scurrility and biting words to any man, for a wound given by a word is oftentimes harder to be cured than that given with the sword. Be you rather a hearer and bearer away of other men's talk than a beginner and procurer of speech; otherwise you shall be counted to delight to hear yourself speak. If you hear a wise sentence or an apt phrase, commit it to your memory with respect of the circumstance when you shall speak it. Let never oath be heard to come out of your mouth, nor word of ribaldry; detest it in others—so shall custom make to yourself a law against it in yourself.

Be modest in each assembly, and rather be rebuked of light fellows for maiden-like shamefastness than of your sad friends for pert boldness. Think upon every word you will speak before you utter it.

Above all things, tell no untruth, no, not in trifles ; the custom of it is naughty. And let it not satisfy you that, for a time, the hearers take it for truth, for after it will be known as it is, to your shame, for there cannot be a greater reproach to a gentleman than to be accounted a liar. Study and endeavour yourself to be virtuously occupied ; so shall you make such a habit of well-doing in you that you shall not know how to do evil.

Remember, my son, the noble blood you are descended of by your mother's side ; and think that only by virtuous life and good action you may be an ornament to that illustrious family ; otherwise, through vice and sloth, you shall be counted one of the greatest curses that can happen to man.

Well, my little Philip, this is enough for me, and too much, I fear, for you. But if I shall find that this light meal of digestion nourish anything in the weak stomach of your capacity I will, as I find the same grow stronger, feed it with tougher food.

Your loving father, so long as you live in the fear of God,

H. Sidney

What Shadows We Are, and What Shadows We Pursue

Edmund Burke, realising in the midst of a contest at Bristol that he would not be elected, declined the election in this famous short speech, one phrase of which (referring to the death of a candidate) has become a familiar quotation.

GENTLEMEN, I decline the election. It has ever been my rule through life to observe a proportion between my efforts and my objects. I have never been remarkable for a bold, active, and sanguine pursuit of advantages that are personal to myself.

I have not canvassed the whole of this city in form ; but I have taken such a view of it as satisfies my own mind that your choice will not ultimately fall upon me. Your city, gentlemen, is in a state of miserable distraction ; and I am resolved to withdraw whatever share my pretensions may have had in its unhappy divisions. I have not been in haste. I have tried all prudent means. I have waited for the effect of all contingencies. If I were fond of a contest, by the partiality of my numerous friends (whom you know to be among the most weighty and respectable people of the city) I have the means of a sharp one in my hands ; but I thought it far better, with my strength unspent and my reputation unimpaired, to do early and from foresight that which I might be obliged to do from necessity at last.

I am not in the least surprised, nor in the least angry, at this view of things. I have read the book of life for a long time, and I have read other books a little. Nothing has happened to me but what has happened to men much better than me, and in times and in nations full as good as the age and country that we live in. To say that I am no way concerned would be neither decent nor true . . . but, gentlemen, I will see nothing except your former kindness, and I will give way to no other sentiments than those of gratitude. From the bottom of my heart I thank you for what you have done for me. You have given me a long term, which is now expired. I have performed the conditions, and enjoyed all the profits to the full; and I now surrender your estate into your hands without being in a single tile or a single stone impaired or wasted by my use.

I have served the public for fifteen years; I have served you in particular for six. What is past is well stored. It is safe, and out of the power of fortune. What is to come is in wiser hands than ours, and He in whose hands it is best knows whether it is best for you and me that I should be in Parliament, or even in the world.

Gentlemen, the melancholy event of yesterday reads to us an awful lesson against being too much troubled about any of the objects of ordinary ambition. The worthy gentleman who has been snatched from us at the moment of the election, and in the middle of the contest, while his desires were as warm and his hopes as eager as ours, has feelingly told us what shadows we are, and what shadows we pursue.

It is no plaything you are about. I tremble when I consider the trust I have presumed to ask. I confided perhaps too much in my intentions. They were really fair and upright; and I am bold to say that I ask no ill thing for you when, on parting from this place, I pray that whomever you choose to succeed me, he may resemble me exactly in all things except in my abilities to serve and my fortune to please you.

A Bunch of Violets

THREE times this lovely thought of violets comes into English literature the same thought in the mind of Shakespeare, Herrick, and Tennyson.

Shakespeare puts it into Hamlet, where the angry brother of the drowned Ophelia cries to the churlish priest at her graveside:

> Lay her i' the earth,
> And from her fair and unpolluted flesh
> May violets spring! I tell thee, churlish priest,
> A ministering angel shall my sister be
> When thou liest howling.

Herrick puts it into his epitaph on his faithful maid Prue:

> In this little urn is laid
> Prudence Baldwin, once my maid,
> From whose happy spark here let
> Spring the purple violet.

Tennyson puts it into In Memoriam at the grave of Arthur Hallam:

> Tis well, tis something, we may stand
> Where he in English earth is laid,
> And from his ashes may be made
> The violet of his native land.

A World Crisis in the Dark Ages

There is in old letters a remarkable picture of one of the rulers of the world trying to get in touch with the greatest scholar in Europe in the midst of a world crisis. This glimpse of it is from a few letters which passed between Rome and Basle at the end of 1522, each letter taking a month by special messenger.

From Pope Adrian the Sixth to Erasmus:

IT lies with you, God helping, to recover those who have been seduced by Luther from the right road, and to hold up those who still stand. I need not tell you with what joy I shall receive back these heretics without need to smite them with the rod of the Imperial law. You know how far are such rough methods from my own nature. I am still as you knew me when we were students together. Come to me to Rome.

Erasmus to Pope Adrian:

This is no ordinary storm. Earth and air are convulsed—arms, opinions, authorities, factions, hatreds, jarring one against the other. If your Holiness will hear from me what I think you should do to make a real cure, I will tell you in a secret letter. If you approve my advice you can adopt it. If not let it remain private between you and me. We little dreamt when we jested together in our early years what times were coming. With the Faith itself in peril we must beware of personal affections.

The Pope to Erasmus:

Open your mind to me. Speak freely. I am not alarmed for myself. I am not alarmed for the Holy See. I am distressed for the myriads of souls who are going to perdition. Be swift and silent. Come to me if you can, and come quickly.

Erasmus to the Pope:

I would come to you with pleasure if my health allowed. But the road over the Alps is long. The lodgings on the way are dirty and inconvenient. The smell from the stoves is intolerable. The wine is sour and disagrees with me.

Meanwhile you shall have my honest heart in writing. Your eyes and mine will alone see my letter. If you like it—well. . . .

Those counsel you best who advise gentle measures. Some others think there is no remedy but force. That is not my opinion. The question is not what heresy deserves but how to deal with it wisely. Things have gone too far for cautery. If you mean to try prisons, lashes, confiscations, stake, and scaffold you need no help from me. For myself I should say, Discover the roots of the disease. Clean out those to begin with. Punish no one. Let what has taken place be regarded as a chastisement sent by Providence and grant a universal amnesty.

If God forgives so many sins, God's vicar may forgive. If possible there should be a check on the printing presses. Then let the world see and know that you mean in earnest to reform the abuses which are justly cried out against, and, if your Holiness desires to know what the roots are to which I refer, send persons whom you can trust to every part of Latin Christendom. Let them consult the wisest men that they can find in the different countries and you will soon know.

You say to me " Come to Rome, Write a book against Luther. Declare war against his party."

Come to Rome ? Tell a crab to fly. The crab will say " Give me wings." I say " Give me back my youth and strength."

Portrait of Erasmus by Sir Thomas More

You adjure me to beware of Erasmus. Gratitude for your concern for my soul obliges me to thank you for your alarms. It is my duty also to point out to you that you are yourself walking among precipices. . . .

Erasmus has published volumes more full of wisdom than any which Europe has seen for ages. You have turned to poison what to others has brought only health. I read with real sorrow your intemperate railing at such a man. You defame his character. You call him a vagabond. You say he is a heretic, a schismatic, a forerunner of Antichrist.

Before you were a priest you had candour and charity ; now that you have become a monk some devil has possession of you. You say you do not give him these names yourself. You pretend that he is so described by Almighty God. Are you not ashamed to bring in God when you are doing the devil's work in slandering your neighbour ? God has revealed it, you pretend, to someone that you know. I am not to be frightened by an idiot's dreams.

I knew you once an innocent and affectionate youth : why are you now charged with spite and malice ? You complain of Erasmus's satire and you yourself worry him like a dog. Take all the hard things he has said of anyone. It is a handful of dust to the pyramid of invective which you have piled over a man who was once kind to you. Is a boy like you to fall foul of what the Vicar of Christ approves ? Is the head of the Christian Church, speaking from the citadel of faith, to give a book his sanction, and is it to be befouled by the dirty tongue of an obscure little monk ? Erasmus, forsooth, does not know Scripture ! He has studied Scripture for more years than you have been alive. You yourself quote Scripture like a rogue in a play. . . .

Erasmus is the dearest friend that I have. You claim him a vagabond because he has moved from place to place to carry on his work. A saint, I suppose, must remain fixed like a sponge or an oyster. You forget your own mendicants. They wander wide enough, and you think them the holiest of mankind. Jerome travelled far, the Apostles travelled far.

Look into your own heart. You, for sooth, are never angry, never puffed up, never seek your own glory. My friend, the more conscious you are of your own faults, the more likely you are to be a profitable servant. This I pray may be your care, and mine, and Erasmus's also. You hint that you are not yourself implacable : if Erasmus will correct his errors you will again take his hand. Doubtless he will bow to so great a man, and will correct them when you point them out ; so far you have only exposed your own. In what you call errors he has substituted pure Latin for bad, cleared obscurities, corrected mistakes, and has pointed out blunders of copyists. To please so great a man as you he may perhaps undo all this, forfeit the respect of the wise, and console himself with the sense of your forgiveness.

But a truce to satire. You say that the blots you indicate are trifles. Well, you cannot regard heresy and schism and precursing and Antichrist as trifles. I presume, therefore, that those charges are withdrawn. I will let the rest drop, and our tragedy may end as a comedy. Farewell ! If the cloister is good for your soul, make the best of it, but spare us for the future these effervescenes of genius.

*Written by Sir Thomas More to a young
priest who had written him criticising Erasmus*

Portrait of Sir Thomas More by Erasmus

NOT everyone understands More, who is as difficult a subject as Alexander or Achilles.

He is of middle height, well shaped, complexion pale, without a touch of colour in it save when the skin flushes. The hair is black shot with yellow, or yellow shot with black ; beard scanty, eyes grey, with dark spots—an eye supposed in England to indicate genius, and to be never found except in remarkable men. The expression is pleasant and cordial, easily passing into a smile, for he has the quickest sense of the ridiculous of any man I ever met. The right shoulder is rather higher than the left, the result of a trick in walking, not from a physical defect. The rest is in keeping. The only sign of rusticity is in the hands, which are slightly coarse.

From childhood he has been careless of appearance, but he has still the charm which I remember when I first knew him. His health is good, though not robust, and he is likely to be long-lived. His father, though in extreme old age, is still vigorous. He is careless in what he eats. (I never saw a man more so.) Like his father, he is a water-drinker. His food is beef, fresh or salt, bread, milk, fruit, and especially eggs. His voice is low and unmusical, though he loves music ; but it is clear and penetrating. He articulates slowly and distinctly, and never hesitates.

He dresses plainly ; no silks, or velvets, or gold chains. He has no concern for ceremony, expects none from others, and shows little himself. He holds forms and courtesies unworthy of a man of sense, and for that reason has hitherto kept clear of the Court. All Courts are full of intrigue. There is less of it in England than elsewhere, for there are no affectations in the King ; but More loves freedom, and likes to have his time to himself. He is a true friend. When he finds a man to be of the wrong sort he lets him drop, but he enjoys nothing so much as the society of those who suit him and whose character he approves. Gambling of all kinds (balls, dice, and such like) he detests. None of that sort are to be found about him. In short, he is the best type of companion.

His talk is charming, full of fun, but never scurrilous or malicious. He used to act plays when young; wit delights him, though at his own expense; he writes smart epigrams; he can make fun of anything. He is wise with the wise, and jests with fools—with women especially, and his wife among them. He is fond of animals of all kinds, and likes to watch their habits. All the birds in Chelsea come to him to be fed. He has a menagerie of tame beasts, a monkey, a fox, a ferret, and a weasel. He buys any singular thing which is brought to him. His house is a magazine of curiosities, which he delights in showing off.

He controls his family with the same easy hand : no tragedies, no quarrels. If a dispute begins it is promptly settled. He has never made an enemy nor become an enemy. His whole house breathes happiness, and no one enters it who is not the better for the visit. He is indifferent to money. He sets apart so much of his income as will make a future provision for his family; the rest he spends or gives away.

More has been never known to accept a present. Happy the commonwealth where the magistrates are of such material ! Elevation has not elated him or made him forget his humble friends, and he returns whenever he can to his beloved books. He is always kind, always generous. Some he helps with money, some with influence. When he can give nothing else he gives advice. He is Patron-General to all poor devils.

He has a fine intellect and an excellent memory, information all arranged and pigeon-holed to be ready for use. He is so ready in argument that he can puzzle the best divines on their own subjects. Colet, a good judge on such points, says More has more genius than any man in England. He is religious, but without superstition. He has his hours for prayer, but he uses no forms, and prays out of his heart. He will talk with his friends about a life to come, and you can see that he means it and has real hopes.

Such is More, and More is an English courtier, and people fancy that no Christians are to be found outside monasteries. The King not only admits such men into his Court, but he invites them, forces them, that they may be in a position to watch all that he does, and share his duties and his pleasures. He prefers the companionship of men like More to that of silly youths or girls, or the rich, or the dishonest, who might tempt him to foolish indulgences or injurious courses. If you were here in England you would leave off abusing Courts. A galaxy of distinguished men now surrounds the English throne. *Erasmus in England to a friend on the Continent*

Erasmus Writes to Bluebeard

THE heart of a king is in the hands of God. When God means well to any nation he gives it a king who deserves a throne. Perhaps after so many storms He now looks on us with favour, having inspired the present reigning monarchs with a desire for peace and the restoration of piety.

To you is due the highest praise. No prince is better prepared for war and none more wishes to avoid it, knowing as you do, how deadly a scourge is war to the mass of mankind, while you have so well used your respite that you have cleared the roads of robbers, so long the scourge and reproach of England ; you have suppressed vagabonds ; you have strengthened your laws, repealed the bad ones, and supplied defects. You have encouraged learning. You have improved discipline among the monks and clergy. You have recognised that a pure and noble race of men is a finer ornament to your realm than warlike trophies or splendid edifices.

You make yourself the pattern of what you prescribe for others. The king's command goes far, but the king's example goes farther. Who better keeps the law than you keep it ? Who less seeks unworthy objects ? Who is truer to his word ? Who is juster and fairer in all that he does ? In what household, in what college or university, will you find more wisdom and integrity than in the Court of England ?

The poet's golden age, if such age ever was, comes back under your Highness. What friend of England does not now congratulate her ? What enemy does not envy her good fortune ? By their monarch's character realms are ennobled or depraved. Future ages will tell how England throve, how virtue flourished in the reign of Henry the Eighth, how the nation was born again, how piety revived, how learning grew to a height which Italy may envy, and how the prince who reigned over it was a rule and pattern for all time to come.

Once I avoided kings and courts. Now I would gladly migrate to England if my infirmities allowed. I am but a graft upon her, not a native, yet when I remember the years I spent there, the friends I found there, the fortune (small though it be) which I owe to her, I rejoice in England's felicity as if she were my natural mother.

For yourself, the intelligence of your country will preserve the memory of your virtues, and scholars will tell how a king once reigned there who in his own person revived the virtues of the ancient heroes.

Letter to Henry the Eighth

It Might Have Been

OF all sad words of tongue or pen
The saddest are these, It might have been.

Whittier

ELIZABETH KNIGHTING RALEIGH, BY A. K. LAWRENCE

HENRY THE EIGHTH, BY HOLBEIN

EDWARD THE SIXTH, BY HOLBEIN

A CHINESE PRIEST OF THE
TANG DYNASTY

THE MOURNING WOMAN, BY A
SCULPTOR OF OLD GREECE

I Mourn No More My Vanished Years

I MOURN no more my vanished years :
  Beneath a tender rain,
An April rain of smiles and tears,
  My heart is young again.

The west-winds blow, and, singing low,
  I hear the glad streams run ;
The windows of my soul I throw
  Wide open to the sun.

I break my pilgrim staff, I lay
  Aside the toiling oar ;
The angel sought so far away
  I welcome at my door.

Enough that blessings undeserved
  Have marked my erring track ;—
That, whereso'er my feet have swerved,
  His chastening turned me back ;

That more and more a Providence
  Of love is understood,
Making the springs of time and sense
  Sweet with eternal good :

That all the jarring notes of life
  Seem blending in a psalm,
And all the angels of its strife
  Slow rounding into calm.

And so the shadows fall apart,
  And so the west-winds play ;
And all the windows of my heart
  I open to the day.
            Whittier's Psalm

A Story of a Dark and Lonely Night

ABOUT seven hundred lambs, which were once under my care at weaning time, broke up at midnight and scampered off in three divisions across the hills, in spite of all that I and an assistant lad could do to keep them together. Sirrah, my man ! said I in great affliction, they are awa'.

The night was so dark that I could not see Sirrah, but the faithful animal heard my words, words such as of all others were sure to set him most on the alert ; and without much ado he silently set off in search of the recreant flock. We spent the whole night in scouring the hills for miles around, but of neither the lambs nor Sirrah could we obtain the slightest trace. It was the most extraordinary circumstance that had occurred in my pastoral life. We had nothing for it (day having dawned), but to return to our master and inform him that we had lost his whole flock of lambs.

F.T.—14

On our way home, however, we discovered a body of lambs at the bottom of a deep ravine, and the indefatigable Sirrah standing in front of them, looking all around for some relief but still standing true to his charge.

The sun was then up ; and when we first came in view of them we concluded that it was one of the divisions which Sirrah had been unable to manage until he came to that commanding situation, but what was our astonishment when we discovered that not one lamb of the whole flock was wanting !   How he had got all the divisions collected in the dark is beyond my comprehension.   The charge was left entirely to himself from midnight until the rising of the sun ; and if all the shepherds in the forest had been there to have assisted him they could not have affected it with greater propriety.   All that I can further say is that I never felt so grateful to any creature below the sun as I did to my honest Sirrah that morning.

Story told by James Hogg, the Ettrick Shepherd

The Slave to His Master

In the Festival of Saturn the slave of ancient Rome might do as he pleased, for all were equal during Saturnalia.   Here the poet Horace makes a slave talk to his master freely in those days of privilege.

You praise the fortune and the manners of men of old, and yet, if on a sudden some god were for taking you back to those days, you would refuse.   What if you are found to be a greater fool even than I, who cost you five hundred drachmas ?

Are you my master, you, a slave to the dominion of so many men and things—you whom the praetor's rod, though placed on your head three or four times over, never frees from base terror ?   Why, you who lord it over me are the wretched slave of another master, and you are moved like a wooden puppet by wires that others pull.

Who, then, is free ?   The wise man who is lord over himself, whom neither poverty nor death nor bonds affright, who bravely defies his passions, and scorns ambition, who in himself is a whole, smoothed and rounded, so that nothing from outside can rest on the polished surface, and against whom Fortune in her onset is ever maimed.

Of these traits can you recognise any one as your own ?   You cannot, for you have a master, and no gentle one, plaguing your soul, pricking your weary side with the sharp spur, and driving you on against your will.

If I am tempted by a smoking pasty, I am a good-for-naught, but you—does your heroic virtue defy rich suppers ?

And you cannot bear to be in your own company, you cannot employ your leisure aright, you shun yourself, a runaway, a vagabond, seeking now with wind and now with sleep to baffle Care.   In vain : that black consort dogs you and follows your flight.

I Am Dying, Egypt, Dying

ANTHONY: I am dying, Egypt, dying :
  My spirit is going ; I can no more.

Cleopatra : Noblest of men, woo 't die ?
Hast thou no care of me ? Shall I abide
In this dull world, which in thy absence is
No better than a sty ? O, see, my women,
The crown o' the earth doth melt. My lord !
O, withered is the garland of the war,
The soldier's star is fallen : young boys and girls
Are level now with men ; the odds is gone,
And there is nothing left remarkable
Beneath the visiting moon.   *Shakespeare*

I AM dying, Egypt, dying,
  Ebbs the crimson life-tide fast,
And the dark Plutonian shadows
  Gather on the evening blast ;
Let thine arms, O Queen, enfold me,
  Hush thy sobs and bow thine ear ;
Listen to the great heart-secrets,
  Thou, and thou alone, must hear.

Though my scarred and veteran legions
  Bear their eagles high no more,
And my wrecked and scattered galleys
  Strew dark Actium's fatal shore,
Though no glittering guards surround me,
  Prompt to do their master's will,
I must perish like a Roman,
  Die the great Triumvir still.

Let not Caesar's servile minions
  Mock the lion thus laid low ;
Twas no foeman's arm that felled him,
  Twas his own that struck the blow ;
His who, pillowed on thy bosom,
  Turned aside from glory's ray,
His who, drunk with thy caresses,
  Madly threw a world away.

I am dying, Egypt, dying ;
  Hark ! the insulting foeman's cry.
They are coming ! quick, my falchion,
  Let me front them ere I die.
    Ah ! no more amid the battle
      Shall my heart exulting swell ;
    Isis and Osiris guard thee !
      Cleopatra, Rome, farewell !
          William Haines Lytle

The Old Man Broken

KATHARINE: Didst thou not tell me, Griffith, as thou led'st me,
That the great child of honour, Cardinal Wolsey,
Was dead ?

Griffith : Well, the voice goes, madam :
For after the stout Earl Northumberland
Arrested him at York, and brought him forward,
As a man sorely tainted, to his answer,
He fell sick suddenly, and grew so ill
He could not sit his mule.

Katharine : Alas, poor man !

Griffith : At last, with easy roads, he came to Leicester,
Lodged in the abbey ; where the reverend abbot,
With all his covent, honourably received him ;
To whom he gave these words, *O, father abbot,*
An old man, broken with the storms of State,
Is come to lay his weary bones among ye ;
Give him a little earth for charity !
So went to bed ; where eagerly his sickness
Pursued him still : and, three nights after this,
About the hour of eight, which he himself
Foretold should be his last, full of repentance,
Continual meditations, tears, and sorrows,
He gave his honours to the world again,
His blessed part to heaven, and slept in peace.

Katharine : So may he rest ; his faults lie gently on him !

Shakespeare's Henry the Eighth

A Riddle from Hamlet

FIRST GRAVEDIGGER: Come, my spade. There is no ancient
gentlemen but gardeners, ditchers, and grave-makers : they hold
up Adam's profession. What is he that builds stronger than either
the mason, the shipwright, or the carpenter ?

Second Gravedigger : The gallows-maker, for that frame outlives
a thousand tenants.

First Gravedigger : I like thy wit well, in good faith : the gallows
does well ; but how does it well ? It does well to those that do ill.
Now thou dost ill to say the gallows is built stronger than the church ;
argal, the gallows may do well to thee. Cudgel thy brains no more
about it, for your dull ass will not mend his pace with beating ; and
when you are asked this question next, say a grave-maker : the houses
that he makes last till Doomsday.

From the scene at Ophelia's grave

Poor Richard's Advice for Hard Times

Poor Richard's Almanack was published for twenty-five years by Benjamin Franklin. One of its famous chapters is a summing-up of Poor Richard's homely counsel, given here in the form of a talk by an old countryman.

I STOPPED my horse lately where a great number of people were collected at an auction. The hour of the sale not being come, they were conversing on the badness of the times, and one of the company called to a plain, clean old man with white locks, " Pray, Father Abraham, what think you of the times ? Will not these heavy taxes quite ruin the country ? How shall we ever be able to pay them ? What would you advise us to do ? "

Friends (says he) the taxes are indeed very heavy ; and, if those laid on by the Government were the only ones we had to pay we might more easily discharge them ; but we have many others, much more grievous to some of us. We are taxed twice as much by our idleness, three times as much by our pride, and four times as much by our folly ; and from these taxes the Commissioners cannot ease or deliver us. However, let us hearken to good advice, and something may be done for us. God helps them that help themselves, as Poor Richard says.

It would be thought a hard government that should tax its people one-tenth part of their time to be employed in its service ; but idleness taxes many of us much more : sloth, by bringing on diseases, absolutely shortens life. Sloth, like rust, consumes faster than labour wears, while the used key is always bright, as Poor Richard says. But dost thou love life, then do not squander time, for that is the stuff life is made of. How much more than is necessary do we spend in sleep, forgetting that the sleeping fox catches no poultry.

If time be of all things the most precious, wasting time must be, as Poor Richard says, the greatest prodigality, since lost time is never found again. Let us then up and be doing, and doing to the purpose, so by diligence shall we do more with less perplexity. Sloth makes all things difficult, but industry all easy, and he that riseth late must trot all day and shall scarce overtake his business at night, while laziness travels so slowly that poverty soon overtakes him.

But with our industry we must likewise be steady, settled, and careful, oversee our own affairs with our own eyes, and not trust too much to others, for, as Poor Richard says :

> I never saw an oft removed tree,
> Nor yet an oft removed family,
> That throve so well as those that settled be.

Three removes are as bad as a fire. Keep thy shop and thy shop will keep thee. A little neglect may breed great mischief. For want of a nail the shoe was lost ; for want of a shoe the horse was lost ; and for want of a horse the rider was lost, being overtaken and slain by the enemy—all for want of a little care about a nail.

So much for industry, and attention to one's own business ; but to these we must add frugality. A man may keep his nose all his life to the grindstone, and die not worth a groat at last. A fat kitchen makes a lean will. The Indies have not made Spain rich because her out-goes are greater than her in-comes.

Away, then, with your expensive follies, and you will not have so much cause to complain of hard times, heavy taxes, and chargeable families. What maintains one vice would bring up two children. You may think perhaps that a little punch now and then, diet a little more costly, clothes a little finer, can be no great matter ; but remember many a little makes a mickle. Beware of little expenses ; a small leak will sink a great ship, as Poor Richard says. Who dainties love shall beggars prove ; and, moreover, fools make feasts and wise men eat them. Here you are all got together to this sale of fineries and nick-nacks. You call them goods, but if you do not take care they will prove evils to some of you. You expect they will be sold cheap, but if you have no occasion for them they must be dear to you. Remember that Poor Richard says, Buy what thou hast no need of, and ere long thou shalt sell thy necessaries. Many have been ruined by buying good pennyworths. Silks and satins, scarlet and velvets, put out the kitchen fire. By these and other extravagances the greatest are reduced to poverty and forced to borrow. When the well is dry they know the worth of water.

Again, Pride is as loud a beggar as Want, and a great deal more saucy. When you have bought one fine thing you must buy ten more, that your appearance may be all of a piece, but Poor Dick says, it is easier to suppress the first desire than to satisfy all that follow it. And it is as truly folly for the poor to ape the rich, as for the frog to swell in order to equal the ox. It is, however, a folly soon punished ; for, as Poor Richard says, Pride that dines on vanity sups on contempt ; Pride breakfasted with Plenty, dined with Poverty, and supped with Infamy. And after all, of what use is this pride of appearance, for which so much is risked, so much is suffered ? It cannot promote health, nor ease pain ; it makes no increase of merit in the person ; it creates envy, it hastens misfortune.

And now to conclude. Experience keeps a dear school, but fools will learn in no other. However, remember this : They that will not be counselled cannot be helped, and, further, that if you will not hear reason she will surely rap your knuckles, as Poor Richard says.

Thus the old gentleman ended his harangue. The people heard it and approved the doctrine, and immediately practised the contrary, just as if it had been a common sermon ; for the auction opened and they began to buy extravagantly. Though I had at first determined to buy stuff for a new coat, I went away, resolved to wear my old one a little longer. *Benjamin Franklin*

The Laws of the King of Babylon

Written on a stone about eight feet high are the laws of King Hammurabi, King of Babylon, 4000 years ago. They are engraved in 3614 lines which have been translated for us by Mr C. H. W. Johns. It is one of the remarkable documents of human history, and these are some of its decrees.

IF a man weave a spell upon a man and has not justified himself, he shall be put to death.

If a man has uttered threats against witnesses in a capital suit, that man shall be put to death ; if he has offered money to witnesses he shall himself bear the sentence.

If a judge has judged a judgment and afterwards altered it, he shall be expelled from his judgment seat.

If a man has carried on brigandage he shall be put to death ; if the brigand has not been caught the city and governor in whose land the brigandage took place shall render back what was lost.

If a man's house is on fire and a man coming to extinguish it should take the property of the owner, that man shall be thrown into that fire.

If a constable on an errand of the king goes not or sends one in place of himself, he shall be put to death.

If one should leave his field or his garden or his house to waste, and they should be taken by another for three years, they shall not be given back to him who returns.

If a man has taken a field to cultivate and has not caused the corn to grow, he shall be put to account and compelled to give corn like its neighbour.

If a man has neglected to strengthen his bank of the canal and the waters have carried away the meadow, the man who neglected the bank shall render back the corn which is lost.

If a man has lost nothing but says he has lost something, he shall be compelled to give whatever he has claimed.

If a woman hates her husband and says " Thou shalt not possess me " the matter shall be enquired into, and if she has been economical and has no vice she shall take her marriage portion and go to her father's house. If she has not been economical and has wasted her house, has gone about, and belittled her husband, she shall be drowned.

If a man should strike his father, his hands shall be cut off ; if he causes the loss of a gentleman's eye, he himself shall lose an eye. If he shatters a gentleman's limb, he himself shall lose a limb ; if he shatters a poor man's limb, he shall pay a mina of silver. If a man makes the tooth of a man who is his equal to fall out, he himself shall lose a tooth. If he makes the tooth of a poor man to fall out, he shall pay in silver.

If a man has struck the strength of a man who is great above him, he shall be struck in the assembly with sixty strokes of a cow-hide whip.

If a builder has built a house which falls and causes the death of its owner, the builder shall be put to death. If it causes the death of the owner's son the builder's son shall die.

If a man has refloated a ship which was aground, he shall receive half its value.

If a wild bull has gored a man and caused him to die, that case has no remedy.

Nebuchadnezzar Calling

On two barrel cylinders in the British Museum is an impressive statement by Nebuchadnezzar of the things he did. These few words are taken from them.

NEBUCHADNEZZAR, the exalted prince, the supreme lord, the beloved lord, the beloved of the god Nebo, the unwearied prince of the gate, the restorer of the temples, the messenger of the great gods, the King of Babylon am I.

I caused to be completed the great fortresses, upon the threshold of its gates mighty lords and poisonous snakes I set up, the which never had any king made. The paths of the ancient quays I built up with bitumen and brick. The quay which my father had worked at I excavated. I caused its foundations to be laid and raised up its summit like a mountain.

The palace of heaven and earth, the seat of tranquillity, the temple of the gods, the dwelling-place of the divine king of heaven and earth, I caused them to be covered with shining gold and I made them brilliant as the day.

The temple, the foundation of heaven and earth, the tower of Babel I built anew. The temple beloved of Nebo with gold and sculptured stones I made like the brilliance of heaven.

An account of my magnificent works and of my restorations of the temples of the great gods I wrote, and I set it up for future days.

O God, the king of Marad, lord of all warriors, sweep away the disobedient, smash their weapons, devastate the lands of the enemies, sweep them all away. In the presence of Marduk, king of heaven and earth, upon my works pronounce blessing, command my prosperity.

King Alfred Dreams of a New Day for Old England

Is there not something curiously interesting today in this remarkable letter from King Alfred, addressed to one of his bishops over a thousand years ago?

KING ALFRED bids greet Bishop Waerferth with his words lovingly and with friendship.

I let it be known to thee that it has very often come into my mind what wise men there formerly were throughout England, both church and lay folk, and how happy times there were then throughout England, and how the kings who had power over the nation in those days obeyed God and His ministers, and preserved peace, morality, and order at home, and at the same time enlarged their territory abroad, and prospered both in war and in wisdom ; and how zealous were God's ministers in teaching and in learning, and in all the services they owed Him ; and how men came from oversea in search of instruction, which we should now have to get from thence if we would have them.

So far has it fallen in England that few there are on this side Humber who understand the English of their service or can translate a letter from Latin, nor are there many, I know, beyond Humber more learned. There were so few of them that I cannot remember one south of Thames when I first began to reign. God be thanked that we have any teachers among us now.

Therefore I command thee, as I believe thou wouldst, to free thyself from worldly matters and apply the wisdom which God had given thee as thou art able. Consider what punishment shall fall upon us for the sake of this world if we have neither loved wisdom ourselves nor suffered other men to obtain it, if we have loved the name of Christian only, and very few of us its duties. When I considered all this I remembered I had seen, before the land had been ravaged and burnt, how its churches stood filled with treasures and books, and with a multitude of His servants, but they had very little knowledge of the books, and could not understand them, for they were not written in their own language.

Therefore it seems well to me, if ye think so, for us also to translate the books most needful for all men to know into the speech which all men know, and (as we are well able if we have peace) to make all the youth in England of free men rich enough to devote themselves to it, to learn while they are unfit for other occupation till they are well able to read English writing ; and let those be afterwards taught Latin who are to continue learning and be promoted to higher rank.

When I remembered how Latin-learning had decayed in England, and yet many could read English, I began during the various and manifold troubles of this realm to translate into English the book which is called in Latin Cura Pastoralis, and in English Shepherd's Book, sometimes word for word, and sometimes according to the sense, as I had learned it from Plegmund my archbishop, and Asser, my bishop, and Grimbold and John my mass-priests.

When I had learned it as I could best understand and most clearly interpret it, I translated it into English ; and I will send a copy to every bishopric in my kingdom ; and on each there is a clasp worth 50 marcus. I command in God's name that no man take the clasp from the book or the book from the minster.   *Alfred*

The King of Great Sorrow

IN the year 878 the army of the pagans drove many by force and poverty and fear to sail over the sea, and they subdued almost all the dwellers in that region under their sway.

In those days King Alfred, with a few of his nobles and with some soldiers and vassals, passed his life in great sorrow and unrest amid the woods and marshes of the land of Somerset ; nor had he anything wherewith to support life, save that which by constant raids he might take from the pagans, or from Christians who had submitted to the pagan yoke.   *From Asser's Life of Alfred*

Amid the Troubles of This World

I BESOUGHT my trusty friends that out of God's books of the lives and miracles of the saints they would set down for me the instruction which follows, so that, strengthened in my mind through memory and love, I may, amid the troubles of this world, sometimes think of the things of heaven.   *Alfred's preface to one of his books*

Alfred and His Memory

I HAVE sought to live worthily, and after my life to leave to them that come after me a remembering of me in good works.   *Alfred*

The King Makes Himself Known to His Son

Now for the story of Richard Plantagenet. In the year 1720 I waited on Lord Heneage, Earl of Winchelsea, at Eastwell House, and found him sitting with the register of the parish of Eastwell open before him. He told me he had been looking there to see who of his own family were mentioned in it. But, says he, I have a curiosity here to show you, and then showed me, and I immediately transcribed it into my almanac :

Richard Plantagenet was buried the 22d day of December, anno ut supra. Ex Registro de Eastwell, sub anno 1550.

This is all the registers mention of him. The story my lord told me was this.

When Sir Thomas Moyle built Eastwell Place he observed his chief bricklayer, whenever he left off work, retired with a book. Sir

Thomas had curiosity to know what book the man read, and, looking into it, found it to be Latin. Hereupon he examined him, and finding he pretty well understood that language, inquired how he came by his learning. Thereupon the man told him, as he had been a good master to him, that he was boarded with a Latin schoolmaster, without knowing who his parents were, till he was fifteen or sixteen ; a gentleman came once a quarter and paid for his board, and took care to see that he wanted nothing. One day this gentleman took him to a fine great house, where he passed through several stately rooms, in one of which he left him, bidding him stay there.

Then a man, finely dressed, with a star and garter, came to him, asked him some questions, talked kindly to him, and gave him some money.

Some time after the gentleman came to him again and told him he must take a journey into the country. They went into Leicestershire and came to Bosworth Field ; and he was carried to King Richard's tent. The king embraced him and told him he was his son. " But, child," says he, " tomorrow I must fight for my crown. And, assure yourself, if I lose that, I will lose my life too : but I hope to preserve both. Do you stand in such a place (directing him to a particular place) where you may see the battle, out of danger, and when I have gained the victory, come to me ; I will then own you to be mine, and take care of you. But if I should be so unfortunate as to lose the battle, then shift as well as you can, and take care to let nobody know that I am your father ; for no mercy will be shown to any one so nearly related to me." Then the king gave him a purse of gold, and dismissed him.

He followed the king's directions ; and when he saw the battle was lost, and the king killed, he hasted to London, sold his horse and fine clothes, and, the better to conceal himself from all suspicion of being son to a king, and that he might have means to live by his honest labour, put himself apprentice to a bricklayer. But, having a competent skill in the Latin tongue, he was unwilling to lose it ; and having an inclination also to reading, and no delight in the conversation of those he was obliged to work with, he generally spent all the time he had in reading by himself.

Sir Thomas said, " You are now old, and almost past your labour ; I will give you the running of my kitchen as long as you live." He answered, " Sir, you have a numerous family ; I have been used to live retired ; give me leave to build a house of one room for myself, in such a field, and there, with your good leave, I will live and die." Sir Thomas granted his request ; he built his house, and there continued to his death.

From a Letter written in 1733 by Dr Thomas Brett to Dr William Warren and published in Peck's Desiderata Curiosa

No Name in History Like This

ALFRED is the most perfect character in history. A saint without superstition, a scholar without ostentation, a warrior all whose wars were fought in the defence of his country, a conqueror whose laurels were never stained by cruelty, a prince never cast down by adversity, never lifted up to insolence in the day of triumph, there is no other name in history to compare with his. *Professor Freeman*

The Fame of Francis Drake

THE stars above would make thee known
    If men here silent were :
The sun himself cannot forget
    His fellow voyager.   *Ben Jonson*

Queen Elizabeth Passes By

We take this little-known picture of Elizabeth from a description by a visitor to her Court. He was Paul Hentzner, who was tutor to a young German nobleman and brought his pupil to England in 1598. This is one of the things he wrote.

WE arrived at the royal palace of Greenwich. It was here Elizabeth, the Queen, was born, and here she resides.

We were admitted into the Presence Chamber, hung with rich tapestry, and the floor after the English fashion, strewed with hay. At the door stood a gentleman dressed in velvet.

It was Sunday, when there is usually the greatest attendance of nobility. In the same hall were the Archbishop of Canterbury, the Bishop of London, a great number of Counsellors of State, Officers of the Crown, and Gentlemen, who waited the Queen's coming out ; which she did from her own apartment, when it was time to go to prayers. First went Gentlemen, Barons, Earls, Knights of the Garter, all richly dressed and bareheaded. Next came the Chancellor, bearing the seals in a red-silk purse, between two, one of which carried the Royal Sceptre, the other the Sword of State, in a red scabbard, studded with golden Fleur-de-Lys.

Next came the Queen, in the sixty-fifth year of her age, as we are told, very majestic ; her face oblong, fair, but wrinkled ; her eyes small, yet black and pleasant ; her nose a little hooked ; her lips narrow ; and her teeth black.

She had in her ears two pearls, with very rich drops ; she wore false hair, and that red ; upon her head she had a small crown, reported to be made of some of the gold of the celebrated Lunebourg Table. Her bosom was uncovered, as all the English ladies have it till they marry ; and she had on a necklace of exceeding fine jewels. Her hands were small, her fingers long, and her stature neither tall nor low. Her air was stately, her manner of speaking mild and obliging.

As she went along in all this state and magnificence she spoke very graciously, first to one, then to another, whether foreign ministers or those who attended for different reasons, in English, French, and Italian.

Whoever speaks to her, it is kneeling ; now and then she raises some with her hand. While we were there, W. Slawata, a Bohemian baron, had letters to present to her ; and she, after pulling off her glove, gave him her right hand to kiss, sparkling with rings and jewels, a mark of particular favour. Wherever she turned her face everybody fell on their knees.

The ladies of the court followed next to her, very handsome and well-shaped, and for the most part dressed in white. She was guarded on each side by the Gentlemen Pensioners, fifty in number, with gilt battle-axes. In the ante-chapel petitions were presented to her, and she received them most graciously, which occasioned the acclamation of *Long live Queen Elizabeth*! She answered it with, *I thank you, my good People*.

In the chapel was excellent music ; as soon as it and the service was over, which scarce exceeded half an hour, the Queen returned in the same state and order and prepared to go to dinner. But while she was still at prayers we saw her table set out with the following solemnity.

A Gentleman entered the room bearing a rod, and along with him another who had a table-cloth, which, after they had both kneeled three times with the utmost veneration, he spread upon the table, and after kneeling again they both retired. Then came two others, one with the rod again, the other with a salt-cellar, a plate, and bread. When they had kneeled and placed what was brought upon the table, they too retired with the same ceremonies performed by the first. At last came an unmarried lady, dressed in white silk, who, when she had prostrated herself three times in the most graceful manner, approached the table and rubbed the plates with bread and salt, with as much awe as if the Queen had been present.

When they had waited there a little while the Yeomen of the Guard entered, bare-headed, clothed in scarlet, with a golden rose upon their backs, bringing in at each turn a course of 24 dishes, served in plate most of it gilt. These dishes were received by a gentleman in the same order they were brought, and placed upon the table, while the lady-taster gave to each of the Guard a mouthful to eat of the particular dish he had brought, for fear of any poison. During the time that this Guard were bringing dinner, twelve trumpets and two kettle-drums made the hall ring for half an hour together.

At the end of this ceremonial a number of unmarried ladies appeared, who, with particular solemnity, lifted the meat off the table and conveyed it into the Queen's inner chamber.

The Shadows Close About the Queen

THE triumph of Mountjoy flung its lustre over the last days of Elizabeth, but no outer triumph could break the gloom which gathered round the dying queen. Lonely as she had always been, her loneliness deepened as she drew towards the grave.

The statesmen and warriors of her earlier days had dropped one by one from her Council-board ; and their successors were watching her last moments, and intriguing for favour in the coming reign. Her favourite, Lord Essex, was led into an insane outbreak of revolt which brought him to the block. The old splendour of her court waned and disappeared.

As she passed along in her progresses the people whose applause she courted remained cold and silent. The temper of the age, in fact, was changing, and isolating her as it changed. Her own England, the England which had grown up around her, serious, moral, prosaic, shrank coldly from this brilliant, fanciful, unscrupulous child of earth and the Renascence. She had enjoyed life as the men of her day enjoyed it, and now that they were gone she clung to it with a fierce tenacity.

She hunted, she danced, she jested with her young favourites, she coquetted and scolded and frolicked at sixty-seven as she had done at thirty. "The Queen," wrote a courtier a few months before her death, "was never so gallant these many years, nor so set upon jollity." She persisted in her gorgeous progresses from country-house to country-house. She clung to business as of old.

But death crept on. Her face became haggard, and her frame shrank almost to a skeleton. At last her taste for finery disappeared, and she refused to change her dresses for a week together. A strange melancholy settled down on her : " she held in her hand," says one who saw her in her last days, " a golden cup, which she often put to her lips : but in truth her heart seemed too full to need more filling." Gradually her mind gave way. She lost her memory, the violence of her temper became unbearable, her very courage seemed to forsake her. She called for a sword to lie constantly beside her, and thrust it from time to time through the arras, as if she heard murderers stirring there. Food and rest became alike distasteful. She sate day and night propped up with pillows on a stool, her finger on her lip, her eyes fixed on the floor, without a word. If she once broke the silence it was with a flash of her old queenliness. When Robert Cecil asserted that she must go to bed, the word roused her like a trumpet. " Must ! " she exclaimed ; " is Must a word to be addressed to princes ? Little man, little man, thy father, if he had been alive, durst not have used that word."

Then as her anger spent itself, she sank into her old dejection. " Thou art so presumptuous," she said, " because thou knowest I shall die." She rallied once more when the ministers beside her bed named Lord Beauchamp, the heir to the Suffolk claim, as a possible successor. " I will have no rogue's son," she cried hoarsely, " in my seat." But she gave no sign, save a motion of the head, at the mention of the King of Scots. She was in fact fast becoming insensible ; and early the next morning the life of Elizabeth, a life so great, so strange and lonely in its greatness, passed quietly away.

John Richard Green in his Short History

The Schoolmaster to the Young Gentlemen of England

IT is your shame (I speak to you all, you young gentlemen of England) that one maid should go beyond you all in excellency of learning and knowledge of divers tongues. Point forth six of the best given gentlemen of this court and all they together show not as much goodwill, spend not so much time, bestow not so many hours (daily, orderly, and constantly) for the increase of learning and knowledge as doth the Queen's Majesty herself.

Yea, I believe that, beside her perfect readiness in Latin, Italian, French, and Spanish, she readeth here now at Windsor more Greek every day than some Prebendary of this church doth read Latin in a whole week.

Among all the benefits God hath blessed me with, next the knowledge of Christ's true religion I count this the greatest—that it pleased God to call me, one poor minister, in setting forward these excellent gifts of learning in this most excellent prince, whose example, if the rest of our nobility would follow, then might England be in learning and wisdom a spectacle to all the world.

Roger Ascham on Queen Elizabeth

Carry No Tales

CARRY no tales, be no common teller of news, be not inquisitive of other men's talk, for those that are desirous to hear what they need not, commonly be ready to babble what they should not.

Roger Ascham

Martin Luther Can Do No Other

IT was not the thought that he would be condemned and led to the stake that shook the Reformer on the morning of his second appearance before the Imperial Diet. It was something more terrible than to die. The crisis had come and he felt unable to meet it. Let us draw near :

O God, my God, hearest thou my need ? I am ready to lay down my life for thy truth. I will never separate myself from thee, though the world should be filled with devils, though my body should be slain, should be racked on the wheel.

It is one of those solemn points in history where the seen touches the unseen, where earth and heaven meet.

Luther rises from his knees, and in the calm reigning in his soul feels that he has received an answer to his prayer.

At four of the clock the grand marshal and the herald presented themselves. Through crowded streets was the Reformer conducted to the town hall. When Luther should be admitted no one could say. One hour passed, and then another ; the Reformer was still standing amid the hum and clamour of the multitude. But his tranquillity did not forsake him. He was in a sanctuary apart.

The night began to fall ; torches were kindled in the hall. At last the door opened and Luther entered. He stood before the Emperor with an air of dignity, and looked on the assembly of princes with a calm, steadfast eye.

The Chancellor rose and demanded his answer. The fate of ages hangs upon it. The Emperor leans forward, the princes sit motionless, the guards are still, all eager to catch the first words of the monk.

He salutes the Emperor, the princes, and the lords. Of the volumes on the table, the authorship of which he acknowledged, there were three sorts, he said. There was one class in which he expounded with simplicity and plainness the first principles of faith and morals. In the second class he had waged war against the Papacy, the errors in doctrine, the scandals in life, and the tyrannies in government, by which it had fettered and entangled the conscience, blinded the reason, and depraved the morals of men. There was a third class of his writings in which he had attacked those who defended the errors which corrupted the faith, the scandals which disgraced the priesthood, and the exactions which robbed the people and ground them into dust.

He could not retract it, but if he had spoken evil let them bear witness of it. He was but dust and ashes, liable to err, and therefore it well became him to invite all men to examine what he had written. Let him but be convinced that he was in error and he would throw his books into the flames.

He warned this assembly of monarchs of a judgment to come, a judgment not from the grave only but on this side of it. They were on their trial. They, their kingdoms, their crowns, their dynasties stood at a great bar. It was to them the day of visitation ; it was now to be determined whether they were to be planted in the earth, whether their thrones should be stable, or whether they should be swept away in a deluge of wrath and eternal desolation.

Luther sat down and rested, and he then rose once more and repeated in Latin what he had said in German. The princes found

COUNTESS OF PEMBROKE, BY GHEERAEDTS

HAMO THORNYCROFT'S CROMWELL

that a change came over the scene.   Luther no longer stood at their bar ;   they had suddenly to stand at his.

The Chancellor rose and with a fretted air said to Luther, " You have not yet answered the question put to you.   We demand a direct and precise answer.   Will you or will you not retract ? "

Luther stood unmoved, and this is what he said :

I cannot submit my faith either to the Pope or to the Councils, because they have frequently erred and contradicted one another.   Unless I am convinced by scripture, or on plain and clear grounds of reason, I cannot and will not retract, for it is neither safe nor wise to do anything contrary to conscience.   Here I stand.   I can do no other.   God help me.
                                        A History of Protestantism

Cromwell Comes

IT was about the noon of a glorious day of June
    That we saw their banners dance and their cuirasses shine,
And the man of blood was there, with his long essenced hair,
    And Astley, and Sir Marmaduke, and Rupert of the Rhine.

Like a servant of the Lord, with his Bible and his sword,
    The General rode along us to form us for the fight ;
When a murmuring sound broke out, and swelled into a shout,
    Among the godless horsemen upon the tyrant's right.

And hark ! like the roar of the billows on the shore,
    The cry of battle rises along their charging line :
For God !   For the cause !   For the Church !   For the laws !
    For Charles, King of England, and Rupert of the Rhine !

The furious German comes, with his clarions and his drums,
    His bravoes of Alsatia and pages of Whitehall :
They are bursting on our flanks ! Grasp your pikes ! Close your
    ranks !
    For Rupert never comes but to conquer or to fall.

They are here ; they rush on ; we are broken ; we are gone ;
    Our left is borne before them like stubble on the blast.
O Lord, put forth Thy might !   O Lord, defend the right !
    Stand back to back in God's name, and fight it to the last !

Stout Skippen hath a wound, the centre hath given ground.
    Hark !   Hark !   What means the trampling of horsemen on our
    rear ?
Whose banner do I see, boys ? Tis he ! Thank God ! tis he, boys
    Bear up another minute !   Brave Oliver is here !

Their heads all stooping low, their points all in a row,
    Like a whirlwind on the trees, like a deluge on the dikes,
Our cuirassiers have burst on the ranks of the accurst,
    And at a shock have scattered the forest of his pikes.
                                        Macaulay

F.T.—15

John Wycliffe Waits for the End

COURTENAY, Bishop of London, summoned Wycliffe before him. Forty years ago the reformer had come up to the university: Oxford had become his home, and now it was turning against him. Weakened by labours, by trials, by that ardent soul which preyed upon his feeble body, he might have refused to appear. But Wycliffe, who never feared the face of man, came before them with a good conscience.

We may conjecture that there were among the crowd some disciples who felt their hearts burn at the sight of their master; but no outward sign indicated their emotion. The solemn silence of a court of justice had succeeded the shouts of enthusiastic youths.

Yet Wycliffe did not despair; he raised his venerable head, and turned to Courtenay with that confident look which had made the regents of Oxford shrink away. Growing wrath against the priests of Baal, he reproached them with disseminating error in order to sell their masses. Then he stopped and uttered these simple and energetic words, " The truth shall prevail." Having thus spoken, he prepared to leave the court : his enemies dared not say a word ; and, like his divine Master at Nazareth, he passed through the midst of them and no man ventured to stop him. He then withdrew to Lutterworth.

Living peacefully among his books and his parishioners, Wycliffe looked upon his end as near and entertained no idea that it would come in peace. A dungeon on one of the Seven Hills, or a burning pile in London, was all he expected. " Let the blow fall; I await its coming."

The stroke was spared him. Wycliffe therefore continued tranquilly to preach Jesus Christ; and on the 29th of December, 1384, as he was in his church at Lutterworth, in the midst of his flock, at the very moment that he stood before the altar and was elevating the host with trembling hands, he fell upon the pavement struck with paralysis. He was carried to his house by the affectionate friends around him, and after lingering forty-eight hours resigned his soul to God on the last day of the year.

Thus was removed from the church one of the boldest witnesses to the truth. The seriousness of his language, the holiness of his life, and the energy of his faith had intimidated the popedom. Travellers relate that if a lion is met in a desert it is sufficient to look steadily at him, and the beast turns away roaring from the eye of man. Wycliffe had fixed the eye of a Christian on the Papacy, and the affrighted Papacy had left him in peace. Hunted down unceasingly while living, he died in quiet. The Reformation in England had begun.   *J. H. Merle D'Aubigné*

The Prayer of Columbus

A BATTERED, wrecked old man,
Thrown on this savage shore, far, far from home,
Pent by the sea, and dark rebellious brows, twelve dreary months
Sore, stiff with many toils, sickened, and nigh to death,
I take my way along the island's edge,
Venting a heavy heart.

I am too full of woe !
Haply I may not live another day ;
I cannot rest, O God, I cannot eat or drink or sleep,
Till I put forth myself, my prayer, once more to Thee.

All my emprises have been filled with Thee !
My speculations, plans, begun and carried on in thoughts of Thee
Sailing the deep or journeying the land for Thee.
Oh I am sure they really come from Thee !
The urge, the ardour, the unconquerable will,
These sped me on.
The end I know not, it is all in Thee.

One effort more, my altar this bleak sand ;
That Thou, O God, my life hast lighted,
With ray of light, steady, ineffable, vouchsafed of Thee,
For that, O God—be it my latest word, here on my knees,
Old, poor, and paralysed—I thank Thee.

My terminus near,
The clouds already closing in upon me,
The voyage baulked, the course disputed, lost,
I yield my ships to Thee.

Steersman unseen ! henceforth the helms are Thine ;
Take Thou command.
My hands, my limbs, grow nerveless ;
My brain feels racked, bewildered ;
Let the old timbers part—I will not part,
I will cling fast to Thee, O God, though the waves buffet me ;
Thee, Thee, at least I know.

What do I know of life ?   What of myself ?
I know not even my own work ;
Dim, ever-shifting guesses of it spread before me,
Of newer, better worlds.

And these things I see suddenly—what mean they ?
As if some miracle, some hand divine, unsealed mine eyes,
Shadowy vast shapes smile through the air and sky,
And on the distant waves sail countless ships,
And anthems in new tongues I hear saluting me.

Walt Whitman

The Beggar Man and His Little Son

IN the springtime of the year 1471, and at noon of day, under a burning sun which turned to ashes the roads of Andalusia, upon a hill about half a league from the small seaport of Palos, two strangers fared afoot, their shoes worn with walking, their clothes (in which might be detected the remains of a certain costliness) sullied with dust, paused to seat themselves in the shadows of the gateway of a small monastery, called Santa Maria de Rabida.

One of them was a man who had scarcely reached the middle of life, of tall stature, robust in figure, majestic in his bearing, with a noble brow, an open countenance, a pensive gaze, and mild and gracious lips. His hair, of a blond lightly tinted with brown in his early youth, was prematurely marked at the temples by those grey shadows which misfortune and mental labour hasten. His forehead was lofty ; his complexion was paled by thought and bronzed by sun and sea. The tones of his voice were manly, sonorous, and penetrating, like the accents of a man accustomed to give utterance to profound ideas.

The other was a child of eight to ten. His features, more feminine but already matured by the fatigues of his life, had so lively a resemblance to those of the first stranger that it was impossible not to recognise in him either his son or brother.

These two strangers were Christopher Columbus and his son Diego. The monks, touched by the noble aspect of the father and the gracefulness of the child, invited them to enter and offered them shelter. While Columbus and his child refreshed themselves with water, bread, and olives at the table of their hosts, the monks informed their prior of the arrival of the two strangers, and the strange interest attaching to their distinguished appearance in opposition to their poverty. The prior descended to converse with them.

This head of the convent of Rabida was Juan Peres de Marchenra, former confessor of Queen Isabella, who with Ferdinand then ruled over Spain. A man of sanctity, science, and erudition, he had preferred the shelter of his cloister to the honours and intrigues of the court ; but his very retreat had preserved for him a great reputation in the palace, and a powerful influence over the mind of the Queen.

The prior saluted the stranger, embraced the child, and gently made himself acquainted with the circumstances which had forced them to travel on foot the most unfrequented routes of Spain and borrow the shelter of the humble roof of a poor and solitary monastery. Columbus told the story of his obscure life, and laid bare to the attentive monk his grand conceptions. The prior, affected at first with compassion, was soon afterwards stirred into enthusiasm. He saw in him one of those messengers of God who are repulsed from the threshold of princes, whither they bear in the hands of want the invisible treasures of truth.   *Alphonse Louis de Lamartine*

Columbus Dying

COLUMBUS perceived that life was about to fail him. He called to one of his servants, the last companion of his wanderings, of his glory and his misery, to bring to his bedside a little breviary, the gift of Pope Alexander at a time when sovereigns treated him as a sovereign. He wrote his will on a page of this book, to which he attributed a virtue of divine consecration.

Strange spectacle for his poor servant! This old man, forsaken by the world, and stretched upon a pauper's bed in a hired house of Segovia, gave away in his will seas, hemispheres, islands, continents, nations, empires!

" I pray my sovereigns and their successors," said he, " to observe for ever my wishes in the distribution of my rights, my wealth, and my offices. I who, born at Genoa, came to serve them in Castile, and who discovered in the West the mainland, the islands, and the Indies! My son shall possess my dignity of Admiral of that part of the ocean which lies to the west of a line drawn from one pole to the other." Passing from this point to the distribution of the revenues which had been secured him by his treaty with Isabella and Ferdinand, the old man divided, with liberality and wisdom, the millions which ought to return to his family among his sons and Bartholomew his brother.

He had a thought for that city of Genoa where time had garnered up his paternal house, but where still remained a far-off kinsman, like the roots which live in the earth after the tree has been felled. " I command my son, Diego," he wrote, " to support for ever in the city of Genoa a member of our family, who shall reside there with his wife and to assure him an honourable livelihood, as shall become a person who is allied to us. I wish this kinsman to preserve his footing and nationality in that city, in the quality of a citizen ; for it is there that I was born, and it is from thence that I have come."

Columbus, this duty done, surrendered all his thoughts to that God whom he had always considered as a single and veritable Sovereign, as if he was lifted up directly by that Providence of which he felt himself to be the peculiar instrument and minister. Resignation and enthusiasm, the two supports of his life, did not fail him in his death. He humbled himself under the hand of nature and rose again under that of God, which he had always beheld in his triumphs and reverses, and which he saw more closely at the moment of his departure from earth.

He was wholly lost in penitence for his errors and hope of his two-fold immortality. A poet at heart, as we see him in his compositions, he yielded to the sacred poetry of the Psalms the last aspirations of his soul and the last faint utterances of his lips. He pronounced in Latin his farewell of the world, and with a loud voice returned his soul into the hands of his Creator—a servant satisfied with his work, and released from the visible world whose boundaries he had enlarged, to enter the world unseen, and conquer the immeasurable space of the boundless universe.

All the qualities of the truly great man were combined in Columbus : genius, work, patience ; obscurity of condition vanquished by strength of nature ; steadfastness, gentle but inflexible to the end ; resignation to the will of Heaven, wrestling with the world, long-brooding thought in solitude, heroic execution of thought in action, intrepidity and coolness against the elements in tempests and against death in rebellions, confidence in the star—not of man, but of humanity ; life hazarded with temerity and without looking behind him, in casting himself into that unknown and phantom-crowded ocean, a Rubicon of 1500 leagues, far more irrepassable than that of Caesar ! A fitness, nobility, and dignity of outward form which revealed the greatness of his soul and enchained the eyes and minds of all ; language harmonising with the elevation of his thoughts ; an eloquence which convinced kings and subdued the seditious spirit of his crews ; an immense, ardent, and active love of humanity ; the wisdom of a legislator and the mildness of a philosopher in the administration of his colonies ; a paternal compassion for the Indians ; forgetfulness of injuries, majesty of pardon towards his enemies ; a constant presence of God in the mind, of justice in the conscience, of pity in the heart ; gratitude in success, resignation in suffering, adoration everywhere and always—such was Columbus.

We know of no man more perfect. He contained in his sole self several men. He was worthy of personifying the ancient world before that unknown world which he was the first to enter, and to bear to the men of another race all the virtues of the old continent without any of its vices. No one by the grandeur of his influence has better deserved the name of the Civiliser.

His influence on civilisation was without limit. He completed the universe ; he perfected the physical oneness of the globe. It was his to advance, far beyond what had been done before him, the work of God, the moral unity of the human race. The work in which Columbus thus co-operated was too grand to be recompensed by the imposition of his name on the fourth continent of the earth. America does not bear his name ; mankind, brought together and re-united through his labours, shall bear it over all the globe. *Alphonse de Lamartine*

Pursuing Fame

Once in the keen pursuit of fame
I, schoolboy-like, pursued a bubble ;
But death, before I gained a name,
Stepped in and saved a world of trouble.
By Sir Walter Scott's friend John Leyden

The Widow's Song

Sleep, little darling, sleep ;
God watch o'er thee.
Thou'rt all that's left i'th world
To comfort me. *Edwin Waugh*

Plant Daisies at His Feet

The son of Sussex peasants, Robert Realf emigrated to America and did mission-ary work in the slums of New York.

When the controversy over slavery broke out he started a paper and met John Brown, who proposed to make him Secretary-of-State in his Government! After Brown was captured Realf joined the Army, cheering many a camp-fire with his songs. Domestic troubles bowed him down, and he died tragically by his own hand in California. He left for posterity this picture of himself as he saw himself.

SAY naught but good of the dead, and when
For me this end has come and I am dead,
And the little voluble chattering daws of men
Peck at me curiously, let it then be said
By some one brave enough to speak the truth :
Here lies a great soul killed by cruel wrong.
Down all the balmy days of his fresh youth
To his bleak, desolate noon, with sword and song,
And speech that rushed up hotly from the heart,
He wrought for liberty, till his own wound
(He had been stabbed), concealed with painful art
Through wasting years, mastered him, and he swooned,
And sank there where you see him lying now
With the word *Failure* written on his brow.

But say that he succeeded.   If he missed
World's honours and world's plaudits, and the wage
Of the world's deft lacqueys, still his lips were kissed
Daily by those high angels who assuage
The thirstings of the poets (for he was
Born unto singing) and a burthen lay
Mightily on him, and he moaned because
He could not rightly utter to the day
What God taught in the night.   Sometimes, nathless,
Power fell upon him, and bright tongues of flame,
And blessings reached him from poor souls in stress ;
And benedictions from black pits of shame,
And little children's love, and old men's prayers,
And a Great Hand that led him unawares.

So he died rich.   And if his eyes were blurred
With big films—silence ! he is in his grave.
Greatly he suffered ; greatly, too, he erred ;
Yet broke his heart in trying to be brave,
He was a-weary, but he fought his fight,
And stood for simple manhood ; and was joyed
To see the august broadening of the light
And new Earths heaving heavenward from the void.
He loved his fellows, and their love was sweet ;
Plant daisies at his head and at his feet.

Overcome Evil With Good

LET love be without dissimulation. Abhor that which is evil; cleave to that which is good. Be kindly affectioned one to another, with brotherly love, in honour preferring one another; not slothful in business, fervent in spirit, serving the Lord; rejoicing in hope; patient in tribulation; continuing instant in prayer; distributing to the necessity of saints; given to hospitality.

Bless them which persecute you; bless, and curse not.

Rejoice with them that rejoice, and weep with them that weep.

Be of the same mind one toward another. Mind not high things, but condescend to men of low estate. Be not wise in your own conceits.

Recompense to no man evil for evil. Provide things honest in the sight of all men. If it be possible, live peaceably with all men.

Dearly beloved, avenge not yourselves, but rather give place unto wrath, for it is written, Vengeance is mine, I will repay, saith the Lord. Therefore if thine enemy hunger, feed him; if he thirst, give him drink, for in so doing thou shalt heap coals of fire on his head.

Be not overcome of evil, but overcome evil with good.

Let every soul be subject to the higher powers, for there is no power but of God; the powers that be are ordained of God. Whosoever therefore resisteth the power resisteth God.

Render to all their dues; tribute to whom tribute is due; custom to whom custom; fear to whom fear; honour to whom honour.

Owe no man anything, but to love one another, for he that loveth another hath fulfilled the law. Love worketh no ill to his neighbour; therefore love is the fulfilling of the law.   *St Paul to the Romans*

Plato, Thou Reasonest Well

IT must be so—Plato, thou reason'st well,
    Else whence this pleasing hope, this fond desire,
This longing after immortality?
Or whence this secret dread and inward horror
Of falling into nought? Why shrinks the soul
Back on herself and startles at destruction?
Tis the Divinity that stirs within us,
Tis Heaven itself that points out an Hereafter,
And intimates Eternity to man.
Eternity!—thou pleasing-dreadful thought!
Through what variety of untried being,
Through what new scenes and changes must we pass!
The wide, the unbounded prospect lies before me;
But shadows, clouds, and darkness rest upon it.
Here will I hold: If there's a Power above us
(And that there is, all Nature cries aloud
Through all her works), he must delight in Virtue;
And that which he delights in must be happy:

But when ?—or where ?—*This* world was made for Caesar.
I'm weary of conjectures : this must end them.
(Laying his hand on his sword)
Thus I am doubly armed ; my death and life,
My bane and antidote, are both before me.
This in a moment brings me to an end,
But this informs me I shall never die.
The soul, secured in her existence, smiles
At the drawn dagger and defies its point.
The stars shall fade away, the Sun himself
Grow dim with age, and Nature sink in years ;
But thou shalt flourish in immortal youth,
Unhurt amidst the war of elements,
The wrecks of matter, and the crush of worlds.   *Addison*

What Cromwell Saw in Ludgate Circus

IT is the year 1630, and Cromwell is still in his early manhood.
One bright morning, with St Paul's to his back, Cromwell entered
Ludgate Circus.   In the midst of the Circus stood a scaffold, and
around it was a great throng, crowding and pressing toward the place
of torture.   At the foot of the scaffold was a venerable scholar, his
white hair flowing upon his shoulders, a man of stainless character
and spotless life, renowned for his devotion, eloquence and patriotism.
When the executioner led the aged pastor up the steps, the soldiers
tore off his garments.   He was whipped until blood ran in streams
down his back, both nostrils were slit and his ears cropped off, hot
irons were brought and two letters, " S-S "—sower of sedition—were
burned into his forehead.

What crime has this pastor committed ?   Perhaps he had lifted
a firebrand upon the King's palace ; perhaps he had organised some
foul gunpowder plot to overthrow the throne itself.   Perhaps he had
been guilty of treason, or some foul and nameless sin against the
State.   Not so.   The reading of the decision of the judge and the
decree of the punishment made clear the truth.   It seemed that a
fortnight before, the aged pastor had been commanded to give up his
extempore prayers and the singing of the Psalms, and has been commanded to read the written prayers and sing the hymns prescribed
by the State Church.   But the gentle scholar had disregarded the
command, and on the following Sunday, walked in the ways familiar
and dear to him by reason of long association.

He had dared to sing the same old Psalms and lift his heart to
God in extempore prayer, after the manner of his fathers.
Newell Dwight Hillis

We Are Not Always Free

IF it be my liberty to walk abroad in the fields it is not my wisdom
to do so when my house is on fire.
Cromwell, justifying a limitation of liberty

Cromwell's Last Prayer

In the tumult of the winds the dying Oliver was heard uttering
words like these, preserved for us by his faithful attendant.

LORD, though I am a miserable and wretched creature, I am in covenant with Thee through grace. And I may, I will, come to Thee, for Thy people. Thou hadst made me, though very unworthy a mean instrument to do them some good, and Thee service ; and many of them have set too high a value upon me, though others wish and would be glad of my death ; Lord, however Thou do dispose of me, continue and go on to do good for them. Give them consistency of judgment, one heart and mutual love ; and go on to deliver them, and with the work of reformation ; and make the Name of Christ glorious in the world. Teach those who look too much on Thy instruments, to depend more upon Thyself. Pardon such as desire to trample upon the dust of a poor worm, for they are Thy people too. And pardon the folly of this short prayer :—even for Jesus Christ's sake. And give us a good night, if it be Thy pleasure. Amen.

For two or three days life still flickered and to his wife and children weeping round his bed he said, Love not this world ; it is not good that you should love this world.

On September 3, the day of Worcester and Dunbar, he sighed deeply and passed to his inheritance.

From accounts of Cromwell's Death

Oliver Cromwell's Lamp Goes Out

IN the beginning of September the symptoms appeared upon him and, asking one of his physicians what he thought of his case, the doctor answered, My lord, there is no more oil in that lamp which has given so much light to both Church and State.

The dying Protector replied, with a magnanimity worthy of him, When do you think it will go out ? The physician told him in two days at the farthest, upon which Cromwell said, It is time, then, to settle my mind.   *From an old paper of the time*

BEFORE his plans could be realised the overtaxed strength of the Protector suddenly gave way. He saw too clearly the chaos into which his death would plunge England and was unwilling to die. " Do not think I shall die," he burst out with feverish energy to the physicians who gathered round him.

Prayer rose from every side for his recovery, but death grew steadily nearer till even Cromwell felt that his hour was coming. " I would be willing to live," the dying man murmured, " to be further serviceable to God and His people, but my work is done. Yet God will be with His people."

A storm which tore roofs from houses and levelled huge trees in every forest seemed a fitting prelude to the passing away of this mighty spirit.   *John Richard Green*

Something Has Been Gained

THEIR works follow them—as I think this Oliver Cromwell's works have done and are still doing. Somewhat has been gained for poor mankind. Men's ears are not now slit off; star chambers, branding irons, are gone.   *Carlyle*

On the Storm in which Cromwell Died

WE must resign ! Heaven his great soul does claim
      In storms as loud as his immortal fame ;
His dying groans, his last breath, shake our isle,
And trees uncut fall for his funeral pile.
                                              Edmund Waller

Charles Stuart's Advice to His Son

SON, if these papers come to your hands, they may be so far useful to you as to state your judgment aright in what hath passed ; and they may also give you some directions how to remedy the present distempers, and prevent the like for time to come.

I had rather you should be Charles le Bon than le Grand, Good than Great ; I hope God hath designed you to be both.

With God I would have you begin and end, who is King of Kings, the Sovereign Disposer of the kingdoms of the world, who pulleth down one and setteth up another. The best government and highest sovereignty you can attain to is to be subject to Him, that the sceptre of His word and spirit may rule in your heart.

The true glory of princes consists in advancing God's glory, in the maintenance of true religion and the Church's good ; also in the dispensation of civil power with justice and honour to the public peace.

Take heed of abetting any factions, or applying to any public discriminations in matters of religion, contrary to what is in your judgment and the Church well settled. Your partial adhering to any one side gains you not so great advantage in some men's hearts (who are prone to be of their King's religion) as it loseth you in others. Take such a course as may either with calmness and charity quite remove seeming differences and offences by impartiality ; or so order affairs that you shall not need to fear or flatter any faction. For if ever you stand in need of them, or must stand to their courtesies, you are undone : the serpent will devour the dove.

When you have done justice to God, your own soul, and His Church, in the profession and preservation both of truth and unity in religion, the next main hinge on which your prosperity will depend and move is that of civil justice, wherein the settled laws of these kingdoms, to which you are rightly heir, are the most excellent rules you can govern by—which, by an admirable temperament, give very much to subjects, industry, liberty, and happiness, and yet reserve enough to the majesty of any king who owns his people as subjects, not as slaves.

Never charge your head with such a crown as shall by its heaviness oppress the whole body.   Your prerogative is best shewed and exercised in remitting rather than exacting the rigour of the laws, there being nothing worse than legal tyranny.

Take heed that outward circumstances and formalities of religion devour not all or the best encouragements of learning, industry, and piety ; but with an equal eye and impartial hand distribute favours and rewards to all men, as you find them for their real goodness, both in abilities and fidelity, worthy and capable of them.   This will be sure to gain you the hearts of the best, and the most, too ; who, though they be not good themselves, yet are glad to see the severer ways of virtue sweetened by temporal rewards.

Time will dissipate all factions, when once the rough horns of men's covetous and ambitious designs shall discover themselves, which were at first wrapped up and hidden under the soft and smooth pretensions of religion, reformation, and liberty.   As the wolf is not less cruel, so he will be more justly hated, when he shall appear no better than a wolf under sheep's clothing.

But as for the train of the vulgar, who in their simplicity follow those disguises, my charge and counsel to you is that as you study really to exceed, in true and constant demonstrations of goodness, piety, and virtue, even all those men that make the greatest noise and ostentations of religion, so you shall neither fear any detection, nor shall you frustrate the just expectations of your people.

Let no passion betray you to any study of revenge upon those whose own sin and folly will punish them in due time.

It is all I have now left me, a power to forgive those that have deprived me of all ; and I thank God I have a heart to do it.

Be confident, as I am, that the most of all sides who have done amiss have done so not out of malice, but misinformation or misapprehension of things.

None will be more loyal and faithful to me and you than those subjects who, sensible of their errors and our injuries, will feel in their own souls most vehement motives to repentance, and earnest desires to make some reparations.   As your quality sets you beyond any duel with any subject, so the nobleness of your mind must raise you above the meditating any revenge.   You will have more inward complacency in pardoning one than in punishing a thousand.

If God shall see fit to restore me to those enjoyments the laws have assigned to us, and no subjects without a high degree of guilt and sin can divest us of, then may I have better opportunity, when I shall be so happy to see you in peace, to let you more fully understand the things that belong to God's glory, your own honour, and the kingdom's peace.

But if you never see my face again, and God will have me buried in such a barbarous imprisonment and obscurity wherein few hearts that love me are permitted to exchange a word or a look with me, I do require and entreat you, as your father and your King, that you never suffer your heart to receive the least check against or disaffection from the true religion.

Nor would I have you to entertain any dislike of parliaments; which in their right constitution, with freedom and honour, will never injure or diminish your greatness, but will rather be as interchangings of love, loyalty, and confidence between a prince and his people. Nothing can be more happy for all than in fair, grave, and honourable ways to contribute their counsels in common, enacting all things by public consent, without tyranny or tumults.

And, if neither I nor you be ever restored to our rights, I hope God will give me and you that grace which will teach and enable us to want as well as to wear a crown, which is not worth taking up or enjoying upon sordid, dishonourable, and irreligious terms. Keep you to true principles of piety, virtue, and honour, you shall never want a kingdom.

My prayer to God Almighty is (whatever becomes of me, who am, I thank God, wrapt up and fortified in my own innocency and His grace) that He would be pleased to make you an anchor, or harbour rather, to these tossed and weather-beaten kingdoms. When they have destroyed me (for I know not how far God may permit the malice and cruelty of my enemies to proceed, and such apprehensions some men's words and actions have already given me), as I doubt not but my blood will cry aloud for vengeance to Heaven, so I beseech God not to pour out His wrath upon the people who have either deserted me, or engaged against me, through the artifice and hypocrisy of their leaders, whose inward horror will be their first tormentor.

For those that loved me, I pray God they may have no miss of me when I am gone. For those that repent of any defects in their duty toward me, as I freely forgive them in the word of a Christian king, so I believe you will find them truly zealous to repay with interest that loyalty and love to you which was due to me. What good I intended, do you perform, when God shall give you power.

I pray God bless you, and establish your kingdoms in righteousness, your soul in true religion, and your honour in the love of God and your people.

John Brown Goes to His Reward

HE stepped out of gaol with a bright serene countenance, holding his head like a victorious hero going to his reward.   Close to the door stood a Negro woman with a child in her arms.

Good-bye, Captain, said his cell companion, I know you are going to a better land.

I know I am, said Brown.

As his eye fell on the soldiers he straightened himself up proudly. As they ascended a little eminence the scaffold broke upon his sight, but it did not cause him even a flutter of fear.   His eye roamed over the landscape tracing the dim outline of the Blue Ridge Mountains. " This is a beautiful country," he said.   At the foot of the scaffold he was assisted out of the waggon, and turning to the mayor and others, he said, " Gentlemen, good-bye," and walked with firm step and erect frame up the scaffold steps.

The sheriff asked, Shall I give you a handkerchief and let you drop it as a signal ? and he said No ; I am ready at any time, but do not keep me needlessly waiting.

Virginia refused this last request of John Brown, and for ten minutes he was kept while the military, among them John Wilkes Booth, the murderer of Lincoln, went through a series of aimless evolutions until the civilians began to cry Shame.

John Brown was buried at the foot of a rock about fifteen yards from his door.   " Blow ye the trumpet, blow," the hymn with which he lulled his little ones to sleep, was sung around his grave.   Then Wendell Phillips spoke :

How feeble words seem here !   How can I hope to utter what your hearts are full of !   I fear to disturb the harmony which his life breathes round this home.   One and another of you, his neighbours, say, " I have known him five years," " I have known him ten years." It seems to me as if we had none of us known him.   How our admiring, loving wonder has grown, day by day, as he has unfolded trait after trait of earnest, brave, and tender Christian life !   We see him walking with radiant, serene face to the scaffold, and think what an iron heart, what a devoted faith !   We take up his letters and this iron heart seems all tenderness.   Marvellous old man !   Your neighbour farmer went, surrounded by his household, to tell the slaves there were still hearts and right arms ready and nerved for their service.

He has abolished slavery in Virginia.   History will date Virginian Emancipation from Harper's Ferry.

True, the slave is still there.   So, when the tempest uproots a pine on our hills, it looks green for months, a year or two.   Still, it is timber, not a tree. Thus has John Brown loosened the roots of the slave system.

Surely such a life is no failure. How vast the change in men's hearts! Insurrection was a harsh, horrid word to millions a month ago. John Brown went a whole generation beyond it, claiming the right for white men to help the slave to freedom by arms. Harper's Ferry was no single hour, standing alone—taken out from a common life ; it was the flowering of fifty years of single-hearted devotion. He must have lived wholly for one great idea, when those who owe their being to him and those whom love has joined group so harmoniously around him, each accepting serenely his and her part. I feel honoured to stand under such a roof. Hereafter you will tell children standing at your knees, " I saw John Brown buried ; I sat under his roof."

God make us all worthier of him whose dust we lay among these hills he loved. Here he girded himself and went forth to battle. Fuller success than his heart ever dreamed God has granted him. He sleeps in the blessings of the crushed and the poor, and men believe more firmly in virtue now that such a man has lived.

Adapted from a Life of John Brown

Where Old John Brown is Laid

NOT any spot six feet by two
   Will hold a man like thee ;
John Brown will tramp the shaking earth
   From Blue Ridge to the sea,
Till the strong angel come at last
   And opes each dungeon door,
And God's Great Charter holds and waves
   O'er all his humble poor.

And then the humble poor will come
   In that far-distant day,
And from the felon's nameless grave
   They'll brush the leaves away ;
And grey old men will point the spot
   Beneath the pine-tree shade,
As children ask with streaming eyes
   Where Old John Brown is laid.

Written by Edmund Sears at the Memorial
Service at the grave of John Brown

What He Must Do

I AM not bound to win, but I am bound to be true. I am not bound to succeed, but I am bound to live up to what light I have. I must stand with anybody that stands right ; stand with him while he is right, and part with him when he goes wrong.

Abraham Lincoln

Abraham Lincoln Finds Himself Famous

In his struggling days as a lawyer Abraham Lincoln leaped into instant fame by a cross-examination which convicted a murderer. This is it.

LINCOLN : You were with the murdered man just before, and saw the shooting ?

Witness : Yes.

You stood near the two men ?

Yes.

Was it in the open field ?

No ; in the timber.

What kind of timber ?

Beech timber.

The leaves of beech are rather thick in autumn ?

Rather.

You could see the prisoner shoot ?

Yes.

How near did this happen to the meeting-place ?

Three-quarters of a mile away.

Where were the lights ?

Up by the minister's stand.

That was three-quarters of a mile away ?

I have already said so.

Was there a candle where the prisoner was standing ?

No. What would he want a candle for ?

Then how did you see the shooting ?

By moonlight.

You saw this shooting, at ten o'clock at night, in beech timber, three-quarters of a mile away from the lights ? Saw the man point the pistol and fire ? Saw it all by moonlight ?

Yes, I have already said so.

Then the young lawyer slowly drew from his pocket an almanac, and showed that on the night of the crime the moon was not visible.

His Monument a People Free

HIS grave a nation's heart shall be,
His monument a people free.
Caroline Atherton Mason on Lincoln

In Brief

THE world is my country : to do good is my religion.
Thomas Paine

ABRAHAM LINCOLN'S SHRINE IN WASHINGTON

SUNSET AT STONEHENGE

His Soul Goes Marching On

JOHN BROWN's body lies a-mould'ring in the grave,
  John Brown's body lies a-mould'ring in the grave,
  John Brown's body lies a-mould'ring in the grave,
    But his soul goes marching on.

He captured Harper's Ferry with his nineteen men so true,
And he frightened old Virginia till she trembled through
    and through,
They hung him for a traitor, themselves the traitor crew,
    But his soul goes marching on.

Fooling the People

YOU may fool some of the people all the time, you may fool all the
  people some of the time, but you never can fool all the people all
the time.   *Abraham Lincoln*

Abraham Lincoln Stands Alone

THE tragic events of the future were mercifully hidden. Mr
  Lincoln was planning yet another generous offer to shorten the
period of conflict. He remembered that the rebels, notwithstanding
all their offences and errors, were yet American citizens, members of
the same nation, brothers of the same blood. He remembered, too,
that the object of the war was the maintenance of one Government
and one Union. Not only must hostilities cease, but dissension,
suspicion, and estrangement be eradicated. Filled with such thoughts
and purposes, he designed a new proposal as a peace offering to the
States in rebellion, a liberal indemnity for the loss of State property
on absolute cessation of the war and the abolition of slavery by the
Southern States.

He called his Cabinet together and read to them the draft of a
proclamation offering the Southern States four hundred million
dollars, a sum equal to the cost of the war for 200 days.

This was indeed going to the extreme of magnanimity, and it
turned out that he was more humane and liberal than his constitutional advisers. The indorsement in his own handwriting on the
manuscript draft records the result of his appeal and suggestion :

*February 5, 1865. Today these papers, which explain themselves,
were drawn up and submitted to the Cabinet, and unanimously dis-
approved by them.—A. Lincoln.*

With the words, " You are all opposed to me, sadly uttered,
the President folded up the paper and ceased the discussion.
                                        Adapted from a Life of Lincoln

Sayings of Abraham Lincoln

Lincoln to a religious deputation urging immediate Emancipation

I AM approached with the most opposite opinions and advice by religious men who are equally certain that they represent the divine will. I am sure that either the one or the other class is mistaken in their belief. I hope it will not be irreverent for me to say that, if God would reveal His will to others on a point so connected with my duty, it might be supposed that He would reveal it directly to me. I can assure you that the subject is on my mind by day and night, more than any other. Whatever shall appear to be God's will I will do.

Lincoln to his Cabinet on September 2, 1862

WHEN the rebel army was at Frederick I determined, as soon as it should be driven out of Maryland, to issue a proclamation of Emancipation. I said nothing to anyone, but I made the promise to myself and (here he hesitated a little) to my Maker. The rebel army is now driven out and I am going to fulfil that promise.

I have got you together to hear what I have written down. I know very well that many others might do better than I can, and if I was satisfied that the public confidence was more fully possessed by any one of them, and knew of any constitutional way in which he could be put in my place, he should have it. But there is no way in which I can have any other man put where I am. I am here ; I must do the best I can, and bear the responsibility for the course I feel I ought to take.

Lincoln in a Speech to Congress

FELLOW citizens, we cannot escape history. We of this Congress and this Administration will be remembered in spite of ourselves. No personal significance or insignificance can spare one or another of us. The fiery trial through which we pass will light us down in honour or dishonour to the latest generation. We say we are for the Union. The world will not forget that we say this. We know how to save the Union. The world knows we do know how to save it. We—even we here, hold the power and bear the responsibility. In giving freedom to the slave we assure freedom to the free—honourable alike in what we give and what we preserve. We shall nobly save or meanly lose the last, best hope of Earth. Other means may succeed ; this could not fail. The way is plain, peaceful, generous, just ; a way which, if followed, the world will forever applaud and God must forever bless.

From the Emancipation Proclamation

. . . that on the first day of January in the year of Our Lord 1863 all persons held as slaves within any State shall be then, thenceforward, and for ever free . . . and upon this act, sincerely believed to be an act of Justice, warranted by the Constitution upon military necessity, I invoke the considerate judgment of mankind and the gracious favour of Almighty God.

There is no Name so Loved

THERE is no name in all our country's story
    So loved as his today :
No name which so unites the things of glory
    With life's plain common way.
Robert Whitaker on Abraham Lincoln

The Civil War Draws Near Its Close

ON the occasion corresponding to this four years ago all thoughts
    were anxiously directed to an impending Civil War. All dreaded
it ; all sought to avert it. Both parties deprecated war ; but one of
them would make war rather than let the nation survive ; and the
other would accept war rather than let it perish. And the war came.

Neither party expected for the war the magnitude or the duration
which it has already attained. Neither anticipated that the cause of
the conflict might cease with, or even before, the conflict itself should
cease. Each looked for an easier triumph, and a result less funda-
mental and astounding. Both read the same Bible and pray to the
same God ; and each invokes His aid against the other. It may
seem strange that any men should dare to ask a just God's assistance
in wringing their bread from the sweat of other men's faces ; but let
us judge not, that we be not judged. The prayers of both could not
be answered—that of neither has been answered fully.

The Almighty has His own purposes. " Woe unto the world
because of offences ! for it must needs be that offences come ; but
woe to that man by whom the offence cometh." If we shall suppose
that American slavery is one of those offences which, in the providence
of God, must needs come, but which, having continued through His
appointed time, He now wills to remove, and that He gives to both
North and South this terrible war, as the woe due to those by whom the
offence came, shall we discern therein any departure from those divine
attributes which the believers in a living God always ascribe to Him ?
Fondly do we hope, fervently do we pray, that this mighty
scourge of war may speedily pass away. Yet, if God wills that it
continue until all the wealth piled by the bondman's two hundred
and fifty years of unrequited toil shall be sunk, and until every drop
of blood drawn with the lash shall be paid by another drawn with the
sword—as was said three thousand years ago, so still it must be said,
The judgments of the Lord are true and righteous altogether.

With malice towards none ; with charity for all ; with firmness
in the right as God gives us to see the right, let us strive on to finish
the work we are in ; to bind up the nation's wounds, to care for him
who shall have borne the battle, and for his widow, and his orphan—
to do all which may achieve and cherish a just and lasting peace
among ourselves and with all nations.

Lincoln on his second election, during the war

The Tragic Drama of the Last Hour of Abraham Lincoln

No one, not even the comedian who uttered them, can ever remember the last words of the piece that was spoken that night —the last Abraham Lincoln heard upon earth. The tragedy in the box turned play and players to the most unsubstantial of phantoms.

Here were five human beings in a narrow space : the greatest man of his time in the glory of the most stupendous success of our history ; his wife, proud and happy ; a pair of betrothed lovers with all the promise of felicity that wealth and social position could give them ; and this handsome young actor, the pet of his little world. The glitter of fame, happiness, and ease was upon the entire group, yet in an instant everything was to be changed.

Quick death was to come to the central figure, the central figure of the century's great and famous men. Over the rest hung fates from which a mother might pray early death to save her children in their infancy. One was to wander with the stain of murder upon his soul, in frightful physical pain with a price upon his head and the curse of a world upon his name, until he died a dog's death in a burning barn ; the wife was to pass the rest of her days in melancholy and madness ; and one of the lovers was to slay the other and end his life a raving maniac.

The murderer seemed to himself to be taking part in a play. Holding a pistol in one hand and a knife in the other, he opened the box door, put the pistol to the President's head, and fired.

Then, rushing forward, Booth placed his hand on the railing of the box and vaulted to the stage. It was a high leap, but nothing to such an athlete. He would have got safely away but for his spur catching in the flag that draped the front of the box. He fell, the torn flag trailing on his spur, but though the fall had broken his leg he rose instantly and, shouting *Sic Semper Tyrannis*, fled rapidly across the stage and out of sight.

The cry rang out, " He has shot the President," and from the audience, stupid at first with surprise and wild afterward with excitement and horror, two or three men jumped upon the stage in pursuit of the assassin. But he ran through the familiar passages, leapt upon his horse, rewarding with a kick and a curse the boy who held him, and escaped into the night.

The President scarcely moved ; his head drooped forward slightly, his eyes closed. He was carried to a house across the street and laid upon a bed in a small room. The wound would have brought instant death to most men, but his vital tenacity was remarkable. He was, of course, unconscious from the first, but he breathed a regular and slow respiration throughout the night. As the dawn came and the moonlight grew pale his pulse began to fail, but his face even then was scarcely more haggard than those of the sorrowing men around him. His automatic moaning ceased, a look of unspeakable peace came upon his worn features, and at twenty-two minutes after seven he died. Stanton broke the silence by saying " Now he belongs to the ages."

Booth had been recognised by dozens of people as he stood before the footlights, but his swift horse quickly carried him beyond hap-hazard pursuit. He rode into Maryland, being very soon joined by David Herold. The assassin and his wretched acolyte came at midnight to Mrs Surratt's Tavern and afterwards pushed on through the moonlight to the house of a surgeon named Mudd, who set Booth's leg and gave him a room. After parting with him they were given into the charge of a Thomas Jones, a contraband trader. He kept Booth and Herold hiding at the peril of his life for a week, feeding and caring for them in the woods near his house, watching for an opportunity to ferry them across the Potomac. But there is no final escape than suicide for an assassin with a broken leg. At each painful move their chance of discovery increased. Jones was able, after repeated failures, to row his fated guests across the Potomac. Arriving on the Virginia side, they lived the lives of hunted animals for two or three days longer, finding to their horror that they were received by the staunchest Confederates with more of annoyance than enthusiasm, though none indeed offered to betray them.

Booth had by this time seen the comments in the newspapers on his work, and bitterer than death and bodily suffering was the blow to his vanity. He confided his feelings of wrong to his diary, com-paring himself favourably with Brutus and William Tell, and com-plaining : I am abandoned with the curse of Cain upon me, when, if the world knew my heart, that one blow would have made me great.

On the night of April 25 he and Herold were surrounded as they lay sleeping in a barn. When called upon to surrender Booth refused. Herold came out. The barn was fired, and while it was burning Booth, clearly visible through the cracks in the building, was shot by a sergeant of cavalry.

Upon the hearts of a people glowing with the joy of victory the news of the President's assassination fell as a great shock. It was the first time the telegraph had been called upon to spread over the world tidings of such deep and mournful significance. In the stunning effect of the unspeakable calamity the country lost sight of the national success of the past week, and it thus came to pass that there was never any organised expression of the general rejoicing in the North over the downfall of the rebellion.

As soon as it was announced that Mr Lincoln was to be buried at Springfield, Illinois, every town and city on the road begged that the train might halt within its limits and give its people the opportunity of testifying their grief and reverence. The train went up the Hudson River by night, and at every town and village on the way vast waiting crowds were revealed by the fitful glare of torches, and dirges and hymns were sung. The day spent at Cleveland was unexampled in the depths of emotion it brought to light; some of the guard of honour have said that it was at this point they began to appreciate the place that Lincoln was to hold in history.

The ceremonies at the grave were simple and touching. Bishop Simpson delivered a pathetic oration, but the weightiest and the most eloquent words uttered anywhere that day were those of the Second Inaugural, which the committee had wisely ordained to be read over his grave, as the friends of Raphael chose the incomparable canvas of the Transfiguration to be the chief ornament of his funeral.

John G. Nicolay

Punch Apologises to Abraham Lincoln

Punch made much fun of Abraham Lincoln during the Civil War, and at his death offered this brave apology to his memory.

You lay a wreath on murdered Lincoln's bier,
  You, who with mocking pencil wont to trace,
Broad for the self-complaisant British sneer,
  His length of shambling limb, his furrowed face,

His gaunt, gnarled hands, his unkempt, bristling hair,
  His garb uncouth, his bearing ill at ease,
His lack of all we prize as debonair,
  Of power or will to shine, of art to please;

You, whose smart pen backed up the pencil's laugh,
  Judging each step as though the way were plain;
Reckless, so it could point its paragraph,
  Of chief's perplexity or people's pain.

Beside this corpse, that bears for winding-sheet
  The Stars and Stripes he lived to rear anew,
Between the mourners at his head and feet,
  Say, scurrile jester, is there room for *you*?

Yes: he had lived to shame me from my sneer,
  To lame my pencil and confute my pen;
To make me own this hind of princes peer,
  This rail-splitter a true-born king of men.

My shallow judgment I had learned to rue,
  Noting how to occasion's height he rose;
How his quaint wit made home-truth seem more true;
  How, iron-like, his temper grew by blows;

How humble, yet how hopeful he could be;
  How in good fortune and in ill the same;
Nor bitter in success, nor boastful he,
  Thirsty for gold, nor feverish for fame.

Tom Taylor

When Abraham Lincoln Died

THOSE who mourned most deeply were the blacks. They were the only ones who had blessed him heartily as their saviour in life. They sang songs in his honour and said that their Messiah was now in Heaven. Tad, who lived only a few years more, believed the same thing. When he stood beside the coffin at the White House he asked, " Is Father in heaven now ? Then I am glad, for he was not really happy here."

Never again, since Abraham Lincoln lived and died, has an innocent man worn fetters in the United States. Since he lived, worked, and was slain, all men to whom God has given the gift of life are there born free. *Emil Ludwig*

They Come Beset by Riddling Hail

This stirring chorus comes into Thomas Hardy's famous Epic of the Dynasts, and deals with the Battle at Albuera in Spain, between the British and Spanish on the one side and Napoleon's forces on the other.

THEY come beset by riddling hail,
    They sway like sedges in a gale ;
They fail, and win, and win, and fail.   Albuera !

They gain the ground there, yard by yard,
Their brows and hair and lashes charred,
Their blackened teeth set firm and hard.

Their mad assailants rave and reel,
And face, as men who scorn to feel,
The close-lined, three-edged prongs of steel.

Till faintness follows closing-in,
When, faltering headlong down, they spin
Like leaves.   But those pay well who win Albuera.

Out of six thousand souls that sware
To hold the mount, or pass elsewhere,
But eighteen hundred muster there.

Pale colonels, captains, ranksmen lie,
Facing the earth or facing sky ;
They strove to live, they stretch to die.

Friends, foemen, mingle ; heap and heap.
Hide their hacked bones, Earth !—deep, deep, deep,
Where harmless worms caress and creep.

Hide their hacked bones, Earth !—deep, deep, deep,
Where harmless worms caress and creep.
What man can grieve ? what woman weep ?
Better than waking is to sleep !   Albuera !

Thomas Hardy

Let Him Not Be Forgotten

SUFFER no pomp at my funeral. Lay me quietly in the earth and put a sundial over my grave, and let me be forgotten.

Last words of John Howard

Youth Above All

THERE is a feeling of Eternity in youth which makes us amends for everything. To be young is to be as one of the Immortals.

William Hazlitt

The Spark Divine

NOT hopeless, round this calm sepulchral spot,
　A wreath presaging life we twine ;
If God is Love, what sleeps below was not
　Without a spark divine.

Sir Francis Doyle on a favourite dog

The Laughing and the Weeping

WHEN a friend laughs it is for him to disclose the subject of his joy ; when he weeps it is for me to discover the cause of his sorrow. *Joseph Francois Desmahis*

The Death Roll of Ideas

THE number of the soldiers killed in the Great War is known. The number of the ideas and beliefs destroyed by it remains still unknown. *Gustave Le Bon*

All We Like Sheep

SHOW me half a dozen people whom I can persuade that it is not the sun that gives light, and I should not despair of whole nations holding the same opinions. *Fontenelle*

The Emperor Looks Back

WHAT an egregious fool must I have been to have squandered so much blood and treasure in an absurd attempt to make men think alike when I cannot even make a few watches keep time together. *The Emperor Charles the Fifth amusing himself as a watchmaker after his abdication*

So Many to So Few

THE gratitude of every home, except in the abodes of the guilty, goes out to the British airmen who, undaunted by odds, unwearied by their constant challenge and mortal danger, are turning the tide of world war by their prowess and by their devotion. Never in the field of human conflict was so much owed by so many to so few.

Winston Churchill

The Saddest Story of the English Throne

This word-picture of George the Third is one
of the most pathetic passages in Thackeray

GEORGE THE THIRD and his queen lived in a very unpretending but elegant-looking house. The king's mother inhabited Carlton House. A shrewd, hard, domineering, narrow-minded woman, she educated her children according to her lights. She kept him very close ; she held the tightest rein over him ; she had curious prejudices and bigotries.

His mother's bigotry and hatred he inherited with the courageous obstinacy of his own race ; but he was a firm believer where his fathers had been free-thinkers, and a true and fond supporter of the Church of which he was the titular defender.

The king lamented, not without pathos, in his after life that his education had been neglected. He was a dull lad brought up by narrow-minded people. The cleverest tutors in the world could have done little probably to expand that small intellect, though they might have improved his taste, and taught his perceptions some generosity.

But he admired as well as he could. There is little doubt that a letter written by the little Princess Charlotte of Mecklenburg-Strelitz . . . struck the young monarch greatly, and decided him upon selecting the young princess as the sharer of his throne. They met, and they were married, and for years they led the happiest lives. It is said the king winced when he first saw his homely little bride ; but, however that may be, he was a true and faithful husband to her, as she was a faithful and loving wife. They had the simplest pleasures—little country dances, to which a dozen couples were invited, after which delicious excitement they would go to bed without any supper and get up quite early the next morning, and perhaps the next night have another dance ; or the queen would play on the spinet, or the king would read to her a paper out of The Spectator, or one of Ogden's sermons.

O Arcadia ! what a life it must have been ! There used to be Sunday drawing-rooms at Court, but the young king stopped these as he stopped all godless gambling. Many stories, mirthful and affecting, are told of his behaviour at the concerts he ordered. When he was blind and ill he chose the music for the Ancient Concerts once, and the music and words he selected were from Samson Agonistes, and all had reference to his blindness, his captivity, and his affliction.

There is something exceedingly touching in that simple early life of the king. As long as his mother lived he was a shy, awkward boy under the tutelage of that hard parent. She must have been a clever, domineering, cruel woman. She kept her household lonely and in gloom.

What virtue he knew he tried to practise ; what knowledge he could master he strove to acquire. He was for ever drawing maps, for example, and learned geography with no small care and industry. He knew all about the family histories and genealogies of his gentry, and pretty histories he must have known. He knew the whole Army List, and all the facings and the exact number of the buttons, all the tags and laces, and the cut of all the cocked-hats, pigtails, and gaiters in his army. . . .

Yet there is something grand about his courage. The battle of the king with his aristocracy remains yet to be told by the historian who shall view the reign of George more justly than the trumpery pane-gyrists who wrote immediately after his decease. It was he, with the people to back him, who made the war with America ; it was he and the people who refused justice to the Roman Catholics ; and on both questions he beat the patricians.

His courage was never to be beaten. It trampled North under foot ; it bent the stiff neck of the younger Pitt ; even his illness never conquered that indomitable spirit. As soon as his brain was clear it resumed the scheme, only laid aside when his reason left him ; as soon as his hands were out of the strait-waistcoat they took up the pen and the plan which had engaged him up to the moment of his malady.

Even Americans, whom he hated and who conquered him, may give him credit for having quite honest reasons for oppressing them. Remember that he believed himself anointed by a Divine com-mission ; remember that he was a man of slow parts and imperfect education ; that the same awful will of Heaven which placed a crown upon his head, which made him tender to his family, pure in his life, courageous and honest, made him dull of comprehension, obstinate of will, and at many times deprived him of reason. He was the father of his people ; his rebellious children must be flogged into obedience.

Wars and revolutions are, however, the politician's province ; let us return to our Court gossip. Yonder sits our little queen, sur-rounded by many stout sons and fair daughters. The history of the daughters, as little Miss Burney has painted them to us, is delightful. They were handsome : she calls them beautiful ; they were most kind, loving, and ladylike ; they were gracious to every person, high and low, who served them. They had many little accomplishments of their own. This one drew : that one played the piano ; they all worked most prodigiously, and fitted up whole suites of rooms with their needles.

A quieter household, a more prosaic life, cannot be imagined. Rain or shine, the king rode every day for hours, poked his red face into hundreds of cottages round about, and showed that shovel hat and Windsor uniform to farmers, to pig-boys, to old women making apple-dumplings ; to all sorts of people, gentle and simple, about whom countless stories are told. Nothing can be more undignified than these stories. He used to give a guinea sometimes ; sometimes feel in his pockets and find he had no money ; often ask a man a hundred questions : about the number of his family, about his oats and beans, about the rent he paid for his house, and ride on. Our fathers read these simple tales with fond pleasure ; liked the old man who poked his nose into every cottage ; who lived on plain wholesome roast and boiled ; who despised your French kickshaws ; who was a true hearty English gentleman.

Their Majesties were very sociable potentates : and the Court Chronicler tells of numerous visits which they paid to their subjects, gentle and simple ; with whom they dined ; at whose great country houses they stopped ; or at whose poorer lodgings they affably partook of tea and bread-and-butter. Some of the great folk spent enormous sums in entertaining their sovereigns.

The king rose every morning at six, and had two hours to himself. He thought it effeminate to have a carpet in his bedroom. Shortly before eight the queen and the royal family were always ready for him, and they proceeded to the king's chapel in the castle. There were no fires in the passages ; the chapel was scarcely alight ; princesses, governesses, equerries grumbled and caught cold ; but, cold or hot, it was their duty to go ; wet or dry, light or dark, the stout old George was always in his place to say Amen to the chaplain.

All the world knows the story of his malady. History presents no sadder figure than that of the old man, blind and deprived of reason, wandering through the rooms of his palace, addressing imaginary parliaments, reviewing fancied troops, holding ghostly courts. I have seen his picture as it was taken at this time hanging in the apartment of his daughter. The poor old father is represented in a purple gown, his snowy beard falling over his breast, the star of his famous Order still idly shining on it. He was not only sightless ; he became utterly deaf. All light, all reason, all sound of human voices, all the pleasures of this world of God, were taken from him. Some slight lucid moments he had ; in one of which the queen, desiring to see him, entered the room and found him singing a hymn and accompanying himself at the harpsichord. When he had finished he knelt down and prayed aloud for her, and then for his family, and then for the nation, concluding with a prayer for himself that it might please God to avert his heavy calamity from him ; but, if not, to give him resignation to submit. He then burst into tears, and his reason again fled.

O brothers, I said to those who heard me first in America, O brothers ! speaking the same dear mother-tongue, O comrades ! enemies no more, let us take a mournful hand together as we stand by this royal corpse, and call a truce to battle ! Low he lies to whom the proudest used to kneel, and who was cast lower than the poorest.

Hush ! Strife and Quarrel, over the solemn grave ! Sound, trumpets, a mournful march ! Fall, dark curtain, upon his pageant, his pride, his grief, his awful tragedy ! *W. M. Thackeray*

The Crime of Being Young

THE atrocious crime of being a young man which the honourable gentleman has with such spirit and decency charged upon me, I shall neither attempt to palliate nor deny; but content myself with wishing that I may be one of those whose follies may cease with their youth, and not of that number who are ignorant in spite of experience.   *The first William Pitt replying to Robert Walpole*

Thomas Carlyle Writes to Benjamin Disraeli

SIR, Yesterday to my great surprise I had the honour to receive your letter containing a magnificent proposal for my benefit, which will be memorable to me for the rest of my life.

Allow me to say that the letter, both in purport and expression, is worthy to be called magnanimous and noble, that it is without example in my own poor history, and I think it is unexampled, too, in the history of governing persons towards men of letters at the present or at any time; and that I will carefully preserve it as one of the things precious to memory and heart. A real treasure or benefit *it*, independent of all results from it.

This said to yourself and reposited with many feelings in my own grateful mind, I have only to add that your splendid and generous proposals for my practical behoof must not any of them take effect; that titles of honour are, in all degrees of them, out of keeping with the tenor of my own poor existence hitherto in this epoch of the world, and would be an encumbrance, not a furtherance, to me; that as to money, it has, after long years of rigorous and frugal, but also (thank God and those that are gone before me) not degrading poverty, become in this latter amply abundant, even superabundant; more of it, too, now a hindrance, not a help to me; so that royal or other bounty would be more than thrown away in my case; and, in brief, that except the feeling of your fine and noble conduct on this occasion, which is a real and permanent possession, there cannot anything be done that would not now be a sorrow rather than a pleasure.

With thanks more than usually sincere, I have the honour to be, Sir, your obliged and obedient servant,   T. CARLYLE

   5 Cheyne Row, Chelsea, December 29, 1874.

George the Third to James the Great

GEORGE THE THIRD TO JAMES WATT: Well, my man, and what have you to sell?

   James Watt to George the Third: What kings covet, may it please your Majesty—Power.

The Times to Queen Victoria

A profound sensation was caused throughout England by the appearance
of the following leading article in The Times on December 15, 1864.

YESTERDAY was the third anniversary of the death of the late
Prince Consort, and it was marked by a touching ceremonial.
Her Majesty and the younger members of the Royal Family visited
the beautiful mausoleum which has been erected over the prince's
remains and paid a fresh tribute of affection to his memory. It
seems but the other day that the Queen and the nation suffered this
great bereavement, but in the meantime how many changes have
taken place !

In the queen's own family the Prince of Wales has passed from
youth into manhood, and now there is an heir to the throne in the
second generation. One more daughter has left her royal mother's
house for a foreign home.

In the affairs of the world there has been constant movement, wars
and revolutions, immense social and commercial activity, bringing
ever new duties to all classes, and particularly to those who stand
highest and are nearest to the throne. Yet the lapse of time has not
yet brought a due alleviation of sorrow to the chief sufferer.

Oppressed by a great grief, Her Majesty has retired from the
world, and devoted her life to recollections of the past. Never has a
husband been more justly mourned than the eminent man who was so
suddenly snatched away three years since ; but in all bereavements
there is a time when the days of mourning should be looked upon as
past. The living have their claims as well as the dead ; and what
claims can be more imperative than those of a great nation and the
society of one of the first European capitals ? We might also speak
of Her Majesty's own youthful family, whose introduction into the
social life which belongs to their station depends on the resumption
by the Court of its ordinary habits. But we will confine ourselves to
the public functions which the occupant of the Throne may be
expected to fulfil, and ask, in all duty and loyalty, whether the time
has not now come when they should once more be performed in person.

The Queen's most loyal subjects are precisely those who think it is
not a matter of indifference whether the sovereign should be seen and
take part in public matters and in social intercourse. No reigning
house can afford to confirm in their views those who suggest that the
throne is only an antiquarian relic and royalty itself a ceremony, who
think that the less that is seen or heard of a Court the better.

The great mass of the nation are, happily for the interests of
royalty, not of this opinion. They desire that the highest personage
in the realm, the hereditary chief magistrate, should even in political
affairs use an individual judgment and a discretion apart from the
counsels of any set of politicians. The balance of the Constitution
depends, in fact, on the sovereign being able on certain occasions to

rise superior to party suggestions and stand as the representative of the nation and the guardian of the Executive.   But, for any sovereign to be able to fulfil this high duty when required, a proper intercourse with the world and a knowledge which seclusion soon loses are absolutely necessary.

The Court of England in recent times has always been so conducted as to give the sovereign a familiarity with the most trustworthy opinions of the time by means of intercourse with the ablest and most respected persons in the land.   To relinquish these means of learning what English people think and feel on all subjects, to dry up the sources of the royal tact which is the most valuable quality a constitutional sovereign can possess, is to abandon something of the prerogative of the Crown.   It is impossible for a recluse to occupy the British Throne without a gradual weakening of that authority which the sovereign has been accustomed to exert.   The regulation of a household may be in the power of such a ruler, but the real sway of an empire will be impossible.

For the sake of the Crown as well as of the public we would, therefore, beseech Her Majesty to return to the personal exercise of her exalted functions. . . . In the early days of Her Majesty's reign nothing was more gratifying to the public than to learn that there was a royal speech at the opening or closing of the Session, and not a Message.   Equally beneficial was it to the interests of the Constitution that with the chief enterprises of the day the name of the queen should be connected.   Whether it was an industrial exhibition, or a naval review, or a new public building, it pleased the people and strengthened the throne when Her Majesty was on the spot.   Such influences have a constitutional value in a State like ours.

It is also fair to say that the society of England requires its chief hostess and its natural leader.   It may be that in time the London season may accustom itself to do without the Palace, but it is not desirable that we should attain that point of republican simplicity. For every reason we trust that, now that three years have elapsed and every honour that affection and gratitude could pay to the memory of the Prince Consort has been offered, Her Majesty will think of her subjects' claims and the duties of her high station, and not postpone them longer to the indulgence of an unavailing grief.

The Triumph of the Cross

WE are trying to readjust the life of the world ; what is to be the ultimate principle dominating that process of readjustment ? Is it to be Christian or pagan ?   It may be either, but a choice has to be made.   Is the Cross or materialism to become supreme ?   One or the other must prevail.

That is the stark, the ultimate reality which Good Friday compels us to face.   Mankind has been beset by appeals to the baser motives, by voices that deride as foolish the idea of permitting Christian ethics to regulate mundane affairs. Good Friday brings a pause to such clamour. It dies down, and we become aware of another appeal when we stand before the Cross of Calvary.

To be emotionally stirred by that spectacle of august and suffering love is not enough; the message of the Cross calls to thought, to resolve, to action. It entreats us to discern, beneath all our secondary troubles, the plain issue of life or death, of Christianity or paganism, that confronts us today. It urges, with a truth which bitter experience has made unquestionable, that eager and strenuous concern for material things alone can bring no peace either to a world or an individual soul. It insists that true riches and true happiness have to be sought along a road other than that which we supposed would bring us to prosperity. It does not promise that, if we are wholeheartedly Christian, we shall be able to mould circumstances to our liking. But we shall try to mould them to GOD's liking, and that effort, even if it fails to change the circumstances, infallibly will change ourselves. It will give us a part in the one victory that matters—the victory of Good Friday, the triumph of the Cross.

We incline to think of the Crucifixion as the world's supreme tragedy. That, in a sense, it was; though the real tragedy lay not in the Crucifixion but in the sin and hatred which brought it about. But on Good Friday the disciples were in no mood for such distinctions. To them, as to all their contemporaries, the Cross was a word of horror. And the candour of the Gospels pictures the unrelieved tragedy of the Cross for the disciples on the first Good Friday.

They had shrunk aghast and uncomprehending from their MASTER's reiterated predictions. It was impossible to link Him in thought with that awful ignominy; impossible to doubt, to the last moment, that somehow He would triumph over His enemies. Yet the gloom steadily deepened, no Divine power intervened, JESUS was crucified, and the disciples fled in an extremity of despair. If ever there was a symbol of hideous disaster and irretrievable defeat, that symbol was the Cross on Good Friday. Then came Easter, making all things new. Yet the character of that change is often misunderstood. It seems natural to contrast the tragedy of Good Friday with the victory of Easter. That was not the view of the early Christians. Such a view has no resemblance to that found in the New Testament.

There the Passion is regarded as central; each detail of the story is set down with scrupulous care, and the Resurrection is given less space, as being not the contradiction of the Passion but its consequence. So far from wishing his converts to forget the Cross or to speak of it with horror, ST PAUL would have them glory in it. It was on the Cross, and not in spite of the Cross, that JESUS conquered. He is acclaimed as overthrowing the banded powers of evil, triumphing over them, not in the Resurrection but in the Cross. The Cross, rather than the empty sepulchre, was to become the Christian sign of triumph, was to lead processions and crown the churches and gleam from their altars.

When, accordingly, we turn our thoughts to the malice and obtuseness of which human nature is capable, and contemplate what they brought about on Calvary, we shall rightly keep Good Friday as a day of profound penitence. When again we place ourselves in imagination beside the first disciples and attempt to view the Crucifixion through their eyes, we shall think of the scene as supremely tragic. But when we regard the Cross as did ST PAUL and the rest of the early Church, we shall glory in it with high thanksgiving.

If on Good Friday we can return to this New Testament belief in the triumph of the Cross, we shall not merely replace one abstract opinion by another. The change will have consequences of a practical kind, and of a kind that will have a special value in the present circumstances of the world. We shall gain new courage and a changed outlook.

It is something if we have learned already from Holy Week and Easter to believe that, after the endurance of tribulation and seeming defeat, miraculous victory may follow, when our buried hopes will rise to fulfilment from the grave of despair. But it is far more to discern that endurance of tribulation is itself the victory. No miracle, but the inevitable operation of GOD's law will bring about the resurrection of all that is good.

We live at a time in history when the forces of evil are strong, when peace and civilisation and Christianity often seem endangered. On the other hand, religious faith is making progress in unexpected ways, while brave and resolute men and women throughout the world are striving for goodwill and trying to win a happier future for the human race. To dedicate to such ends whatever of influence we possess, to endure through the darkest days with serene courage, to think little of our own needs and much of our neighbour's, to be unashamed in our religion and frank in making the FATHER's Will our supreme rule in conduct—to do that is to fulfil the teaching of Good Friday, to follow so far as we may the supreme example of the Crucified, and to share in the triumph of the Cross.

For after nineteen centuries the Cross remains the Sign of victory, and in this Sign we shall conquer. *From the leading article in The Times on Good Friday 1933*

The Man Who Forgot

*T*o *one who thought Sir Thomas More had offended him Erasmus wrote :*

What you write about More is all nonsense; why, he does not even remember grave injuries.

PORTRAIT OF A LADY, BY REMBRANDT

CHINESE CAMEL FROM A TANG TOMB

Three Friends Meet in English Literature

A hundred years and more ago there died in New York Joseph Rodman Drake, and his great friend FitzGreene Halleck wrote this beautiful tribute to his memory.

GREEN be the turf above thee,
 Friend of my better days !
None knew thee but to love thee,
 None named thee but to praise.

Tears fell, when thou wert dying,
 From eyes unused to weep,
And long, where thou art lying,
 Will tears the cold turf steep.

When hearts whose truth was proven,
 Like thine, are laid in earth,
There should a wreath be woven
 To tell the world their worth.

It should be mine to braid it
 Around thy faded brow,
But I've in vain assayed it,
 And feel I cannot now.

While memory bids me weep thee,
 Nor thoughts nor words are free,
The grief is fixed too deeply
 That mourns a man like thee.

Nearly sixty years passed by, and John Greenleaf Whittier paid this tribute to FitzGreene Halleck, who had passed on to the "friend of his better days."

NOT his the soldier's sword to wield,
 Nor his the helm of State,
Nor glory of the stricken field,
 Nor triumph of debate.

He toiled and sang ; and year by year
 Men found their homes more sweet,
And through a tenderer atmosphere
 Looked down the brick-walled street.

Alive, he loved, like all who sing
 The echoes of his song ;
Too late the tardy meed we bring,
 The praise delayed so long.

Our lips of praise must soon be dumb,
 Our grateful eyes be dim ;
O, brothers of the days to come,
 Take tender charge of him !

New hands the wires of song may sweep,
 New voices challenge fame ;
But let no moss of years o'er creep
 The lines of Halleck's name.

The Royal Visit

No one knows who wrote this rare and vivid poem. It was found in Christ Church Library at Oxford, and is a seventeenth-century manuscript. From its abrupt opening it might be a fragment, yet it is so perfect that we would not have it a line longer or shorter.

YET if his majesty, our sovereign lord,
   Should, of his own accord
Friendly himself invite,
And say, " I'll be your guest tomorrow night,"
How should we stir ourselves, call and command
All hands to work ! " Let no man idle stand !
Set me fine Spanish tables in the hall,
See they be fitted all ;
Let there be room to eat,
And order taken that there want no meat !
See every sconce and candlestick made bright
That without tapers they may give a light !
Look to the presence : are the carpets spread,
The dais o'er the head,
The cushions in the chairs,
And all the candles lighted on the stairs ?
Perfume the chambers, and in any case
Let each man give attendance in his place."
Thus, if the king were coming, would we do,
And twere good reason too ;
For tis a duteous thing
To show all honour to an earthly king,
And after all our travail and our cost,
So be he pleased, to think no labour lost.
But at the coming of the King of Heaven
All's set at six and seven :
We wallow in our sin,
Christ cannot find a chamber in the inn.
We entertain him always as a stranger,
And, as at first, still lodge Him in the manger.

Not the Way to Heaven

WE may not go to heaven in feather beds ; it is
   not the way.   *Sir Thomas More*

A Celebrated Problem

TWAS a celebrated problem among the ancient mythologists
what was the Strongest thing, what the Wisest, and what the
Greatest ? Concerning which twas this determined, that the
strongest thing was Necessity, the wisest was Time, and the greatest
was the Heart of Man.   *Norris of Bemerton in the 17th century*

The Prophecies that Came True

Erasmus Darwin Looking Forward in 1792

SOON shall thy arm, Unconquered Steam, afar
  Drag the slow barge, or drive the rapid car ;
Or on the wide-waving wings expanded bear
The flying-chariot through the fields of air.
Fair crews triumphant, leaning from above,
Shall wave their fluttering kerchiefs as they move ;
Or warrior-bands alarm the gaping crowd,
And armies shrink beneath the shadowy cloud.

From the Botanic Garden

Tennyson Looking Forward in 1842

MEN, my brothers, men the workers, ever reaping something new :
  That which they have done but earnest of the things that they
  shall do :

For I dipt into the future, far as human eye could see,
Saw the vision of the world and all the wonder that would be ;

Saw the heavens fill with commerce, argosies of magic sails,
Pilots of the purple twilight, dropping down with costly bales ;

Heard the heavens fill with shouting, and there rained a ghastly dew
From the nations' airy navies, grappling in the central blue ;

Far along the world-wide whisper of the south-wind rushing warm,
With the standards of the people plunging through the thunder-
  storm ;

Till the war drums throbbed no longer and the battle-flags were
  furled
In the Parliament of man, the Federation of the world.

There the common sense of most shall hold a fretful realm in awe,
And the kindly earth shall slumber, lapt in universal law.

From Locksley Hall

Four Things Small and Wise

THERE be four things which are little upon the earth, but they are
  exceeding wise :

*The ants are a people not strong, yet they prepare their meat in the
summer ;*

*The conies are but a feeble folk, yet make they their houses in
the rocks ;*

The locusts have no king, yet go they forth all of them by bands ;

The spider taketh hold with her hands, and is in kings' palaces.

Solomon

James Watt is Dead

Mr James Watt, the great improver of the steam-engine, died on August 25, 1819, in the eighty-fourth year of his age. This name fortunately needs no commemoration of ours, for he that bore it survived to see it crowned with undisputed and unenvied honours ; and many generations will probably pass away before it shall have gathered all its fame.

We have said that Mr Watt was the great improver of the steam-engine ; but in truth he should rather be described as its inventor. It was by his inventions that its action was so regulated as to make it capable of being applied to the finest and most delicate manufactures, and its power so increased as to set weight and solidity at defiance. By his admirable contrivance it has become a thing stupendous alike for its force and its flexibility—for the prodigious power it can exert, and the ease and precision and ductility with which that power can be varied, distributed, and applied. The trunk of an elephant, that can pick up a pin or rend an oak, is as nothing to it. It can engrave a seal, crush masses of obdurate metal before it, draw out without breaking a thread as fine as gossamer, and lift a ship of war like a bauble in the air. It can embroider muslin and forge anchors, cut steel into ribands, and impel loaded vessels against the fury of the winds and waves.

It would be difficult to estimate the value of the benefits which these inventions have conferred upon this country. There is no branch of industry that has not been indebted to them ; and in all the most material they have not only widened most magnificently the field of its exertions, but multiplied a thousandfold the amount of its productions. It was our improved steam-engine that fought the battles of Europe, and exalted and sustained, through the late tremendous contest, the political greatness of our land. It is the same great power which now enables us to pay the interest of our debt, and to maintain the arduous struggle in which we are still engaged with the skill and capital of countries less oppressed with taxation.

But these are poor and narrow views of its importance. It has increased indefinitely the mass of human comforts and enjoyments, and rendered cheap and accessible all over the world the materials of wealth and prosperity. It has armed the feeble hand of man, in short, with a power to which no limits can be assigned ; completed the dominion of mind over the most refractory qualities of matter ; and laid a sure foundation for all those future miracles of mechanic power which are to aid and reward the labours of after generations.

It is to the genius of one man, too, that all this is mainly owing. Certainly no man ever bestowed such a gift on his kind. The blessing is not only universal, but unbounded ; and the fabled inventors of the plough and the loom, who were deified by the erring gratitude of their rude contemporaries, conferred less important benefits on mankind than the inventor of our steam-engine.

This will be the fame of Watt with future generations : and it is sufficient for his race and his country. But to those to whom he more immediately belonged, who lived in his society and enjoyed his conversation, it is not, perhaps, the character in which he will be most frequently recalled, most deeply lamented, or even most highly admired.

Independently of his great attainments in mechanics, Mr Watt was an extraordinary and in many respects a wonderful man. Perhaps no individual in his age possessed so much and such varied and exact information—had read so much, or remembered what he had read so accurately and well. He had infinite quickness of apprehension, a prodigious memory, and a certain rectifying and methodising power of understanding which extracted something precious out of all that was presented to it. His stores of miscellaneous knowledge were immense, and yet less astonishing than the command he had at all times over them.

There was nothing of effort or impatience, any more than of pride or levity, in his demeanour. He had in his character the utmost abhorrence for all sorts of forwardness, parade, and pretensions, and never failed to put all such impostures out of countenance, by the manly plainness and honest intrepidity of his language and deportment.

In his temper and dispositions, he was not only kind and affectionate, but generous, and considerate of the feelings of all around him ; and gave the most liberal assistance and encouragement to all young persons who showed any indications of talent or applied to him for patronage or advice. His health, which was delicate from his youth upwards, seemed to become firmer as he advanced in years ; and he preserved up almost to the last moment of his existence not only the full command of his extraordinary intellect, but all the alacrity of spirit and the social gaiety which had illumined his happiest days. *Obituary in the Edinburgh Review, 1819*

I Will Lift up Mine Eyes Unto the Hills

I WILL lift up mine eyes unto the hills, from whence cometh my help. My help cometh from the Lord, which made heaven and earth.

He will not suffer thy foot to be moved ; he that keepeth thee will not slumber.

The sun shall not smite thee by day, nor the moon by night.

The Lord shall preserve thee from all evil ; he shall preserve thy soul.

The Lord shall preserve thy going out and thy coming in from this time forth, for evermore. *Psalm 121*

The Butchers

AMONG those foolish pursuers of pleasure the people of Utopia reckon all that delight in hunting, or gaming, of whose madness they have only heard, for they have no such things among them. But they have asked us : What sort of pleasure is it that men can find in throwing the dice ?　And what pleasure can one find in hearing the barking and howling of dogs ?　Nor can they comprehend the pleasure of seeing dogs run after a hare, more than seeing one dog run after another.

But if the pleasure lies in seeing the hare killed and torn by the dogs this ought rather to stir pity that a weak, harmless and fearful hare should be devoured by strong, fierce, and cruel dogs.　Therefore all this business of hunting is, among the Utopians, turned over to their butchers, and the butchers are all slaves, and they look on hunting as one of the basest parts of a butcher's work, for they account it both more profitable and more decent to kill those beasts that are more useful to mankind, whereas the killing and tearing of so small and miserable an animal can only attract the huntsman with a false show of pleasure, from which he can reap but small advantage. They look on the desire of the bloodshed, even of beasts, as a mark of a mind that is corrupted with cruelty, or that at least, by too frequent returns of so brutal a pleasure, must degenerate into it.

Sir Thomas More

Remember Thy Creator

REMEMBER now thy Creator in the days of thy youth, while the evil days come not, nor the years draw nigh, when thou shalt say, I have no pleasure in them ;

While the sun, or the light, or the moon, or the stars, be not darkened, nor the clouds return after the rain :

In the days when the keepers of the house shall tremble, and the strong men shall bow themselves, and the grinders cease because they are few, and those that look out of the windows be darkened, and the doors shall be shut in the streets, when the sound of the grinding is low, and he shall rise up at the voice of the bird, and all the daughters of musick shall be brought low ;

Also when they shall be afraid of that which is high, and fears shall be in the way, and the almond tree shall flourish, and the grasshopper shall be a burden, and desire shall fail : because man goeth to his long home and the mourners go about the streets :

Or ever the silver cord be loosed, or the golden bowl be broken, or the pitcher be broken at the fountain, or the wheel broken at the cistern.　　　　　　　　　　　　　　　*Ecclesiastes*

Moses to His People

Moses said unto the Lord, O my Lord, I am not eloquent, but am slow of speech.

WHEN thou art in tribulation, if thou turn to the Lord thy God he will not forsake thee. Thou shalt love the Lord thy God with all thy heart and with all thy soul and with all thy mind.

Ye have been rebellious against the Lord from the day that I knew you. I fell down before the Lord forty days and forty nights and said, O Lord God, destroy not thy people which thou hast redeemed.

The Lord hearkened unto me at that time and would not destroy thee. And now what doth the Lord require of thee but to fear God, to walk in all his ways, and to love him ? The Lord had a delight in thy fathers to love them, and he choose their seed after them, you above all people. Thy fathers went down into Egypt with threescore and ten persons, and now the Lord thy God hath made thee as the stars of heaven for multitude.

If ye shall diligently keep all these commandments, to do them, to love the Lord your God, to walk in all his ways, and to cleave unto him, then will the Lord drive out all nations before you, and ye shall possess greater nations, and mightier than yourselves. Every place your feet shall tread shall be yours. There shall no man be able to stand before you.

But it shall come to pass, if thou wilt not hearken unto the voice of the Lord thy God, that curses shall come upon thee. Thy sons and thy daughters shall be given unto another people, and there shall be no might in thine hand. The fruit of thy land, and all thy labours, shall a nation which thou knowest not eat up. Thou shalt be oppressed and crushed alway. Thou shalt become an astonishment, a proverb, and a byword among all nations. Thou shalt carry much seed out into the field and shalt gather but little in, for the locust shall consume it. Thou shalt have olive trees throughout all thy coasts but thou shalt not anoint thyself with oil, for thine olive shall cast its fruit. Thou shalt beget sons and daughters but shalt not enjoy them, for they shall go into captivity.

The Lord shall bring a nation against thee from afar, from the end of the earth, as swift as the eagle flieth ; a nation whose tongue thou shalt not understand, a nation of fierce countenance, which shall not regard the old, nor show favour to the young, and shall eat the fruit of thy cattle, and the fruit of thy land, until thou be destroyed. Ye shall be left few in number, whereas ye were as the stars of heaven for multitude, because thou wouldest not obey the voice of the Lord thy God. The Lord shall scatter thee among all people, from the one end of the earth to the other ; and among these nations shalt thou find no ease, neither shall the sole of thy foot have rest ; but the Lord shall give thee there a trembling heart, and failing of eyes, and sorrow of mind, and thy life shall hang in doubt before thee ; and thou shalt fear day and night. In the morning thou shalt say, Would God it were even ! and at even thou shalt say, Would God it were morning ! And the Lord shall bring thee into Egypt again, and there ye shall be sold unto your enemies for bondmen and bond-women, and no man shall buy you.

This commandment which I command thee this day, it is not hidden from thee, neither is it far off. The word is very nigh unto thee, in thy mouth and in thy heart, that thou mayest do it.

See, I have set before thee this day life and good, and death and evil. I call heaven and earth to record this day that I have set before you life and death, blessing and cursing : therefore choose life, that both thou and thy seed may live, that thou mayest love the Lord thy God, and obey his voice and cleave unto him, for he is thy life, and the length of thy days. *Old Testament*

Proverbs of Solomon

BETTER is a dinner of herbs where love is than a stalled ox and hatred.

Go to the ant, thou sluggard ; consider her ways and be wise.

A word fitly spoken is like apples of gold in pictures of silver.

A wise son maketh a glad father, but a foolish son is the heaviness of his mother.

Better is a little with righteousness than great revenues without right.

Hatred stirreth up strifes ; but love covereth all sins.

Where no counsel is the people fall ; but in the multitude of counsellors there is safety.

He that trusteth in his riches shall fall, but the righteous shall flourish.

Poverty and shame shall be to him that refuseth instruction, but he that regardeth reproof shall be honoured.

He that walketh with wise men shall be wise, but a companion of fools shall be destroyed.

Righteousness exalteth a nation, but sin is a reproach to any people.

A soft answer turneth away wrath, but grievous words stir up anger.

A merry heart maketh a cheerful countenance, but by sorrow of the heart the spirit is broken.

Pride goeth before destruction, and a haughty spirit before a fall.

The hoary head is a crown of glory, if it be found in the way of righteousness.

He that is slow to anger is better than the mighty ; and he that ruleth his spirit than he that taketh a city.

Three Things Too Wonderful

THERE be three things that be too wonderful for me, yea, four which I know not.

The way of an eagle in the air ; the way of a serpent on a rock ; the way of a ship in the midst of the sea ; and the way of a man with a maid.
                                                                    Solomon

Six Things the Lord Doth Hate

THESE six things doth the Lord hate : yea, seven are an abomination unto him :

A proud look, a lying tongue, hands that shed innocent blood, a heart that deviseth wicked imaginations, feet swift in running to mischief, a false witness that speaketh lies, and he that soweth discord among brethren.   *Solomon*

Through All Generations

LORD, thou hast been our dwelling-place in all generations.

Before the mountains were brought forth, or ever thou hadst formed the earth and the world, even from everlasting to everlasting thou art God.

Thou turnest man to destruction ; and sayest Return, ye children of men.

For a thousand years in thy sight are but as yesterday, when it is past, and as a watch in the night.

Thou carriest them away as with a flood ; they are as a sleep : in the morning they are like grass which groweth up.

In the morning it flourisheth, and groweth up ; in the evening it is cut down, and withereth.

For we are consumed by thine anger, and by thy wrath are we troubled.

Thou hast set our iniquities before thee, our secret sins in the light of thy countenance.

For all our days are passed away in thy wrath : we spend our years as a tale that is told.

The days of our years are threescore years and ten ; and if by reason of strength they be fourscore years, yet is their strength labour and sorrow ; for it is soon cut off, and we fly away.

So teach us to number our days, that we may apply our hearts unto wisdom.   *Psalm 90, written about 3400 years ago*

The Path of the Just is as the Shining Light

HAPPY is the man that findeth wisdom, and the man that getteth understanding,

For the merchandise of it is better than the merchandise of silver, and the gain thereof than fine gold.

She is more precious than rubies, and all the things thou canst desire are not to be compared unto her.

Length of days is in her right hand, and in her left hand riches and honour.

Her ways are ways of pleasantness, and all her paths are peace.

Hear, ye children, the instruction of a father, and attend to know understanding.

Get wisdom, get understanding : forget it not ; neither decline from the words of my mouth.

Forsake her not, and she shall preserve thee ; love her, and she shall keep thee.

Wisdom is the principal thing ; therefore get wisdom, and with all thy getting get understanding.

Exalt her, and she shall promote thee ; she shall bring thee to honour, when thou dost embrace her.

She shall give to thine head an ornament of grace ; a crown of glory shall she deliver to thee.

Take fast hold of instruction. Let her not go : keep her, for she is thy life.

Enter not into the path of the wicked, and go not in the way of evil men.

Avoid it, pass not by it, turn from it, and pass away, for they sleep not ; they eat the bread of wickedness, and drink the wine of violence.

But the path of the just is as the shining light, that shineth more and more unto the perfect day.   *Solomon*

Surely He Shall Deliver Thee

HE that dwelleth in the secret place of the Most High shall abide under the shadow of the Almighty.

Surely he shall deliver thee from the snare of the fowler, and from the noisome pestilence.

Thou shalt not be afraid for the terror by night, nor for the arrow that flieth by day, nor for the pestilence that walketh in darkness, nor for the destruction that wasteth at noonday.

A thousand shall fall at thy side, and ten thousand at thy right hand ; but it shall not come nigh thee.   *From Psalm 91*

Her Price is Far Above Rubies

WHO can find a virtuous woman ?   Her price is far above rubies. The heart of her husband doth safely trust in her, so that he shall have no need of spoil.

She will do him good and not evil all the days of her life.

She seeketh wool, and flax, and worketh willingly with her hands.

She is like the merchant's ships : she bringeth her food from afar.

She riseth while it is yet night, and giveth meat to her household, and a portion to her maidens.

She considereth a field, and buyeth it ; with the fruit of her hands she planteth a vineyard.

She girdeth her loins with strength, and strengtheneth her arm.

She perceiveth that her merchandise is good ; her candle goeth not out by night.

She layeth her hands to the spindle, and her hands hold the distaff.

She stretcheth out her hand to the poor ; yea, she reacheth forth her hands to the needy.

She maketh fine linen, and selleth it ; and delivereth girdles unto the merchant.

Strength and honour are her clothing, and she shall rejoice in time to come.

She openeth her mouth with wisdom, and in her tongue is the law of kindness.

She looketh well to the ways of her household, and eateth not the bread of idleness.

Her children arise up and call her blessed ; her husband also and he praiseth her.

Many daughters have done virtuously, but thou excellest them all.

Solomon

As for Man, His Days Are as Grass

LIKE as a father pitieth his children, so the Lord pitieth them that fear him.   For he knoweth our frame ; he remembereth that we are dust.

As for man, his days are as grass ; as a flower of the field, so he flourisheth.   For the wind passeth over it, and it is gone ; and the place thereof shall know it no more.

But the mercy of the Lord is from everlasting to everlasting upon them that fear him, and his righteousness unto children's children.

From Psalm 103

Sayings From the Psalms

THE Lord is my light and my salvation; whom shall I fear? The Lord is the strength of my life; of whom shall I be afraid?

This poor man cried, and the Lord heard him, and saved him out of all his troubles.

The young lions do lack and suffer hunger, but they that seek the Lord shall not want any good thing.

A little that a righteous man hath is better than the riches of many wicked.

The meek shall inherit the earth, and shall delight themselves in the abundance of peace.

I have been young and am now old, yet have I not seen the righteous forsaken, nor his seed begging bread.

Create in me a clean heart, O God, and renew a right spirit within me.

Yea, the sparrow hath found a house, and the swallow a nest where she may lay her young.

O sing unto the Lord a new song, for he hath done marvellous things; with trumpets and sound of cornet make a joyful noise before the King. Let the sea roar, the world, and they that dwell therein; let the clouds clap their hands; let the hills be joyful together before the Lord, for he cometh to judge the earth. With righteousness shall he judge the world, and the people with equity.

I will lift up mine eyes unto the hills from whence cometh my help.

The Lord is gracious and full of compassion; slow to anger, and of great mercy.

The Lord looseth the prisoners; the Lord openeth the eyes of the blind; the Lord raiseth them that are bowed down; the Lord loveth the righteous; the Lord preserveth the strangers; he relieveth the fatherless and widow; but the way of the wicked he turneth upside down.

They Shall Mount Up with Wings as Eagles

HAST thou not known? Hast thou not heard, that the everlasting God, the Lord, the Creator of the ends of the earth, fainteth not, neither is weary? There is no searching of his understanding. He giveth power to the faint; and to them that have no might he increaseth strength. Even the youths shall faint and be weary, and the young men shall utterly fall, but they that wait upon the Lord shall renew their strength; they shall mount up with wings as eagles, they shall run and not be weary, they shall walk and not faint.

Isaiah

God is Our Refuge and Strength

GOD is our refuge and strength, a very present help in trouble. Therefore will not we fear, though the earth be removed, and though the mountains be carried into the midst of the sea;

Though the waters roar and be troubled, though the mountains shake with the swelling thereof.

There is a river the streams whereof shall make glad the city of God, the holy place of the tabernacles of the Most High.

God is in the midst of her; she shall not be moved. God shall help her, and that right early.

He maketh wars to cease unto the end of the earth. He breaketh the bow, and cutteth the spear in sunder. He burneth the chariot in the fire.

Be still, and know that I am God : I will be exalted in the earth.

From Psalm 46

A Little Child Shall Lead Them

THE people that walked in darkness have seen a great light. They that dwell in the land of the shadow of death, upon them hath the light shined. For unto us a child is born, unto us a son is given; and the government shall be upon his shoulder; and his name shall be called Wonderful, Counsellor, The Mighty God, The Everlasting Father, The Prince of Peace.

Righteousness shall be the girdle of his loins, and faithfulness the girdle of his reins. The wolf shall dwell with the lamb, and the leopard shall lie down with the kid, and the calf and the young lion and the fatling together; and a little child shall lead them.

Isaiah

They Shall Learn War No More

HE shall judge among the nations, and shall rebuke many people; they shall beat their swords into plough-shares and their spears into pruning hooks; nation shall not lift up sword against nation, neither shall they learn war any more.   *Isaiah*

The Widow's Mite

JESUS sat over against the treasury, and beheld how the people cast money in. Many that were rich cast in much, and there came a certain poor widow, and she threw in two mites, which make a farthing.

He called unto him his disciples, and saith, Verily I say unto you that this poor widow hath cast more in than all they which have cast into the treasury; for all they did cast in of their abundance, but she of her want cast in all that she had, even all her living.

The Good Samaritan

A CERTAIN lawyer stood up, and tempted him, saying, Master, what shall I do to inherit eternal life ? He said unto him, What is written in the law ? How readest thou ? And he answering said, Thou shalt love the Lord thy God with all thy heart, and with all thy soul, and with all thy strength, and with all thy mind ; and thy neighbour as thyself. And he said unto him, Thou hast answered right : this do, and thou shalt live.

But he, willing to justify himself, said unto Jesus, And who is my neighbour ? And Jesus said :

A certain man went down from Jerusalem to Jericho, and fell among thieves, which stripped him of his raiment, and wounded him, and departed, leaving him half dead.

By chance there came down a certain priest that way ; and when he saw him he passed by on the other side. Likewise a Levite, when he was at the place, came and looked on him, and passed by on the other side.

But a certain Samaritan, as he journeyed, came where he was ; and when he saw him he had compassion on him, and went to him, and bound up his wounds, pouring in oil and wine, and set him on his own beast, and brought him to an inn, and took care of him.

On the morrow, when he departed, he took out two pence, and gave them to the host, and said, Take care of him ; and whatsoever thou spendest more, when I come again I will repay thee. Which now of these three, thinkest thou, was neighbour unto him that fell among thieves ?

And he said, He that shewed mercy on him. Then said Jesus unto him, Go, and do thou likewise.   *St Luke*

Letter of a Prodigal Son
Antonius Longus to Nilous, his mother.

M ANY greetings. I continually pray that you are in good health, and make supplication for you before our Lord Serapis.

I would have you know that I never expected you were coming up to the city. This was why I never came into it. But I was ashamed to come up to Karanis, for I am going about in rags.

I write to tell you that I have not any clothes. I entreat you, mother, to be reconciled to me. But I know what I have brought on myself. I have been chastised as I have been because I have sinned.

I heard from Postumus, who found you in Arsinoe county, and he has unseasonably told you all. Don't you know I would rather become a cripple than know that I owed anybody twopence ?

Come yourself, I beseech. Don't fail.

Written in the Second Century after Christ

The Rich Young Ruler

AND, behold, one came and said unto him, Good Master, what good thing shall I do that I may have eternal life ? He said unto him, Why callest thou me good ? There is none good but God. But if thou wilt enter into life, keep the commandments. The young man saith unto him, All these things have I kept from my youth up ; what lack I yet ? Jesus said unto him, If thou wilt be perfect, go and sell that thou hast, and give to the poor, and thou shalt have treasure in heaven ; and come and follow me.

But when the young man heard that saying he went away sorrowful, for he had great possessions. *St Matthew*

The Ride Into Jerusalem

Nineteen centuries separate these two descriptions of a ride into Jerusalem. The first is written in the first century of our Era and the second in the twentieth.

WHEN they drew nigh unto Jerusalem, and were come to Bethphage, unto the mount of Olives, then sent Jesus two disciples, saying unto them, Go into the village over against you, and straightway ye shall find an ass tied, and a colt with her : loose them, and bring them to me. If any man say aught unto you ye shall say, The Lord hath need of them, and straightway he will send them.

The disciples did as Jesus commanded them, and brought the ass, and the colt, and put on them their clothes, and they set him thereon.

A very great multitude spread their garments in the way ; others cut down branches from the trees, and strawed them in the way ; and the multitudes cried, saying, Hosanna, to the Son of David ! Blessed is he that cometh in the name of the Lord ! Hosanna in the highest ! *St Matthew*

WHEN fishes flew and forests walked
   And figs grew upon thorn,
Some moments when the moon was blood,
   Then surely I was born.

With monstrous head and sickening cry
   And ears like errant wings,
The devil's walking parody
   On all four-footed things.

The tattered outlaw of the earth,
   Of ancient crooked will ;
Starve, scourge, deride me : I am dumb,
   I keep my secret still.

Fools ! For I also had my hour ;
   One far fierce hour and sweet :
There was a shout about my ears,
   And palms before my feet.

      G. K. Chesterton (The Donkey)

Blessed Are They

The chief foundation-stone of our English language is the Bible. This is how it has grown up, shown in one of its noblest passages as written by John Wycliffe, as improved by William Tyndale, and as perfected by the forty-nine translators in the Jerusalem Chamber at Westminster.

BLESSID be pore men in spirit, for the kyngdom of heuenes is hern.

Blessid be mylde men, for thei schulen weeld the erthe.

Blessid be thei that mournen, for thei schulen be counfortid.

Blessid be thei that hungren and thirsten rightewisnesse, for thei schulen be fulfillid.

Blessid ben merciful men, for thei schulen gete merci.

Blessid ben thei that ben of clene herte, for thei schulen se god.

Blessid be pesible men, for thei schulen be cleped goddis children.

Blessid ben thei that suffren persicusioun for rightewisnesse, for the kyngdom of heuenis is hern.

Wycliffe's Bible, about 1382

BLESSED are the povre in sprete, for theirs is the kyngdome of heven.

Blessed are they that morne, for they shalbe conforted.

Blessed are the meke, for they shall inherit the erth.

Blessed are they which honger and thurst for rightewesnes, for they shalbe filled.

Blessed are the mercifull, for they shall obteyne mercy.

Blessed are the pure in herte, for they shall se God.

Blessed are the peacemakers, for they shalbe called the chyldren of God.

Blessed are they which suffre persecucion for rightewesnes sake, for theirs ys the kyngdome of heuen.

Tyndale's Testament, 1535

BLESSED are the poor in spirit, for theirs is the kingdom of heaven.

Blessed are they that mourn, for they shall be comforted.

Blessed are the meek, for they shall inherit the earth.

Blessed are they which do hunger and thirst after righteousness, for they shall be filled.

Blessed are the merciful, for they shall obtain mercy.

Blessed are the pure in heart, for they shall see God.

Blessed are the peacemakers, for they shall be called the children of God.

Blessed are they which are persecuted for righteousness' sake, for theirs is the kingdom of heaven.

Authorised Version, 1612

MADONNA AND CHILD WITH ST. JOHN, BY RAPHAEL

MADONNA AND CHILD, BY RAPHAEL

MADONNA IN THE NATIONAL MUSEUM, FLORENCE

The Book Our Lord Immortalised

Some of the familiar words of Jesus have a striking resemblance to passages in one of the popular works of his day, The Testaments of the Twelve Patriarchs. It cannot be doubted that Jesus read this book and that it influenced his thought. These parallel passages make it quite clear.

Words of Jesus

WITH what measure ye mete, it shall be measured to you again.
The Sermon on the Mount

Whosoever shall do and teach them, the same shall be called great in the Kingdom of Heaven.
Sermon on the Mount

Thou shalt love the Lord thy God with all thy heart, and with all thy soul, and with all thy mind.
Thou shalt love thy neighbour as thyself. *St Matthew*

So likewise shall my heavenly Father do also unto you if ye from your hearts forgive not every one of their trespasses.
St Matthew

I was a-hungered, and ye gave me meat.

I was thirsty, and ye gave me drink.

I was a stranger, and ye took me in ;

Naked, and ye clothed me.

I was sick, and ye visited me.

I was in prison, and ye came unto me. *St Matthew*

Take heed to yourselves. If thy brother trespass against thee, rebuke him ; and if he repent, forgive him. *St Luke*

Words of the Patriarchs

EVEN as a man doeth to his neighbour even so will the Lord do to him.
Testament of Zebulun

Whosoever teaches noble things and does them shall be enthroned with kings.
From the Testament of Levi

Love the Lord through all your life,
And one another with a true heart.
From the Testament of Dan

If he be shameless and persisteth in his wrong-doing, even so forgive him from the heart, and leave to God the avenging.
Testament of Gad

I was sold into slavery, and the Lord of all made me free.

I was taken into captivity, and His strong hand succoured me.

I was beset with hunger, and the Lord Himself nourished me.

I was alone, and God comforted me. I was sick, and the Lord visited me.

I was in prison, and my God showed favour unto me ;

In bonds, and He released me ;

Slandered, and He pleaded my cause. *Testament of Joseph*

Love ye one another from the heart. If a man speak against thee, speak peaceably to him, and in thy soul hold not guile. If he repent and confess, forgive him.
Gad

The Prodigal Son

A CERTAIN man had two sons, and the younger of them said to his father, Father, give me the portion of goods that falleth to me. And he divided unto them his living.

Not many days after the younger son gathered all together, and took his journey into a far country, and there wasted his substance with riotous living. When he had spent all there arose a mighty famine in that land; and he began to be in want; and he joined himself to a citizen of that country, and he sent him into his fields to feed swine. And he would fain have filled his belly with the husks that the swine did eat; and no man gave unto him.

When he came to himself, he said, How many hired servants of my father's have bread enough and to spare, and I perish with hunger! I will arise, and go to my father, and will say unto him, Father, I have sinned again heaven, and before thee, and am no more worthy to be called thy son; make me as one of thy hired servants.

And he arose, and came to his father; but when he was yet a great way off his father saw him, and had compassion, and ran, and fell on his neck, and kissed him.

The son said unto him, Father, I have sinned against heaven, and in thy sight, and am no more worthy to be called thy son. But the father said to his servants, Bring forth the best robe, and put it on him; and put a ring on his hand, and shoes on his feet; and bring hither the fatted calf, and kill it, and let us eat, and be merry, for this my son was dead, and is alive again; he was lost, and is found. And they began to be merry.

Now his elder son was in the field, and as he came and drew nigh to the house he heard music and dancing; and he called one of the servants, and asked what these things meant.

He said unto him, Thy brother is come; and thy father hath killed the fatted calf, because he hath received him safe and sound.

He was angry, and would not go in; therefore came his father out, and intreated him. And he said to his father, Lo, these many years do I serve thee, neither transgressed I at any time thy commandment; and yet thou never gavest me a kid, that I might make merry with my friends; but as soon as this thy son was come, which hath devoured thy living, thou hast killed for him the fatted calf.

And he said unto him, Son, thou art ever with me, and all that I have is thine. It was meet that we should make merry, and be glad; for this thy brother was dead and is alive again; and was lost, and is found.   *St Luke*

The Pharisee and the Publican

HE spake this parable unto certain which trusted in themselves that they were righteous, and despised others.

Two men went up into the temple to pray, the one a Pharisee, and the other a publican. The Pharisee stood and prayed thus with himself: *God, I thank thee that I am not as other men are, extortioners, unjust, or even as this publican. I fast twice in the week, I give tithes of all I possess.* And the publican, standing afar off, would not lift up so much as his eyes unto heaven, but smote upon his breast, saying, *God be merciful to me a sinner.* St Luke

Behold, I Show You a Mystery

BEHOLD, I show you a mystery: We shall not all sleep, but we shall all be changed, in a moment, in the twinkling of an eye, at the last trump: for the trumpet shall sound, and the dead shall be raised incorruptible, and we shall be changed. For this corruptible must put on incorruption, and this mortal must put on immortality.

So when this corruptible shall have put on incorruption, and this mortal shall have put on immortality, then shall be brought to pass the saying that is written, Death is swallowed up in victory. O death, where is thy sting? O grave, where is thy victory?

The sting of death is sin; and the strength of sin is the law. But thanks be to God, which giveth us the victory through our Lord Jesus Christ. Therefore, my beloved brethren, be ye stedfast, unmoveable, always abounding in the work of the Lord, forasmuch as ye know that your labour is not in vain in the Lord. St Paul

Who Shall Separate Us?

WHO shall separate us from the love of Christ? Shall tribulation, or distress, or persecution, or famine, or nakedness, or peril, or sword? Nay, in all these things we are more than conquerors, through him that loved us, for I am persuaded that neither death nor life, nor angels, nor principalities, nor powers, nor things present, nor things to come, nor height, nor depth, nor any other creature, shall be able to separate us from the love of God.

From Paul's Letter to the Romans

This Nightingale

IT were a heavenly health,
It were an endless wealth,
A life for God himself,
To hear this nightingale . . .

John Skelton, 16th-century Poet Laureate

Sayings of St Paul

THE kingdom of God is not meat and drink, but righteousness and peace.

God hath chosen the foolish things of the world to confound the wise, and the weak to confound the mighty.

All things are lawful unto me, but all things are not expedient ; all things are lawful for me, but I will not be brought under the power of any.

We look not at the things which are seen, but at the things which are not seen, for the things which are seen are temporal, but the things which are not seen are eternal.

If a man be overtaken in a fault, restore such a one in the spirit of weakness, considering thyself, lest thou also be tempted.

Bear ye one another's burdens, and so fulfil the law of Christ.

Be not deceived ; God is not mocked, for whatsoever a man soweth, that shall he also reap.

Let us not be weary in well doing, for in due season we shall reap, if we faint not.

Let all bitterness, and wrath, and anger, and evil speaking, be put away from you.

Whatsoever things are true, whatsoever things are honest, whatsoever things are just, whatsoever things are pure, whatsoever things are lovely, whatsoever things are of good report, if there be any virtue, and if there be any praise, think on these things.

Be at peace among yourselves. Be patient toward all men. See that none render evil for evil. Rejoice evermore. Pray without ceasing. In everything give thanks. Prove all things. Hold fast that which is good. Abstain from all appearance of evil.

Charge them that are rich in this world that they be not high-imnded, nor trust in uncertain riches.

Follow righteousness, faith, charity, peace, but foolish and un-learned questions avoid, knowing that they gender strifes.

The just shall live by faith. Faith is the substance of things hoped for, the evidence of things not seen.

I am ready to be offered, and the time of my departure is at hand. I have fought a good fight ; I have finished my course ; I have kept faith ; henceforth there is laid up for me a crown of righteousness.

What Doth the Lord Require of Thee ?

WHAT doth the Lord require of thee but to do justly, and to love mercy, and to walk humbly with thy God ? *Micah*

The Philosophy of Galilee

WHAT shall it profit a man if he shall gain the whole world and lose his own soul ?

Thou shalt love the Lord thy God with all thy heart, and with all thy soul, and with all thy mind ; and thou shalt love thy neighbour as thyself.

Beware of covetousness, for a man's life consisteth not in the abundance of things which he possesseth.

If any man desire to be first, he shall be last, and servant of all.

They that take the sword shall perish with the sword.

Render unto Caesar the things which are Caesar's, and unto God the things which are God's.

Give not that which is holy unto the dogs, neither cast ye your pearls before swine.

Every idle word that men shall speak they shall give account of in the day of judgment, for by thy words thou shalt be justified, and by thy words thou shalt be condemned.

There is nothing from without a man that entering into him can defile him, but the things which come out of him are they which defile a man.

Every kingdom divided against itself is brought to desolation.

How can one enter into a strong man's house and spoil his goods except he first bind the strong man ?

He that is not with me is against me.

Take heed that ye do not your alms before men ; do not sound a trumpet before thee as hypocrites do. When thou doest alms let not thy left hand know what thy right hand doeth.

Lay not up for yourselves treasures upon earth, where moth and dust doth corrupt and thieves break through and steal ; but lay for yourselves treasures in heaven, for where your treasure is, there will your heart be also.

No man can serve two masters, for either he will hate the one and love the other or he will hold to the one and despise the other. Ye cannot serve God and mammon

Take no thought for what ye shall eat or drink, nor what ye shall put on. Is not the life more than meat, and the body than raiment ? Behold the fowls of the air, for they sow not, neither do they reap, nor gather into barns ; yet your heavenly Father feedeth them.

Consider the lilies of the field, how they grow ; they toil not, neither do they spin, yet even Solomon in all his glory was not arrayed like one of these. If God so clothe the grass of the field, shall he not much more clothe you ? Therefore take no thought, saying,

What shall we eat, or What shall we drink ? but seek first the kingdom of God and his righteousness, and all these things shall be added unto you.

Take no thought for the morrow, for the morrow shall take thought for the things of itself. Sufficient unto the day is the evil thereof.

Of all things whatsoever ye would that men should do unto you, do ye even so to them.

Enter ye in at the strait gate, for wide is the gate and broad is the way that leadeth to destruction, but strait is the gate and narrow is the way which leadeth unto life.

Beware of false prophets which come in sheep's clothing, but inwardly are ravening wolves. Ye shall know them by their fruits. Do men gather grapes of thorns, or figs of thistles ? A good tree cannot bring forth evil fruit, nor a corrupt tree bring forth good fruit.

Judge not, that ye be not judged. Why beholdest thou the mote that is in thy brother's eye but not the beam that is in thine own eye ? First cast out the beam of thine own eye, and then shalt thou see clearly to cast out the mote of thy brother's eye.

If thy brother shall trespass against thee, go and tell him of his fault alone, but if he will not hear thee, then take with thee one or two more. If he shall neglect to hear them, tell it unto the church, but if he neglect to hear the church let him be unto thee as a heathen man.

If thou bring thy gift to the altar and remember that thy brother hath brought aught against thee, first be reconciled to thy brother and then offer thy gift. Agree with thine adversary quickly, lest the adversary deliver thee to the judge and thou be cast into prison.

If thy hand or thy foot offend thee, cast them off.

Resist not evil. Whosoever shall smite thee on thy right cheek, turn to him the other. If any man take away thy coat, give him thy cloak also, and whosoever shall compel thee to go a mile, go with him twain.

Give to him that asketh thee.

Love your enemies, bless them that curse you, do good to them that hate you, and pray for them which despitefully use you.

Behold a sower went forth to sow. Some seeds fell by the wayside, and the fowls came and devoured them up. Some fell upon stony places, and because they had no root they withered away. Some fell among thorns, and the thorns sprung up and choked them. But other fell into good ground and brought forth fruit, some thirty, some sixty, some a hundredfold.

The kingdom of heaven is like unto leaven, which a woman took and hid in three measures of meal till the whole was leavened. It is like a merchantman seeking goodly pearls, who, when he had found one pearl of great price, went and sold all that he had and bought it.

Except ye become as little children ye shall not enter the kingdom of heaven. Whoso shall offend one of these little ones it were better for him that a millstone were hanged about his neck and that he were drowned in the depth of the sea. Woe unto the world for offences, for it needs be that offences come, but woe to that man by which the offence cometh.

Woe unto you, scribes and Pharisees! for ye devour widows' houses, and for a pretence make long prayers.

Woe unto you, ye blind guides, for ye pay tithe of mint and anise and cummin, and have omitted the weightier matters of the law— Judgment, Mercy, and Faith. Why strain ye at a gnat and swallow a camel? Ye make clean the outside of the cup and platter, but within they are full of extortion and excess. Cleanse first that which is within, and the outside may be clean also.

No man having put his hand to the plough and looking back is fit for the kingdom of God.

Every one that doeth evil hateth light, but he that doeth truth cometh to the light.

If thou canst believe all things are possible. If ye have faith as a grain of mustard seed ye shall say unto this mountain, Remove hence, and it shall be removed.

He that is faithful in that which is least is faithful also in much.

Unto whom much is given of him shall much be required.

Collected from the Sayings of Jesus

Love Letter from a Coffee House

MADAM, It is the hardest thing in the world to be in love and yet attend to business. As for me, all who speak to me find me out, and I must lock myself up, or other people will do it for me.

A gentleman asked me this morning what news from Lisbon, and I anserd she's exquisitely handsome. Another desired to know when I had been last at Hampton Court. I reply'd twill be on Tuesday come se'ennight. Prithee allow me at least to kisse your hand before that day, that my mind may be in some composure. O love!

A thousand torments dwell about thee,
Yet who would live to live without thee?

Methinks I could write a volume to you, but all the language on earth would fail in saying how much, and with what disinterested passion, I am ever yours, RICHD STEELE.

Written in St James's Coffee House, September 1, 1707

The Old Lady Remembering

BENEATH her lids the pictures flit
Of memories far away ;
Her look has not a hint in it
Of what she sees today.   *Thomas Ashe*

Honour Most Of All

I COULD not love thee, Dear, so much
Loved I not honour more.   *Richard Lovelace*

The Cook Without a Kitchen

PEOPLE say that the German has no talent for politics ;
but how can a man learn to cook if he is forbidden to
enter the kitchen ?   *Prince Lichnowsky*

Some Valiant Deed

MY hour at last has come ;
Yet not ingloriously or passively
I die, but first will do some valiant deed
Of which mankind shall hear in after time.
Homer's Iliad

Stay, Traveller, Stay

STAY, weary traveller, stay !
Beneath these boughs repose ;
A step out of the way
My little fountain flows.
And never quite forget
The monumental urn
Which Simus here hath set
His buried child to mourn.
From Ancient Greece, translated by C. Merivale

A Child's Prayer

FATHER, we thank Thee for the night
And for the pleasant morning light,
For rest and food and loving care,
And all that makes the world so fair.
Help us to do the thing we should,
To be to others kind and good,
In all we do, in all we say,
To grow more loving every day.
By a Writer Unknown

The Green Caravanserai

THE bed was made, the room was fit,
　By punctual eve the stars were lit ;
The air was still, the water ran ;
No need there was for maid or man,
When we put up, my ass and I
At God's green caravanserai.

Old Play

Envy Me Not

O MAN, whosoever thou art, and whensoever thou cometh (for come
　I know thou wilt), I am Cyrus, the founder of the Persian Empire ; envy me not the little earth that covers my body.

The Epitaph which much moved
Alexander on his visit to Persia

To an Ass, Long Ago

SWEET ass, go gently, go
　By night and day, sang she ;
Rock gentle as a cradle
　Or a mother's knee,
For thou must bear my Baby
　As thou must bear me ;
O do not break His slumber,
　Go gently, go, sang she.

By a Writer Unknown

More and More and Less and Less

A SPECIALIST is a man who keeps on learning more and more about
　less and less until ultimately he knows everything about nothing,
while the politician is a man who keeps on learning less and less about
more and more until ultimately he knows nothing about everything.

A Twentieth-century Saying

The Little Child so High

UPON this tall pagoda's peak
　My hand can nigh the stars enclose ;
I dare not raise my voice to speak,
　For fear of startling God's repose.

A Chinese poet of the tenth century on being
taken as a child to the top of a pagoda

Fortune's Smile

IF Fortune smiles, who doesn't ?　If Fortune doesn't,
who does ? 　　　　　　　　　 *Chinese Proverb*

Warm for Three Winters

ONE kind word will keep you warm for three winters.

Chinese Proverb

The Rider on the Tiger

HE who rides a tiger cannot dismount.

Chinese Proverb

Poor Man's Grace

HEAVENLY Father bless us,
And keep us all alive,
There's ten of us to dinner
And not enough for five.

By a Writer Unknown

The King to His Friends

KING JAMES advising his friends to go to their country houses :

Gentlemen, at London you are like ships at sea which show like nothing, but in your country villages you are like ships in a river which look like great things.

The King Stoops

JUST before the charge was read out to Charles Stuart at the Trial the silver head of his staff happened to fall off, at which he wondered.   But no man moved to pick it up and *the King stooped for it himself.*   *Record of the Trial*

The Slanderer

WHO loves another's name to stain,
He must not dine with me again.

On Augustine of Hippo's dining-table

Farewell to an Eastern Traveller

THY journey be auspicious ; may the breeze,
Gentle and soothing, fan thy cheek ; may lakes
All bright with lily cups delight thine eye,
The sunbeam's heat be cooled by shady trees,
The dust beneath thy feet the pollen be
Of lotuses.

From a Sanskrit play 1600 years old

What He Knew

I NEVER learned how to tune a harp or to play upon a lute, but I know how to raise an obscure city to wealth and greatness.

Themistocles

Horace Walpole Gives Thanks

THANK you for your lamentations on my gout ; it was, in proportion to my size, very slender ; when I had what I called big shoes I could have danced a minuet on a silver penny.

The Comedy and the Tragedy

LIFE is a comedy to him who thinks and a tragedy to him who feels. *Horace Walpole*

The Ghost

THE ghost of Raleigh pursued the House of Stuart to the scaffold. *Professor Trevelyan*

So Goes the Round

WAR begets Poverty ; Poverty, Peace ;
  Peace begets Plenty, then riches increase.
Riches bring Pride, and Pride is War's Ground.
War begets Poverty—so goes the round.
Written by Robert Hayman in 1630

The Difference

THE witty and learned Duchess of Milan having asked a company of guests what was the difference between herself and a clock, Bernard Fontenelle, the French scholar, answered, " The difference is this—that a clock marks the hours but your Grace makes us forget them."

The Little Ship in the Great Sea

THEY say that I am small and frail,
  And cannot live in stormy seas ;
It may be so ; yet every sail
  Makes shipwreck in the swelling breeze.
Not strength nor size can then hold fast,
  But Fortune's favour, Heaven's decree :
Let others trust in oar and mast,
  But may the gods take care of me.
From the Greek Anthology

White as Snow

O GOD, the cleanest offering
  Of tainted earth below
Unblushing to Thy feet we bring :
  A leper white as snow !
*John Bannister Tabb on Father
Damien, who became a leper*

The Good We Do

THE good we do today becomes
The happiness of tomorrow.

Hindu Proverb

Sir Humphry Davy Looks Back

THE source of the little information and intelligence I possess I
must refer to a restless activity of spirit, a love of glory which
ever belonged to my infancy, and a sensibility easily excited.

Accident opened to me in early youth a philosophical career,
which I pursued with success. In manhood fortune smiled on me
and made me independent; I then really became a philosopher, and
pursued my travels with the object of instructing myself and benefit-
ing mankind. I have seen most parts of Europe, and conversed, I
believe, with all the illustrious men of science belonging to them.
I have added some little to the quantity of human knowledge, and
I have endeavoured to add something to the quantity of human
happiness. *Humphry Davy shortly before he died*

I Tell Thee, Priest

I TELL thee, priest, when shoemakers make shoes
That are well sewed, with never a stitch amiss;
When tailors steal no stuff from gentlemen;
When tanners are with curriers well agreed,
And both so dress their hides that we go dry;
When tinkers make no more holes than they found;
When thatchers think their wages worth their work;
When colliers put no dust into their sacks;
When Davy Diker digs and dallies not;
When smiths shoe horses as they would be shod;
When brewers put no baggage in their beer;
When vintners mix no water with their wine;
When printers pass no errors in their books;
When pewterers infect no tin with lead;
When searchers see all corners in a ship;
When sycophants can find no place in court,
But are espied for echoes, as they are;
When all these things are ordered as they ought,
And see themselves within my glass of steel:
Even then, my priest, may you make holiday,
And pray no more but ordinary prayers.

George Gascoigne

At Rest

HERE lies my wife! here let her lie!
Now she's at rest, and so am I.

John Dryden

A Very Early Riser

AT the Last Day, while all the rest
Are soundly sleeping underground,
He will be up, clean-shaved and dressed,
An hour before the trumpets sound.

Gerald Massey

God Gives Every Bird Its Food

GOD gives every bird its food, but does not throw
it into the nest.   *Old Proverb*

The First Casualty

THE first casualty when war comes is truth.

Hiram Johnson

These Above All

IN things essential Unity; in things doubtful Liberty;
in all things Charity.   *Old Saying*

A Rare Spirit

HE could always be made happy when tired if
someone mentioned the name of Shakespeare.

Life of Temple Gairdner

The Great Conqueror

HE is twice a conqueror who conquers himself in
the moment of victory.   *Publilius Syrus*

They Never Happened

I AM an old man and have had many troubles, but most
of them never happened.   *Carved over a mantelpiece*

Let Us Do It Now

I SHALL pass through this world but once.   Any good thing
therefore that I can do, or any kindness I can show to
any human being, let me do it now.   Let me not defer nor
neglect it, for I shall not pass this way again.

By a Writer Unknown

Why They Loved Him

WE love him for the enemies he has made.

Said of a President of America

The Slaves

SLAVERY enchains a few, but more enchain
themselves to slavery.   *Seneca*

His Nets in Many Streams

I CAST my nets in many streams
To catch the silver fish of dreams.
Karle Wilson Baker

Alas Poor Brother

P OOR Cleon out of envy died,
His brother thief to see
Nailed near him to be crucified
Upon a higher tree.
Translated by Francis Hodgson from the Greek Lucilius

Ask Your Purse

A SK your purse what you should buy.
German Proverb

A Beggar

B ETTER to die a beggar than to live one.
Old Proverb

Knowing All

T o understand all is to forgive all.
French Saying

Two Men Looked Out

T WO men looked out through prison bars ;
The one saw mud, the other stars.
Writer unknown

The Poet's Shoe-strings

P OETRY has never brought in enough to buy shoe-strings.
Wordsworth

Keeping War Alive

N O one ever has succeeded in keeping nations
at war except by lies.   *Salvador de Madariaga*

The Valiant and the Virtuous

H ER name was Margaret Lucas, youngest sister to Lord Lucas of
Colchester, a noble familie, for all the brothers were valiant and
all the sisters virtuous.   *Epitaph on Margaret, Duchess of Newcastle*

The Three Johns

T HERE are three Johns : the real John, known only to his Maker ;
John's ideal John, never the real one, and often very unlike him ;
Thomas's ideal John, never the real John, nor John's John, but often
very unlike either.   *Oliver Wendell Holmes*

Two Friends in Arabia

THE MYSTIC : All that he knows I see.
The Philosopher : All that he sees I know.

Inscriptions on Three Gates

ON the First : Be Bold.
On the Second : Be bold, be very bold.
On the Third : Be not too bold.

The Bigot, the Fool, and the Slave

HE that will not reason is a bigot ; he that cannot reason is a fool :
he that dare not reason is a slave.

William Drummond

His Country's Friend

A MAN who would give his life to serve his country but would not
do a base thing to save it.

Said of Lord Saltoun, in the 17th century

The World of Fools

THE world of fools has such a store,
That he who would not see an ass
Must bide at home and bolt his door,
And break his looking-glass.

Writer Unknown

The Little Beauty

THIS is a little work, but beautiful to look upon like a rose in a
garden, or a violet in a basket of flowers.

Inscription on a small bath in ancient Greece

Adam and Eve

WHEN Adam delved and Eve span
Who was then a gentleman ?

Cry of the Peasants in the Rising of 1381

The Bathers

THE immortals bathe when the bath is first opened, at the fifth
hour the demi-gods, and later all the rubbish.

On a bath in ancient Greece

Delivering the Goods

IT is the cock that does the crowing but the hen
delivers the goods. *Familiar Saying*

Nonsense

I FLATTER myself that we are almost the only people who understand nonsense.   *Hazlitt on the English*

Every Man Decideth

To every man there openeth
A high way and a low,
And every man decideth
The way his soul shall go.
John Oxenham

The Beggar and the Prince

I WOULD recommend every young man to take to heart the following lines.   There are

two points in the adventure of the diver :
One when, a beggar, he prepares to plunge,
One when, a prince, he rises with his pearl.
Sir Ernest Shackleton

Our Paradise

MEMORY is the only Paradise from which we cannot be turned out.   *Jean Paul Richter*

The Adventure of Being Alive

MERELY to be alive is adventure enough in a world like this, so erratic and disjoined ; so lovely and so odd, and mysterious and profound.   It is, at any rate, a pity to remain in it half-dead.
Walter de la Mare

Down to Kew in Lilac Time

Go down to Kew in lilac-time, in lilac-time, in lilac-time ;
Go down to Kew in lilac-time (it isn't far from London)
And you shall wander hand in hand with love in summer's wonderland ;
Go down to Kew in lilac-time (it isn't far from London).
Alfred Noyes

Our Little Maid

HERE lies, but seven years old, our little maid,
Once of the darkness, oh, so sore afraid !
Light of the World, remember that small fear,
And when not moon nor stars do shine, draw near.
Epitaph on a little child, by Walter de la Mare

Upstairs

I CAME upstairs into the world, for I was born in a cellar.
William Congreve

PRINCE BALTHASAR CARLOS, BY VELASQUEZ

PRINCESS MARGARET, BY VELASQUEZ

The Broken Vow

I LOVED thee, beautiful and kind,
And plighted an eternal vow ;
So altered are thy face and mind,
Twere perjury to love thee now.

Robert Nugent

The Good and the Bad

O GOD, show pity toward the wicked, for on the
good Thou hast already bestowed mercy in
having made them good.   *Sadi the Persian*

The Pearls

IF the diver were to think of the jaws of the
crocodile he would never find the pearls.

Sadi the Persian

He Was Not Born For That

I WILL love with you ; I will not hate with you.
I was not born for that.   *Sophocles*

A Great Man Leaving the World

I CANNOT bear to leave the world with all the
misery in it.   *Lord Shaftesbury, dying*

Socrates Does Without

How many things are here which I do not want !

Socrates at a Fair

The Fourth Kingdom

KING JAMES said to the fly, Have I three kingdoms,
and thou must needs fly into my eye ?

John Selden

A Sad Day for Bottom the Weaver

*It was the punishment of a man who played Bottom the Weaver on
a Sunday in Puritan England to carry these lines in front of him :*

GOOD people, I have played the beast,
And brought ill things to pass :
I was a man, but thus have made
Myself a silly ass.

Alas For His Country

I TREMBLE for my country when I reflect that
God is just.   *Thomas Jefferson*

Today and Tomorrow

WE have to live today by what truth we can get, and be ready tomorrow to call it falsehood. *William James*

The Stars and the Rocks

IT is often a temptation to throw the compass overboard and steer by the stars, but those who do are apt to get on the rocks.   *J. A. Spender*

It Does Not Follow

IT does not follow that because old men have made mistakes young men are infallible. *J. A. Spender*

Do Not Write It Down

OH, no, do not write it down. If you write it it can be rescinded.   - *St Francis*

Stronger Than Evil

THE Gates of Thought are stronger than the Gates of Hell.   *Hegel*

Quiet Conversation

SILENCE—a conversation with an Englishman.
Heinrich Heine

The Rainbow

IF life an empty bubble be,
How sad for those who cannot see
The rainbow in the bubble.
Frederick Locker-Lampson

His Best Friends

COME, my best friends, my books, and lead me on.
Abraham Cowley

All He Wanted

DIOGENES who lived in a tub was sitting in the sun one day when Alexander passed by, and, seeing a man of such simple needs, the emperor said to him, What can I do for you ?
Please get out of my light, said Diogenes.

The Pride of Humility

DIOGENES : I tread the ambition of Plato under my feet.

Plato : Yet in how great pride swellest thyself, O Diogenes, while thou thinkest thyself to tread any man's pride under thy feet.

The Ladye of Our Race to a Little One in Its Cradle

In these verses, written on the eve of revolutions which shook all Europe in 1848, Lord Macaulay imagines a curtained room in an old mansion where lies a sleeping infant, and by its cradle come the fairy queens who rule our birth according to the fairy tales. One by one they come.

Nor deigning on the boy a glance to cast
　　Swept careless by the gorgeous Queen of Gain ;
More scornful still, the Queen of Fashion passed
　　With mincing gait and sneer of cold disdain.

The Queen of Power tossed high her jewelled head ;
　　And o'er her shoulder threw a wrathful frown :
The Queen of Pleasure on the pillow shed
　　Scarce one stray rose-leaf from her fragrant crown.

Still Fay in long procession followed Fay ;
　　And still the little couch remained unblest :
But, when those wayward sprites had passed away,
　　Came One, the last, the mightiest, and the best.

Oh, glorious lady, with the eyes of light
　　And laurels clustering round thy lofty brow,
Who by the cradle's side didst watch that night,
　　Warbling a sweet strange music, who wast thou ?

Yes, darling, let them go (so ran the strain).
　　Yes ; let them go, Gain, Fashion, Pleasure, Power,
And all the busy elves to whose domain
　　Belongs the nether sphere, the fleeting hour.

Without one envious sigh, one anxious scheme,
　　The nether sphere, the fleeting hour resign.
Mine is the world of thought, the world of dream,
　　Mine all the past, and all the future mine.

Fortune, that lays in sport the mighty low,
　　Age, that to penance turns the joys of youth,
Shall leave untouched the gifts which I bestow,
　　The sense of beauty and the thirst of truth.

There are who, while to vulgar eyes they seem
　　Of all my bounties largely to partake,
Of me as of some rival's handmaid deem,
　　And court me but for gain's, power's, fashion's sake.

To such, though deep their lore, though wide their fame,
　　Shall my great mysteries be all unknown ;
But thou, through good and evil, praise and blame,
　　Wilt not thou love me for myself alone ?

Yes ; thou wilt love me with exceeding love ;
　　And I will tenfold all that love repay,
Still smiling, though the tender may reprove,
　　Still faithful, though the trusted may betray.

For aye mine emblem was, and aye shall be,
　The ever-during plant whose bough I wear,
Brightest and greenest then, when every tree
　That blossoms in the light of time is bare.

In the dark hour of shame, I deigned to stand
　Before the frowning peers at Bacon's side :
On a far shore I smoothed with tender hand,
　Through months of pain, the sleepless bed of Hyde :

I brought the wise and brave of ancient days
　To cheer the cell where Raleigh pined alone ;
I lighted Milton's darkness with the blaze
　Of the bright ranks that guard the eternal throne.

And even so, my child, it is my pleasure,
　That thou not then alone should'st feel me nigh,
When in domestic bliss and studious leisure,
　Thy weeks uncounted come, uncounted fly ;

Not then alone, when myriads, closely pressed
　Around thy car, the shout of triumph raise ;
Nor when in gilded drawing-rooms, thy breast
　Swells at the sweeter sound of woman's praise.

No : when on restless night dawns cheerless morrow,
　When weary soul and wasting body pine,
Thine am I still, in danger, sickness, sorrow,
　In conflict, obloquy, want, exile, thine ;

Thine, where on mountain waves the snowbirds scream
　Where more than Thule's winter barbs the breeze,
Where scarce, through lowering clouds, one sickly gleam
　Lights the drear Mayday of Antarctic seas ;

Thine, when around thy litter's track all day
　White sandhills shall reflect the blinding glare ;
Thine, when through forests breathing death, thy way
　All night shall wind by many a tiger's lair.

Thine most, when friends turn pale, when traitors fly,
　When, hard beset, thy spirit, justly proud,
For truth, peace, freedom, mercy, dares defy
　A sullen priesthood and a raving crowd.

Amidst the din of all things fell and vile,
　Hate's yell, and Envy's hiss, and Folly's bray,
Remember me ; and with an unforced smile
　See riches, baubles, flatterers pass away.

Yes : they will pass away ; nor deem it strange :
　They come and go, as comes and goes the sea :
And let them come and go : thou, through all change,
　Fix thy firm gaze on virtue and on me.

Macaulay

To a Soul Going Out Into the Dark

MY pretty soul, my fleeting soul,
 Who guest and comrade wert to me,
To what dim undiscovered goal,
 Pale little spectre, now wilt flee,
On timid wings of frigid fear,
Forgetting all thy wonted cheer ?
    Hadrian, Roman Emperor of Britain

A Little While the Rose

A LITTLE while the rose,
 And after that the thorn ;
An hour of dewy morn,
And then the glamour goes.
Ah, love in beauty born,
A little while the rose !
    Translated by Henry Van Dyke

His Life Summed Up

HE slept beneath the moon
 He basked beneath the sun ;
He lived a life of going to do
And died with nothing done.
   Old epitaph written by James Albery

Beauty

IF Beauty grows old, share it before it be gone ; and if it abides, why fear to give it away ?   *From the Greek Anthology*

The Secret

WHEN a German knows he is going to die his emotions all break forth and he weeps pitifully. A Frenchman sobs and calls for his mother. But Tommy Atkins is silent as if he had a secret with the Almighty. *Walter Hines Page, American Ambassador*

His Watch

I AM to be shot in an hour's time. Dearest, your hubby will die with your name on his lips, your face before his eyes.

I cannot tell you, sweetheart, how much it means to me to leave you alone, you and my sweet little Annie. I leave my medals to my father, and *my watch to the officer who is executing me*, because I believe him to be a gentleman. *An English officer captured by Irish rebels in 1921, writing to his wife*

Good Comfort

BE of good comfort, maisters, for I have espied land.
Diogenes to his pupils, on coming
to a blank page in a long lecture

Cabbages and Kings

ARISTIPPUS TO DIOGENES : If you knew how to flatter kings you
would not need to live on herbs.

Diogenes : If you knew how to live on herbs you would not need to
flatter kings.

The Master of Demosthenes

DIOGENES was taking his breakfast in a small shop when he saw
Demosthenes pass, and called to him. As he took no notice,
Diogenes said, " So you are ashamed to be seen in a shop, are you ?
Why, your master, the common people, comes here every day."
Aelian

The Sentry At His Post

THE highest of us is but a sentry at his post.
George John Whyte-Melville

The Poorest Way

THE poorest way to face life is to face it with a sneer.
Theodore Roosevelt

Civilisation

CIVILISATION is being poisoned by its own waste products.
Dean Inge

This Field Is Never Quiet

THE battle of freedom is never done ; that
field is never quiet. *H. W. Nevinson*

Fools

THE ultimate result of sheltering men from the effects of
folly is to fill the world with fools. *Herbert Spencer*

The Fairy Tale

EVERY man's life is a fairy tale written by God's fingers.
Hans Christian Andersen

I HAVE not seen one who loves virtue as he loves beauty.
Confucius

A Man and His Dog

I WOULD not give much for that man's Christianity
whose dog did not benefit by it. *Rowland Hill*

The Immortal Legacy of the Unconquered Dead

The immortal legacy of the unconquered dead is that they were unconquered. They gave us that that none could take away, their faith in the things that matter more than the breath in our bodies. Yet there is another legacy.

No one has yet been able to give the world a list of those men whose genius had set them already on the way to fame when the war took them. The group of poems in the next few pages is either the work of these fallen poets or appreciations of them by other poets.

O Valiant Hearts Who to Your Glory Came

O VALIANT hearts who to your glory came
  Through dust of conflict and through battle-flame ;
Tranquil you lie, your knightly virtue proved,
Your memory hallowed in the Land you loved.

Proudly you gathered, rank on rank to war,
As who had heard God's message from afar ;
All you had hoped for, all you had, you gave
To save Mankind—yourselves you scorned to save.

Splendid you passed, the great surrender made,
Into the light that never more shall fade ;
Deep your contentment in that blest abode,
Who wait the last clear trumpet-call of God.

Long years ago, as earth lay dark and still,
Rose a loud cry upon a lonely hill,
While in the frailty of our human clay,
Christ our Redeemer passed the selfsame way.

Still stands His cross from that dread hour to this
Like some bright star above the dark abyss ;
Still through the veil the Victor's pitying eyes
Look down to bless our lesser Calvaries.

These were His servants, in His steps they trod,
Following through death the martyred sons of God ;
Victor He rose ; victorious too shall rise
They who have drunk His cup of sacrifice.

O risen Lord, O shepherd of our dead,
Whose cross has brought them and whose staff has led,
In glorious hope their proud and sorrowing Land
Commits her children to Thy gracious Hand.

*By Sir John Arkwright, sung at the
burial of America's Unknown Warrior*

The Things That Will Remain

B UT the things I love in nature are the height, the depth, the length
  Of the mountains and the ocean and the plain,
All the things that tell so wondrously the magnitude and strength
Of the hand that made the things which will remain.

Brian Brooke

Better Far to Pass Away

BETTER far to pass away
  While the limbs are strong and young,
Ere the ending of the day,
  Ere Youth's lusty song be sung.
Hot blood pulsing through the veins,
  Youth's high hope a burning fire,
Young men needs must break the chains
  That hold them from their heart's desire.

My friends, the hills, the sea, the sun,
  The winds, the woods, the clouds, the trees :
How feebly, if my youth were done,
  Could I, an old man, relish these !
With laughter, then, I'll go to meet
  What Fate has still in store for me,
And welcome Death if we should meet,
  And bear him willing company.

My share of fourscore years and ten
  I'll gladly yield to any man,
And take no thought of where or when,
  Contented with my shorter span.
For I have learned what love may be,
  And found a heart that understands,
And known a comrade's constancy,
  And felt the grip of friendly hands.

Come when it may, the stern decree
  For me to leave the cheery throng,
And quit the sturdy company
  Of brothers that I work among.
No need for me to look askance,
  Since no regret my prospect mars.
My day was happy—and perchance
  The coming night is full of stars.
                    Richard Molesworth Dennys

His Temple

I HAVE a temple I do not
  Visit, a heart I have forgot,
A self that I have never met,
A secret shrine—and yet, and yet,

This sanctuary of my soul
Unwitting I keep white and whole,
Unlatched and lit, if Thou should'st care
To enter or to tarry there.
                    Charles Hamilton Sorley

The God We Make

I THINK we all have made our God too small.
There was a Young Man, a good while ago,
Who taught that doctrine . . . but they murdered him
Because he wished to share the Jewish God
With other folk.

        They are long-lived, these fierce
Old hating gods of nations ; but at last
There surely will be spilled enough of blood
To drown them all !

Sad jesting ! If there be no God at all,
Save in the heart of man, why, even so—
Yea, all the more—since we must make our God,
Oh, let us make Him large enough for all,
Or cease to prate of Him !

        Yet it is hard
To make Him big enough ! For me, I like
The English and the Germans and the French,
The Russians, too ; and Serbians, I should think,
Might well be very interesting to God.

What was it he said so long ago
(The Young Man who outgrew the Jewish God) ?
Not a sparrow falleth ? Ah, God, God,
And there shall fall a million murdered men !

          Karle Wilson Baker

The Poplars

O, A lush green English meadow—it's there that I would lie,
A skylark singing overhead, scarce present to the eye,
And a row of wind-blown poplars against an English sky.

The elm is aspiration, and death is in the yew,
And beauty dwells in every tree from Lapland to Peru ;
But there's magic in the poplars when the wind goes through.

When the wind goes through the poplars and blows them silver white,
The wonder of the universe is flashed before my sight :
I see immortal visions ; I know a god's delight.

And so I sing the poplars ; and when I come to die
I will not look for jasper walls, but cast about my eye
For a row of wind-blown poplars against an English sky.

         Bernard Freeman Trotter,
         about to die in France

Comrades, Farewell

IN a wood they call the Rouge Bouquet
There is a new-made grave today,
Built by never a spade nor pick
Yet covered with earth ten metres thick.
There lie many fighting men,
Dead in their youthful prime,
Never to laugh nor love again
Nor taste the Summertime.
For Death came flying through the air
And stopped his flight at the dug-out stair,
Touched his prey and left them there,
Clay to clay.
He hid their bodies stealthily
In the soil of the land they sought to free
And fled away.

Now over the grave abrupt and clear
Three volleys ring ;
And perhaps their brave young spirits hear
The bugle sing :
Go to sleep ! Go to sleep !
Danger's past ;
Now at last, Go to sleep !

There is on earth no worthier grave
To hold the bodies of the brave
Than this place of pain and pride
Where they nobly fought and nobly died.
Never fear but in the skies
Saints and angels stand
Smiling with their holy eyes
On this new-come band.

Farewell ! Farewell !
Comrades true, born anew, peace to you !
Your souls shall be where the heroes are
And your memory shine like the morning star.
                                    Joyce Kilmer

On a Friend Who Fell

O BROTHER, I have sung no dirge for thee :
    Nor for all time to come
Can song reveal my grief's infinity :
    The menace of thy silence makes me dumb.
                        Robert Sterling, killed on
                        St George's Day, 1915

Now God Be Thanked

Now God be thanked Who has matched us with His hour,
And caught our youth, and wakened us from sleeping. . .
Rupert Brooke, died on St George's Day, 1915

I Have a Rendezvous With Death

I HAVE a rendezvous with Death
At some disputed barricade,
When Spring comes round with rustling shade
And apple blossoms fill the air.
I have a rendezvous with Death
When Spring brings back blue days and fair.

It may be he shall take my hand
And lead me into his dark land
And close my eyes and quench my breath;
It may be I shall pass him still.
I have a rendezvous with Death
On some scarred slope of battered hill,
When Spring comes round again this year
And the first meadow flowers appear.

God knows twere better to be deep
Pillowed in silk and scented down,
Where love throbs out in blissful sleep,
Pulse nigh to pulse, and breath to breath,
Where hushed awakenings are dear.
But I've a rendezvous with Death
At midnight in some flaming town,
When Spring trips north again this year,
And I to my pledged word am true,
I shall not fail that rendezvous. *Alan Seeger*

To His Daughter Betty, the Gift of God

IN wiser days, my darling rosebud, blown
To beauty proud as was your mother's prime,
In that desired, delayed, incredible time,
You'll ask why I abandoned you, my own,
And the dear heart that was your baby throne,
To dice with death. And oh! they'll give you rhyme
And reason: some will call the thing sublime,
And some decry it in a knowing tone.
So here, while the mad guns curse overhead,
And tired men sigh with mud for couch and floor,
Know that we fools, now with the foolish dead,
Died not for Flag, nor King, nor Emperor,
But for a dream, born in a herdsman's shed,
And for the secret Scripture of the poor. *Tom Kettle*

Sailor, What of the Debt We Owe You?

SAILOR, what of the debt we owe you?
  Day or night is the peril more?
Who so dull that he fails to know you,
  Sleepless guard of our island shore?

Safe the corn to the farmyard taken;
  Grain ships safe upon all the seas;
Homes in peace and a faith unshaken:
  Sailor, what do we owe for these?

Andrew John, Viscount Stuart

The Sea Is His

THE Sea is His: He made it,
  Black gulf and sunlit shoal
From barriered bight to where the long
  Leagues of Atlantic roll:
Small strait and ceaseless ocean
  He bade each one to be:
The Sea is His: He made it,
  And England keeps it free.

Count me the splendid captains
  Who sailed with courage high
To chart the perilous ways unknown:
  Tell me where these men lie!
To light a path for ships to come
  They moored at Dead Man's Quay;
The Sea is God's—He made it,
  And these men made it free.

Oh little land of England,
  Oh Mother of hearts too brave,
Men say this trust shall pass from thee
  Who guardest Nelson's grave.
Aye, but these braggarts yet shall learn
  Who'd hold the world in fee,
The Sea is God's, and England—
  England shall keep it free.

R. E. Vernede

March On

THEN lift the flag of the Last Crusade!
  And fill the ranks of the Last Brigade!
March on to the fields where the world's re-made,
And the ancient dreams come true!

Tom Kettle

A Little Boy in the Morning

HE will not come, and still I wait.
He whistles at another gate
Where angels listen. Ah, I know
He will not come, yet if I go
How shall I know he did not pass
Barefooted in the flowery grass?

The moon leans on one silver horn
Above the silhouettes of morn,
And from their nest sills finches whistle
Or, stooping, pluck the downy thistle.
How is the morn so gay and fair
Without his whistling in its air?
The world is calling, I must go.
How shall I know he did not pass
Barefooted in the shining grass?

Francis Ledwidge

A Young Man's Prayer

BY all the glories of the day
And the cool evening's benison,
By that last sunset touch that lay
Upon the hills when day was done,
By beauty lavishly outpoured
And blessings carelessly received,
By all the days that I have lived,
Make me a soldier, Lord.

By all of all man's hopes and fears
And all the wonders poets sing,
The laughter of unclouded years
And every sad and lovely thing,
By the romantic ages stored
With high endeavour that was his,
By all his mad catastrophes,
Make me a man, O Lord.

I, that on my familiar hill
Saw with uncomprehending eyes
A hundred of Thy sunsets spill
Their fresh and sanguine sacrifice,
Ere the sun swings his noonday sword,
Must say goodbye to all of this:
By all delights that I shall miss,
Help me to die, O Lord.

William Noel Hodgson two days before he fell in France

Home Thoughts in Laventie

GREEN gardens in Laventie !
   Soldiers only know the street
Where the mud is churned and splashed about
   By battle-wending feet ;
And yet beside one stricken house there is a glimpse of grass,
Look for it when you pass.

Beyond the church whose pitted spire
   Seems balanced on a strand
Of swaying stone and tottering brick
   Two roofless ruins stand,
And here behind the wreckage where the back wall should have been
We found a garden green.

The grass was never trodden on,
   The little path of gravel
Was overgrown with celandine,
   No other folk did travel
Along its weedy surface, but the nimble-footed mouse
Running from house to house.

Hungry for Spring I bent my head,
   The perfume fanned my face,
And all my soul was dancing
   In that little lovely place,
Dancing with a measured step from wrecked and shattered towns
Away—upon the Downs.

I saw green banks of daffodil,
   Slim poplars in the breeze,
Great tan-brown hares in gusty March
   A-courting on the leas ;
And meadows with their glittering stream, and silver scurrying dace,
Home—what a perfect place.   *Edward Wyndham Tennant*

The Quiet Song

PEACE, God's own peace,
   This it is I bring you
The quiet song of sleep,
Dear tired heart, I sing you.
Dream, softly dream,
Till solemn death shall find you,
With coronals of roses
Tenderly to bind you.
Peace past understanding,
Dear tired heart, I bring you ;
The quiet song of evening
Softly I sing you.
    Ivar Campbell

The Strenuous Life

ON the cabin-roof I lie
  Gazing into vacancy.
Make no noise and break no jest,
I am peaceful and at rest.

Somewhere back in days gone by
I did something—was it I ?
Do not ask : I have forgot
Whether it was I or not.

Sometime I may have to do
Something else ; but so may you.
Do not argue, but admit
That we need not think of it.

Thought has ever been my foe ;
That is so. Yes. That is so.
On the cabin-roof I lie
Gazing into vacancy.   *Arthur Hugh Sidgwick*

> *Written on the boat of Mr C. C. Lynam's School at
> Oxford, twenty-one years before the poet fell in France.*

Into Battle

THE naked earth is warm with Spring,
  And with green grass and bursting trees
Leans to the sun's gaze glorying,
  And quivers in the sunny breeze ;
And Life is Colour and Warmth and Light,
  And a striving evermore for these ;
And he is dead who will not fight ;
  And who dies fighting has increase.

The fighting man shall from the sun
  Take warmth, and life from the glowing earth ;
Speed with the light-foot winds to run,
  And with the trees to newer birth ;
And find, when fighting shall be done,
  Great rest, and fullness after dearth.

All the bright company of Heaven
  Hold him in their high comradeship,
The Dog-Star and the Sisters Seven,
  Orion's Belt and sworded hip.

The woodland trees that stand together,
  They stand to him each one a friend ;
They gently speak in the windy weather ;
  They guide to valley and ridges' end.

The kestrel hovering by day,
  And the little owls that call by night
Bid him be swift and keen as they,
  As keen of ear, as swift of sight.

The blackbird sings to him, Brother, brother,
  If this be the last song you shall sing,
Sing well, for you may not sing another;
  Brother, sing.

In dreary, doubtful, waiting hours,
  Before the brazen frenzy starts,
The horses show him nobler powers;
  O patient eyes, courageous hearts!

And when the burning moment breaks,
  And all things else are out of mind,
And only Joy-of-Battle takes
  Him by the throat, and makes him blind,

Through joy and blindness he shall know,
  Not caring much to know, that still
Nor lead nor steel shall reach him, so
  That it be not the Destined Will.

The thundering line of battle stands,
  And in the air Death moans and sings;
But Day shall clasp him with strong hands
  And Night shall fold him in soft wings.
                              Julian Grenfell

The World of One

L IFE and I were alone together;
    The world and I were one.
Earth and sea were mine to tether,
  Mine was the golden Sun.

Life ran clear as a limpid river;
  The seas were charted seas.
God was a kind and generous giver,
  Giver of gifts to please.

I dreamed and slept in shadow and Sun;
  I lipped the goblet's brim,
And I was one in a world of one
  That span to my will and whim.

But out of this has come a day
  When I heard a bugle call,
And forth I go from a world of one
  To serve for a world of all.
                              Leslie Coulson

THE GREAT PYRAMID

THE COLOSSEUM, ROME

THE CAPITOL, WASHINGTON

ST. PETER'S, ROME

In Flanders Fields

IN Flanders fields the poppies blow
Between the crosses, row on row,
That mark our place ; and in the sky
The larks, still bravely singing, fly
Scarce heard amid the guns below.

We are the Dead. Short days ago
We lived, felt dawn, saw sunset glow,
Loved and were loved, and now we lie
In Flanders fields.
Take up our quarrel with the foe :

To you from failing hands we throw
The torch ; be yours to hold it high.
If ye break faith with us who die
We shall not sleep, though poppies grow
In Flanders fields.

John McCrae in Punch

The Sound of Running Feet

I HEARD a sound of running feet,
And all along the dusty street
A multitude came sweeping by.
On every shoulder was a load,
Each drove his neighbour with a goad
I saw one stop, and heard his cry :
Why drive ye in this dreadful race,
Why urge ye such an awful pace,
What treasure do ye look to find ?
They turned upon him in amaze
And gaped at him with owlish gaze.
And suddenly I saw them—blind !
Where to ?   We neither know nor care,
But hurry, hurry onward there.
The multitude was called Mankind.

Colwyn Philipps

Kismet

OPAL fires in the Western sky
(For that which is written must ever be),
And a bullet comes droning, whining by,
To the heart of a sentry close to me.

For some go early, and some go late
(A dying scream on the evening air),
And who is there that believes in Fate
As a soul goes out in the sunset flare ?

R. B. Marriott-Watson

Surely They Sleep Content

SURELY they sleep content, our valiant dead,
  Fallen untimely in the savage strife :
They have but followed whither duty led,
  To find a fuller life.

Who, then, are we to grudge the bitter price
  Of this our land inviolate through the years,
Or mar the splendour of their sacrifice
  That is too high for tears ?

God grant we fail not at the test—that when
  We take, mayhap, our places in the fray,
Come life, come death, we quit ourselves like men,
  The peers of such as they.

*Written by Arthur Lewis Jenkins, a Marlborough boy,
of those Marlborough boys killed in the war before him*

There Is No Fitter End

THERE is no fitter end than this,
  No need is now to yearn or sigh ;
We know the glory that is his,
  The glory that can never die.

Surely we knew it all before ;
  Knew all along that he was made
For a swift radiant morning, for
  A sacrificing swift nightshade.

*Written by Charles Sorley, a Marlborough boy, of Sidney Clay-
ton Woodroffe, a Marlborough boy killed in the war before him*

How Long, O Lord?

How long, O Lord, how long, before the flood
  Of crimson-welling carnage shall abate ?
From sodden plains in West and East the blood
  Of kindly men steams up in mists of hate,
Polluting Thy clean air ; and nations great
  In reputation of the arts that bind
The world with hopes of heaven, sink to the state
  Of brute barbarians, whose ferocious mind
  Gloats o'er the bloody havoc of their kind,
Not knowing love or mercy. Lord, how long
  Shall Satan in high places lead the blind
To battle for the passions of the strong ?
  Oh, touch Thy children's hearts that they may know
Hate their most hateful, pride their deadliest, foe.

Robert Palmer

To My Brother

THIS will I do when we have peace again,
    Peace and return, to ease my heart of pain.
Crouched in the brittle reed-beds, wrapt in grey,
I'll watch the dawning of the winter's day,
The peaceful, clinging darkness of the night
That mingles with mysterious morning light,
And graceful rushes melting in the haze ;
While all around in winding waterways,
The wildfowl gabble cheerfully and low,
Or wheel with pulsing whistle to and fro,
Filling the silent dawn with joyous song,
Swelling and dying, as they sweep along. . . .

Until the watchful heron, grim and gaunt,
Shows ghostlike, standing at his chosen haunt,
And jerkily the moorhens venture out,
Spreading swift-circled ripples round about,
And softly to the ear, and leisurely,
Querulous comes the plaintive plover's cry ;
And then maybe some whispering near by,
Some still small sound as of a happy sigh,
Shall steal upon my senses soft as air,
And, Brother, I shall know that you are there.
                    Miles Jeffrey Game Day

No One Cares Less Than I

No one cares less than I,
    Nobody knows but God,
Whether I am destined to lie
    Under a foreign clod,
Were the words I made to the bugle call in the morning.

But laughing, storming, scorning,
    Only the bugles know
What the bugles say in the morning,
    And they do not care, when they blow
The call that I heard and made words to early
    this morning.   *Edward Thomas*

The Lamps Are Going Out

THE lamps are going out all over Europe ; we shall not
    see them lit again in our lifetime.
            *Lord Grey to Mr J. A. Spender, looking out from
            Foreign Office windows on the night of August 4, 1914*

Outward Bound

THERE's a waterfall I'm leaving
   Running down the rocks in foam,
There's a pool for which I'm grieving
   Near the water-ouzel's home,
And it's there that I'd be lying
   With the heather close at hand,
And the curlews faintly crying
   Mid the wastes of Cumberland.

Though the high gods smite and slay us,
   Though we come not whence we go,
As the host of Menelaus
   Came there many years ago ;
Yet the selfsame wind shall bear us
   From the same departing place
Out across the Gulf of Saros
   And the peaks of Samothrace.

We shall pass in summer weather,
   We shall come at eventide,
When the fells stand up together
   And all quiet things abide ;
Mixed with cloud and wind and river,
   Sun-distilled in dew and rain,
One with Cumberland for ever
   We shall go not forth again.
           Nowell Oxland

And Wave Beyond the Stars That All is Well

BECAUSE of you we will be glad and gay,
   Remembering you we will be brave and strong ;
And hail the advent of each dangerous day,
And meet the dark adventure with a song.
And, as you proudly gain your jewelled gift,
We'll give our lesser offering with a smile,
Nor falter on the path where, all too swift,
You led the way and leapt the golden stile.
Whether new paths, new heights to climb, you find,
Or gallop through the unfooted asphodel,
We know you know we shall not lag behind,
Nor halt to waste a moment on a fear ;
And you will speed us onward with a cheer,
And wave beyond the stars that all is well.
           Maurice Baring to Julian Grenfell

I Looked into the Eyes of Time

I LOOKED into the eyes of Time,
  And musingly I said,
There'll come a day when you and I
  Will both of us be dead.
But I shall rise again, to count
  No hours that come and go,
And quiet you will ever bide
  With Death as bedfellow.   *Harold Parry*

There Was a Whispering in My Hearth

THERE was a whispering in my hearth,
  A sigh of the coal,
Grown wistful of a former earth
  It might recall.

I listened for a tale of leaves
  And smothered ferns ;
Frond-forests, and the low, sly lives
  Before the fawns.

My fire might show steam-phantoms simmer
  From Time's old cauldron,
Before the birds made nests in summer,
  Or men had children.

But the coals were murmuring of their mine,
  And moans down there
Of boys that slept wry sleep, and men
  Writhing for air.

And I saw white bones in the cinder-shard.
  Bones without number,
For many hearts with coal are charred
  And few remember.

I thought of some who worked dark pits
  Of war and died,
Digging the rock where Death reputes
  Peace lies indeed.

Comforted years will sit soft-chaired
  In rooms of amber ;
The years will stretch their hands, well-cheered
  By our lives' ember.

The centuries will burn rich loads
  With which we groaned,
Whose warmth shall lull their dreaming lids
  While songs are crooned.
But they will not dream of us poor lads
  Lost in the ground.   *Wilfred Owen*

He Had Flung Away His Idols and Met God

GOD, it is glorious to think of a soul so wholly devoid of the pettiness and humbug, the cynicism and dishonesty, of so much that we see.

There is a story in one of Miss Kingsley's books of a West African medicine-man who found himself at death's door. He applied all his herbs and spells, and conducted all his well-known rites before his idols, and with his friends' intercessions without any effect. At last he wearied of his hocus-pocus, and took his idols and charms down to the seashore and flung them into the surf ; and he said, " Now I will be a man and meet my God alone."

Julian from the time I knew him had flung away his idols and had met God. *Charles Lister on Julian Grenfell*

Was There More to Do ?

To have laughed and talked (wise, witty, fantastic, feckless),
   To have mocked at rules and rulers, and learned to obey,
To have led your men with a daring adored and reckless,
   To have struck your blow for Freedom, the old straight way ;

To have hated the world and lived among those who love it,
   To have thought great thoughts, and lived till you knew them true,
To have loved men more than yourself and have died to prove it—
   Yes, Charles, this is to have lived ; was there more to do ?

C. A. Alington on Charles Lister

The King's Story

This story from the life of Walter Page is from the days immediately following America's entry into the War, when the Ambassador and Mrs Page were invited by George the Fifth to spend the night at Windsor.

I ARRIVED during the middle of the afternoon (writes Page), and he sent for me to talk with him in his office.

" I've a good story on you," said he. " You Americans have a queer use of the word Some to express mere bigness or emphasis. We are taking that use of the word from you over here. Well, an American and an Englishman were riding in the same railway compartment. The American read his paper diligently—all the details of a big battle. When he had done he put the paper down and said, ' Some fight ! '

And some don't ! said the Englishman.

The King roared. " A good one on you ! "

" The trouble with that joke, sir," I ventured to reply, " is that it's out of date."

Nothing Like it Ever Seen on This Planet

As for the British, there never was such a race. They absolutely hold the Seven Seas. They sent to France the largest army any people ever sent over the sea. They are financing most of their allies and they have turned this whole island into gun and shell factories. They made a great mistake at the Dardanelles and they are slower than death to change their set methods, but no family in the land, from charcoal burners to dukes, hesitates one moment to send its sons into the army. When the news comes of their death they never whimper. When you come right down to hard facts, the courage and the endurance of the British and the French excel anything ever before seen on this planet. All the old stories of bravery from Homer down are outdone every day by these people. *Walter Page*

Talking to George the Third

HAD it not been for the fact that both Page and Grey had an understanding sense of humour, neutrality would have proved a more difficult path than it actually was.

One of the curious memorials preserved in the British Foreign Office is the cancelled £3,000,000 cheque with which Great Britain paid the Alabama claims. That the British should frame this memento of their great diplomatic defeat, and hang it in the Foreign Office is an evidence of the fact that the English are excellent sportsmen. Sir Edward Grey used frequently to call Page's attention to this document.

One day the two men were discussing certain detentions of American cargoes—high-handed acts which, in Page's opinion, were unwarranted. Suddenly his eye was attracted by the framed Alabama cheque. He leaned over, peered at it intently, and then quickly turned to the Foreign Secretary : " If you don't stop these seizures, Sir Edward, some day you'll have your entire room papered with things like that."

Not long afterwards Sir Edward scored on Page. The Ambassador called to present one of the many State Department notes. It not infrequently happened that these notes could not be presented to the British Government ; they were so rasping and undiplomatic. On such occasions it was the practice of the London Embassy to smooth down the language before handing the paper to the Foreign Secretary. The present note was one of this kind, but Page decided to transmit the communication in its original shape.

Sir Edward glanced over the document, looked up, and remarked, with a twinkle in his eye, " This reads as though they thought they are still talking to George the Third."

The roar of laughter that followed was something quite unprecedented amid the dignified walls of the Foreign Office.

Life and Letters of Walter Page

Sir Edward Grey Speaking

SIR EDWARD energetically rose ; his figure straightened, his eyes were fairly flashing.

"England would be for ever contemptible," Sir Edward said, "if we should sit by and see this treaty violated. We have told Germany that if this assault on Belgium's neutrality is not reversed England will declare war."

"Do you expect Germany to accept it ? " asked the Ambassador. Sir Edward shook his head.

"No. Of course everybody knows that there will be war."

There was a moment's pause, and then the Foreign Secretary spoke again.

"Yet we must remember that there are two Germanys. There is the Germany of men like ourselves—of men like Lichnowsky and wagow. Then there is the Germany of men of the war party. The Jar party has got the upper hand."

At this point Sir Edward's eyes filled with tears.

"Thus the efforts of a lifetime go for nothing. I feel like a man who has wasted his life."

"I came away," the Ambassador said, "with a sort of stunned sense of the impending ruin of half the world."

From the Life of Walter Page, Ambassador

Peace and Justice Shall Reign

GERMANY has once more said that force and force alone shall decide whether peace and justice shall reign in the affairs of man.

There is but one response possible from us—force, force to the utmost, force without stint or limit, the righteous and triumphant force that shall make Right the law of the world and cast every selfish dominion down in the dust.

President Wilson on America coming into the War

The British People to America's Soldiers

SOLDIERS of the United States, the people of the British Isles welcome you on your way to take your stand beside the armies of many nations now fighting in the Old World the battle for human freedom. The Allies will gain new heart and spirit in your company. I wish I could shake the hand of each one of you and bid you godspeed on your mission. *King George's welcome to the first American army that ever touched our shores*

The Love That Maketh Rich

I WOULD rather belong to a poor nation that was free than to a rich nation that had ceased to be in love with liberty. We shall not be poor if we love liberty. *Woodrow Wilson*

She Can Do No Other

IT is a fearful thing to lead this great peaceable people into war, into the most terrible and disastrous of all wars, civilisation itself seeming to be in the balance.

But right is more precious than peace, and we shall fight for the things which we have always carried in our hearts—for democracy, for the right of those who submit to authority to have a voice in their own governments, for the rights and liberties of small nations, for a universal dominion of right by such a concert of free peoples as shall bring peace and safety to all nations and make the world itself at last free.

To such a task we can dedicate our lives and our fortunes, everything that we are and everything that we have for the pride of those who know that the day has come when America is privileged to spend her blood and her might for the principles that gave her birth and happiness and the peace she has treasured. God helping her, she can do no other. *Woodrow Wilson*

The Resting Place

In loving memory of one who was killed in action, aged 20.

A LITTLE while your grave will be o'ertrodden,
  Soon the frail cross have fallen in the breeze.
No loving hands are there to tend and cherish
That grave in foreign soil beyond the seas.
Somewhere in France—oh, surely, my beloved,
Though sign and token all be swept away,
It is not in that land of desolation,
But in my heart that you will rest alway.
From a London newspaper

1908 Looks into 1918

LORD ROBERTS in 1908 : We sleep under a false security, for I do not hesitate to affirm that we shall have a frightful war in Europe, and that England and France will have the hardest experience of their existence. They will see defeat very near, but the war will finally be won by the genius of a French general named Foch.

Somebody to Foch in 1918 : How did you win the war ?

Foch : By smoking my pipe, not getting excited, and reserving all my strength for the task in hand.

The Eleventh Hour of the Eleventh Day
of the Eleventh Month

IT was a few minutes before the eleventh hour of the eleventh day of the eleventh month. I stood at the window of my room looking up towards Trafalgar Square, waiting for Big Ben to tell that the war was over. . . . Suddenly the first stroke of the chime.

I looked again at the broad street beneath me. It was deserted. From the portals of one of the large hotels absorbed by Government Departments darted the slight figure of a girl clerk, distractedly gesticulating while another stroke of Big Ben resounded. Then from all sides men and women came scurrying into the street. Streams of people poured out of all the buildings. The bells of London began to clash. I could see that Trafalgar Square was already swarming.

Around me in our very headquarters disorder had broken out. Doors banged. Feet clattered down corridors. Everyone rose from the desk and cast aside pen and paper. All bounds were broken. The tumult grew. It grew like a gale, but from all sides simultaneously. The street was now a seething mass of humanity. Flags appeared as if by magic. Streams of men and women flowed from the Embankment. They mingled with torrents pouring down the Strand on their way to acclaim the King.

Almost before the last stroke of the clock had died away the strict, war-straitened, regulated streets of London had become a triumphant pandemonium. At any rate it was clear that no more work would be done that day. Yes, the chains which had held the world were broken. Links of imperative need, links of discipline, links of brute force, links of self-sacrifice, links of terror, links of honour which had held our nation, nay, the great part of mankind, to grinding toil, to a compulsive cause—every one had snapped upon a few strokes of the clock. *Winston Churchill*

As The Curtain Falls

IT is difficult to turn our attention elsewhere while our eyes and minds are centred on the unfolding of the last act in one of the great dramas in history.

Some people think that it is characteristic of a tragedy that it should have what is technically known as an unhappy ending. The ending in this case is not going to be in that sense an unhappy one. But in all the essentials of tragedy (the ups and downs of fortune, the alternations of hope and fear, the interplay of heroism and suffering and sacrifice, and let us add, the final triumph of the good cause), the war upon which the curtain is about to fall has been unique and supreme. It is not too much to say that it has cleansed and purged the whole atmosphere of the world. *Mr Asquith on November 2, 1918*

A Spectacle to Appal Mankind

WHEN the great organisations of this world are strained beyond breaking point their structure often collapses at all points simultaneously. There is nothing on which policy, however wise, can build ; no foothold can be found for virtue or valour, no authority or impetus for a rescuing genius.

The mighty framework of German Imperial Power, which a few days before had overshadowed the nations, shivered suddenly into a thousand individually disintegrating fragments. All her Allies whom she had so long sustained fell down broken and ruined, begging separately for peace. The faithful armies were beaten at the front and demoralised from the rear. The proud, efficient Navy mutinied. Revolution exploded in the most disciplined and docile of States. The Supreme War Lord fled.

Such a spectacle appals mankind ; and a knell rang in the ear of the victors, even in their hour of triumph. *Winston Churchill*

They Told Him So

I GAVE my life for freedom—This I know,
For those who bade me fight had told me so.
W. N. Ewer

Is It the End?

THE curtain falls upon the long front in France and Flanders. The soothing hands of Time and Nature, the swift repair of peaceful industry, have already almost effaced the crater fields and the battle lines which in a broad belt from the Vosges to the sea lately blackened the smiling fields of France. The ruins are rebuilt, the riven trees are replaced by new plantations. Only the cemeteries, the monuments and stunted steeples, with here and there a mouldering trench or huge mine-crater lake, assail the traveller with the fact that twenty-five millions of soldiers fought here and twelve millions shed their blood or perished in the greatest of all human contentions.

Merciful oblivion draws its veils ; the crippled limp away ; the mourners fall back into the sad twilight of memory. New youth is here to claim its rights, and the perennial stream flows forward even in the battle zone, as if the tale were all a dream.

Is this the end ? Is it to be merely a chapter in a cruel and senseless story ? Will a new generation in their turn be immolated to square the black accounts of Teuton and Gaul ? Will our children bleed and gasp again in devastated lands ? Or will there spring from the very fires of conflict that reconciliation of the three giant combatants which would unite their genius and secure to each in safety and freedom a share in rebuilding the glory of Europe ?
Winston Churchill

Like Withered Leaves

I HAVE spent the week at Versailles. It was a wonderful week. Walking through the beautiful forests, the leaves were falling, but not these alone. Empires and kingdoms, kings and crowns, were falling like withered leaves. *Mr Lloyd George at the Guildhall Banquet*

Three Men Lie Dying

THERE are two other men lying near me, and I do not think there is much hope for them, either. One is an officer of a Scottish regiment and the other a private in the Uhlans. They were struck down after me, and when I came to myself I found them bending over me, rendering first aid.

The Britisher was pouring water down my throat from his flask, while the German was endeavouring to stanch my wound with an antiseptic preparation served out to their troops by the medical corps. The Highlander had one of his legs shattered, and the German had several pieces of shrapnel buried in his side.

In spite of their own sufferings, they were trying to help me, and when I was fully conscious again the German gave us a morphia injection and took one himself. His medical corps had also provided him with the injection and the needle, together with printed instructions for their use.

After the injection, feeling wonderfully at ease, we spoke of the lives we had lived before the war. We all spoke English, and we talked of the women we had left at home. Both the German and the Britisher had been married only a year.

I wondered (and I suppose the others did) why we had fought each other at all. I looked at the Highlander, who was falling to sleep, exhausted, and, in spite of his drawn face and mud-stained uniform, he looked the embodiment of freedom. Then I thought of the Tricolour of France and all that France had done for liberty. Then I watched the German, who had ceased to speak. He had taken a prayer book from his knapsack, and was trying to read a service for soldiers wounded in battle. And while I watched him I realised what we were fighting for. He was dying in vain, while the Britisher and myself, by our deaths, would probably contribute something toward the cause of civilisation and peace. *A French officer dying on the field in Flanders in 1915*

That Fateful Morning

THUS, Mr Speaker, at eleven o'clock this morning, came to an end the cruellest and most terrible war that has ever scourged mankind. I hope we may say that thus, this fateful morning, came to an end all wars. *Mr Lloyd George in the House of Commons*

The Great War is Over

NEVER did the welkin ring in London as it rang today. Parliament Street and Whitehall were packed with people. The day was grey and chill with a threat of rain, but no one minded the weather. There prevailed everywhere throughout London an irresistible impulse to let business go hang, to get into the streets and yell and sing and dance and weep.

I could distinguish the hooting of motors, the ringing of handbells, the banging of tea-trays, the shrilling of police whistles, and the screaming of toy trumpets. And why not? The war was over, the war which, sick at heart, we were beginning to think would never end. Yes, the infernal war is over, the catastrophes, alarms, fears, uncertainties, anxieties of four and a half years, the air-raids, the sinking of food ships, the daily desolation of family circles, have culminated in victory.

If anyone entertained a lingering doubt as to whether war was really finished, the mad follies of the girl clerks in the Government offices in Whitehall must have removed it. They actually showered down upon our heads from the windows masses of official forms relating to the war.

It was bank holiday on Hampstead Heath, on a vastly stupendous scale. . . . But while the holiday crowd are almost entirely wage-earners, persons of the most select social relations took part in today's revels. The males in the civilian section of the roysterers had two other peculiarities: they were almost all middle-aged and looked a shabby lot in their well-worn clothes. . . . We are in truth an enormous family party engaged in what may be called a stupendous house-warming, and everyone taking part is, as befits the unparalleled occasion, in high spirits of the most extravagantly irresponsible kind —utterly forgetful of self-propriety, pretentiousness, absorbed in the desire to contribute something to the Pandean frolic.

As I moved about I heard not a single hard word of Germany, not a single expression of glee that she was lying crippled, perhaps for ever.
Michael MacDonagh writing on November 11, 1918

Surely for History it is Enough

IN the sphere of force human records contain no manifestation like the eruption of the German volcano.

For four years Germany fought and defied the five continents of the world by land and sea and air. The German Armies upheld her tottering confederates, intervened in every theatre with success, stood everywhere on conquered territory, and inflicted on their enemies more than twice the bloodshed they suffered themselves. To break their strength and science, and curb their fury, it was necessary to bring all the greatest nations of mankind into the field against them. Overwhelming populations, unlimited resources, measureless sacrifice, the sea blockade, could not prevail for fifty months. Small states were trampled down in the struggle; a mighty Empire was battered into unrecognisable fragments; and nearly twenty million men perished or shed their blood before the sword was wrested from that terrible hand. Surely, Germans, for history it is enough!

Winston Churchill

The Fall of Lord Kitchener

THE failure of the Dardanelles Expedition was fatal to Lord Kitchener. The conduct of the Gallipoli Campaign showed only too plainly the limitations of this great figure at this period of his life and in this tremendous situation, both as an organiser and a man of action. His advocacy of the offensive in France which had failed so conspicuously at Loos and in Champagne was upon record. Under the agony of the Gallipoli evacuation his will power had plainly crumpled, and the long series of contradictory resolves which had marked his treatment of this terrible question was obvious to all who knew the facts.

Already in November had come direct rebuff. His plan for a fresh landing in the Gulf of Alexandretta, though devised by him in the actual theatre of operations, had been decisively vetoed. In a series of telegrams, the inclination of which could scarcely be obscure, he was encouraged to transform his definite mission at the Dardanelles into a general and extensive tour of inspection. On December 3 the War Committee determined to recreate the Imperial General Staff. . . .

The end of his great story is approaching; the long life full of action, lighted by hard-won achievement, crowned by power such as a British subject had rarely wielded and all the regard and honour that Britain and her Empire could bestow, was now declining through the shadows. The sudden onrush of the night, the deep waters of the North, were destined to preserve him and his renown from the shallows.

> *Better to sink beneath the shock*
> *Than moulder piecemeal on the rock.*

The solemn days when he stood forth as Constable of Britain, beneath whose arm her untrained people braced themselves for war, were ended. His life of duty could only reach its consummation in a warrior's death. His record in the Great War as strategist, administrator, and leader will be judged by the eyes of other generations than our own. Let us hope they will also remember the comfort his character and personality gave to his countrymen in their hours of hardest trial.

Winston Churchill

A Great Man Betrayed by His Country

I ALWAYS thought our people were at least as capable as those of any other nation. But I liked to study what other nations had accomplished. I had gone to Germany too often, and had read her literature too much, not to give ground to narrow-minded people to say that Germany was my spiritual home.

Anyhow, in August 1914, a formidable section of the public here had turned against me. I did not think that this was good for the Government, and in the autumn of 1914 I felt bound to go to the Prime Minister and to say that, as the attacks on me must obviously affect the general position, it would probably be better that I should not remain in office. He laughed at the idea of this, but I took a more serious view of it.

I was never depressed by even the most violent abuse. I was well content to endure, for if the Army came home victorious I believed that it would return with witnesses in my defence whose testimony would be irresistible. So it proved in the end.

But before the war ended in our victory I had, of course, a disagreeable time. I was threatened with assault in the street, and I was on occasions in some danger of being shot at. But on the other hand I had a multitude of loyal and devoted friends whose hopes had through years rested on my efforts. . . . My special adherents in the Army, and outside it, were firm as rocks.

After the victory in France came, and the British troops had returned to London, with the victorious Commander-in-Chief, Douglas Haig, riding with the King at their head, all London was in a state of rejoicing. I was left alone, solitary in my study at Queen Anne's Gate. It was after dark that evening when my servant came upstairs to me and said that there was an officer who wanted to see me, but who would not give his name. The door was opened, and who should enter but a friend who was indeed intimately known to me, Field-Marshal Douglas Haig, come from a triumphant ride with his Sovereign along the Mall.

" I am not going to remain," he exclaimed ; " my purpose is to leave with you a book in which I have written something." With that he insisted on going away. The book was a volume containing his Despatches, and on the page at the beginning he had written these affectionate words :

To Viscount Haldane of Cloan, the greatest Secretary of State for War England has ever had. In grateful remembrance of his successful efforts in organising the Military Forces for a war on the Continent, notwithstanding much opposition from the Army Council and the half-hearted support of his Parliamentary friends.—Haig, F.M.

A page from the Autobiography of Lord Haldane

The Bag of Pearls

I SAW an Arab sitting in a circle of jewellers and relating as follows: Once on a time, having missed my way in the desert and having no provisions left, I gave myself up for lost, when I happened to find a bag full of something. I shall never forget the relish and delight that I felt on supposing it to be fried wheat; nor the bitterness and despair which I suffered on discovering that the bag contained pearls.

A Persian writer of the 12th century

No Man Slept the Night He Died

No man in England slept the night he died:
The harsh, stern spirit passed without a pang,
And freed of mortal clogs his message rang.
In ever wakeful mind the challenge cried:
Think not of me: one servant less or more
Means nothing now: hold fast the greater thing:
Strike hard, love truth, serve England and the King!

Servant of England, soldier to the core,
What does it matter where his body fall?
What does it matter where they build his tomb?
Five million men, from Calais to Khartoum,
These are his wreath and his memorial.

Christopher Morley on Lord Kitchener,
drowned during the Great War

The Hand That Ceased to Write

AMONG the drivers of the Balkan Convoy was a young Irishman who had vainly tried to enter the British Army but had been rejected for ill-health, and who died in Salonica. In his last letter he wrote:

The risks, as the days go by, seem of smaller and smaller account. I miss many, very many, of the little luxuries at home, but I have enough and to spare. We are all so prone to put our own selves before the part we are playing in stemming the tide of human suffering that never seems to ebb.

While in the main we are happy, we never cease to talk of home. Daily we conjure up what we shall do when that great day of peace shall dawn, the hours we shall laze in the morning between sheets of snowy white, the meals we shall have, the visits to our old haunts. There is much to do in the meantime, work which will daily bring us near to suffering and self-sacrifice, and teach us perhaps some lessons in unselfishness and bring us nearer to finding our souls. On the whole there is renewed courage out here, and the hope of brighter——

The letter ends abruptly, for the writer's hand was cold.

Laurence Binyon

PORTRAIT OF A BOY, BY CARL VAN LOO

TUTANKHAMEN AND HIS QUEEN

An Englishman Gives Thanks

This is an Englishman's thankoffering to his country after the Great War. The letter appeared in The Times in 1919, when all were looking forward to the Great Peace.

No one knew the writer then, and his example was not widely followed; but it is now known that the man who laid this tribute on the altar of his country was Stanley Baldwin.

IT is now a truism to say that in August 1914 the nation was face to face with the greatest crisis in her history. She was saved by the freewill offerings of her people.

The best of her men rushed to the colours; the best of her women left their homes to spend and to be spent; the best of her older men worked as they had never worked before, to a common end, and with a sense of unity and fellowship as new as it was exhilarating. It may be that in four and a half years the ideals of many became dim, but the spiritual impetus of those early days carried the country through to the end.

Today, on the eve of peace, we are faced with another crisis, less obvious but none the less searching. The whole country is exhausted. By a natural reaction, not unlike that which led to the excesses of the Restoration after the reign of the Puritans, all classes are in danger of being submerged by a wave of extravagance and materialism.

It is so easy to live on borrowed money; so difficult to realise that you are doing so. It is so easy to play; so hard to learn that you cannot play for long without work. A fool's paradise is only the afternoon to a fool's hell.

How can the nation be made to understand the gravity of the financial situation, that love of country is better than love of money?

This can only be done by example, and the wealthy classes have today an opportunity of service which can never recur.

They know the danger of the present debt; they know the weight of it in the years to come. They know the practical difficulties of a universal statutory capital levy. Let them impose upon themselves, each as he is able, a voluntary levy. It should be possible to pay the Exchequer within 12 months such a sum as would save the taxpayer 50 millions a year.

I have been considering this matter for nearly two years, but my mind moves slowly; I dislike publicity, and I hoped that someone else might lead the way. I have made as accurate an estimate as I am able of the value of my own estate and I have arrived at a total of about £580,000. I have decided to realise 20 per cent. of that amount or, say £120,000, which will purchase £150,000 of the new War Loan, and present it to the Government for cancellation.

I give this portion of my estate as a thankoffering in the firm conviction that never again shall we have such a chance of giving our country that form of help which is so vital at the present time.

The Caravan of Humanity is on the March

IF the future peace of the world is to be maintained, it will not be sufficient merely to erect an institution for the purpose of settling international disputes after they have arisen ; it will be necessary to devise an instrument of government which will deal with the causes and sources of disputes. The need is there, and the end of the Great War has brought an unequalled opportunity for dealing with it.

For not only are men's minds prepared for the new peaceful order, but the sweeping away of the imperial systems of Europe leaves the space vacant which the new institution must occupy. The need, political and psychological, is imperative ; the opportunity is unique ; and only the blindness of statesmen could now prevent the coming of the new institution which will, more than anything else, reconcile the people to the sufferings they have endured in this war. It will be the only fitting monument to our heroic dead. It will be the great response to the age-long cry from the human heart for Peace on earth, Goodwill among men. It will nobly embody and express the universal spirit which must heal the deep self-inflicted wounds of humanity. And it must be the wise regulator, the steadying influence, in the forward movement now set going among the nations of the earth.

For there is no doubt that mankind is once more on the move. The very foundations have been shakened and loosened, and things are again fluid. The tents have been struck, and the great caravan of humanity is once more on its march. Vast social and industrial changes are coming—perhaps upheavals which may, in their magnitude and effects, be comparable to war itself. A steadying, controlling, regulating influence will be required to give stability to progress, and to remove that wasteful friction which has dissipated so much social force in the past, and in this war more than ever before. These great functions could only be adequately fulfilled by the League of Nations. Responding to such vital needs and coming at such a unique opportunity in history, it may well be destined to mark a new era in the government of man, and become to the peoples the guarantee of peace, to the workers of all races the great international, and to all the embodiment and living expression of the moral and spiritual unity of the human race.

From General Smuts's plan for a League of Nations,
written for the Allies in the last weeks of the war

A Thousand Ages

MAY our Lord
Live for a thousand ages
Until the pebbles
Become a rock
Overgrown with moss.

A Japanese National Anthem, 1000 years old

King George the Fifth to His Very Dear People

The Broadcast to the Nation by George the Fifth at the close of his Jubilee Day

AT the close of this memorable day I must speak to my people everywhere, yet how can I express what is in my heart ?

As I passed this morning through cheering multitudes to and from St Paul's Cathedral, as I thought there of all these 25 years have brought to me and to my country and my Empire, how could I fail to be most deeply moved ? Words cannot express my thoughts and feelings. I can only say to you, my very dear people, that the Queen and I thank you from the depth of our hearts for all the loyalty and (may I say ?) the love with which this day and always you have surrounded us. I dedicate myself anew to your service for the years that may still be given to me.

I look back on the past with thankfulness to God. My people and I have come through great trials and difficulties together. They are not over. In the midst of this day's rejoicing I grieve to think of the numbers of my people who are still without work. We owe to them, and not least to those who are suffering from any form of disablement, all the sympathy and help that we can give. I hope that during this Jubilee Year all who can will do their utmost to find them work and bring them hope.

Other anxieties may be in store, but I am persuaded that with God's help they may all be overcome, if we meet them with confidence, courage, and unity. So I look forward to the future with faith and hope.

It is to the young that the future belongs. I trust that through the Fund inaugurated by my dear son the Prince of Wales to commemorate this year many of them throughout this country may be helped in body, mind, and character to become useful citizens.

To the children I would like to send a special message. Let me say this to each of them whom my words may reach : *The King is speaking to* YOU. *I ask you to remember that in days to come you will be the citizens of a great Empire. As you grow up always keep this thought before you ; and when the time comes be ready and proud to give your country the service of your work, your mind, and your heart.*

I have been greatly touched by all the greetings which have come to me today from my Dominions and Colonies, from India, and from this Home Country. My heart goes out to all who may be listening to me now wherever you may be—here at home in town or village, or in some far-off corner of the Empire, or it may be on the high seas.

Let me end my words to you with those which Queen Victoria used after her Diamond Jubilee, 38 years ago. No words could more truly or simply express my own deep feeling now : *From my heart I thank my beloved people. May God bless them.*

The Whole Earth Leapt Forward

In that great year when Peace came back, at the Eleventh hour of the Eleventh day of the Eleventh month of 1918, the earth itself appears to have leapt for joy, for it is true that the earth took a sudden step forward.

IT has been made known as a scientific fact that when the war ended the old earth received a sudden jolt. It was such a shock that the lengthening earth's day was shortened by a twenty-five-millionth.

Dr de Sitter, of the University of Leyden, who has disclosed this strange and sudden alteration of the length of the Earth's day, has spent many years in examining the reasons why the day seems to alter. It appears to be lengthening, and the month which the Moon occupied in going round the Earth appears to be shortening. At present the length of the Moon's month is lessened by less than a thirtieth of a second in a hundred years. The length of the day increases even less in a century.

In that fateful year of 1918 the length of the day changed in a very short time from more than a six-hundredth of a second longer to less than a five-hundredth of a second shorter. The day lost a twenty-five-millionth of its length at the same time that the Armistice was signed. In short, *the Earth leapt forward.*

Dr de Sitter calculates that if the whole Earth had shrunk by about five inches all over the surface the result would have quickened the Earth to about that extent. But, as that evidently did not take place, the explanation has to be sought in some unknown displacement of the lower strata of the Earth. It may be that the earthquakes that have since been experienced are symptoms of it. At any rate, whatever the cause, it is surely a remarkable thing that this should have happened on the day when the heart of the whole world was lifted up with joy.

Edwin Sharpe Grew

We Have Kept Our Heritage

George the Fifth to the representatives of the Empire in St James's Palace

THERE is a word which gladdens me, more especially when I hear it used by friends from overseas, many of whom say when they visit this country that they are coming Home. It is in this spirit that the Queen and I meet you today; we welcome one and all to our home.

Before I succeeded my father, the Queen and I had the privilege of studying at first hand the Dominions Overseas and India. We were fellow-travellers, then as now, comparing notes and sharing impressions. We treasure these memories and keep them alive; moreover, what we forget our four sons are now able to recall. Many years before our happy partnership began I had as a midshipman sailed the Seven Seas: I realised early that the Empire has many climes but one spirit.

I regard this as a unique gathering, where we can tell one another of our successes, and also of our failures and mistakes. But there will be no sharp criticism nor vain regrets, for we are in sympathy one with another, conscious that we have acted according to our lights for the good name and ordered prosperity of the family.

We are sometimes told that we are lacking in logic, our political institutions loose and undefined. But I look back on the trying and testing time through which we have passed and wonder whether a less flexible system would have withstood the strains to which we have been subjected. With commonsense and goodwill as our shield and buckler we have kept, in spite of all difficulties, our heritage of liberty, alike for the individual and for our many constituent races. The numberless and invisible ties of sentiment and tradition which bind us together are indeed delicate ; but many strands make a cable, strong to bind in times of adversity. It is my prayer, no less than my firm belief, that this bond of the spirit may prove also the bond of peace.

To the Schools of London

These are the last words George the Fifth sent to the children of London schools

YOU are the heirs of a great past ; but the future is yours, and is your high responsibility. Each of you must try to be a good citizen in a good city. To this end you must make the best of all your powers. Strive to grow in strength, in knowledge, and in grace. If you persist bravely in this endeavour you will work worthily for your family, your city, your country, and for mankind.

So to live, in whatever sphere, must be noble and may be great. My confident trust is in you.

None Shall Make Us Afraid

George the Fifth to both Houses of Parliament assembled in the
famous Westminster Hall under the roof built by William Rufus

THE Mother of Parliaments and her children, grown to full estate, stand now upon equal terms in common allegiance to the Crown. The unity of the British Empire is no longer expressed by the supremacy of the time-honoured Parliament that sits here at Westminster.

The Crown is the historic symbol that unites this great family of nations and races scattered over every quarter of the Earth.

The United Kingdom and the Dominions, India, the numerous Colonies and dependencies embrace such wide varieties of speech, culture, and form of government as have never before in the world's history been brought into a commonwealth of peace.

In these days when fear and preparation for war are again astir in the world, let us be thankful that quiet government and peace prevail over so large a part of the Earth's surface, and that under our flag of freedom so many millions eat their daily bread in far distant lands and climates with none to make them afraid.

This my Palace of Westminster, in the mighty heart of our Empire, is the very cradle of our envied Parliamentary institutions. Here is the anvil whereon our common law was forged to become the joint inheritance of the United States of America and our own community of peoples.

Beneath these rafters of medieval oak, the silent witnesses of historic tragedies and pageants, we celebrate the present under the spell of the past.

It is to me a source of pride and thankfulness that the perfect harmony of our Parliamentary system with our constitutional Monarchy has survived the shocks that have in recent years destroyed other empires and other liberties.

Our ancient Constitution, ever adaptable to change, has during my reign faced and conquered perils of warfare never conceived in earlier days, and has met and satisfied new democratic demands both at home and overseas.

The system bequeathed to us by our ancestors, again modified for the needs of a new age, has been found once more, as of old, the best way to secure government by the people, freedom for the individual, the ordered strength of the State, and the rule of law over governors and governed alike.

The complex forms and balanced spirit of our Constitution were not the discovery of a single era, still less of a single party or of a single person. They are the slow accretion of centuries, the outcome of patience, tradition, and experience constantly finding channels old and new for the impulse toward liberty, justice, and social improvement inherent in our people down the ages.

In looking back over the 25 years of my reign the thankfulness that I feel today is chiefly for escape from danger greater than ever before threatened our land. I can never forget how the peril from without at once united all the parties, classes, Governments, and races of the Empire ; men and women played their parts ; the ranks were closed, and in the issue strength upheld the free.

Let us not, in this hour of thanksgiving, fail to remember those who gave their lives or who live now maimed or blinded that we might continue to enjoy the blessings of life.

Through later years our path has led uphill. In the aftermath of war, in a world exhausted by its ordeals and impoverished by its destruction, we set ourselves to resume our normal ways to recreate the structure of our industry and commerce, and to respond to the urgent desire to improve the conditions of life.

We were treading unfamiliar and broken ground, for there had been far-reaching changes, especially in economic conditions. Everywhere a feeling of uncertainty and lack of confidence hung like a shadow over human endeavour.

But we have made headway by the earnest goodwill, prudence, and stability of my people, and the country has attained to a measure of industrial success which gives it confidence in the future.

I am very conscious that these years have brought hardship and often disappointment, and I have been moved with profound admiration for the greatheartedness of my people and for the steadfast fortitude and unbending will to overcome which they have ever shown in their anxieties.

I sympathise deeply with those who have endured the sadness and burden of unemployment. It is a source of comfort to me to feel that from these times of trial there has grown up throughout our community a stronger feeling of fellowship one with another.

I give thanks to Almighty God, who has thus far sustained me and my people, and I pray that we may continue to pursue the cause of freedom and progress in a spirit of peace, tolerance, and understanding.

The Passing of the King

THE King's life is moving peacefully towards its close.

The message broadcast while George the Fifth lay dying

I AM rather glad to think that the King has taken his trumpeter with him to the other side.

A lady on hearing that Kipling, Poet of the Empire, passed away just before King George

A Little Talk Heard by the World

This is the little talk of the Archbishop of Canterbury to the Duke and Duchess of Kent at their wedding, heard all over the world

NEVER in history, we may dare to say, has a marriage been attended by so vast a company of witnesses. For by a new and marvellous invention of science countless multitudes in every variety of place and home are joining in this service.

The whole nation (nay, the whole Empire) are the wedding guests : and more than guests, members of the family. For this great assembly in the Abbey, the crowds waiting outside its walls, and the multitude of listening people regard the family of our beloved King and Queen as in a true sense their own.

It must be most moving to you, dear Bride and Bridegroom, to know that this wealth of good wishes and goodwill is being offered to you as their wedding gift. Yet in the midst of all the voices which have acclaimed you in your coming here, and will again acclaim you as you leave, will you let one voice for a few minutes sound a deeper note ? It may not be easy for you in all this happy excitement to listen ; but perhaps some echo of my words may linger among the memories of this great day. At least, you know that the words will not be merely formal but spoken from the heart of a friend and Father in God.

We all wish you happiness ; but our wishes cannot give it. Nor can it come from outward circumstance. It can only come from yourselves, from the spirit that is within you. You cannot choose what changes and chances are to befall you in the coming years. But you can choose the spirit with which you will meet them. Let it be the spirit of the noble vows in which you have just plighted your troth each to the other. If you will take these vows not as a form but as a bond of honour which you will keep with unswerving loyalty, then whatever may come you will have that inward happiness which no pleasures of themselves can give and no sorrows can take away. Then the home-life which awaits you will be both an abiding security to yourselves and a welcome example to others.

Today your separate lives, with their own memories and hopes, temptations and trials, are merged in one. Will you bring into this new life, each for the sake of the other, the best that you can be ? Let your deepest bond of union be in that inward region of the soul where conscience and true ideals dwell. For there you come near to God and God comes near to you. Keep there a reverent remembrance of Him. Then His protecting hand will guide you, and by His eternal love the love you bear each other will be ever strengthened and enriched.

One more word. As you think of the good wishes with which the people of this nation and Empire are surrounding you, you will, I know, resolve that you will ever be eager to help and serve them in such ways as you can. You, Sir, have already and fully taken your place in this service of the community. And you, dear Bride, as your husband's comrade, will find a new happiness in sharing the joys and sorrows, and in ministering to the needs of the good British folk who have already, with a warmth so swift and so spontaneous, taken you into their heart. I am sure that that heart is now speaking through my words as I say : God bless you both, God guide you, God keep you always.

The Marriage of Queen Elizabeth

CONCERNING marriage, I have been long since persuaded that I was sent into this world by God to do those things chiefly which may tend to His glory. I have already joined myself in marriage to a husband, namely the Kingdom of England. And do not upbraid me with miserable lack of children, for everyone of you, and as many as are Englishmen, are children and kinsmen to me.

Queen Elizabeth's answer to Parliament,
which had urged her to marry

The Gift He Gave to England

HIS eyes are bright and eager, with the brightness of the Sun,
(England, he gives them you).
His hands are strong for climbing and his feet are swift to run,
(England, he gives them you).
He has knowledge of the meadows, in the dreamy autumn days,
The brown hill and the gold hill, and the green, forgotten ways
(But he leaves them now for you).
There's a certain ancient city where he once was free and young,
(But he leaves it now for you),
Where Oxford tales are spoken, and Oxford ways are sung,
(But he leaves them now for you),
And his heart is often weary for that dear old river shore,
And he thinks a little sadly of the days that come no more
(But he gives them up for you).
If his dust is one day lying, in an unfamiliar land
(England, he went for you).
Oh, England, sometimes think of him, of thousands, only one,
In the dawning, or the noonday, or the setting of the Sun
(As once he thought of you).　　　*H. Rex Freston*

People, He Must Not Die

NO, Freedom ! People, No ! He must not die.
Twould be too simple, too unscorned an end,
After all law destroyed, the hour brought nigh
　　When holy shame must back to heaven ascend.

By this man's deed, ephemeral Emperor,
　　Daughters and sons are fatherless and sad ;
The widow weeps, kneels, sobs, her anguish o'er ;
　　The mother seems a ghost in mourning clad.

The reels which weave his robes of royalty,
　　Deep dyed, are wound about with blood-stained thread ;
Montmartre's boulevard doth the vat supply,
　　And steeps his mantle in imperial red !

When livid Treason, of his crimes the guide,
　　Raps at his door, he welcomes his ally.
He is the fratricide, the parricide :
　　People, on this account he must not die.

Keep the man living. Noble punishment !
　　Would that, some day, him we may wandering find,
Naked, crouched, shivering, like reed tempest-bent,
　　Beneath the execration of mankind.

Clasped by the past—crammed with those crimes of his,
　　As with a crown all bristling o'er with nails,
Seeking dark spots—the forest, the abyss ;
　　Pale, scared, and whom the wolf as kindred hails.

In some vile hulks, fetters his only sound,
  Telling to the deaf rocks his vain despair;
Alone, alone, Silence and Hate around—
  Men nowhere near, and spectres everywhere!

Aged, rejected by Death's scornful hand,
  Doomed, abject, trembling, through long years to plod:
People, avoid that man, marked by a brand:
  Let Cain pass by, for he belongs to God.

Victor Hugo on Napoleon the Third

A Prince of Learning Writes to a Rich Lady

*Erasmus, in desperate need of money, yielded to the
temptation to write to a rich lady; this is from his letter.*

IT is unworthy of me (a man of letters and a philosopher) to be so
cast down as I am, when you who were born to rank and luxury
endure your trials so patiently.

But let Fortune thunder as she will, I will not be crushed and
leave my work undone while I have my Princess for a Cynosure to
shine upon me. Malice cannot rob me of the learning I have gained.
A little money will enable me to make use of it, and this you can
supply out of your abundance.

My muse I shall owe to you, and she shall henceforth be dedicated
to your services. Thee, dear nurse of my soul, I would not change
for Augustus and Maecenas, and future ages will marvel that in
this far corner of the world, when learning lay prostrate from neglect
and ignorance, a woman rose, who, by her benevolence, restored
learning from dust to life. When Erasmus was mocked by promises
which were not observed to him, when he had been robbed and flung
out to buffet with the waves of fortune, you, Lady, did not suffer him
to drown in penury. Continue the work which you have begun. My
writings, your own children, reach out their suppliant hands to you.

Erasmus

A Dialogue at the Gate of Heaven

*There appeared in Paris in 1514 a play set at the Gate of Heaven, where Pope
Julius appeared to demand admission. This is from the conversation between the
Pope and St Peter, anonymous but thought to be written by Erasmus.*

JULIUS: Hey there, porter; are you asleep or drunk? Open
the gates, I say. Why is there no one to receive me?

Peter: Here is fine talk. Who are you, I say?

Julius: You know this key, I suppose, and the triple crown, and
the pallium?

Peter: No admission without merits.

Julius: What do you mean by merits?

Peter: Have you taught true doctrine?

Julius: I have been too busy fighting. There are monks to look
after doctrine.

Peter : Have you been diligent in your prayers ?

Julius : The invincible Julius ought not to answer a beggarly fisherman, but you shall know who and what I am. I have done more for the Church and Christ than any pope before me. I have set all the princes of Europe by the ears, torn up treaties, kept great armies in the field, covered Rome with palaces, and left five millions in the Treasury.

Peter : Invincible warrior ! All this is quite new to me, pardon my simplicity, but how comes it that the princes are so ready to take up arms for you, while to us they were the worst enemy we had ?

Julius : By my triple crown and by my victories I will make you know who Julius is if you provoke me farther.

Peter : Poor worldly madman, will you boast of your treaty-breaking and your accursed wars ? These are Satan's arts. Power with you is joined with madness and vanity. What sign have you ever shown of an apostle ? Have you increased the Church ?

Julius : I found it poor : I have made it splendid. I have filled Rome with palaces, trains of mules and horses, troops of servants, armies and officers ; with purple and gold, with revenues so vast that kings are poor beside the pope.

Peter : Pray, inform me. The Church had nothing of all this when it was founded by Christ.

Julius : You are thinking of the old affair, when you starved as pope with a handful of poor hunted bishops about you. Time has changed all that. Look now at our gorgeous churches, bishops like kings, cardinals in purple gloriously attended, horses decked with jewels, and shod with gold and silver.

Peter : He who was Lord of all became the scorn of all, and ended with a death of shame.

Julius : He will not find many imitators in these times. The world will not respect us and the Church will go to pieces if we are poor and cannot defend ourselves. Money is power.

Peter : If the world saw the gifts of Christ in you it would think more of you and not less for being poor. Then the Church would flourish again. You call the Church flourishing when it is drunk with luxury. We are not of your communion in this place. You have an army of sturdy rogues behind you ; go build a paradise of your own.

Julius : I will do better than that. I will wait till I have a larger force and will take your place by storm.

Is It Nothing to You, All Ye that Pass By ?

How doth the city sit solitary, that was full of people ! She that was great among the nations, and princess among the provinces, how is she become tributary ! She weepeth sore in the night, and her tears are on her cheeks.

Among all her lovers she hath none to comfort her. All her friends have dealt treacherously with her, they are become enemies. Judah is gone into captivity because of affliction; she dwelleth among the heathen; she findeth no rest.

The ways of Zion do mourn, because none come to the solemn feasts. All her gates are desolate; her priests sigh, her virgins are afflicted, and she is in bitterness.

Is it nothing to you, all ye that pass by? Behold, and see if there be any sorrow like unto my sorrow.

The young and the old lie on the ground in the streets;

My virgins and my young men are fallen by the sword; our persecutors are swifter than the eagles; they pursued us upon the mountains, they laid wait for us in the wilderness.

The joy of our heart is ceased; our dance is turned into mourning.

Thou, O Lord, remainest for ever; thy throne from generation to generation. Wherefore dost thou forget us for ever, and forsake us so long time? Turn thou us unto thee, O Lord, and renew our days as of old.
From the Lamentations of Jeremiah

The Voice From Mount Sinai
And the Lord spake, saying

Do not drink wine nor strong drink when ye go into the tabernacle, lest ye die; it shall be a statute for ever throughout your generations. Ye shall keep my sabbaths and reverence my sanctuary. Regard them not that have familiar spirits, neither seek after wizards.

If a stranger sojourn with thee in your land thou shalt love him as thyself.

Ye shall do no unrighteousness in judgment, in meteyard, in weight, or in measure. Just balances, just weights, shall ye have.

When ye reap the harvest thou shalt not make clean the corners of thy field, neither shalt thou gather any gleaning of thy harvest; thou shalt leave them to the poor and to the stranger.

The Lord spake on Mount Sinai, saying

Six years thou shalt sow thy field and prune thy vineyard and gather in the fruit, but the seventh year shall be a sabbath for the Lord, a year of rest unto the land.

Thou shalt number seven sabbaths, seven times seven years, and ye shall hallow the fiftieth year and proclaim liberty throughout the land unto all the inhabitants. A jubilee shall that fiftieth year be. It shall be holy unto you. In the year of this jubilee ye shall return every man to his possession.

The land shall not be sold for ever, for the land is mine. Ye are strangers and sojourners with me.
Old Testament

All Men Are Equal

WHEN, in the course of human events, it becomes necessary for one people to dissolve the political bands which have connected them with another, and to assume, among the Powers of the earth, the separate and equal station to which the laws of Nature and of Nature's God entitle them, a decent respect to the opinions of mankind requires that they should declare the causes which impel them to the separation.

We hold these truths to be self-evident :

That all men are created equal ;

That they are endowed by their Creator with certain unalienable rights ;

That among these are life, liberty, and the pursuit of happiness ;

That, to secure these rights, governments are instituted among men, deriving their just powers from the consent of the governed ;

That, whenever any form of government becomes destructive of these ends, it is the right of the people to alter or to abolish it, and to institute a new Government, laying its foundation on such principles, and organising its powers in such form, as to them shall seem most likely to effect their safety and happiness.

Prudence, indeed, will dictate that governments long established should not be changed for light and transient causes ; and accordingly all experience hath shown that mankind are more disposed to suffer, while evils are sufferable, than to right themselves by abolishing the forms to which they are accustomed. But when a long train of abuses and usurpations, pursuing invariably the same object, evinces a design to reduce them under absolute despotism, it is their right, it is their duty, to throw off such government, and to provide new guards for their future security. Such has been the patient sufferance of these colonies, and such is now the necessity which constrains them to alter their former systems of government. The history of the present King of Great Britain is a history of repeated injuries and usurpations, all having in direct object the establishment of an absolute tyranny over these States. To prove this, let facts be submitted to a candid world.

He has refused his assent to laws the most wholesome and necessary for the public good. He has forbidden his Governors to pass laws of immediate and pressing importance, unless suspended in their operation till his assent should be obtained ; and, when so suspended, he has utterly neglected to attend to them. He has refused to pass other laws for the accommodation of large districts of people, unless those people would relinquish the right of representation in the Legislature—a right inestimable to them, and formidable to tyrants only. He has called together legislative bodies at places unusual, uncomfortable, and distant from the repository of their public records, for the sole purpose of fatiguing them into compliance with his measures. He has dissolved Representative Houses repeatedly, for opposing, with manly firmness, his invasions on the rights of the people. He has refused, for a long time after such dissolutions, to cause others to be elected; whereby the legislative powers, incapable of annihilation, have returned to the people at large for their exercise, the State remaining, in the meantime, exposed to all the dangers of invasion from without, and convulsions within.

He has endeavoured to prevent the population of these States; for that purpose obstructing the laws for naturalisation of foreigners, refusing to pass others to encourage their migration hither, and raising the conditions of new appropriations of lands. He has obstructed the administration of justice by refusing his assent to laws for establishing judiciary powers. He has made judges dependent on his will alone for the tenure of their offices, and the amount and payment of their salaries. He has erected a multitude of new offices, and sent hither swarms of officers to harass our people, and eat out their substance.

He has kept among us, in times of peace, standing armies, without the consent of our Legislatures. He has affected to render the military independent of, and superior to, the civil power. He has combined with others to subject us to a jurisdiction foreign to our constitution, and unacknowledged by our laws: giving his assent to their acts of pretended legislation for quartering large bodies of armed troops among us; for protecting them, by a mock trial, from punishment for any murders which they should commit on the inhabitants of these States; for cutting off our trade with all parts of the world; for imposing taxes on us without our consent; for depriving us, in many cases, of the benefits of trial by jury; for transporting us beyond seas to be tried for pretended offences; for abolishing the free system of English laws in a neighbouring province, establishing therein an arbitrary government, and enlarging its boundaries so as to render it at once an example and fit instrument for introducing the same absolute rule into these colonies; for taking away our charters, abolishing our most valuable laws, and altering, fundamentally, the forms of our governments; for suspending our own Legislatures, and declaring themselves invested with power to legislate for us in all cases whatsoever.

He has abdicated government here by declaring us out of his protection, and waging war against us. He has plundered our seas, ravaged our coasts, burnt our towns, and destroyed the lives of our people. He is at this time transporting large armies of foreign mercenaries to complete the works of death, desolation, and tyranny, already begun with circumstances of cruelty and perfidy scarcely paralleled in the most barbarous ages, and totally unworthy the head of a civilised nation.

He has constrained our fellow-citizens, taken captive on the high seas, to bear arms against their country, to become the executioners of their friends and brethren, or to fall themselves by their hands. He has excited domestic insurrections amongst us, and has endeavoured to bring on the inhabitants of our frontiers the merciless Indian savages, whose known rule of warfare is an undistinguished destruction of all ages, sexes, and conditions.

In every stage of these oppressions we have petitioned for redress in the most humble terms : our repeated petitions have been answered only by repeated injury. A prince whose character is thus marked by every act which may define a tyrant, is unfit to be the ruler of a free people.

Nor have we been wanting in attentions to our British brethren. We have warned them, from time to time, of attempts by their Legislature to extend an unwarrantable jurisdiction over us. We have reminded them of the circumstances of our emigration and settlement here. We have appealed to their native justice and magnanimity, and we have conjured them, by the ties of our common kindred, to disavow these usurpations, which would inevitably interrupt our connections and correspondence. They too have been deaf to the voice of justice and of consanguinity. We must therefore acquiesce in the necessity which denounces our separation, and hold them, as we hold the rest of mankind—enemies in war, in peace friends.

We, therefore, the representatives of the United States of America, in General Congress assembled, appealing to the Supreme Judge of the world for the rectitude of our intentions, do, in the name and by the authority of the good people of these colonies, solemnly publish and declare that these United Colonies are, and of right ought to be, FREE AND INDEPENDENT STATES ; that they are absolved from all allegiance to the British Crown, and that all political connection between them and the State of Great Britain is, and ought to be, totally dissolved ; and that, as free and independent States, they have full power to levy war, conclude peace, contract alliances, establish commerce, and to do all other acts and things which independent States may of right do. And for the support of this declaration, with a firm reliance on the protection of Divine Providence, we mutually pledge to each other our lives, our fortunes, and our sacred honour.   *American Declaration of Independence*

The Fool and the Wise Man

A FOOL can ask more questions than a wise man can answer, but a wise man cannot ask more questions than he will find a fool ready to answer.   *Archbishop Whately*

The Mind that Leaves its Mortal House

Do not suppose that when I have departed from you I shall be nowhere or no being. Neither while I was with you did you see my mind, but supposed it to be in this body from the actions which I performed. Believe, therefore, that the same still exists even though you behold none. Nor, in truth, would the honours of illustrious men continue after death if their minds were inefficacious toward our longer retaining them in memory. I certainly can never be persuaded that minds live so long as they are in mortal bodies and, when they have departed out of these, wholly die.

The dying Cyrus to his sons

Sir Thomas Browne's Good-Night

The night is come, like to the day,
    Depart not thou, great God, away,
Let not my sins, black as the night,
Eclipse the lustre of Thy light :
Keep still in my horizon, for to me
The sun makes not the day, but Thee.
Thou, Whose nature cannot sleep,
On my temples sentry keep ;
Guard me 'gainst those watchful foes,
Whose eyes are open while mine close.
Let no dreams my head infest
But such as Jacob's temples blest.
While I do rest, my Soul advance ;
Make my sleep a holy trance,
That I may, my rest being wrought,
Awake into some holy thought ;
And with as active vigour run
My course, as doth the nimble sun.
Sleep is a death ; O make me try,
By sleeping, what it is to die ;
And as gently lay my head
On my grave as now my bed.
Howe'er I rest, great God, let me
Awake again at last with Thee ;
And, thus assured, behold I lie
Securely to awake or die.
These are my drowsie days ; in vain
I do now wake to sleep again :
O come that hour, when I shall never
Sleep again but wake for ever.

Written in the Seventeenth Century